ARCH HERETIC, UNKNOWN GENIUS

J.M. Robertson:
An Introduction and Guide

MARTIN PAGE

'I know he is, they know he is –
A most arch heretic'

Shakespeare, *Henry VIII*, Act V, Scene 1

'the world will find no difficulty in admitting …
his radicalism and his rationalism, both – such is
the prophetic power of genius "dreaming on things
to come" – of a late nineteenth century pattern'

John Dover Wilson, *The Criterion*, 1930

Ivan Scheer and Martin Page
London, England

First published by Ivan Scheer
and Martin Page 2024
394 Muswell Hill Broadway, London, N10 1DJ

ISBN 979-8-89238-181-9

Printed by Mixam UK Limited,
6 Hercules Way, Leavesden, Watford, WD25 7GS

DEDICATED

TO

The memory of five stalwarts
who in various ways supported and encouraged me
in the preparation of this book:
J.M. Robertson's daughter Guenn
Geoffrey Andrews
Professor Stanislav Andreski
Jack Benjamin
Chris Tame

TO

Those Afghans who have worked and suffered in the cause of an
Afghanistan free from religious extremism and respectful of human
rights for all

and

TO

The millions of victims in the Middle East, Europe and Asia of
Vladimir Putin, child and devotee of the Soviet Union, latter-day
barbarian and monstrous war criminal

By the same author

Britain's Unknown Genius: An Introduction to the Life-Work of John Mackinnon Robertson

Crimefighters of London: A History of the Origins and Development of the London Probation Service 1876-1965

Fighter for Britain's Freedom: Letters to the Press by Reg Simmerson, 1971-98 (editor)

Wilma's Story: Growing Up in Nazi Germany and Colonial Rhodesia (editor)

Homelessness and Mental Illness: The Dark Side of Community Care (co-editor)

The Rights of Old People (contributor: foreword by Richard Crossman)

Martin Page has also addressed a variety of historical, political, social and literary topics in periodic lectures, articles and book reviews, of which the earliest was perhaps his book review in the South Place *Ethical Record* for October 1968 of Bernard Porter's *Critics of Empire*.

CONTENTS

SOME BACKGROUND INFORMATION ON MARTIN PAGE

Martin Page was educated at what was then Colfe's Grammar School in Lewisham, and at Oxford University, where he is understood to have founded his college's first Humanist Society. After graduation he went on a holiday visit to a republic that craved official recognition, Communist East Germany, where in a mass question and answer session for foreign visitors and tourists addressed by a Government Minister (who he believes was most probably Otto Winzer), he angrily raised the case of Peter Fechter, who was less than six months younger than Martin Page himself, and who had been left to die in his own blood at the Berlin Wall after being shot while attempting to escape East Germany. In an article in the *Freethinker* in June 1970 Martin Page branded the regime of the Greek Colonels "a Fascist State". A month or so later, while very briefly in Greece in transit, he inadvertently attended the tail-end of the very public Athens funeral of the junta's Foreign Minister Panagiotis Pipinelis. In his article Martin Page had indicated that a coming revolution could be heralded by an outbreak of internal dissension in the ruling class, which "may yet spell the downfall of the present junta in Greece" - a prospect fulfilled four years later with the Turkish invasion of Cyprus and Greek student unrest. Martin Page became Associate Editor of the then South Place *Ethical Record*, a regular contributor to the *Freethinker*, and General Secretary of the British National Secular Society, stressing the N.S.S. links with the then anti-apartheid movement and participating in the Society's deputation to the Foreign Office to oppose selling arms to South Africa. He was later appointed the first head office social work co-ordinator at the Zimbabwe Ministry of Health in Harare, campaigned against the disastrous closure of British psychiatric hospitals and worked for a combined total of about thirty years in the public service in Britain and Zimbabwe.

PREFACE

This book may be considered polemical in the sense that it is based on the belief that the works, accomplishments and endeavours of the freethinker and Radical John Mackinnon Robertson ("J.M.R.": 1856-1933) are not as widely or as well known as they deserve to be. Indeed, I regard Robertson as one of the most remarkable scholars, men of letters and public intellectuals thrown up by Western civilization during the half century between the election of the atheist and freethinker Charles Bradlaugh to the British Parliament in 1880 and the rise of Adolf Hitler in Germany during 1930-33. But my admiration for Robertson is not unconditional or unqualified. In the present volume many of the numerous notes on a selection of his writings include criticisms, overt or implicit, by me or others, of aspects of his work or approach. He was inevitably a child of his age, although it is submitted that he transcended it in various ways through the combination of his qualities of originality, imagination, intellectual power and application, and a wealth of insights into both the past and the future that, viewed in the round, could entitle him to be considered a genius.

On Robertson's death his writer-friend and admirer Eden Phillpotts praised "his many-sided genius" at the same time as another correspondent in the rationalist press compared J.M.R. with "that critical and artistic genius of last century,

Ernest Renan" (*LG*, February 1933, pp. 37, 47). Then in 1969 the veteran American freethinker Jack Benjamin described Robertson as "this most unusual genius", and a decade later Professor Stanislav Andreski hailed J.M.R. as "a forgotten genius" (*Question 12*, R.P.A., April 1979). In some respects J.M.R. seems a latter-day genius of the Enlightenment.

A genius is by no means infallible; and it is not pretended that Robertson was infallible. But at the very least it is contended that whatever may have been the limitations within which he operated, he bequeathed a body of work of enduring value in diverse fields of which any man, or woman, would be proud. As his economist friend J.A. Hobson declared of him in 1933: "So capacious a memory, such prolonged intellectual industry, so much courage and independence of mind, such absolute honesty of conviction, and so firm a belief that reason must prevail – such a combination has been very rare in the whole history of 'homo sapiens'" (quoted in *BRUG*, 1984, p. 73).

Equally, readers or critics with a strong religious faith should at least be willing to recognize that, as the literary writer Eden Phillpotts remarked soon after Robertson's death, "he first wrote and fought against such a triumphant tyranny of Church and Law as this more fortunate generation of thinkers can hardly imagine". Phillpotts's point, I believe, is illustrated by the first part of my book, on Robertson's Scottish years (1856-84), which presents the only detailed published account known to me of the life and activities of a secularist group or branch in Scotland between 1877 and 1884.

Through his writings and lectures Robertson had a direct influence on British youth. The music critics Ernest Newman and, later, Neville Cardus recorded their debt to J.M.R.; and in 1928 the philosopher Cyril Joad declared, referring to his debating opponent Chapman Cohen, a leading freethinker and secularist: "All that Mr. Chapman Cohen has owed to Mr. Robertson I, too, have owed; Mr. Robertson has had an incalculable influence in moulding the thought of my generation, perhaps even more than that of Mr. Chapman Cohen's generation." In 1933 the South Place Ethical Society and University lecturer C. Delisle Burns paid a similar tribute to J.M.R.'s influence, as did the anarchist art critic and scholar Herbert Read in 1938. In 1936 Ernest Newman recorded of his friend Robertson: "he was not only intellectually the greatest, but in character the best, man I have ever known or am ever likely to know" (*HF*, p. xxii).

In more detail than *Britain's Unknown Genius* (1984) – which was the first known book on Robertson to be published in Britain – the present volume offers many examples of J.M.R.'s undoubted, ostensible or indirect influence on others. A similar instance which may have escaped notice may relate to his line of thought that the dynamics of international trade (with his emphasis on free trade) had become instrumental in promoting democracy, co-operation and social progress. He concluded *The Political Economy of Free Trade* (1928), after a reference to Free Land, by declaring "lose Free Trade, and every other social ideal will fall from your hands". In 1929 he added that the United Kingdom "had been inwoven with the whole progress of the world for two hundred years, stirring the literatures, thrilling the democracies, rousing the hopes of all the peoples in turn" only to be brought low by "traders" (*The Decadence*, p. 107). Very many years later the historians Niall Ferguson (in *Empire*) and Stephen Kotkin would make similar claims in pointing to the strength of the West's assets *vis-à-vis* totalitarian régimes. Comments by Robertson could also have seemed germane or telling decades later when the Labour leader and Prime Minister Tony Blair told the 2001 Labour Party Conference: "The kaleidoscope has been shaken. The pieces are in flux. … let us reorder this world around us." Blair's words could have suggested a throw-back to the kind of Victorian imperialism attacked in Robertson's article "Fabian Imperialism" (in *The Reformer*, January 1901).

Finally, I have been as scrupulously accurate and careful as possible regarding the factual reliability of my text. If freethought encompasses free speech and freedom of thought generally without being confined to criticism of religious dogma and pretensions, Robertson's values, as reflected in his life-work, retain relevance, vitality, importance and a source of inspiration in the world today.

MARTIN PAGE
5 January - 6 June 2024

ACKNOWLEDGEMENTS

In the course of the preparation of this book I benefited hugely from access to, and ready assistance from, the following libraries and/or academic institutions and their staff: first and foremost, the British Library, London; the Bodleian Library, Oxford; Bristol University; Conway Hall Ethical Society (previously known as South Place Ethical Society), London; various London local authority public libraries; the London School of Economics; the National Liberal Club, London; the National Library of Scotland; the National Reform Union records, Dunford House, Midhurst; the National Secular Society, London; Reading University (Professor Stanislav Andreski, who had already noticed J.M.R.'s *The Evolution of States* in 1954); and Dr. Williams's Library, originally based in London.

I also wish to express my thanks and gratitude to the following individuals who have helped me in various ways since I began my research: J.M. Robertson's daughter Guenn in the United States; Geoffrey Andrews (who lived with Robertson and his family for some months before the First World War); Jack Benjamin, New York; Ralph Blumenau; Ian Hebdon; Elaine Newman for her secretarial assistance; Clive Ogden; my father Leslie R. Page, whose library at home introduced me to J.M.R.'s *History of Freethought Ancient and Modern* (1936) when I was about 18 or 19; Edwina Palmer (S.P.E.S.); Frank Ridley (to whom *Britain's*

Unknown Genius is dedicated); Dr. W.A. Smeaton; Chris Tame; Dame Rebecca West; and Louis Yearsley. Needless to say, none of the above is responsible for any factual errors that may have crept into my text, or necessarily shares any of the opinions I have expressed.

The photo of John Robertson which is reproduced on p.xv originally appeared on p. 83 of James C. Inglis's *Brodick Old and New*, which gives no publication date, but seems over 90 years old. The lack of a beard suggests the photo may have been taken in about 1877 by a photographer who has not been identified or traced. The photo of J.M.R. on the cover appeared in *The Reformer* for 15 July 1900.

My Appendix on Robertson, Marxism and Communism may also have benefited in some way from a chance and very pleasant conversation I had with Professor Ralph Miliband of the L.S.E. at Conway Hall in about 1968 (Miliband was a pupil of Robertson's friend Harold Laski). I certainly have to acknowledge that at about that time – with no direct personal refutation known to me then or since by Soviet apologists – I began publicly to criticise the lack of free speech and the crackdown on dissent in Soviet Russia, including one occasion in September 1970 when, two decades before the Soviet Union collapsed, I ventured to forecast "we may be confronted with the preliminary birth-pains of another Russian Revolution".

Finally, the Index has absorbed much of my time; and my wife has proved her stoicism.

MARTIN PAGE
5 January - 6 June 2024

GUIDE TO ABBREVIATIONS

BRUG	*Britain's Unknown Genius* (1984) (by Martin Page)
Charles Bradlaugh: A Record	*Charles Bradlaugh: A Record of His Life and Work* (1894) (by Hypatia Bradlaugh Bonner and J.M. Robertson)
EEN	*Edinburgh Evening News*
HF	*A History of Freethought Ancient and Modern to the Period of the French Revolution* (1936) (by J.M. Robertson)
HFNC	*A History of Freethought in the Nineteenth Century* (1929)
J.M.R.	John Mackinnon Robertson [1856-1933]
LG	*Literary Guide*
ML	*The Meaning of Liberalism* (1925 or 1912 edition)
NR	*National Reformer*

N.S.S.	National Secular Society
OC	*Our Corner*
R.P.A.	Rationalist Press Association
SC	*Secular Chronicle*
SR	*Secular Review*
S.S.U.	Scottish Secular Union

J.M. Robertson, London
(when a young man)

ROBERTSON AND THE PRIVY COUNCIL

(partly based on information from the Privy Council Office, London)

An intriguing aspect of Robertson's life relates to his membership of the secretive Privy Council. According to the Privy Council Office: "Our records show that the Right Honourable J.M. Robertson was appointed, on affirmation, a member of the Privy Council on 16th June 1915" at a Privy Council meeting held at Buckingham Palace. (This was probably to help shore up Herbert Asquith's premiership, but about a month after he was forced to introduce a form of wartime coalition government in which Conservatives were prominent.) The Privy Council Office add: "We do not have any further information regarding whether he attended subsequent Privy Council meetings … At the meetings the Lord President reads out the business and The Monarch says 'approved' or 'referred' in response to each item … - there is no discussion. … routine Privy Council meetings are generally only attended by Privy Counsellors who are part of the Government of the day." The reigning monarch throughout the World War and up to the era of Robertson's death was George V, for whom as a person Robertson evidently had respect and sympathy as a "faithful and well-beloved King … slowly climbing back to health" (*The Decadence*, 1929, p. 106). In June 1889 the republican atheist Bradlaugh was considered a "trusty and well-beloved" counsellor by Queen Victoria. No religious service or ceremony seems to have preceded or accompanied Privy Council meetings in modern times.

CHRONOLOGY

1856   (14 November) John Robertson born on the island of Arran, Scotland.

1870   (early to mid) Believed to have left school in Stirling to earn a living, initially as a railway telegraph clerk there.

1877   (March) Heard Charles Bradlaugh lecture in Edinburgh and thereby was introduced to the freethought and secularist movement. Quite probably worked as a solicitor's assistant at this time.

1878   (late) Became leader writer for the *Edinburgh Evening News*, succeeding his friend William Archer.

1883   Made a selection published in Edinburgh as *Winnowings from Wordsworth* from the latter's poetry, to which Robertson added an unsigned critical preface (see *NR*, 10.4.1892, p. 233).

1884   (July onwards) Credited with providing arguably the first major personal influence in leading Annie Besant towards socialism, Robertson was recruited by her, with Bradlaugh's blessing, to join the *National*

Reformer staff in London, where J.M.R. initially stayed as a lodger in her St. John's Wood house. Published *Walt Whitman, Poet and Democrat.*

1885   *Socialism and Malthusianism.*

1886   *The Perversion of Scotland: An Indictment of the Scottish Church*, arguably marking Robertson's novitiate as a historian. He gained first class passes in the organic chemistry, electricity and magnetism examinations at the Hall of Science school in London.

1887   (late) – 1888 (early) Stayed in Germany (with Professor Ludwig Büchner at the latter's home in Darmstadt) and then in Vienna to improve his knowledge of German and associated literature and culture.

1888   (June onwards) Supported Annie Besant's active involvement in the organisation of the seminal Bryant and May's match girls' agitation and strike: at one solidarity meeting where strike fund contributions were distributed, Robertson seated the strikers in pre-arranged sections. *Thomas Paine: An Investigation.*

1891   President of the North Middlesex Secular Federation; became editor (February) of the *National Reformer* on Bradlaugh's death. *Modern Humanists.*

1892   *The Fallacy of Saving.*

1893   *The Eight Hours Question*, where, two decades and more before the Russian Revolution, he rejected (p. 150) "a crude Marxian economics" (consistent with the later Soviet-style command and control economy); and for him a macro-economic perspective indicated that a blanket eight hours working day law, rigidly enforced by the state, highlighted the need for a division or balance between the free market and state control or regulation. Married Maud Mosher, an American.

1895   *Buckle and His Critics.* Unsuccessfully contested Northampton (Bradlaugh's old seat) in the General Election. At this time "apprehending money pressures, I began to work out an old scheme of mine for a sensational story to be subtitled 'Treasure England'… to make some money to pay my debts". As quoted (in G.A. Wells, ed., 1987, p. 22), J.M.R. did not refer to any novel of his previously published in his youth "as a pot-boiler, to eke out the slender family finances" as would be claimed by J.P. Gilmour in 1936 (*HF*, pp. vii-viii).

1896-7 *Papers for the People.*

1897   *The Saxon and the Celt*; *The Dynamics of Religion* (the latter under pseudonym 'M.W. Wiseman'); *New Essays towards a Critical Method*.

1897-8 Lecturing tour in the United States, including Washington and some of the leading Universities.

1899   *Patriotism and Empire* (noticed in Patricia Knight's 1968 Ph.D. thesis on British imperialist sentiment from 1880 to 1900).

1900   *Christianity and Mythology* (also 1910); *Studies in*

Religious Fallacy. Robertson's edition (2 vols., 1900) of the Earl of Shaftesbury's *Characteristics* would be commended in 1924 by Benedetto Croce and later cited by Walter McIntosh Merrill (1949: also noticing J.M.R.'s *HF* and *A Short History of Morals*), Isaac Kramnick (also listing *Bolingbroke* and *Walpole*) (1968), Ian MacKillop (1987), Steven Shapin (1994), Thomas Mautner (1997), and Terry Eagleton (2003). Quite a few of J.M.R.'s works would be reprinted during the 1960s or 1970s, including his edition of *Characteristics.* A contributor to *J.M. Robertson* (ed. G.A. Wells, 1987, p. 39) did not seem to realise that J.M.R.'s absence as a candidate in the 1900 'Khaki' General Election was not directly due to his "anti-jingo stance" as such, but because between June and October he was in South Africa investigating the ongoing Boer War and therefore could not participate as a candidate in September in the British General Election.

1901   *Wrecking the Empire*, based on his South African war letters, taken together with his subsequent lectures in Britain on the subject, caused quite a stir.

1903   *Pagan Christs* (also 1911).

1904   *Essays in Sociology* (2 vols.). Edited Buckle's *Introduction to the History of Civilization in England.* Attended the International Freethought Congress in Rome.

1905   *Did Shakespeare Write 'Titus Andronicus'?* Edited *The Philosophical Works of Francis Bacon. Letters on Reasoning* (also 1902).

1906   In the General Election he won Tyneside for the
        Liberals – he was one of the ten Rainbow Circle
        M.P.s then elected (G.A. Wells, ed., 1987, p. 40) –
        and thereafter he spoke in Parliament on a very wide
        range of issues of concern to Liberals and Radicals.
        (Re-elected 1910.)

1907   *Pioneer Humanists*. Visited Egypt following the
        notorious Denshawai Affair.

1908   *Trade and Tariffs:* influenced Walter Citrine, a future
        Trades Union Congress General Secretary. (J.M.R.'s
        book would be noticed – unindexed – in 1997 in
        Anthony Howe's *Free Trade and Liberal England
        1846-1946*, p. 247.) Robertson read a paper in the
        Reichstag (German Parliament) when it was lent to
        the Inter-Parliamentary Union (18 September).

1909   *Montaigne and Shakespeare* (also 1897): noticed
        in 1972 by Ivor Morris in *Shakespeare's God.* "Until
        1908, there was not a single copy of any of Paine's
        works in the local library" in Thetford, his birthplace
        (Chapman Cohen in his undated edition of *The Age
        of Reason*, circa 1938?, p. vi). This gave added
        point to Robertson's speech in Thetford on Paine
        on 1 July 1909 to mark the centenary of his death,
        and at a similar later event, on 17 October, he
        took the opportunity to move a resolution (passed
        unanimously) in the Leicester Secular Hall
        condemning the Spanish Government's show trial
        and atrocious execution on 13 October of Francisco
        Ferrer.

1911   Read a paper on "The Rationale of Autonomy" to an

international congress in London on race.

1912   *The Evolution of States* (also 1900 under different title).

1913   *The Baconian Heresy.*

1915   Made his affirmation before the Lord Chancellor as a new Justice of the Peace for the Tunbridge Wells Division (12 May). Due to the advent of a form of wartime Government coalition, J.M.R. ceased (25 May) to be Parliamentary Secretary to the Board of Trade, to which he had been appointed in 1911. But he was promptly made a Privy Counsellor by Asquith, who was still Prime Minister (Jim Herrick was at least misleading in referring at this point to "Asquith's fall").

1916   *The Historical Jesus* (noticed in 1963 by Joel Carmichael in *The Death of Jesus*). *The Germans. The Future of Militarism* (by "Roland"): this and the preceding book listed here were noticed in *The Choice Before Us* (1917) by the political scientist G. Lowes Dickinson, who may have known or suspected that these two works were from the same hand. *Shipping after the War* (quoted approvingly by J.A. Hobson). Robertson – by now Chairman of the Liberal Publication Department (*The Times*, 7.1.1933) – was appointed Chairman of a wartime Government Committee on Food Prices (June).

1917   *War and Civilization* (September: also January 1916). *Shakespeare and Chapman. The Jesus Problem.*

1918   *The Economics of Progress*. Defeated in the General
        Election.

1919   *Bolingbroke and Walpole*. *The Problem of 'Hamlet'*:
        influenced T.S. Eliot.

1920   *A Short History of Morals*. President, National Liberal
        Federation (until 1923).

1921   *Liberalism and Labour*. (See *BRUG*, pp. 82-3.)

1922   *The Shakespeare Canon*; then similar studies by
        J.M.R. bearing this title (1923-32) published.

1923   *Mr. Lloyd George and Liberalism*. Unsuccessfully
        contested Hendon as Liberal Party candidate in the
        General Election.

1925   *The Meaning of Liberalism* (also 1912). *Mr. Shaw
        and 'The Maid'* (discussed in Charles A. Berst's 1994
        article "As Kingfishers Catch Fire: The Saints and
        Poetics of Shaw and T.S. Eliot").

1926   *The Dynamics of Religion* (also 1897). *The Problems
        of the Shakespeare Sonnets* (includes references to
        his own work entitled *The Shakespeare Canon*). (14
        November) Seventieth birthday dinner event.

1927   Elected (11 February) a Vice-President of the very
        recently formed Liberal Council. *Modern Humanists
        Reconsidered*. *Jesus and Judas*.

1928   *The Political Economy of Free Trade*. Chaired debate
        in London between Cyril Joad and Chapman Cohen

on materialism (September). Attended complimentary dinner as chief guest of the National Reform Union at the Reform Club, Manchester, where he gave "an excellent fighting Free Trade speech" (November: see Richard D. Holt's political diary).

1929   Attended opening of Down House, Darwin's old home (June). *A History of Freethought in the Nineteenth Century. The Decadence.*

1931   *Fiscal Fraud and Folly* (revealed – p. 149 – he had once attended an international economic conference in Brussels). *Electoral Justice. A Short History of Christianity* (also 1902 and 1913).

1932   *Courses of Study* (third edition, voicing concern – p. 404 – about "the imperfect machinery … for the prevention of war").

1933   (5 January) Died at his London home, leaving his *magnum opus* on the history of freethought up to the era of the French Revolution unpublished until 1936.

1934   The *Autobiography* of the former Labour Chancellor of the Exchequer Philip Snowden declared that Robertson was one of the two best debaters he had known in the House Commons (see *BRUG*, 1984, p. 17, and Odin Dekkers, op. cit. 1998, p. 41, for details).

J. M. ROBERTSON:
THE SCOTTISH YEARS, 1856 – 1884
I: ARRAN

STRANGE as it may seem, the wild, beautiful, sparsely populated and, for years, rather inaccessible island of Arran, off the west coast of Scotland, produced a man hailed, decades after his death in 1933, by one scholar as "one of the more remarkable figures of British history" and by another as "of authentic world stature as writer and scholar".[1] This historic son of Arran, and of Scotland, was John Mackinnon Robertson (1856 – 1933), a humanist in the tradition of Diderot, a man who seemed to take virtually all knowledge as his province. A pioneering radical in diverse fields and arguably the most notable self-educated encyclopaedic scholar of plebeian origins to be born and bred in Britain during the century following Queen Victoria's accession to the throne in 1837, Robertson exerted quite a significant influence on members of his own and a later generation. An amazingly prolific polymath, he made original, path-breaking or imaginative contributions in areas of study such as historiography, sociology, freethought, Christian origins and comparative mythology, Shakespearean scholarship and literary criticism, "the fallacy of saving" in economics, the theory and practice of imperialism and racism, and radical political programmes.[2]

Robertson was intellectually active until the day he died; and his long life was inspired by what he termed "precious and passionate love of knowledge" and an intense respect and relentless quest for "tested truth"[3], both for their own sake and as agents of mental and social progress. In the service of his liberal creed he combined a scholarship that was both profound and wide-ranging with a militant and fighting spirit. Not only was there a high degree of consistency within his system of thought; but also there was considerable unity of theory and practice, and cohesion of thought and action, in his life-work as a whole. He was a keen and fearless polemicist; a noted debater; an able, eloquent and sometimes inspirational speaker and lecturer; an authoritative exponent of both free trade and freethought and their history; and a much respected Parliamentary Secretary to the Board of Trade who performed his duties with zeal and skill in a great British reforming administration.[4] Buttressed by his general commitment to knowledge and reason, he devoted his immense learning and gladiatorial energies to what he believed to be human betterment, with his friend the noted economist J.A. Hobson declaring in 1933 that "a clearance of intellectual 'slums' was his great life-work".[5] It is not known what Robertson thought of the later Stone Age burial chambers or chambered cairns, or of the Bronze Age monuments, on Arran. But as a distant relation of his, Mr. J.M. Mackinnon, remarked somewhat sardonically to the present writer concerning Robertson: "Arran of his day was certainly a place to inspire him with a curiosity about man's spiritual history." During Robertson's early years the English biologist and physiologist William Benjamin Carpenter began to spend summers on Arran, which encouraged this Unitarian scientist – through his developing dredging and sampling techniques, for example – to initiate valuable "research on the biology and physical conditions of the oceans": a concern that would resonate some 150 years later.

The Isle of Arran

On Robertson's death in London in January 1933 an admirer described him in the *Ardrossan and Saltcoats Herald*, which circulated on Arran, as "surely Arran's most distinguished son" who "deserves a statue to his memory in his native island".[6] Yet when an American friend of Robertson's daughter soon afterwards visited Arran to convey his respects he discovered that none of the people he met in its capital Brodick knew anything about its most illustrious son; and he had considerable difficulty finding the house where Robertson was born. It was then occupied by the Scotsman's elderly cousin, Miss Helen McKinnon, who showed the unknown admirer the room in which Scotland's greatest humanist scholar and freethinker of his time first saw the light of day; and there the American visitor hung on the wall a wreath of box and laurel which he had brought with him, bearing an inscription he had composed. Thus did the New World redeem the neglect of the Old.

The difficulties which beset this American visitor were replicated almost three decades later when Frank A. Ridley, erudite President of Britain's National Secular Society (with which Robertson had been associated for years), landed on Arran, accompanied by a native of Arran who was also curator of a relatively local museum, to locate Robertson's birthplace. In the straggling village of Brodick, the island's Lilliputian capital, Ridley encountered near total ignorance of J.M. Robertson's existence and learned that there was no monument to him on his natal isle. Eventually Ridley and his two companions traced Robertson's birthplace (at least to the museum curator's satisfaction) in Low Glencloy within sight of Goatfell, Arran's highest peak, which towered over Brodick. The small, inconspicuous house where Robertson was born looked across Brodick Bay towards the Scottish mainland, which was clearly visible. (The island featured in the poetry of William Wordsworth, who was the subject of the 1883 anthology *Winnowings from Wordsworth*, which was the first of a score of works in book form to carry an introduction by Robertson.)

Although the little house on Arran passed into the hands of owners unconnected with Roberson's relatives and was altered, an opportunity arose to remedy the neglect of Arran's eminent son, thanks to the generosity of the late Archie M. McDonald, a native of Arran who was almost certainly aware of F.A. Ridley's visit. McDonald, an enthusiastic freethinker, was a shoemaker in Lamlash (about four miles south of Brodick by road) and a member of London's South Place Ethical Society and Rationalist Press Association, with both of which Robertson had been associated for more than three decades. For years McDonald travelled from the Scottish Highlands to London and elsewhere in England for meetings held by such organisations; and when he died in 1970 he bequeathed three cottages and some acres of land on the isle of Arran to the South Place Ethical Society (as it then was) as a memorial tribute to J.M. Robertson.

Robertson came from Highland/Lowland stock; and throughout his life he was very conscious of his Highland ancestry which he, if not others, associated with a pugnacious streak in his personality. His friend the heretical economist John A. Hobson would write of him:

When I knew him best, in the nineties, the virtues and at

least one curious defect were exceedingly impressive upon one in general sympathy with his rationalism in all fields of its application. The defect was an excessive combativeness which was apt to pursue every detected falsehood or fallacy to its remotest origins and a related failure to assign the proper scale of importance to the several errors of his "enemies". I remember on one occasion venturing to protest against the ferocity of some indictment, and he answered: "You forget that I am only four generations from a painted Pict." It would be wrong, however, to neglect … the intense "humanism" which underlay his "spirit of revolt" against the popular creeds … he showed a most kindly disposition in all the ordinary affairs of life. It was only when our conversation brought up some controversial topic of the day that the fighting temper was aroused.[7]

In *Buckle and His Critics* (1895) Robertson maintained that the Scottish Highlanders "were certainly semi-savages down till last century". Robertson once told his latter-day surgeon friend Macleod Yearsley that he loved a fight, presumably – he himself suggested – because two hundred years earlier his ancestors were savage Highlanders.[8]

Robertson's parents John Robertson and Susan née McKinnon were married in Edinburgh in March 1852 by the Rev. Donald Masson of the Gaelic Church. (Susan had been brought up on the isle of Arran, where Gaelic was commonly spoken by the local inhabitants until at least 1870. Quite probably, therefore, she not only understood Gaelic, but also spoke it from time to time.) Their first child, James, was born on 17 January 1854 in Edinburgh, where John Robertson senior was working as a servant. Born in Perthshire, John seems to have been a twenty-eight year old butler at the time of his marriage, when his wife Susan was about twenty.

She had lived at home as a seamstress up to about a year before the wedding. She was the eldest daughter of John McKinnon, a mariner and fisherman who fathered at least seven children and who lived at Low Glencloy in the Brodick area. Local people called John McKinnon, apparently born in 1800, "The Baron", as he was believed to be descended from medieval McKinnons who held land on Arran as hereditary crown tenants known in the area as "barons". He evidently "had the dignity and bearing of a man of superior standing and independence of mind. What he thought to be right he clung to tenaciously." Indeed, McKinnon threw open his house as a temporary school (apparently well-attended) following local dissatisfaction with an inefficient parish teacher.[9]

John McKinnon's daughter Susan and her husband stayed in Edinburgh less than three years after the birth of their first child, for Susan's second child, John (who by 1887 would adopt Mackinnon as his middle name), was born at 9 a.m. on 14 November 1856 in "The Baron" 's house (built twenty years earlier) in Low Glencloy. Indeed, the future author of an essay on "Cromwell and the Historians", in which Robertson roundly attacked the religiously fanatical Cromwell, was born not far from where the Protector's troops on Arran had allegedly been put to the sword by the incensed islanders. By 1970 two commentators on the history of Arran had suggested that John Mackinnon Robertson had apparently inherited much of his radical political outlook and controversial vigour from his maternal grandfather (with whom contact was presumably maintained within the family).[10]

J.M. Robertson may also have inherited, through his mother, a number of the attractive gene pool characteristics found on the island of Arran. According to a book about Arran published in 1933 (the year of his death), a demographic survey of the island had reported that "the people are generally tall … athletic, and very well made. Their features are open and regular … The women are decidedly taller, handsomer, and better looking than in most parts of the country. … In mind, they are distinguished for their sound sense, intelligence, acuteness, and liveliness." Less than thirty years after his birth Robertson would be seen by his Scottish friend James Gilmour as "tall, with a well-knit, athletic frame … keen expressive eyes, and a mobile countenance. He was a personable and picturesque figure"; while another freethought friend, Arthur Moss, would describe him as "a fine athletic man with handsome, classical features … with a most impressive style of address, and splendid argumentative powers …"[11]

When Robertson was almost two weeks old, his birth was registered at Lamlash on the island. But the Robertsons did not stay very long on Arran: J.M. Robertson was of a tender age, almost certainly less than three years old[12], when his parents took him to Stirling, which had once been the seat of Scottish kings and of an early Scottish Parliament. The Robertsons may have experienced difficulty in getting permission from the Duke of Hamilton for the building of new accommodation. Robertson later explained: "it is only by the Duke of Hamilton's grace that you can climb Goatfell; and the island of Arran is so absolutely under his rule that not a dog can be kept, or a garret added to a house, save by his permission." He asked, somewhat rhetorically: "what is gained by allowing the Duke of Hamilton to own Arran, Mrs. Colquhoun to own Ben Nevis, or the Highland landowners to keep pedestrians off every Scotch mountain at their pleasure?"[13]

More broadly, the 'translation' of the Robertsons may well have resulted from a lack of adequate economic and even cultural opportunities – the selfsame factors, no doubt, that impelled some of The Baron's descendants to seek their fortune in Panama and the Argentine[14]. Even if John Robertson junior's parents felt his devotion to reading meant he ought to go to University, they would have regarded that aspiration as unrealistic for financial and class reasons. Yet it could be surmised that one or both of his parents suspected that their children's education prospects would be more favourable on the mainland than on the island. Indeed, more than a century after Robertson left the island, Arran children after the age of 14 had to go to the mainland to complete their secondary education, and "if any children have any academic pretensions at all they will never again probably come back to the Island of Arran".[15] What kind of society, then, were the Robertsons approaching as they turned their backs on the birches and willows of Glencloy and sailed across the sea towards the beckoning British mainland?

Britain in the 1850s

By the 1850s Britain's population had grown at what seemed a tremendous rate, having virtually doubled between 1801 and 1851, when it reached 18 million. This growth had been made possible by industrial expansion largely wrought by steam power in driving factory machines, railway engines, and boats. While the British navy, patrolling the oceans of the world, seemed invincible, into the new industrial towns of Britain had poured hordes of uprooted and bewildered men and women, hungry for work and at the mercy of mill-owners and landlords. By 1851 about half the population of Great Britain, excluding Ireland, had become urbanised; and the growth of the working classes was matched by that of the middle classes, which often provided capital, skills and enterprise to meet the needs and demands of a new industrial system that was establishing Britain as the workshop, carrier, clearing-house and banker of the world. The increasing confidence and optimism of the commercial and middle classes were symbolised by the hugely successful Great Exhibition of 1851; and as J.M. Robertson would later observe of trends just prior to 1851: "From the time of the abolition of the Corn Laws, and the passing of the early Factory Acts, the direct opposition between the trading class and the landed class tended to disappear, and the trading class even tended to some extent to amalgamate with the other, since rich merchants were always buying estates, while landowners' sons went into commerce."[16]

Britain's rulers were still largely aristocratic in outlook and origin; prestige clung to the Church, the Bar, the higher Civil Service (with civil servants recruited by patronage until 1855), and the armed forces; while a small proportion, an élite, of the adult population had the vote (women were debarred from voting). By 1850 Chartism, which represented advanced democracy in its day, was, to all intents and purposes, a spent force, although it might have been more successful, as Robertson suggested, if it had co-operated with the Free Trade movement (which ensured the importation of cheap food) instead of practically opposing it. While the Crimean War (1854-56) exposed deficiencies in the organisation of the British army and was, in Robertson's words, "as foolish, as futile, and as ill-managed a war as England ever waged"[17], Britain's increasing imperial pretensions were reflected in the creation in 1855 of a separate Colonial Office. Meanwhile, north of the Tweed, the Commissioner for Mines in Scotland had noted with alarm in 1852 the contagion of socialist ideas in the coal mining districts, where in the spring of 1856 about forty thousand miners went on strike against working conditions, and although they were starved into surrender after three months, trade unions were beginning to represent the growing organisation of the British working classes.

In 1856 less than one third of Scottish factory children, for example, could read or write.[18] Although illiteracy was still widespread in Britain, considerable emphasis was placed on Bible reading, family prayers and church-going; and the reading of sentimental, morbid and didactic religious literature, often focusing on death and dying, was encouraged. The abolition in 1855 of stamp duty on newspapers made them more secure, though the potentialities of photography were still to be fully exploited by newspaper owners. (The telephone, radio, cinema, television and the internet – not to mention the humble typewriter – were all future inventions.)

As Robertson would observe, the world into which he was born included a firm belief in the literal truth of the Bible. In this world the Universities remained bastions of clerical orthodoxy. In Robertson's words: "And this is perhaps the gist of the record of Christian orthodoxy at the English universities in our time, the stultifying of one half of the brains at work there, and the gagging of the tongues of the other half." In 1853 F.D. Maurice had been dismissed from his professorship at King's College, London, because his *Theological Essays* had just called into question the traditional belief in endless future punishment; and when in 1855 Benjamin Jowett's appointment as Regius Professor of Greek at Oxford was opposed on the grounds that he had attacked the doctrine of the Atonement, Jowett was compelled to subscribe in writing to the Church of England's Thirty-Nine Articles. Robertson later commented regarding the 1850s: "Already there had been a falling-off, in England as in Germany, in the numbers of university candidates for clerical ordination."[19] In England growing doubts about the Christian creed found expression in Alfred Tennyson's poem *In Memoriam* (1850), Henry Bowler's painting The Doubt: 'Can these dry bones live?' (exhibited in 1855), and Charles Darwin's scientific treatise *The Origin of Species* (1859).

According to J.M. Robertson, the British working classes in the 1850s were largely anti-religious, though he qualified this by stating that "the middle and working classes of Scotland all through the nineteenth century were at least outwardly more orthodox than those of England".[20] Between 1851 and 1861 about sixty British secularist groups appeared, many of them with Owenite roots or working class connections (Leicester Secular Society, for example, had been founded by 1852). A secular school existed in Edinburgh between 1848 and 1854, and a similar one seems to have been maintained in Glasgow during part of this period.

In Scotland since 1853 public houses had been kept strictly closed on Sundays; and theatres remained closed on the Sabbath in Britain. When in the House of Commons in 1855 the motion put down by Sir Joshua Walmsley, President of the National Sunday League, for the Sunday opening of London museums was overwhelmingly defeated, he was vilified by irate clergymen as "an agent of Satan". Undeterred, he re-introduced this motion in February 1856, though it was again emphatically rejected. Robertson later declared: "The clergy in general oppose the Sunday opening of museums, mainly because it encourages people to stay away from church. Of course they put another face on the matter, saying they are concerned for the Sunday rest of the workers… anything but their own interests, their own power, their own pocket."[21] Moreover, in 1856 the Archbishop of Canterbury was apparently instrumental in preventing military bands from playing in the London parks on Sunday afternoons. But the Anglican hierarchy could not be seen as unfailingly triumphant: the Anglican tests imposed on all undergraduates at Oxford and Cambridge were abolished in 1854 and 1856, respectively.

There were also no blasphemy prosecutions in England between 1843 and 1856. However, in 1857 the Cornish labourer Thomas Pooley was sentenced to twenty-one months' imprisonment for publicly exposing Christianity to ridicule and contempt. This sentence provoked criticism from the philosopher John Stuart Mill in his celebrated essay *On Liberty* (1859) – though Mill added that Pooley was pardoned by the Crown some months later – and vehement condemnation from the historian H.T. Buckle (as Robertson would point out). At about the same time in 1857, according to Mill's *On Liberty*, two leading secularists, the bookseller Edward Truelove and the agitator George Jacob Holyoake, were roundly rejected as jurors because they declared they had no theological beliefs. Mill's account, even in his fourth edition (1869), may have presented these two secularists as more victimised than was strictly justified by the known facts.[22] (Also in 1857 Mill financially supported Holyoake's unsuccessful bid to stand for Parliament, and early the following year Mill rallied to Truelove's defence when the latter was arrested for publishing a pamphlet on tyrannicide.) Moreover, until July 1858 practising Jews elected to the British Parliament could only take their seats as Christians, and it took many years after that to remove similar disabilities confronting M.P.s who were atheists or freethinkers.

A similar repressive and intolerant atmosphere pervaded much of Scotland, certainly the Highlands, where the Free Church was strong. Robertson's longstanding friend and fellow Scot J.P. Gilmour would indicate that quite a few Highlanders in 1899 had once "believed that the theatre was a den of infamy, that dancing was a device of the devil to lure souls to destruction, that instrumental Church music was a purple patch of Papistry, or that God would damn even a Highland gentleman for whistling a profane air on Sunday, or for sitting instead of standing at prayer in Church".[23]

The cholera epidemic of 1853 had caused more than twenty thousand deaths in Britain, mainly in the over-crowded slums of the industrial towns. Over 1,500 people had died in Newcastle-upon-Tyne alone. Lord Palmerston, then Home Secretary, had not been impressed by the Edinburgh Presbytery's appeal in 1853 for a national fast to prevent the spread of cholera. In his classic *The Condition of the Working Class in England in 1844* (published in Germany in 1845), Karl Marx's comrade Friedrich Engels had referred to "the defiance of all considerations of cleanliness, ventilation, and health" which he found in Manchester; and the paucity of reliable healthcare data emanating from Scottish local authorities during the 1850s did not suggest any particular reason for supposing that the health status of people in Scotland in the 1850s was clearly superior to that of people in Manchester, or other industrial centres in northern England, in 1844. The welfare state was as remote as utopia: grinding poverty, associated poor health, destitution and the workhouse were grim prospects facing working class people. Although the press gang had gone and the last notable duel on English soil had been fought in 1852, executions were still held in public, debtors' prisons were still in business, and felons could still be deported from Britain. By 1856, the year of Robertson's birth, the streets of mainland Britain were beginning to be policed on a regular basis and with more success than in India, convulsed by the Indian Mutiny (1857-59) launched by thousands of sepoys against British rule. This resulted in the *Aberdeen Chronicle*, for example, publishing in October 1857 an anguished letter by a Highland soldier (serving in India) who declared "I am in danger of my life every moment" while nurturing the hope of his "return home to Scotland again".[24] Reflecting a search by many in Britain for a better life, the 1850s were years of great domestic migration and emigration, with emigration reaching a peak in 1855.

II: STIRLING

Such was the state of British society when the Robertsons moved to the Scottish mainland. Susan Robertson's third child, this time a girl, was born on 21 September 1859, in the little village of Plean, in the parish of St. Ninians, Stirling. Three days later, Susan's husband was present when the baby girl's birth was registered at St. Ninians, where, centuries before, according to Walter Scott's poem *The Lord of the Isles*, Robert the Bruce, after his victory at Bannockburn, had torches lit in lament for his slain foe de Argentine. This girl was christened Jane, and more than 50 years later "was a spinster, still lived in Scotland, extremely pious and rather old fashioned. A bit of a joke with the family, but they still kept up relations and Robertson used to visit her when on fishing holidays."[25] By March 1861 the Robertson family of five, together with Susan's unmarried younger sister Eliza McKinnon (aged 26), who was acting as a governess, were living in two rooms with at least one window. At this time (when Susan was carrying her fourth child) 38 per cent of the Scottish population lived in two-roomed dwellings; while 27 per cent of the population were in homes consisting of one room, which could be shared by up to 15 people.[26] From these figures it would seem fair to assume that, although J.M. Robertson came from a poor family, whose financial circumstances were challenging, this family was by no means at the very bottom of the social scale. In 1861 Robertson's father was a butler when (at least in England and Wales) domestic servants formed the second largest occupational group, after agricultural workers; and by the time he died he had become a hotel manager (by September 1893). However, the Labour statesman Philip Snowden (the British Labour Party's first Chancellor of the Exchequer) may not have erred in referring, many years later, to J.M. Robertson as "the son of an Arran crofter"[27], which may have been the case at about the time the future Scottish writer was born, although the limited available information suggests that his father usually worked in service. Certainly Snowden erred in his autobiography in declaring that Robertson at twenty-two "became the editor of a Liberal newspaper in Edinburgh".

On 17 May 1861 Susan Robertson's fourth and apparently last child was born, at Plean, and the birth of this child (christened Duncan) was registered ten days later at St. Ninians. The fact that J.M. Robertson later adopted "Robert Duncanson" as a literary pseudonym for himself from his younger brother's name could indicate that he had considerable affection for Duncan. With two brothers and one sister, John Robertson came from a relatively small family, for it was at least a decade later that the large Victorian family began to dwindle and the birth-rate to fall dramatically.

The Victorian family (like society generally) was organised as a hierarchical unit, with children subordinate to their parents and the wife to her husband. Years later J.M. Robertson commented and confessed as an adult: "On the whole the Freethinkers are far the freest from the fault of domineering…

It was from the domineering that my childhood suffered."
Perhaps Robertson's father had difficulty communicating his
affection, and, if so, his difficulty may have been compounded
by the rheumatism from which he certainly suffered much.
Whatever the family dynamics, Robertson would admit that
as a child he himself had engaged in thieving ("which we
sometimes practised just as magpies do") and lying ("which
in a child is often a wholly different thing from the conscious
falsehood of the adult"). Victorians who believed that little
boys should be seen but not heard often had a dark relish
for beating children. As Robertson would ask in adulthood:
"Cannot some of us still recall, with a shudder, the passion of
hatred which was sometimes aroused in us by furious beatings
from our elders for offences the enormity of which we could
not understand?"[28] At one level his fiery outbursts and verbal
broadsides in adult life could be regarded as an extension
of childhood anger and hatred, just as his heterodoxy might
be interpreted, at least in part, as an extension of childhood
rebelliousness. Certainly it seems conceivable that Robertson
turned to reading books for consolation and refuge from
beatings as a child, and that this helped to stimulate his
lifelong quest for knowledge and search for truth fuelled by
intellectual curiosity.

How long Eliza McKinnon stayed in Stirling to look after the
Robertson children is not known, but it may be presumed that
not very long after Duncan was born, John Robertson began
to attend school. At a time when about one child in five in
Scotland attended no school at all – in 1861 there appeared
to be thousands of children of school age in Glasgow alone
who were working ten or twelve hours a day in dye-works
and foundries at the age of eight or nine – J.M. Robertson (as
he was later called) was education at Stirling High School,
known as "The School on the Rock" because it stood on

Castle Hill, where the School's foundation stone had been laid in 1854.[29] The School itself, entered through an imposing archway beneath a central tower, formally opened in May 1856, though its roots could be traced back to the twelfth century. The new School brought the various burgh schools together, and increasingly assimilated them, under one roof. The High School and its local predecessors (including the grammar school) featured some pupils who would make their mark as eminent and distinguished adults, often involved with education and imbued with a sense of public service. These included, over the years before John Robertson's arrival, the following:

The erudite Rector Dr. David Doig, who contributed three articles to the third edition of the *Encyclopaedia Britannica.*

John Anderson (appointed Professor of Oriental Languages), who was an enthusiastic teacher of popular science to artisans, and who, as a democrat, visited revolutionary Paris, where in 1791 he presented the National Convention with the model of a gun he had invented. The virtual founder of Mechanics' Institutions, he bequeathed his estate to inaugurate a university.

Dr. John Burns, who became the first clergyman in Scotland to set up Sunday Schools (before Robert Raikes of Gloucester).

Regius Professor Thomas Thomson, who contributed many articles to the third edition of the *Encyclopaedia Britannica* (which he came to edit), and who established the first laboratory for chemistry teaching in Britain.

John Macfarlane, a very successful merchant and manufacturer who built and equipped a natural history museum at Bridge of Allan, and who, in 1855, founded and endowed a Free Library and Museum in Stirling.

Robert Graham, who became Professor of Botany both in Glasgow and Edinburgh.

William Browne, who became the First Commissioner for the Scotch Lunacy Board formed in 1857.

Edward Horsman, Sir James Anderson and John Ramsay who all became British M.P.s between 1836 and 1885, with Anderson representing Stirling Burghs between 1852 and 1859 and Ramsay doing so in 1868.

Such achievements by previous scholars associated with the School provided a kind of intellectual hinterland, stimulus and foundation that arguably could do much to explain Robertson's own subsequent literary explorations and accomplishments. In the words of a commentator (in 1962) on the history of the High School: "From 1856 onwards, there has been in the background of every High School pupil's consciousness a sense of 'belonging' – of being a member of a community of scholars and teachers stretching far back into a remote and somewhat awe-inspiring past. The architecture of the school encouraged this with its 'studious cloisters' and massive towers." The School was inspected in 1858 and again in 1863, and apparently its condition was considered satisfactory on both occasions. At some point, it seems in 1875, the elementary school component was dispensed with, or, as a historian of the High School put it in 1904, "the elementary teaching was cut off, and the strength of the School concentrated on higher work".[30] Girls, as well as boys, attended the High School, which featured 146 girls and 227 boys in June 1863.

At school with Robertson was, he would recall in 1889, "an unwholesome boy (now, I believe, a deacon) who knew by chapter and verse all the indecent or coarse passages in the Bible; and who was obligingly ready to make them known to others".[31] In this school Robertson, it was later said, received a formal education which, though good in quality, was insufficient in quantity, and which included some Latin and the acquisition of "a style of penmanship, free, flowing, and legible" which retained these features throughout his life.[32] Robertson is not known to have referred, in his later writings, to any of his schoolteachers by name or according to subject taught. But this picture of Robertson suggests a more passive response by him than that presented by another source of information which was probably based on closer and more detailed knowledge of Robertson's schooldays.

While at school Robertson had a fight with a boy (almost exactly the same age as himself) called William Jenkins, who thereafter became Robertson's "chosen chum" at school; and the close relationship which thus began early in life was destined to grow in affection, so that by the time Robertson died more than 60 years later Willie Jenkins, to whom he dedicated his massive *History of Freethought in the Nineteenth Century* (1929), had become his "very oldest friend". It was ironic and fitting, therefore, that Robertson lunched with Jenkins on the day he himself died; and after his death Jenkins reminisced: "We were boys together. Fond of books, we used to read all at school, and others from various quarters outside, which were religiously lent to each other. There was no variation of taste. We both loved the thriller type, as thrillers were known sixty to seventy years ago. To the last he used to turn for change or relaxation to a thriller, and he had grown a competent judge of that class of literature. When at school prize-day came round "J.M.R." carried off piles of books given for excellence on all subjects, much to the mortification of many of his class-mates."[33] As for William Jenkins himself, it may be presumed that he was the only person of that name who, from the nearby town of Denny, was a listed subscriber to the *History of the High School of Stirling* (1904) by A.F. Hutchison, Rector of the High School between 1866 and 1896. (Jenkins would live less than nine months after Robertson's death in January 1933, as would Robertson's widow and also J.M.R.'s dear friend Annie Besant from the 1880s.)

The fact that Robertson and Jenkins had a fight at school might suggest that at least one of them was unduly aggressive. But testimony in, or shortly before, 1900 from a number of other Stirling High School "old boys" indicated that fighting between boys at the School would have been quite common during the 1850s, 1860s and 1870s (in the words of one such 'old boy', "fighting was one of their enjoyments"), and that many of the High School boys were not infrequently thrashed by the schoolmasters during this same period. The "furious beatings from our elders" recalled by Robertson could well have included thrashings at school, particularly perhaps if one "old boy"'s admission is taken into account: "You took your thrashing and said nothing about it, knowing well that if you blubbered about it at home there was another thrashing in store for you."[34]

On the other hand, Robertson as a boy spent "many happy hours" reading the adventure stories of the contemporary Scottish writer R.M. Ballantyne, whose books were to be read by generations of British youth, at least until well into the twentieth century. Robertson also appreciated *The Swiss Family Robinson*, although when, after years of happiness on a desert island, the family's eldest son discovered a neighbouring island on which a young lady had been shipwrecked, and then left his paradise to get married and settle down in Europe, "no words could express my juvenile contempt for his bad taste". Robertson regarded *Robinson Crusoe* as "really a much greater book, going deeper into human character".[35]

Once, when he was immersed in *Robinson Crusoe* at the age of about ten or twelve, Robertson was reproached by his father because he was not reading Hugh Miller's *The Old Red Sandstone* (1841). "I am not at all sure that he was very deep in *The Old Red Sandstone* himself, and the title certainly did not allure me to geology. In a great many minds, as in mine, the scientific interest is late to awaken." Though Robertson, when reproached, stuck to his preference for *Robinson Crusoe*, he later realised that Miller's handling of science had the quality of literature. One of the leaders of the Free Church of Scotland, Miller, who committed suicide in December 1856, "seems to have broken his heart because he could not reconcile Genesis with geology". Decades later Robertson would add "a recollection of the hate and fury with which geologists like Hugh Miller repelled the plain lesson of their own science when it was shown to clash with the sacred myth, and a memory of the roar of derision and disgust which met Darwin".[36] The Darwinian controversy, which raged after the publication of *Darwin's Origin of Species* (1859), had indeed intensified public interest in science.

For much of his life Robertson combined a scientist's devotion to truth with an artist's appreciation of the aesthetic. "In my early youth certainly, my active interests were mainly aesthetic. If I had had a rich father, I should have become an artist – a fourth-rater at that, probably … The aesthetic has always been a very great bias with me; and perhaps it is overwhelming me again in my old age in my devotion to

Shakespeare. But I always seemed to end in working, not with the idea of seeking verisimilitude in fiction, or the production of beauty for its own sake, but just to find out the truth about something."[37] In Robertson's case at least, this drive seemed to be associated with the fact that quite a few of his books would be reprinted in revised editions, often years after their first publication. Moreover, Stirling High School's drawing classes had been put in touch in 1858 with the Government Department of Science and Art, South Kensington, with which they would retain contact over at least four decades, and with which the London-based secularist Hall of Science was similarly in touch during the 1880s (the decade when the Hall's teaching staff would include "J.M.R.").

According to Robertson's testimony in old age, a woman friend of the family comforted his parents by assuring them that, as a result of his perpetual reading in every leisure hour, he would one day be riding in his own carriage. (In his work intended for public consumption J.M. Robertson never seems to have referred to his mother or siblings as separate individuals.) Robertson added, with a hint of dry humour, regarding this family friend: "She was a very shrewd woman, but her economics were fallacious."[38] In fact, during a period of a few months immediately following his death on 5 January 1933, at the age of 76, some tentative signs would emerge that Robertson may well have been living in straitened circumstances towards the end.[39] Be that as it may, decades earlier, in his schooldays, Robertson helped his father at work, probably during 1868-69 when his father was the tenant of the Eagle Inn, Stirling, at 43 Murray Place, which at that time comprised a hotel and a stable, but which between 1900 and 1904 would constitute the address of the first publisher of a book relating to the High School's history.

During his boyhood Robertson also began to develop an interest in public affairs: at about this time "cheap sugar was throwing some men – not many – idle in our sugar refineries; and at that elementary stage I was a juvenile protectionist for one week, or rather an advocate of a special dole for unemployed sugar-refiners".[40]   This was an early indication of Robertson's concern for others.   Moreover, he heard the remarkable adventurer, spy and mystic Laurence Oliphant (who was the Liberal M.P. for Stirling Burghs between 1865 and 1868, later marrying a granddaughter of Robert Owen) described, by those who had seen him on his canvassing tours, as very clever and " 'a bit daft' ".[41]   Oliphant made far less Parliamentary impact than his successor as Liberal M.P. for Stirling Burghs: Henry Campbell-Bannerman, who held this seat for 40 years until his death in 1908 and who became Prime Minister with the 1906 Liberal landslide, which also brought Robertson into Parliament.   Robertson, whose path may have crossed Campbell-Bannerman's in Stirling, later referred to this long-serving M.P. as a trustworthy leader who "set up the most effective Liberal Government of modern times" and who, "with his kindly humour, conciliated all colleagues".[42]

In 1872 Gladstone's first Liberal administration made education in Scotland compulsory between the ages of 5 and 13; but Robertson's formal education had already ended when he left school at 13, "with small Latin and no Greek"[43] (in an echo of Ben Jonson's assessment that William Shakespeare had "small Latin and less Greek"). Schooling after the age of 13 was practically non-existent at that time for Scottish boys, except for those intended for the ministry or the very small number able to go on to become University students (Robertson would later point to men like John Stuart Mill, Herbert Spencer, Henry Thomas Buckle and

Charles Bradlaugh who never went to University, but who made significant contributions to nineteenth century British thought). It is not known what steps, if any, were taken by either or both of his parents, or any of his teachers at what clearly appears to have been a high-achieving school, to try to extend his formal education. The fact that it came to an end when he was 13 has been associated with his family's poverty.

Working for a Living

At a time when expansion of the railway network seemed to represent one of the great liberating experiences of the nineteenth century, Robertson began to work for a living as a railway telegraph clerk at Stirling, apparently on a twelve hour day basis, with intervals for meals.[44] As more than one railway company served Stirling – the Caledonian Railway and also the North British Railway come to mind – it may now be impossible to know for certain which company may have benefited from his services. Nor is it at all clear how young Robertson got this first job, although it was probably through his father, whose known career suggested that he needed to interact with people from different levels of society and to show a degree of drive, initiative and organisational ability. If Robertson began his railway telegraph work within a matter of weeks following his thirteenth birthday, he would have been employed by a private company. But if he was in post only with effect from 5 February 1870 – when he was still 13 – he would have been employed by the Post Office as that was the de facto start date of the nationalisation and Government monopoly of the telegraph system on the railways under the 1869 Telegraph Act. Either way Robertson would have had some awareness at the age of 13 of the impact of nationalisation on the telegraph network; and this may have fed into the crystallization of his later perception of "all the waste involved in competition with none of the usual advantages"[45], which in the 1890s he advanced as part of the case for railway nationalisation. In the development of his political ideas and political programme he may also, at some point, have begun to take account of the fact that in 1871 legislation enabled the Government to take control of the railways in the context of an emergency.

It is not known exactly when or under what circumstances he ceased to work as a railway telegraph clerk; but it may be presumed that he did so to go on to more remunerative employment. In later years he wrote a now little known pamphlet on the case for the telegraph clerk which was used very effectively at a meeting of seventy British M.P.s interested in establishing an official committee to investigate occupational diseases. Indeed, after his election as a Liberal M.P. in 1906 he became the first Member of Parliament to interest himself in workmen's compensation for "telegraph cramp", and Robertson was willingly pressed into service to get telegraphists' cramp legally recognised as an occupational disease.[46]

In 1865 the North British Railway board, for example, had insisted, in the teeth of protests from members of the public, that its Sunday trains provided a public service, "especially to the poorer classes" in Scotland. This situation may have sown a seed of doubt regarding adherence to Christianity in Robertson's mind some years later. But as very few railway workers appeared to be avowed and active freethinkers in 1870[47], it seems unlikely that, in the relatively short time Robertson spent in this industry, any of his fellow-clerks was instrumental in shaking the Christian faith he had inherited from his parents, who were strict Presbyterians and apparently rather dour churchgoers. In later life he did not hesitate to recall the terrible Scottish Sabbath as kept in his parents' home, with two or three religious services, blinds drawn and no reading except of the Scriptures. Robertson could vouch from personal knowledge and experience that (in his family circle at least) "the Sabbath gloom" set in on the Saturday afternoon, and that the simple yet deep-rooted piety portrayed by Robert Burns in *The Cotter's Saturday Night* was "a true picture".[48]

In middle age Robertson expressed the hope that his children would find more help to what he called "right reasoning" in their early environment than he did. As a young adult he dated his progress to freethought from his perusal, at an early age, of Bishop Watson's reply to Thomas Paine. "That respectable, but now neglected, work was welcomed into a household in which the appearance of an intact volume of Paine would have created an excitement such as even the wandering quasi-domestic mouse was powerless to arouse." Perhaps a stirring of doubt in his religious faith was occasioned by his meeting or hearing of a Presbyterian minister who from time to time addressed his congregation in these terms: "Braithren, we here come to a deeficult passage; and, having looked it boldly in the face, we will pass on."[49]

After becoming a convinced freethinker, Robertson publicly referred to "the constant assumption on the part of many Christians that it is not argument but the meeting with 'very poor types of Christianity' that makes men unbelievers. ... I can testify that 'poor types' had nothing whatever to do with my abandonment of orthodoxy in my youth. I was not persecuted: … the Christians I met included some very estimable types as well as some frail ones; and it never occurred to me to make the sins of the sinners a ground for doubting their religion. That is not, in my experience, the way a man's mind moves to Freethought. … He begins to doubt the Christian narratives and doctrines simply because, on critical reflection, he cannot help it. He finally disbelieves them because he finds them incredible, just as are the narratives and doctrines of the other religious systems which he was never taught to believe."[50]

Although Robertson came to reject the theology of Presbyterianism, he retained much of the strict moral code associated with Presbyterianism. During his years in Scotland he does not seem to have explored the extent to which freethinkers and religious believers might uphold some of the same ethical values; but in later years he would set out his views on ethics in *Essays in Ethics, A Short History of Morals*, and *The Dynamics of Religion*, for example. Insofar as the Protestant ethic emphasized work, self-improvement, literacy, thrift, individual conscience, honest dealing and veracity, his reputation was such that he appeared to epitomize such qualities. In his youth he belonged to a Presbyterian Church, receiving instruction in the Shorter Catechism and attending Sunday School, according to one account as a Sunday School teacher.[51] According to a different source of information (also under a pseudonym, though in this case one apparently used by Robertson himself): "Who has not heard in his Sunday School days of the soldier whose Bible in his breast pocket stopped a bullet or a bayonet?"[52] The currency of this salvation story was scarcely surprising in view of the long and close association of Christian Churches with military forces.

The extent to which Robertson may have accessed and used Macfarlane's Free Library in Stirling between, say, 1869 and

1874 is not known. Curiously, *The Free Libraries of Scotland* (1880) by "An Assistant Librarian", recording the fluctuating fortunes of the free library movement north of the Tweed, does not mention Stirling, the urban centre, at all. But Robertson, when almost fifty, remembered being "intensely interested as a boy by Prescott's Conquest of Mexico and Conquest of Peru", both published in the 1840s.[53] In his early teens Robertson did a punctilious translation of the Life of Hannibal (then his favourite hero) from Cornelius Nepos. It can readily be understood how the Carthaginian leader's military genius, epic crossing of the Alps and implacable duel with Rome seem to have fired Robertson's youthful imagination. However, years later he came to feel that military leaders throughout history had rarely proved great constructive statesmen: he maintained that Hannibal and Julius Caesar, for example, could conquer, but failed to regenerate the state or ensure its enduring stability; and he concluded that the life of war ill fitted energetic men to guide the life of peace, as he explained in some detail in *Patriotism and Empire* (1899)."[54] Winston Churchill – who would become a colleague of Robertson's in Parliament and in Government – could be regarded as providing a further example.

Robertson's early poem *A Norland Tower* – published in 1886 - suggested an adolescent interest in classical literature and warfare. But perhaps its reference to Robert Bruce and to Scottish children playing soldiers was at least partly based on memories of Stirling, a market town whose surrounding countryside had often decided Scotland's fate. From the heights of Stirling Castle young Robertson may have looked out across the orchards and fields where, in days of yore, battles such as those of Stirling Bridge, Falkirk and Bannockburn had marked the ebb and flow of the fortunes of national heroes like William Wallace and Robert Bruce.

Perhaps, like the German writer Theodor Fontane, who had visited Stirling in 1858, Robertson gazed in the Castle armoury at one of the rare Lochaber axes found at Bannockburn, or watched off-duty Highland soldiers pitching iron quoits on the great lawn in the Castle forecourt, or saw recruiting sergeants of Highland regiments pacing up and down the steep short streets, some punctuated with ale-houses gas-lit at night, leading down from Castle Hill. (Fontane, who would later win enduring fame as a realist novelist, had enlisted in the Prussian army in 1844 before going on to write as a journalist about Prussia's victorious wars with Denmark (1863 onwards), Austria (1866) and France (1870-71), during the last of which he was taken prisoner by the French.) This was at a time when the conventional heroes of British society were largely military or naval leaders.

This background may help to explain Robertson's attitude towards Britain's armed forces in the wake of the Franco-Prussian War: "about the age of fifteen or seventeen, I was deeply concerned about the fighting strength of our country, not at all realising how immensely more important are its social than its military arrangements."[55] Robertson's words entered the public domain in 1902, and, decades later, historians like W.H. Prescott and Winston Churchill would be criticised for having focused unduly on military and, to some extent, political events at the expense of social, economic and intellectual factors. Robertson added: "I therefore could not appreciate at that age the men and the movements which sought to better the life of peace, with its 'wrongs and shames'; and it needed 'intellectual' experience to enable me to develop my sympathies. …I know few less estimable political types than the adolescent Conservative who has never attained to hoping highly for human betterment because he has never been able to extend his sympathy to the vast world of toiling and heavy-laden humanity."[56]

But Robertson's direct personal experience of having to work for a living from an early age, and the fact that, as he once told the House of Commons, he found his second job at the age of fourteen much more tiring than his first job at thirteen, may still have encouraged him as a thinker to give due weight to the importance of social factors in human history. Even his first job as a telegraph clerk was by no means easy, to judge from closing comments in his 40 page pamphlet *The Case for the Telegraph Clerks* (published in May 1903 by the Central Office of the Postal Telegraph Clerks' Association): "A telegraphist cannot pause at will in the middle of his work, as an ordinary clerk may; he works in a whirl of high pressure, and he is far better entitled than the desk-working civil servant to have his working day reduced to seven hours. And whereas his harassing task ought to be done under the best possible sanitary conditions, it is often done under nearly the worst, the Post Office authorities having significantly refused to open their offices to sanitary inspection by the Government's own officials."

In any attempt to reconstruct, and form a clear picture of, his youth employment record, a number of difficulties emerge. Whether information is gleaned from Robertson's scant and periodic autobiographical asides and snippets scattered virtually at random throughout many of his numerous published writings, or from abridged or imprecise testimony from friends and others who knew him, the fact remains that time and again the names or addresses of companies or firms he worked for have not been given; nor have the start or finishing dates of his various jobs (although the approximate duration of one of them is known); and their urban location is not always clear.

Commentators have copied Robertson's friend James P. Gilmour in suggesting after Robertson's death that Robertson's last job before he joined the *Edinburgh Evening News* in 1878 (when he was almost 22) was working for an insurance company – in an unspecified urban location – for up to "several years". Gilmour gave no source for this information, which, if correct, meant that Robertson was scarcely able to have worked for that company "in my teens" (to use the latter's own words). Gilmour – who came from Glasgow, not Stirling or Edinburgh – seems to have been a dutiful and devoted if not particularly close friend (he incorrectly gave September 1878 as the date for Charles Bradlaugh's 2 March 1877 lecture in Edinburgh on "Giordano Bruno", which Robertson attended).[57] It may therefore be the case that from about November 1870 onwards Robertson found himself in a position where "in my teens I was in the office of a district agency for a Fidelity Guarantee Company".[58] (His wording could suggest this office was in Stirling – and not in the capital, which his context and Gilmour's did not mention.)

Robertson's employment in this capacity - probably his second job – may in some way have been connected with the fact that the North British Railway, which served both Stirling and Edinburgh, had taken out insurance from November 1863 onwards with the Fidelity Guarantee Fund as an employer's protection against fraud or theft by an employee or agent. In fact, while in that job Robertson came across the case of a young man who, becoming a commercial traveller, had quickly resorted to embezzlement (after being recommended by his religious mentors), leaving his devoted sister, a teacher, to scrimp and save for years to pay off his defalcations to save him from prison. As Robertson put it: "He had been seen, in a state of vinous exaltation, in a cab with some loudly-dressed ladies, and the financial complications duly followed."[59] (It is not known where the rogue was seen.)

In Edinburgh at that time, or later, Robertson doubtless saw many enticed or fascinated by the gin and whisky shops selling oblivion, by fervent street preachers hawking tracts and panaceas, by recruiting sergeants offering adventure and glory, by Highland soldiers marching to the beat of drums and the skirl of bagpipes, by barefoot children playing "peevers" (hop-scotch) on the pavement, and by yelling ragamuffins urging on huge panting horses drawing noisy tramcars. If working for the insurance company was his second job (a job which he found hard at the age of fourteen on account of the pretty solid nine hours a day he had to work, with only brief breaks), he would presumably not have stayed in it for as long as the four and a half years or so he spent in a law office.

Enter William Kingdon Clifford

Then, when Robertson was apparently about sixteen years old, occurred an event that seems to have had a significant impact on the crystallization of his thinking and his intellectual development in the direction of rationalism. Sixty years after the event Robertson – in the words of Professor Harold Laski, who heard him speak – "told how, as a young man, brought up in a pious Scottish home, he had heard Kingdon Clifford lecture to a workingmen's Sunday lecture society and came away feeling that a new universe had opened before his eyes. It was impressive to hear him say that no man he had met since seemed to him to have embodied so completely the ideal of the scientific temper as Clifford. Robertson, then a printer's apprentice, wrote to him for books and advice on study; and for three years Clifford directed his reading as a teacher might the work of a disciple for this unknown boy whom he was never actually to meet. The story moved me profoundly; the kind of thing that gives an extra sweetness to life."[60]

Neither J.P. Gilmour's extensive introductory section to Robertson's masterly, posthumously published (1936) edition of *A History of Freethought* nor any other known source of information on Robertson's early life refers to this job as a printer's apprentice. But although Laski's reference to it constitutes the only source of such information that has come to light, there seems to be no particular reason to reject or doubt the accuracy of the account provided by a Professor at the London School of Economics to a fellow scholar (who had recently been a distinguished long-serving Justice of the United States Supreme Court) only a day after Robertson's reminiscence regarding Clifford. Moreover, if Geoffrey Andrews, who lived with J.M. Robertson and his family for a period shortly before the First World War, was correct in his later recollection that one of Robertson's fingers had somehow been damaged in an accident, this could be consistent with the possibility that "J.M.R." (as he became known) had suffered an industrial accident as a printer's apprentice. Robertson could have been attracted to work as such an apprentice through his love of reading and interest in books and their production. Though exceptional, "J.M.R." was not unique in his generation or social class in his thirst for knowledge: born barely three months before Robertson, Keir Hardie, reading in his scanty leisure time as a mining lad, was perhaps no less representative of the self-education of self-made men which often found expression in clandestine reading in factories, mills and offices in nineteenth century Scotland.

William Kingdon Clifford undoubtedly possessed characteristics of genius. He was not only a gifted atheist mathematician and outspoken academic and scholar in a society that was still bound by religion and tradition in many ways. He was also an inspiring teacher and inspired lecturer, a popularizer of science who has been hailed as in a sense anticipating, through some of his insights, aspects of Einstein's theoretical teaching several decades later, and he was a believer in universal education who was also a radical thinker. Nearly all of Clifford's lectures, which proved very popular, appear to have been delivered in London. But he gave one in northern England that young Robertson, despite constraints relating to money, time and distance, could have attended, and, on the basis of Professor Harold Laski's testimony, probably did attend. This was the lecture on "Atoms" Clifford gave in Hulme Town Hall, Manchester, on 20 November 1872 (as it happened, just days after Robertson's sixteenth birthday), a repeat of the lecture Clifford had given to the Sunday Lecture Society in London in January that year.

Robertson later described this lecturer as one of the most lovable men of his time, adding that Clifford "faced the world, and disease, and death, with a cheerful soul, on which none of Nature's loveliness was lost". He was evidently to consider Clifford's untimely death in 1879 at the age of thirty-three an irreparable loss to the rationalist movement – as indeed it was to the Sunday Lecture Society, on whose behalf Clifford gave a number of lectures between 1872 and 1875 in support of the Society's aim to deliver lectures on Science, History, Literature and Art, "especially in their bearing upon the improvement and social well-being of mankind". Robertson later compared Clifford with Winwood Reade, author of *The Martyrdom of Man* (1872), a fellow member of the Sunday Lecture Society, and a brilliant rationalist contemporary who was also struck down before he was forty. With his concepts of "mind stuff" and "tribal self", with stricter reference to science and clearer concern for dialectic than Winwood Reade, and with greater forthright sincerity than the philosopher T.H. Green, Clifford ("an acute and original thinker") – in Robertson's estimation – made "a trumpet call to young readers to shake themselves free of traditional thinking".[61] Robertson would not fail to heed the call.

Looking back at the age of seventy on his outlook at 16, Robertson, with a degree of wry humour, made a revealing confession: "I remember at the age of sixteen, when I do not suppose I passed as a prodigy of discretion in any other respect, saying to myself … 'The thing for me to do is to master Spanish, get into the copper trade, make a reasonable fortune in twenty years or so, and then withdraw and devote myself to my books.' But after having put up that admirable signpost I turned my back on it. Spanish is not a difficult language; but I seemed to find that French and German gave me a great deal more that was interesting; and even the rubbing up of my school Latin in the evening till I could read Livy with a certain fluency seemed more attractive than the Spanish, as there was no money in it." Robertson then added: "If I had gone into copper at the age of sixteen, I might have made a fortune in twenty years; but I am very doubtful whether after the twenty years I should have been satisfied to go back to literature. Copper, they say, has great magnetic properties, financially speaking, and I do not think that I should have had as happy a life."[62]

On a different occasion he suggested that office experience could stimulate "that precious and passionate love of knowledge which a long and thorough schooling seems often to dull and emasculate".[63] He later remembered comparing notes, when about fifteen, with a fellow clerk on Charles Dickens, apparently not very long after the novelist had died. "Our verdict was: 'He makes you think'; and we used to quote his phrases, appreciating their dexterity, their humour, their quaintness." It is conceivable that appreciation of Dickens the humorist could have encouraged Robertson to appreciate Dickens the social critic. However, Robertson never became a worshipper of Dickens, whom he credited in a somewhat double-edged way with being one of the first to popularize the taste for blood in English fiction, declaring: "In Dickens, Jonas Chuzzlewit murders with an amount of mental strain that communicates itself to the reader, so that the episode looms in memory as something lurid and frightful; and similarly, the crime of Bill Sykes bulks blackly and oppressively across the tale. A murder was a murder, so to speak, in Dickens. And in Thackeray, so much less melodramatic, and so fastidious about sensation, we never get a murder at all, save by way of a duel." Later Robertson would sharply if excessively rebuke the devotees of Dickens "who are ardently respectful alike to cheap mannerism and to caricature, to crude melodrama and cruder propaganda".[64]

Carlyle and German culture

During his teenage years Robertson also studied writers, ancient and modern, from continental Europe. He did translations from Catullus, Horace and Boileau, no doubt for his own amusement and edification. Possibly influenced if not guided by W.K. Clifford, who read and translated from German and was familiar with the work of recent German writers and thinkers, Robertson began to read Lessing, Goethe and Heine, not to mention German philosophers and historians, and concluded: "German culture accordingly must have played some part in my development."[65]

Notable Victorians who tried to stimulate awareness in Britain of aspects of German thought and literary culture included Thomas Carlyle, George Eliot, Benjamin Jowett, and Dr. William Smith. Of these, Carlyle, for one, appears to have played some part in Robertson's intellectual history. Robertson paid youthful homage to his fellow Scot "as a kind of inspired censor of men and institutions, whose judgments were to be cherished as oracles and studied as mines of wisdom!" A decade later Robertson was no less critical and recorded his own reaction to the publication of Carlyle's *The Early Kings of Norway* in 1875: "I was still in my teens, and one of Carlyle's most besotted admirers – I mention this to show how a powerful and narrow-minded writer may put stumbling-blocks in the way of young people. Filled with spurious conceptions and insincere convictions from his books, I eagerly read the new work of the Master, as I had read nearly all that went before. Not satisfied with reading his abstract, I devoutly made an abstract of that for myself; and I don't think I shall ever quite forgive him for that particular waste of my then not very valuable time."

Then, almost at the end of his own life, Robertson recalled: "In Edinburgh Carlyle's bust dominated the library of the good old Philosophical Institution, of which he was made honorary President … All young book-lovers in those days were sure to read 'Sartor' [*Sartor Resartus*] and the 'Revolution' [*The French Revolution*]; some of us read them thrice, revelling in their style and diction somewhat as we revelled in the poetry of Keats and Coleridge and Tennyson and the young Swinburne. We could repeat long passages of Carlyle's prose as we could recite whole poems of the others." On this basis the literary critic and academic John Gross was justified in describing Carlyle (in 1969, nearly a century after the high noon of Robertson's hero-worship of him) as Robertson's "first great adolescent passion". But disillusionment began to set in when, as J.M.R. would subsequently remember, "in the later seventies" he himself was one of three youths in Edinburgh who were "foolhardy enough" to send Carlyle, "as avowed admirers", a letter enquiring whether he had actually described Darwinism as "a gospel of dirt": "Needless to say, they received no reply. The phrase was no random fling at Darwinism."[66]

This letter to Carlyle from Robertson and his two friends in Edinburgh was composed and sent at a time later identified by Robertson himself (who was posthumously supported by scholars like Warren Sylvester Smith and W. Warren Wagar) as marking "the turning of the balance of educated intelligence from the current creed to 'unbelief' ", at least in parts of Victorian Britain.[67]

Supernatural Religion

Robertson recalled the attention and criticism *Supernatural Religion* and its anonymous heterodox author received when its first appearance "aroused – and exasperated – the world of British orthodoxy about 1875". He particularly remembered "the displays of temper" by churchmen in their hostile reaction to this monumental, learned and perceptive work which shook the belief of many readers in the divine authority of the Bible. Bishop Lightfoot gave a highly inadequate reply to this work in which, as Robertson maintained many years later, "was collected, by an extraordinarily diligent scholar, the substance of the debate and research of two generations over all the problems of the authenticity and historicity of the Christian gospels".[68] In the fullness of time the unidentified generator of Robertson's admiration was stated to be Walter Richard Cassels, who had once been a prosperous merchant in Bombay, where he was a member of the University Syndicate and Legislative Council. Cassels had retired from trade before he was forty and devoted himself to literary and Biblical studies (rather as Robertson had planned at sixteen to "get into the copper trade, make a reasonable fortune in twenty years or so, and then withdraw and devote myself to my books").

When *Supernatural Religion* first appeared in 1874, its then anonymous author appeared to be a humble if determined truth–seeker, as also, it would seem, was the then unknown and much younger John Robertson, whose faith in orthodox Christianity had dissolved as a result of his own thinking and reading from schooldays onwards. In his teens Robertson critically read the sacred books, certainly of Christianity, to clear his mind first and foremost on the general question of supernaturalism. At about this time he "tried to impress on a venerable relative that there was reason to believe the word 'rib', in the Genesis account of the creation of Eve, was a mistranslation, the Hebrew word meaning simply a piece of the side. I shall never forget the solemnity with which I was answered: '*Moses* says it was a rib; and it is not for us to alter it.' This believer had not attained to the conception of the possibility of a mistranslation of God's word." (More than a century after this exchange of words between Robertson and his unidentified "venerable relative" the King James Study Bible, for example, would acknowledge that in Genesis – the First Book of Moses – 2:21 the relevant wording "would mean 'from his side' or 'from his ribs' ".) On another occasion Robertson asked a cultured and capable man, whose judgement in other respects he esteemed, whether he "rationally believed" the story of Abraham and Isaac to be historical fact. This man (whom Robertson did not identify) flushed as he replied, 'I rationally believe it', leaving Robertson silently convinced that he had never reasoned with himself on the subject at all. More than half a century later, Robertson could still visualise this man's tell-tale face. Moreover, Robertson grappled in his theistic youth with the concept of infinite personality, but rapidly concluded that it represented a contradiction in terms.[69]

III: EDINBURGH: Reaching Out

In the meantime Robertson had started work in a law office, apparently in Edinburgh, as a law clerk or amanuensis to a solicitor, perhaps quite early in 1874. (In an article in 1887 Robertson declared in passing: "I can figure to myself, on a basis of early reminiscence, what would be the sensations of an Edinburgh law-clerk …") John Robertson's tasks included carrying briefs ("which", he recalled, "in Scotland are docketed 'precognitions' ") to a rising young advocate named Thomas Shaw, who had been called to the Scottish Bar, and had become an advocate, in 1875. That latter fact, with its associated date, would make it rather unlikely that J.P. Gilmour was correct in indicating, decades later, that this job was Robertson's very next job after he stopped working as a railway telegraph clerk: for Robertson publicly revealed that he was in his second job (unidentified by him) at the age of 14 and that he worked in a law office for about four and a half years, which could still have meant that he could have left that law office before Shaw was called to the

Bar. Moreover, Robertson would speak of Lord Shaw (as he became) with a certain friendly respect and a degree of warmth which seem to suggest that he had got to know the lawyer over a period of time; and in December 1928 Robertson wrote of him: "Always he will seek to master and sound the available evidence on any problem on which he pronounces judgment." In December 1884 Robertson said he had heard many advocates plead (*NR*, 14.12.84, p. 387) – it sounded as though he was thinking of the relatively recent past – and he was in a position to compare most of them unfavourably with Thomas Shaw, who was destined to be Solicitor-General and then Lord Advocate for Scotland, an M.P. for seventeen years (for some of which Robertson would be a colleague) and a Lord of Appeal for twenty years.[70]

Robertson appears to have been impressed by the Scottish scheme for providing barristers at public cost for those who could not afford to hire them. He wrote in 1890: "A litigant with less than £40 a year (if I recollect rightly) can go to an agent for the poor, who, if he thinks the case feasible, instructs a counsel for the poor, the said agent and counsel being bound to do all the work for nothing, unless in the event of winning, when, if the loser is not also too poor to pay, they may get their costs from him. From youthful experience in a Scotch law-office I can testify that the poor litigant sometimes wins, and that his agent and counsel get their costs. (I do not remember to have heard of a litigation between two persons alike too poor to pay lawyers: under these circumstances, litigation naturally does not tend to arise.)"[71]

Once, after a long session at work, Robertson's solicitor gave him a glass of wine, and this was the first time young Robertson had tasted it. (It may be surmised that the solicitor would have felt less comfortable offering Robertson wine if the latter had been several years younger than it is believed he was at the time.) Many years later, referring to this early period of his life, Robertson would modestly declare: "I claim to have learnt as little law in four years as anyone ever did." This admission may have been associated with his probably studying Christian origins in his spare time after work, or in any free time at work, at the law office, as part of his attempts to trace the history of religion as a matter of anthropology and sociology. Until the age of twenty or more he still firmly believed in the historicity of the Gospel Jesus. But at about this time he was developing a more questioning and critical attitude as a result of his following or studying the work of challenging or unorthodox thinkers and writers like T.H. Huxley, Sir E.B. Tylor, Charles Darwin, David F. Strauss, Ferdinand C. Baur, Ernest Renan (on whom Robertson would compose quite a charming monograph published about half a century later), and Ernest Havet.[72]

Enter Charles Bradlaugh

Then, in March 1877, Robertson first came into contact with a man who was later thought to have spent more time in the law courts than many legal practitioners, and who would have a major and dramatic impact on his life and orientation. That man was Charles Bradlaugh. Although Robertson would refer to himself as "an unprofessional observer in Mr. Bradlaugh's pleading", he would also maintain of that pleading that he had "never heard anything in closer forensic form". But it was not in a court of law that Robertson first saw and heard Bradlaugh: it was in a church hall. Bradlaugh was already a striking orator, debater and pamphleteer in the cause of freethought and atheism, a Radical activist, editor and mainstay of the *National Reformer* for over a decade, and founder and President of the National Secular Society (formed in 1866). Here was a man whom Robertson was to know, love and admire as one of the greatest Englishmen of his era. Robertson later described Bradlaugh as "the most magnetic and in the fullest sense the most powerful personality that it has ever been my fortune to meet", and he wrote of him: "In sheer Titanic oratorical power he was quite unequalled in the England of his day." Robertson had only vaguely heard of Bradlaugh's name as that of a professed republican; but, on being told that Bradlaugh was to lecture in Edinburgh on the martyred heretic Giordano Bruno, Robertson went to hear him.

At the outset of a lecturing tour of Scotland at a time when militant secularism seemed to be at a relatively low ebb there, Bradlaugh lectured on Bruno in St. Mary Street Hall, belonging to the Roman Catholics, on the evening of Friday, 2 March, to a large, attentive and enthusiastic audience. In the anteroom to the lecture hall he could not help looking twice at an oil painting hanging there, a life-size portrait of the current illiberal Pope, Pius IX (who had defined papal infallibility in 1870), and marvelling at the strange irony that he himself should speak in praise of Bruno in a hall belonging to the Church that had burnt him alive.[73] When Bradlaugh strode into the hall to deliver his address, Robertson probably saw a towering, muscular figure dressed in plain black, with a large black tie, white shirt and slender watch chain, a massive, square head, greying hair, close-shaven face, and formidable and commanding, almost menacing, grey-blue eyes, as brilliant as steel, features of a brave, honest and determined fighter. When Bradlaugh spoke, Robertson was doubtless mesmerised, then as later, by the clear enunciation, the earnest and confident tones, the trumpet-like eloquence of a mighty orator who seemed to hold his audience in the palm of his hand.

In his address, Bradlaugh maintained that Bruno had rendered great service to the cause of freedom of thought, and that the forthcoming unveiling in Rome of a statue of Bruno would signal to the world how thought had raised itself against the religion that had crushed him.[74]

Bradlaugh's lecture crystallised Robertson's transition to atheism and freethought: "With that lecture, which first brought me into contact with the freethought movement, I associate the only sensation of pain, and that not a severe one, which attended my abandonment of early beliefs. Thinking inconsecutively for myself, with no freethought literature to guide me save so much of Paine as was contained in Watson's *Apology* – a work which has led probably many more men to freethought than it has established in orthodoxy – I had slowly reasoned myself out of orthodoxy, and only retained a vague belief in a somewhat abstract Deity, with, I think, an equally attenuated notion of immortality. In this lecture on Bruno, Mr. Bradlaugh, then in his unabated strength, discussed incidentally the theistic position, not bringing many batteries to bear on it, but disposing of it with the secure conviction of a thinker who was master of the whole territory. And I remember how one unanswerable sentence showed me the logical impossibility of the doctrine I had loosely held." (More than half a century later, in response to a letter he received from a young man struggling with religious doubts, Robertson intimated that his own parents, who were very religious, had been pained by his irreversible, if gradual, transition to atheism and freethought.)[75]

Indeed, Robertson's last, posthumously published word on

Bruno, martyred by the Inquisition, was that "Bruno expresses from first to last the spirit of freethought and free speech. *Libertas philosophica* is the breath of his nostrils; and by his life and his death alike he upholds the ideal for men as no other before him did. … A philosophic poet rather than a philosopher or man of science, he yet set abroad for the modern world that conception of the physical infinity of the universe which, once psychologically assimilated, makes an end of the mediaeval theory of things."[76] After being incarcerated for some seven years in papal dungeons, culminating in his being condemned to *auto-da-fé* by the Inquisition, the pantheist prophet of the space age is said to have proudly told his judges "Perhaps you are more afraid to pronounce my sentence than I to receive it", and to have spurned the offer of a crucifix in his agony at the stake. Appropriately, during the 1904 International Freethought Congress in Rome Robertson had a pleasant surprise meeting Alexander Orr, the enterprising Edinburgh secularist who had acted as host when Bradlaugh lectured in 1877 on Bruno; and Robertson was apparently among the great crowd of freethinkers who, at the close of the Congress, gathered in tribute around Bruno's statue, finally erected in 1889, on the very spot in the Piazza Campo dei Fiori where in 1600 he had been burnt to death, not far from the Vatican. Then, in 1911, Bradlaugh's former companion Annie Besant would lecture in Paris, at the Sorbonne, on Bruno and his martyrdom. In September 1889 Robertson represented the N.S.S. at the International Freethought Conference in Paris, where the attendees found time to visit the statues of persecuted freethought heroes like Etienne Dolet (burned alive in Paris for heresy), Voltaire and Diderot, and also to affirm equal rights for men and women.

Only a matter of weeks after Bradlaugh delivered his lecture in Edinburgh on Giordano Bruno, the British freethought leader and Mrs. Annie Besant, his no less remarkable colleague and business partner in the Freethought Publishing Company, were prosecuted for obscenity and committed for trial under the Lord Chief Justice for their republication of Dr. Charles Knowlton's contraceptive manual *The Fruits of Philosophy*, which had originally been published in 1832 in America and which had had a trouble-free if unspectacular sale in Britain for over forty years. Bradlaugh had clearly nailed his colours to the mast of birth control, and in retrospect his action in deliberately courting prosecution in this case was seen as the most courageous act of his tumultuous career, with the Knowlton prosecution dividing the British freethought movement into two camps, those sympathetic and those antagonistic to Bradlaugh. Robertson may have contributed in May 1877 to the Bradlaugh-Besant Defence Fund opened in Bradlaugh's weekly *National Reformer*, and in July he probably attended the enthusiastic public meeting convened by Edinburgh secularists (among whom Alexander Orr reported the meeting for the *National Reformer*) to express support for, and solidarity with, Bradlaugh and Mrs. Besant in their legal battle with the Solicitor-General. Although the two co-defendants were found guilty at the end of their historic trial, during which they represented themselves in an impressive way, punishment was in effect set aside thanks to a legal technicality. During this period sales of Knowlton's well-publicised manual soared, and the Malthusian League – of which Robertson was to become a Vice-President years later – was founded in July 1877, with Annie Besant elected Honorary Secretary. Robertson later recorded that while the Knowlton prosecution "added heavily to Mr Bradlaugh's burden of ostracism, and indirectly helped to shorten his life, the battle constituted an enormous gain to the Neo-Malthusian propaganda. It was fought in 1877-78; and from that date begins the fall of the British birth-rate."[77]

Young Robertson apparently attended the second Annual Conference of the Scottish Secular Union held in the hall at 29 North Bridge, Edinburgh, on Sunday 9 September 1877. At this meeting he seems to have played quite an active part in seconding a motion, successfully carried, for appointment of the Union's president for the ensuing year, and also in successfully moving a resolution for appointment of the treasurer, in the latter case with both the seconder and the treasurer apparently residents of Edinburgh. This was at a time when the S.S.U. was regarded as a kind of Scottish version of the National Secular Society[78] (the Union's outgoing secretary appears to have been a firm Bradlaugh supporter).

Less than three weeks later, Robertson was probably present on 27 September when Mrs. Besant (who had separated from her clergyman husband) spoke in Edinburgh for the first time, at the outset of a lecturing tour under the auspices of the Scottish Secular Union, with the chair at her meeting being taken by her companion Charles Bradlaugh (who lectured there, on population, the next day under S.S.U. auspices, as he had on 2 March on Bruno). Charming, magnetic, intelligent, cultured and beautiful, with a sonorous musical voice, the dark-eyed Mrs. Besant was one of the first women in Britain to gain eminence as an eloquent platform speaker; and she was still young. Before addressing some eight hundred people, she toured the city, "whose beauty", she declared, "is unparalleled in Britain". Her tour reflected the attention she devoted on this occasion to some of the Scottish capital's more attractive and historically distinctive sights: the Scott Monument, a memorial to Sir Walter Scott "worthy both of the writer and of his country"; the Castle, built on mighty rock, in stern grey stone; the uncompromising great doors of St. Giles' Cathedral; the old house where the Calvinist reformer John Knox had lived and worked, and the stone beneath which he was buried; the Antiquarian Museum, where she saw the stool supposedly hurled in 1637 by the vegetable seller Jenny Geddes at the Dean who, in St. Giles, had begun to introduce a new Anglican Book of Common Prayer seen as pro-Catholic (Robertson – who would publish *The Perversion of Scotland* in 1886 as an indictment of the Scottish Presbyterian Church – saw the Jenny Geddes story as "a demonstrated myth" and the exhibition of the stool as "a sufficiently impudent absurdity"[79]); and Holyrood Palace (whose association with Mary, Queen of Scots, for example, was noted by Robertson in a poem printed in 1885).

William Archer

If the year 1877 was particularly memorable for Robertson because of his contact with Charles Bradlaugh and, probably, Annie Besant through seeing and hearing them speak in public, it was no less so because at this time he made the acquaintance in Edinburgh of a fellow Scot who was virtually the same age as himself, and who was destined to become a leading drama critic and a lifelong friend: William Archer. Looking for somewhere to live in Edinburgh on his return from Australia in 1877, Archer found lodgings in two "small but snug" attic rooms ("under the slates", as his brother Charles would put it) in a house at the corner of Hanover Street and George Street, on the brow of a hill. Here William Archer lived for the next year, under the care of an excellent landlady, "as diminutive as her rooms".

During this period John Robertson made his acquaintance "in connection with matters dramatic … in Edinburgh, about 1877" (as Robertson rather opaquely remarked in 1925, shortly after

William Archer's death). Regrettably, no solid information has come to light regarding the first meeting between Robertson and Archer. However, Archer's friends already included three artistic and talented young men with whom he would explore critical ideas: Robert Lowe (who concentrated on the theatre) and George Halkett and Edward Dibdin (who both focused on aspects of art). These three men were working in the insurance business, and Archer's brother Charles would claim (in 1931) that from about 1875 onwards "the same or a neighbouring office" in Edinburgh produced Halkett and Dibdin as well as, apparently, Lowe. Then, in 1877, Dibdin decamped for pastures new in Liverpool, but, for William Archer at least, was quite soon replaced. As Archer's brother would claim: "a new friend, John Mackinnon Robertson, who was to play a large part in the coming years, was furnished by the Insurance Office so fertile in talent." Charles Archer did not identify the insurance company concerned or the location of any of its offices. William Archer's subsequent biographer Peter Whitebrook maintained in 1993 that Lowe was "a clerk at the Scottish Union and National Insurance Company", with which Whitebrook did not associate in any way Halkett, Dibdin or even Robertson[80], who restricted himself to stating that "in my teens I was in the office of a district agency for a Fidelity Guarantee Company". It seems clear that Robertson did not know or meet Lowe, Halkett or Dibdin, who were all older than him, before he met William Archer, and he may not have met members of the quartet until early 1878. Nor has any firm indication emerged from writers on William Archer that Robertson worked in an insurance office at the same time as Lowe, Halkett or Dibdin (this would be consistent with Robertson having worked in an insurance office - not necessarily in Edinburgh - between about 1870 and about 1872).

No doubt Robertson, more particularly in the evenings, quite frequently joined Lowe and Halkett in William Archer's eyrie, where Archer and his friends would occasionally – even on the Sabbath – play a card game like euchre (for two, three or four players, and for which Archer had developed a partiality while in Australia). Archer's landlady disapproved of these card games, and the fact that they were 'for love' did not excuse the practice in her eyes. From time to time Lowe entertained the assembled company with his striking impersonations of the contemporary actor Henry Irving as Hamlet or Richard III. These recitations, and the discussions that doubtless accompanied them, whether in Archer's attic or at Robertson's place, may well have helped to stimulate a love of Shakespeare that became a lifelong passion for Robertson, who, on his own admission, "from his youth up scanned everything on Shakespeare that he could lay hands on". Moreover, Ibsen's work might have been introduced to the circle by Archer, whose family had Scandinavian connections, with Robertson, in his recollections of William and Charles Archer, stating in 1931 that "in the translation of Ibsen they were specially associated over *Peer Gynt*". Robertson also recorded of William Archer: "What he felt he always felt deeply. To hear him read the death-scene from *Peer Gynt* in the original was to know this in special ways."[81]

While all the members of what may be termed the Archer quintet (if Dibdin is also counted) made notable contributions in their chosen literary or artistic fields, Robertson would recall regarding his own early friendship with William Archer: "Almost exactly of an age, we disputed Scottishly on all things … Recognising the width of his culture, even at twenty, and the range of his powers, I urged upon him the choice of some greater task than the systematic handling of the current of ephemera which drifted annually over the London stage.

The economic conditions, one argued, practically excluded the production of anything like great drama, as apart from the transient revivals of established classics." Robertson may have felt more confident as a serving solicitor's clerk or amanuensis than as a one-time insurance office clerk in encouraging his friend Archer to undertake legal training in London as a second string to his bow, and not rely solely on the London theatre to generate sufficient income for him as a drama critic. It seems that, with or without the legal training that he had considered at his father's wish, Archer had already concluded that his future prospects best lay in London. Although Robertson was doubtless sincere in his advice to William Archer, there would have come a point when he realised that if and when his friend resigned from the *Edinburgh Evening News* to go to London, he, Robertson, could be in quite a good position to get a job with the newspaper.

By the age of twenty Archer was already outside current conventional religious belief, but, in Robertson's words, "just because he had never had to undergo any struggle to deliver himself from it, he felt no impulse to criticise it in the open". This relatively tolerant attitude towards religious belief and his seemingly low life-expectancy may have been factors which at this juncture, as at the end of his life, predisposed Archer to some sympathy with Spiritualism, which, as an international movement, could be said to have originated in 1848 in America. In 1878, although he regarded the mass of so-called spiritualistic phenomena as fraudulent, he contended that some were not so, but, with Robertson at least, he was never specific on this score.[82] (At about this time Robertson attended a Spiritualist trance séance at which a Scotch carpenter delivered an address from the spirit of Benjamin Franklin which Robertson described as "a tissue of vacuous verbiage".)

Robertson's friendship with William Archer grew and deepened over a period of about a year, during which, in the course of their discussions, whether in Archer's Hanover Street eyrie or in the countryside together, Archer had been much impressed by the power of mind possessed by Robertson, who considered his new friend the best of companions for a long country walk. Perhaps by this time Robertson was "one of the best-read men of his age" (in two senses of the word "age") or "already a walking encyclopaedia" when he was barely twenty-one. Certainly many of the foundations of his encyclopaedic literary knowledge seem to have been laid between the time he left school in Stirling at 13 and subsequently embarked upon journalism in Edinburgh in 1878. During this period – according to his friend J.P. Gilmour – Robertson "wrote his only novel, which appeared as a serial in a provincial newspaper. He always referred to it apologetically, explaining that it had been written as a pot-boiler, to eke out the slender family finances." Unfortunately, Gilmour, who represented the only known source of information regarding this novel (which has not been traced), did not identify the "provincial newspaper" concerned, the region in which it circulated, the title of the novel, its author's name as published, or its approximate publication date. Moreover, Gilmour was misleading in adding that William Archer left Edinburgh "to take up a journalistic appointment in London".

About to leave Edinburgh to undertake legal training at the Middle Temple in London, Archer decided in mid-August 1878 that Robertson was just the man to succeed him as leader writer on the *Edinburgh Evening News*. According to Archer's recollections penned forty-five years later, a few days before his projected departure for London he met

Robertson at the Edinburgh Philosophical Institution, and the two of them went for a walk round Arthur's Seat in the course of which Archer outlined his intentions and explained his desire that Robertson should succeed him as leader writer. After encouraging Robertson to enter journalism in this way, William Archer introduced him to "Mr. John", the paper's acting editor John Wilson (a co-founder of the *Edinburgh Evening News* five years earlier). Archer recommended Robertson as his successor; and during discussion involving the three men, Archer or Robertson may have mentioned the latter's novel (if, indeed, it had already seen the light of day) and its subject-matter or theme to John Wilson. It may also be assumed that Robertson was more likely to be thought suitable for a responsible job with the *News* when he was an amanuensis to a solicitor, with experience of hearing advocates plead in court, than if he was an insurance clerk at the time. It may be added in this context that the newspaper was in a position to cover and report on court cases and legal matters of public interest.

In his 1923 recollections of this situation in Edinburgh in 1878, Archer wrote of Robertson: "He was then, I think, in an insurance office." But Archer's claim in the preceding sentence of his piece that in 1878 he had "a very slight acquaintance" with Robertson serves to highlight the note of doubt admitted in Archer's account regarding the accuracy of his understanding of the nature of Robertson's employment in, say, early August 1878. What may have confused Archer in 1923 was that young Robertson had worked in an insurance office, as had Archer's friends Robert Lowe, George Halkett and Edward Dibdin. If at least two of these friends were working for the same insurance company, at the same office in Edinburgh or in the same line of business at more or less the same time as Robertson, it may seem rather curious that neither Lowe nor Halkett (not to mention Dibdin) seems to have provided the editor of the *Edinburgh Evening News* with a reference or letter of recommendation on Robertson's behalf. Moreover, contrary to Archer's 1923 account it seems distinctly unlikely that he would have nominated Robertson to succeed him as leader writer on the basis merely of a joint walk and discussion by Arthur's Seat following a chance meeting with him at the Philosophical Institution at a time of "a very slight acquaintance" with him. Other records indicate that the friendship between Archer and Robertson had extended and built up over more than six months before the approach to the *Edinburgh Evening News*.

Becoming leader writer with the *Edinburgh Evening News*

Regarding Robertson's appointment as his successor as leader writer, Archer remembered that "matters were arranged without the slightest difficulty; so that I certainly did the paper yeoman's service – in leaving it". Robertson was no less self-deprecating in his own account of the change-over. Referring to Archer, he declared: "At that period he was occupied in the responsible task of instructing the Edinburgh public … in the columns of the *Edinburgh Evening News*. I believe he began that at the mature age of nineteen; and as I followed him at the age of twenty-one with much less natural ripeness of judgment the Edinburgh public gained nothing by the change." [83] Thus did Robertson, on reaching man's estate, become a journalist with the *Edinburgh Evening News*, which was later congratulated (in 1923) on "its 50 years of consistently brilliant work in the cause of all progressive movements" by the accomplished political opportunist and demagogue

Lloyd George, who in the early twentieth century became Robertson's colleague and foe.

Established in May 1873 by the enterprising brothers Hugh, James and John Wilson, the *News* was regarded as the first successful daily newspaper published in Edinburgh. It ran to two editions daily and circulated in Edinburgh, Leith and all the surrounding districts within a 50 mile radius. When Robertson joined, the *News* still had its offices just off the High Street, at no. 9 in the dingy Old Fishmarket Close, where the paper had first seen the light of day. Despite the distraction caused by the babel from the cells of the police office next door, the newspaper premises had the advantage of being centrally situated, within easy reach of the Court of Session and the Council Chambers. The close proximity of such law enforcement agencies, taken into consideration with Robertson's experience as a clerk in an Edinburgh law office, may well have encouraged John Wilson to believe that this would help the new recruit to settle in at the *News*. (Also employed as a journalist by the *Edinburgh Evening News* – albeit years later – was a future Lord Chief Justice of England, Gordon Hewart, who was a journalist with the *Morning Leader* before that paper commissioned Robertson during the second Anglo-Boer War, and who, like Robertson, was a Liberal M.P. between 1913 and 1918.)

The "independent", Liberal *News*, which gave excellent value for its price of a halfpenny and which attracted dedicated staff and able contributors, epitomised high quality Scottish daily journalism. As leader writer with the *Edinburgh Evening News* Archer had received a salary of about £80 a year from 1875 onwards, and Robertson, who recalled "how frugally we could live in the Scotland of my youth", indicated that his own income was some £2 a week at about this time.[84]

The journalist Hector Macpherson, who joined the editorial staff of the *News* shortly before Archer left, and who became editor of the *News* and the author of published studies of Adam Smith, Carlyle and Herbert Spencer, wrote of these early days: "Mr. William Archer was the principal leader writer. In politics he was somewhat detached. Though in the main sharing the view of Mr. J.M. Robertson, he had not the apostolic enthusiasm of his successor. ... Keenly critical, the advocate of extreme views, fearless in expression, Mr. Robertson was a kind of journalistic Ishmaelite. With my intimate knowledge of him I was perfectly certain that in the larger field of London politics and literature he would take high place in the progressive ranks." Macpherson did not give any definition or examples of the "extreme views" he attributed to Robertson, but a clue to his thinking and robust choice of phrase may be provided by the fact that Macpherson was a staunch defender of Protestantism. However, in his *Books To Read and How to Read Them* (1904) Macpherson did quote with approval a long passage from Robertson's weighty survey *An Introduction to English Politics* (1900), which Macpherson, not unjustly, maintained was a misnamed title – although Robertson's book, particularly in its revised version, remains an authoritative guide to the evolution of lesser European states outside Britain.

Macpherson's son later wrote of the *Edinburgh Evening News*, certainly relating to 1877 onwards, that "it appealed to the staunch Liberalism of the middle and working classes. The proprietors were fortunate, too, in securing the services of young men of distinct talent. My father was one of these. Others may be mentioned, all of whom rose to positions of eminence – Mr. J.M. Robertson, afterwards M.P. for Tyneside and a Minister of State, and the late Mr. William Archer, the famous dramatic critic, who afterwards attained eminence as the chief exponent of Ibsen."[85] Robertson was somewhat critical of the elder Macpherson's championing of the social philosopher Herbert Spencer; and, indeed, Hector Macpherson senior was almost certainly the unnamed "editor" of the *Edinburgh Evening News* who, according to J.P. Gilmour, was "a disciple of Herbert Spencer" and once horrified an "Auld Licht" clergyman, asking to what denominations his young colleagues belonged, by declaring, "Oh, they're maistly atheists": Macpherson became the editor in 1894 after having acted as sub-editor over many years. (Ironically, the writer T.S. Eliot would refer in 1927 to "the Auld Licht atheism of our friend Mr. J.M. Robertson".[86])

With the N.S.S. Edinburgh Branch

Meanwhile, at the beginning of September 1878, the Edinburgh Branch of the Scottish Secular Union decided not to affiliate to Bradlaugh's National Secular Society. This decision was quickly followed by the birth of a separate freethought organisation in Edinburgh, the Edinburgh Branch of the National Secular Society. The emergence of this new body, also known as the Edinburgh Secular Society, was doubtless facilitated by the deliberate exclusion and denial of a speaker's platform in that city for Charles Bradlaugh, who found himself forced to cancel speaking engagements there regarding three halls in succession during September (which was the very month, according to J.P. Gilmour, Robertson heard Bradlaugh lecture on Bruno). This hostility towards Bradlaugh was probably connected with the fact that he and Mrs. Besant were still involved to a greater or lesser extent with legal issues relating in some way to the Knowlton birth control pamphlet prosecution (Mrs. Besant had been due to lecture in Edinburgh on 26 September). The Edinburgh Secular Society appointed Alexander Orr as its organising secretary: he was an upholsterer and cabinet-maker, and later the inventor and patentee of a carpet-beating machine. Orr, who was some twenty years older than Robertson, seems to have worked hard to ensure the success of Bradlaugh's lectures in Edinburgh, including the one on Bruno, some eighteen months earlier; and he would remain one of the staunchest freethinkers in "the Athens of the North" for some four or five decades until his death in 1919.

Having embraced the National Secular Society's principles of promoting human happiness through rigorous social and political reform, fighting religion as an obstacle to human progress, and removing legal disabilities and social discrimination oppressing freethinkers, the Edinburgh Secular Society acquired the use of relatively spacious premises, the New Hall, 3 Chambers Street, where the first lecture delivered on that site to the burgeoning Society was devoted to the British Radical and iconoclast William Godwin by Thomas Carlaw Martin on 6 October 1878. Some six years older than Robertson, who esteemed his trusted and talented co-worker, Martin was, at about this time, an administrator with the Post Office in Edinburgh as well as music critic for the *Edinburgh Evening News*. As a music critic, if not as a secularist, Martin would have been acutely aware of the accuracy of the dire picture of Sundays in Edinburgh, for example, drawn by "a Scotchman" in the *Free Sunday Advocate* for February 1877: "A few years ago it was a rare thing to hear the sound of a piano on Sunday, and to discourse even the sacred musical beauties of Haydn, Mozart, Handel, or Beethoven, would have been deemed a most impious thing." It was scarcely surprising, therefore, that, in an attempt to loosen the deadening grip of Sabbatarianism, at the Edinburgh Secular

Society's second reported meeting – on 13 October – "music, of a kind, was introduced for the first time at the meeting".[87]

It was into this enterprising and promising Society that young Robertson stepped, and he quickly followed Martin in addressing its supporters. On 13 October a tailor called Job Bone, who was a vociferous advocate of Christianity, was given the freedom of the Edinburgh Secular Society's platform and – in Alexander Orr's words – "lectured on Attractive Secularism, which he said was very unattractive". Two weeks later, on 27 October 1878, at a crowded meeting, Robertson gave his first known freethought lecture: entitled "A Defence of Secularism", it was, no doubt, a forceful rejoinder to Job Bone, who loved to speak at secularist meetings in Edinburgh, and who was subsequently barred by the Edinburgh Branch of the National Secular Society for at least eighteen months for his excessively coarse language after an address by Mrs. Besant on Evolution. After Robertson's lecture Alexander Orr recorded in Bradlaugh's *National Reformer*: "Mr. Robertson is a well-educated young man, and a good debater."[88]

This was at a time when, as Robertson himself would indicate in *The Dynamics of Religion* (1897), it was still largely the case that "Secularist lectures were almost the only forms of non-religious intellectual excitement that were widely accessible on Sundays in most English towns"; and it seems that this was also broadly true of Scotland as a whole. On 6 March 1879 the untimely death of the esteemed secular lecturer W. Kingdon Clifford was briefly noticed in the *Edinburgh Evening News* (on its back page); but the obituaries of him were no more prominent or informative in the *North Briton*, *Scotsman* or *Edinburgh Daily Review*.

Orr concluded his report in the *National Reformer* for 3

November 1878 by noting: "Since the refusal of the halls to Mr. Bradlaugh and Mrs. Besant there have been crowded audiences every Sunday evening." But by the following March Bradlaugh was back in Edinburgh, lecturing there for the first time since he was denied a public platform during September 1878. On 23 March 1879 Bradlaugh delivered three lectures in the hall at 11 Chambers Street under the auspices of the Edinburgh Branch of the Scottish Secular Union, with large audiences on all three occasions. The next day the *Edinburgh Evening News* journalist (almost certainly Robertson) covering these lectures named Job Bone as having participated in the short discussion that had followed Bradlaugh's morning lecture (on theism), and also reported that the evening lecture was devoted to "The Impeachment of the Tory Ministry" (including a commentary on Britain's declaration of war on Afghanistan in 1878 and subsequent military operations which involved the British Indian Army).

It may be surmised that, with Job Bone as the likely heckler, this evening meeting on 23 March was the meeting referred to, about half a century or more later, by Robertson's friend Dr. Alfred Cox, who recalled:

"J.M.R. [John Mackinnon Robertson] said he was once at a meeting which Bradlaugh was addressing on India. It was either during the Knowlton *Fruits of Philosophy* trial or soon after. Bradlaugh was in the middle of his speech when a man in the audience cried: "But what about Malthusianism?" Bradlaugh paused, gave the man a look which J.M.R. said ought to have withered him, and went on. Again, later, the same interruption. Bradlaugh stopped, fixed the unfortunate man with his eyes, and said: "I came here to talk about India, but since our friend seems curious about Malthusianism let me say that there is such a thing, and I wish his parents had known of it." … As J.M.R. said, and one can well believe it, these devastating retorts, with their crushing finality, made a deep impression on the hearers."[89]

Bradlaugh's daughter Alice started the London Secular Choral Union in 1878, and very soon afterwards, by November of that year, the Edinburgh Secular Society formed a small choir under Mr. Laubach the conductor, in an attempt to extend the cultural, and enhance the social, aspects of life in a secularist community. Such a step could have helped to raise the morale of Edinburgh secularists during the ensuing winter, at about the time that Robertson supposedly wrote his poem *A Birthday Dirge*, with its playful touch of mock-solemnity:

"Oh, why was I in winter born,
In such a leafless time forlorn,
With nought of amber in the light,
And nought of fragrance in the night:
How can I, on my day of birth,
Stir in my veins a pulse of mirth,
In looking on the haggard earth?"

In the poem there was no sign of a romantic relationship or soul mate at that stage in Robertson's life. The sense of desolation or alienation pervading the poem may be related to the assessment reached by the visiting secularist lecturer Charles Watts in February 1879: "It is truly heart-rending to see the poverty which is now casting such a gloom over Scotland."[90] This in turn would appear to be consistent with Robertson's later recollection of "how frugally we could live in the Scotland of my youth".

Befriending Joseph Mazzini Wheeler

On Sunday, 2 March 1879, Robertson himself lectured to the Scottish Secular Union in Edinburgh on "Rational Morality", and, according to Alexander Orr, the lecture and the ensuing discussion were "interesting and instructive". Before that, on 5 January that year, Robertson probably attended "a most able lecture" (in Orr's words) on "The Theory of Evolution" delivered to Edinburgh secularists by the freethinker Joseph Mazzini Wheeler, who was befriended at about this time by the Scot from Arran. Six years older than Robertson, Wheeler was a nervously vivacious, highly-strung and hypersensitive man who was also loyal, brave and modest, and who would emerge as one of the most erudite and lovable of leading late Victorian freethinkers. His father, a Radical journalist, had named him in admiration of the great Italian patriot Mazzini, whose hand, Robertson believed, had been laid on the child's head. After his father's death, Wheeler moved to Edinburgh, where he worked as a lithographer and designer for a colour-printing firm and publishing house; and it was while employed in this capacity that he first met Robertson, who came to regard him as "my old comrade". Although Wheeler as an artist produced some fine landscape paintings, he seemed to prefer reading and writing, illustrated by his contributions to freethought journals. In Robertson's eyes, "he was one of the most variously read men I have ever known. If he could be said to have a speciality it was perhaps the literature of the religions of India … I found that he had perused the whole printed mass of the Elizabethan drama; and in the best European and English literature he was as much at home as in anthropology, in which he might have ranked as an expert. All the while he was versed in the philosophical and scientific discussions of the generation; and whether the talk was of Spencer, or Darwin, or Malthus, or Mill, or Maurice, or Martineau, Wheeler was always among the best informed."

Wheeler would relocate to London in 1881 to assist as sub-editor in the preparation and production of the *Freethinker*, a new journal founded and edited by his friend George William Foote, whom he had known since 1868 and who would eventually succeed Bradlaugh as N.S.S. President. Tragically Wheeler was only forty-eight when he died in 1898, having suffered recurrent mental problems. But although his premature death was a great loss to freethought (one of his works would be remembered by Robertson in the 1932 edition of his *Courses of Study*), perhaps Wheeler's least known mark of distinction was that his Edinburgh lecture of 5 January 1879 on "The Theory of Evolution" was given before British secularists outside London became fully appreciative of the significance of Darwin's contribution, which was largely due to Edward Aveling's extensive articles, devoted to Darwin, in the *National Reformer* from 19 January 1879 onwards.[91] In September that year Dr. Aveling lectured to the Scottish Secular Union on Darwin's *The Descent of Man*.

In addition to Aveling, Bradlaugh and G.W. Foote, the speakers from across the Tweed who came to address the Edinburgh secularists in the course of 1879, and whom young Robertson almost certainly saw and heard at this time, included Charles Watts, Touzeau Parris, Dr. C.R. Drysdale, and Joseph Symes. Of these four, all were involved or associated in some way with the Knowlton (birth control) law case.

Charles Watts, son of a Wesleyan minister, was remembered by Robertson as a "genial and eloquent lecturer". Watts's words, however, had proved to be rather more heroic than his deeds, for although he had himself published an edition of

Knowlton's *Fruits of Philosophy*, he had subsequently pleaded guilty to a charge that, in so doing, he had infringed the Obscene Publications Act – whereas Bradlaugh and Besant resolved to publish a new edition of the book. Regarded by Robertson as an abler lecturer than Watts, Touzeau Parris, who was formerly a Unitarian minister, had succeeded Watts in 1877 as one of Bradlaugh's lieutenants, becoming secretary of the Bradlaugh-Besant defence committee in the Knowlton prosecution, and then a Vice-President of the new Malthusian League. A notable physician, an outspoken rationalist and a lifelong birth control advocate, Charles Robert Drysdale had given evidence on behalf of Bradlaugh and Mrs. Besant at the Knowlton trial. With his enthusiasm, charm and considerable knowledge of the population question, Dr. Drysdale seemed a model propagandist to his audience in Edinburgh, where at about this time he made Robertson's acquaintance, which grew into a friendship broken only by Drysdale's death a quarter of a century later. (Robertson's esteem for Touzeau Parris was indicated by the busy M.P.'s membership of a committee formed in August 1907 to help a now infirm Parris shortly before the latter died.)[92]

Joseph Symes, a former Wesleyan who publicly addressed Edinburgh secularists a number of times in May 1879, had joined the Bradlaugh-Besant defence committee in the Knowlton case. He was later prompted by Bradlaugh to go out to Australia to beat the drum there for freethought and secularism, which Symes did for twenty-two years from 1884 onwards. Strangely, Robertson's *History of Freethought in the Nineteenth Century* (1929) failed to notice Symes's endeavours and those of others in Australia, which, if recorded, would have helped to flesh out a disappointingly thin section in Robertson's book. However, the paths of the two veterans appeared to converge in December 1906 when, with Robertson now M.P. for Tyneside, Symes, just days before his own death, was the centre of public events in Newcastle, where many of those attending were most probably drawn from Robertson's constituency.

Following his visit to Scotland, Symes concluded in early June 1879: "One thing impressed me during my visit – the rapidity with which Scottish orthodoxy is breaking up. … What with heretics at home, Jews and heathens abroad, and demoralisation in their own camp, Presbyterians are just now in a very bad way in Edinburgh, while Freethought is flourishing there." This appeared to be consistent with Alexander Orr's observation, also in Bradlaugh's *National Reformer*, just three weeks earlier: "The propaganda carried on by the Edinburgh society is gradually attracting public attention and gaining the respect of many new sympathisers." By this time, as the late twentieth century historian Stan Shipley noted of Victorian secularists, "in the *National Reformer* they had a weekly newspaper which served as a platform for every radical cause; and a depth of platform speaking power which, at least in London, could not be matched. First as an orator came Charles Bradlaugh…" It seems such an assessment would have been applicable, at least in part, to the situation in Edinburgh in 1879, when a new Sunday science school in the handsome hall at 3 Chambers Street was contemplated for the teaching of science to children above the age of seven. Prominent among Edinburgh secularists promoting and supporting this project was Thomas Carlaw Martin (who within a few years would pen a pamphlet on the custody and guardianship of children), with William Gavazzi King as the school's prospective superintendent.[93]

Lure of the Philosophical Institution

Quite probably at about this time Robertson – settling into his new job as a newspaper leader writer and presumably earning more money than previously – joined the Philosophical Institution, with which he was clearly familiar. Founded in 1846 and based in Queen Street, the Edinburgh Philosophical Institution would be well described as "a body which has little to do with philosophy in the strict sense, but which has for long done much to sustain the general intellectual life of the city by means of its library and the courses of lectures which are held in its hall". It would be seen by different eyes in a more flickering light as "an organisation of some standing, whose main purpose is to provide popular lectures by eminent persons; it possesses a fairly large general library, with a reading-room attached". The Library had over 17,000 volumes by 1869 (rising to 24,000 by 1882); and the distinguished lecturers included Macaulay, Thackeray, Dickens, Charles Kingsley, Trollope, Emerson, Matthew Arnold, R.M. Ballantyne, T.H. Huxley, Ruskin, and Alfred Russel Wallace over the decades. The Institution had over two thousand members by 1878; and many of the lectures were memorably presided over by Dr. William Smith, a self-educated and self-made man, a devoted interpreter of the German thinker Fichte, and a strong Liberal, who was, in Robertson's words, "a most worthy gentleman, whose benignant face I well remember". William Smith died in 1896, in his eightieth year. But Robertson returned to the Philosophical Institution during its 1910-11 session (while he was an M.P.) to give a lecture on "The Glory that was Greece".[94] Arguably the lectures in Edinburgh that Robertson attended during the years 1877-79 formed quite an important part of his education, offering scholarly pointers for further reflection, reading and research, as well as techniques and tips for him to take into account as a public speaker. With his thirst for knowledge, commitment to truth and love of debate, Robertson would certainly have been keen to attend, or receive reports of, lectures given at the Philosophical Institution or by secularist speakers visiting Edinburgh.

In 1876 the telephone had been invented by Scottish-born Alexander Graham Bell, but by 1879 it was not yet in general use, and even telegraph facilities were not always available. "In those days", Robertson later wrote of the staff of the *Edinburgh Evening News*, "we reckoned ourselves enterprising in respect of the establishment of carrier pigeons in a turret". Possibly encouraged by Reuter's success in using a pigeon post on the Continent as relatively early as 1849, the *News* had obtained a consignment of young carrier pigeons from Belgium, and after training they were used in the Edinburgh area to report events within a radius of twenty miles or so. They were installed in the newspaper's office in Old Fishmarket Close and, on the whole, were remarkably effective, though they could be exasperatingly time-wasting. Occasionally they would perch on the branch of a tree or the roof of a house instead of heading straight for home from the scene of the action, or at the end of their flight they might remain on the pinnacle of the turret and refuse to be enticed within, despite the attraction of food plentifully spread inside the landing stage. "Of the old office, my memories are all pleasant", declared Robertson, who moved with the *News* in early 1879 to its new home at 18 Market Street, where, in a building previously used as a warehouse, with what he called "its pleasant situation facing the Princes Street gardens", the newspaper was composed in the top flat and printed in the basement.[95]

Two Political Thunderbolts: Gladstone and Bradlaugh

Then, in November 1879, Edinburgh was struck by a political thunderbolt whose reverberations were heard not only throughout Scotland, but throughout the British Isles. William Ewart Gladstone, who had retired from the Liberal Party leadership in 1875, had accepted an invitation to contest the safe Conservative seat of Midlothian in the Edinburgh area; and just a few weeks short of his seventieth birthday, the Grand Old Man burst out of his four years' retirement and journeyed to Scotland to mount a fierce campaign denouncing, with all of his old eloquence and fire, the record at home and abroad of Disraeli's administration. Enthusiastic crowds, largely of working men, gathered at railway stations through which his train passed between Liverpool and Edinburgh to cheer Gladstone on his triumphant journey north. Although darkness had fallen by the time he reached Edinburgh, dense welcoming crowds lined Gladstone's route along Princes Street to catch a glimpse of the former Prime Minister, with his manly and commanding presence, his tall athletic frame, his wispy white hair, his stern white face, and his restless, flashing dark eyes. Standing erect in Lord Rosebery's carriage, Gladstone, hat in hand, bowed repeatedly to the jubilant spectators. Bonfires illuminated the hills and fireworks irradiated the sky. It was truly an impressive and auspicious start to the fortnight of impassioned speech-making known to history as the first Midlothian Campaign, launched in days when Members of Parliament rarely addressed their constituents between elections and still less indulged in hectic electioneering before an election date had even been announced.

Gladstone's arrival on 24 November elicited favourable comment next day from the *Edinburgh Evening News*, in a leading article probably penned by Robertson: "Few even of his opponents will deny him honour for a roll of achievements in legislation far surpassing in merit and greatness those of any other statesman of the present generation." On 29 November Gladstone addressed some five thousand Liberal supporters from all over Scotland in the Corn Exchange, Grassmarket, while in front of the building a large banner proclaimed: "Welcome to Gladstone, the liberator of the country, guardian of Britain's honour, peace, and prosperity." On his arrival, Gladstone was greeted with great enthusiasm and delivered what Robertson apparently chose to call "a great speech" on Disraeli's economic policy. At this time the *Edinburgh Evening News* was a pioneer among British evening papers in performing feats of rapid production, and Robertson later recorded how, thanks to the reporting staff of the *News* acting in conjunction with the forces of the Press Association ("whose genial chief I well remember") and "dexterous work in the composing room under a masterly foreman", the *News* produced a verbatim report of Gladstone's speech in a special edition that was on sale in the Grassmarket before the last of the orator's audience had dispersed.[96]

In March 1880, misled by two by-election results in England and overlooking electoral implications of signs of an industrial and agricultural depression in Britain, Disraeli announced an early dissolution of Parliament. Gladstone responded by seizing the opportunity to embark on his second Midlothian Campaign within four months. In his campaigning Gladstone espoused the principles of peace and non-intervention abroad, "using language which gave us a right to expect that when in power he would consult Parliament before entering on any war. Of course, he never stood to his words. He not only made fresh wars; he made wars which by his own later confession were unjustifiable, and all without consulting

Parliament. But to-day he is none the less ready for new war; the guilt of past bloodshed having ceased to burden his conscience." These withering criticisms were voiced almost at the end of Gladstone's life by a disillusioned Robertson, who made similar comments, as follows, a few years after the 1880 election: "Nothing could be more impressive, more apparently sincere, than his prae-triumphal declaration that the people of these kingdoms ought to have the power of deliberating in Parliament on the expediency of any war in which Ministers desired to embark; and nothing could be more complete than his virtual repudiation of that principle since. … The reminiscence is an evil one for those who have been deceived in him." Although Robertson was fully aware by 1897 of "the vice in our Constitution which makes it possible to a Cabinet to enter into war without even pretending to consult the representatives of the people"[97], a later British Prime Minister arguably showed more contempt than Gladstone by directly misleading Parliament, disallowing adequate scrutiny and debate regarding a case for war, and encouraging Parliament to vote for war on a deeply flawed and spurious basis, as happened in the run-up to the 2003 Iraq War.

But if chicanery by some, and disillusionment for others, lay ahead, in early 1880 enthusiasm abounded for Gladstone and the stunning Liberal Party victory both in Midlothian and on a national scale in that year's general election. "There can be no doubt that a great share of the remarkable enthusiasm which has led to such very remarkable results on the Liberal side is due to the two series of speeches delivered by Mr. Gladstone in Midlothian. … Bowed with the weight of seventy years, which have been filled with an amount of hard work which no contemporary statesman can pretend to have equalled, he has achieved with apparent ease oratorical performances which would have been magnificent if coming from a man in his prime." Thus declared the *Edinburgh Evening News* on 3 April in a leading article probably penned by Robertson, who later commented on the role of the *News*: "In those days our politics were 'independent', but I doubt whether there was a non-Liberal on the staff; and when the results of the 1880 election were being put up at nights in the office window – above all when we arranged an "illumination" with the Midlothian results for an upper window – the brother proprietors [John and James Wilson] were as joyously juvenile in their Liberal enthusiasm as the rest of us." Indeed, when on the rainy evening of 5 April in Edinburgh, the Midlothian result was declared to reveal that Gladstone had been elected with 1,579 votes to Lord Dalkeith's 1,368 in a 90% poll, the waiting crowd of several thousands erupted into loud cheering and rejoicing. Although he had been vilified by Pope Pius IX as "a viper" and although abhorred by Queen Victoria as "that half-mad firebrand", Gladstone – "the People's William" - became Prime Minister for the second time.[98] This messianic leader evidently believed that "wonderful and nothing less has been the disposing hand of God in all this matter".

If Gladstone the Christian secured a notable personal triumph at Midlothian, Bradlaugh the atheist scored a no less memorable victory at Northampton, where, after unsuccessfully contesting the constituency for some twelve years, he was elected as one of the two M.P.s for the town. In a leading article almost certainly by Robertson, the *Edinburgh Evening News* commented on 16 April: "The influence from which Mr. Bradlaugh suffers most, however, is perhaps not simple bigotry, but rather snobbery. He has to struggle against the weight of that species of popular opinion which is hostile to a man who openly avows himself an Atheist and Republican, but which pays homage to Professors Tyndall and Huxley, despite their Agnosticism, which is practically the same as Atheism; and is friendly to Sir Charles Dilke, whose Republicanism is rendered respectable by his baronetcy." [99] (The leader writer could have added that seven years earlier, in 1873, the Liberal man of letters John Morley, in his study of Rousseau, had spelt God with a small 'g' and Matthew Arnold, in *Literature and Dogma*, had written of the Trinity as "three Lord Shaftesburys".) In a letter of 22 May 1880 to Gladstone, Queen Victoria wrote of Bradlaugh: "It is not only his known atheism, but it is his other horrible principles which make him a disgrace to an assembly like the House of Commons." By contrast, in a letter four days later to her Private Secretary, Lord Halifax declared: "Whatever Bradlaugh's character may be, the legal and constitutional rights of a man chosen by any constituency must not be set aside." Indeed, thousands of electors in Northampton voted for Bradlaugh, whereas none had voted for Victoria to be Queen; and four more elections and six years of bitter struggle were to pass before this openly avowed atheist would be permitted to take his seat in Parliament. During this time one of Bradlaugh's most vociferous Parliamentary enemies was future Prime Minister Arthur Balfour, whose attack on Bradlaugh on the affirmation issue was noticed in Robertson's *Toryism and Barbarism* (1885).

From Across the Tweed

By 1880 Bradlaugh's National Secular Society claimed to have some six thousand members – and many more supporters and sympathisers – and more than sixty active branches throughout the British Isles. One of the more notable centres of freethought in Britain was Edinburgh, where during the first few months of 1880 the speakers from across the Tweed who addressed the Edinburgh secularists, and whom Robertson probably heard at this time, included the libertarian Joseph Hiam Levy, the social reformer Arthur B. Moss, and the Marxian socialist Mrs. Harriet Law. Through their lectures, and the ensuing discussions, these three freethinkers may have helped to shape, extend or modify Robertson's political outlook and sympathies. Levy, who was judged to be a logical and convincing writer and speaker, taught political economy at the City of London College and was also regarded as a competent commentator on Biblical criticism. For Robertson he was "one of the ablest contributors to the *National Reformer*", and Levy and Robertson were courteous opponents when they clashed in its columns in June 1884 following publication of a report by Robertson on the debate between Bradlaugh and the pro-Marxist H.M. Hyndman on socialism. Arthur B. Moss, who was slightly older than Robertson, had attended a grammar school in South London until the age of twelve, when his father lost his job through illness, and young Arthur had to work for a living, initially as an office boy, clerk, and then local reporter. He was a devout Christian until he was 16, when he read Thomas Paine's *The Age of Reason*, and he thereafter began attending lectures at the London Hall of Science in 1874. With these striking similarities to Robertson's early life behind him, Moss gave his first lecture to the Scottish Secular Union in Edinburgh in February 1880 and was "overjoyed" when, in the committee-room after the lecture, he received words of encouragement from Robertson and other committee members. Later Moss was able to assist George Sims in collecting material for his book *How the Poor Live* (1883). Moss lived to become one of the veterans of the modern British freethought movement and, on Robertson's death, to pronounce an eloquent eulogy of the leader he had admired and followed for over forty years.

Marx, Bradlaugh and Holyoake

Rather different, but no less noteworthy, was Mrs. Harriet Law, of whom Robertson is not known to have published his opinion. Like Robertson, but unlike Karl Marx, she was a long-standing supporter of the movement for women's rights and votes for women. None the less, she was (in the words of a respected historian of British secularism) "one of the few Secularists of whom Karl Marx approved". Marx's approval may have been associated with the fact that between 1867 and 1872 this stout ex-Baptist with a thunderous voice was the only female member of the General Council of his (First) International, and that she did not have a positive relationship with Bradlaugh, who in the autumn of 1871 launched a public attack, spilling over into 1872, on both the International and Marx at about the time the former was being split in two by followers of Marx and of the anarchist Bakunin respectively. In July 1871 Engels claimed that he and Marx opposed a Bakuninist proposal to make atheism and materialism essential principles of the International, as to incorporate them "would mean to drive away a vast number of members".[100] From about 1866 onwards Marx criticised British secularist leaders like G.J. Holyoake and, later, Bradlaugh as, it is suggested, he saw an emergent British secularist movement growing in strength and Bradlaugh's ability to rally radical members of the British working class as an obstacle, if not a potential threat, to the smooth progress of the International (which disintegrated by 1876, a year marked by the passing of Bakunin, who not long before he died perceptively foresaw the coming of total war).

After her Edinburgh lecture on 1 February 1880 Harriet Law began to disengage as an active freethought lecturer. But on the ex-Baptist's death *The Reformer* declared in August 1897 (in words probably by the editor Hypatia Bradlaugh Bonner) that "her native eloquence, her fearless outspokenness and earnest conviction won for her many friends and admirers".

Meanwhile, during the early 1880s, Robertson himself was becoming increasingly known in Edinburgh, and farther afield, as a freethinker and secularist (with his regular newspaper work appearing to be anonymous).

In May 1880 the Scottish Secular Union was addressed in Edinburgh by the esteemed social reformer George Jacob Holyoake, who was regarded both as the founder of secularism and as Bradlaugh's rival, though dismissed by Karl Marx as "the thin-voiced, intrusive, consequential Holyoake, who from 'love of the truth' always finds his way into the *Times*". (Holyoake had also found his way to prison in Britain, through blasphemy, unlike the atheist Marx.) Because Holyoake suffered from a prostrating cold, he spoke once only in the Chambers Street Hall; and on the second occasion later the same day he was due to lecture there, his place on the platform was taken – presumably at very short notice – by Robertson, with Holyoake subsequently sending the Edinburgh secularists a message from his sick-bed congratulating them on their "clear and useful programme of secular principles". Half a century later Robertson wrote: "Holyoake never ceased to associate himself actively with freethought propaganda, and remained one of its ablest writers", but eclipsed "in a measure" as an orator and debater by Bradlaugh.[101] Another secularist known to the Edinburgh brethren and to British Marxists was Edward Truelove, commemorated by Engels in 1888 for having published in 1871 Marx's *The Civil War in France*.

Fighting Superstition and Reaction

In early July 1880 a writer in the *Secular Review* (which had been founded by Holyoake) called Edinburgh "this citadel of refined superstition"; and almost a year later "Acid Drops" declared in the first issue of the *Freethinker* : "Secularism in Edinburgh has a good deal of bigotry to contend with. Mr Alexander Orr, the Society's secretary, secured a bookstall in the Waverley Market some time ago, and did a roaring business in Freethought literature, until the authorities became alarmed and turned him out."   In view of such unfavourable circumstances it was perhaps not entirely surprising that in Parliament on 22 June a pro-Bradlaugh petition was presented, favouring a new Affirmation Bill but, so far as Edinburgh was concerned, signed by no more than 92 inhabitants (who almost certainly included Robertson). Less than four weeks later, in July 1880, young Robertson addressed the Secular Union in Edinburgh on two successive Sundays; on the first, 11 July, when he stood in at very short notice for a lecturer who had unexpectedly failed to appear, Robertson gave a closely reasoned defence of atheism, and on the second occasion he read an "able" paper in which he maintained that the emotions growing out of the intellectual life of a freethinker were of a higher order than those cultivated by a religionist.[102]

Two months later he was elected to the Scottish Secular Union's Executive at its annual meeting in the city, where, in early October, he attended a freethought gathering of "most attentive and intelligent ladies and gentlemen" who, as reported by *The Malthusian*, were present (apparently in the hall at 3 Chambers Street) to show support for birth control and to be addressed by Dr. C.R. Drysdale and his co-worker Dr. Alice Vickery of the Malthusian League. Then, on 31 October, the League's Edinburgh Branch was formally inaugurated, with its elected committee including Robertson, Thomas Carlaw Martin, W.E. Snell (a clerk in the Queen's Remembrancer's Office who was also the S.S.U.'s suave, scholarly and University-educated joint secretary), William Gavazzi King (who was also a member of the S.S.U. Executive), and Mr. and Mrs. Marshall (whom Robertson may have subconsciously regarded as his surrogate parents).

William Marshall would have been about sixty and his common-law wife Eliza at least fifty at this time. They were quite a noteworthy couple. Marshall, who worked as a coal agent, would be remembered by Robertson as a friend of liberal causes and as "a man of wide culture and varied experience, conversant with many sciences, and bringing to bear on all themes a penetrating and strong intelligence". He frequently lectured on scientific or economic subjects to the Edinburgh secularists, of whom he and his common-law wife were valued supporters. He gave service as a cellist and she as a pianist, Eliza being a highly intelligent, well-educated woman and a competent musician and linguist who had been ostracised on account of her freethought and free love union with William Marshall. Years later Robertson, who kept in touch, would write of her that her large share of human sorrows had been redressed by the high ministries of love, art and reason, and that "I have known no life of a more beautiful simplicity, no character of more solid worth". Though the Marshalls were always poor, their thrift permitted a simple hospitality which enabled many young freethinkers to get to know one another at their home. It was conceivably thanks to the enterprise of Mr. and Mrs. Marshall that Robertson came to appreciate the music of Beethoven and Schubert (to each of whom he would devote one of his published poems), Eliza being a fiery interpreter of Beethoven's piano sonatas, for example.[103]

Then, in early October 1880, Robertson probably attended the very crowded and very enthusiastic meeting in Edinburgh – addressed by Bradlaugh and presided over by the local Bradlaughite John Lees – at which the programme of Bradlaugh's moderately radical Land Law Reform League (founded in February that year) was endorsed amidst much cheering and with only four dissentients. Less than two weeks later Robertson gave his first known lectures outside Edinburgh. This was when, on 17 October, he gave his first lectures to the Glasgow Eclectic and Secular Institute and Branch of the N.S.S. in a hall at 20 King Street which, although centrally situated, stood in a rather dilapidated and delinquent area inhabited (according to the Glaswegian secularist James Pinkerton Gilmour) by "low Irish and a miscellaneous rabble of somewhat cosmopolitan composition". To approach the hall, which was completely surrounded by other buildings, the lecturer had to walk along a foul, low-roofed passage emerging into a noisy, evil-smelling courtyard. But Robertson was not deterred, and he clearly seems to have been well received. In the morning he talked about "The Future of Faith" (which Gilmour's colleague J. Terris said was "treated in a very able manner"); and that Sunday evening he took "Emotional Religion" as his subject, which was a repeat of the lecture he had given to an appreciative audience in Edinburgh on 18 July. Gilmour commented: "from the very beginning we recognized in him a coming man." A week after his visit to Glasgow Robertson lectured to the Scottish Secular Union in the hall at 3 Chambers Street, Edinburgh, on the life and works of the recently deceased British writer Harriet Martineau, who had opposed slavery in America and elsewhere, supported the Defence Committee for the freethought publisher Edward

Truelove arrested in 1858, commended "the range and mass of knowledge" in Darwin's *Origin of Species*, and espoused feminism in the nineteenth century.[104]

At about this time a visiting American Congregationalist minister much admired in some quarters for his oratory, the Rev. Joseph Cook of Boston, was invited, but declined, to debate with Bradlaugh. On the last Sunday in November 1880, while Cook was addressing working men in Edinburgh on the credibility of Christianity, Robertson was attacking Cook's credibility in a secularist lecture in the same city. According to the *Secular Review*, Robertson "gave a very keen and searching criticism, which evidently went home to the minds of the Christians present". According to the *Edinburgh Courant*, he "virulently attacked Mr. Cook, and declared he had no respect for him whatsoever. Mr. Cook had proved himself to be a snob by having declared in America that freethinkers were impecunious." At the close of Robertson's address the Christian Job Bone replied to some of the lecturer's remarks, and claimed there could be no greater contrast than that between Cook's works and Robertson's "atheistic ravings".[105] Robertson's commitment to the freethought cause, and also, possibly, his status as a single man over Christmas, would be indicated by the fact that he was billed to give an address to the Scottish Secular Union in Edinburgh on 26 December (with a collection for expenses).

Interpreting Shakespeare and Carlyle

As a humanist Robertson combined his critical interest in theological questions and his love of the arts when on Sunday, 30 January 1881 he gave the S.S.U. in Chambers Street what its Corresponding Secretary, W.E. Snell, called "an able lecture, in which he pointed out the thoroughly secular tone of Shakspere's plays". Robertson's lecture was no doubt prepared quite independently of the pro-socialist Anglican clergyman the Rev. Charles W. Stubbs, who, it seems, gave a lecture at about this time to the Leicester Secular Society on "The Religion of Shakespeare" and "was frank enough to say that he could find no evidence in the plays that Shakespeare had any religion except 'The Religion of Humanity' " (in the words of the Leicester secularist Sydney Gimson, who from about 1890 onwards became one of Robertson's close friends). However, a work by a Church of England cleric and writer studied by Robertson in 1881 was *A Short History of the English People* by John Richard Green, of whose book Robertson justifiably wrote half a century later: "Green, if romantic and at times poetically speculative, is notably vivid." Many years later, if not when he delivered his 1881 lecture (which may well have been his first on Shakespeare), Robertson boldly claimed that Green was "the first historical writer to confront his readers with the fact that Shakespeare stood outside the Christian creed". This was an inflated claim which did not rest on an impeccably logical line of argument; although Robertson prayed in aid, so to speak, "Prospero's reverie, and Hamlet's 'The rest is silence', and Macbeth's 'To-morrow and to-morrow and to-morrow' ", regarding Shakespeare's presumed philosophy of life.[106] (Robertson's point of view would be largely supported some eighty years later by the Shakespeare scholar Curtis Brown Watson.)

In the course of his long and intellectually active life Robertson lectured and wrote not only on Shakespeare, but also on Thomas Carlyle, on whose death a leader writer wrote in the *Edinburgh Evening News* for 5 February 1881: "there has now passed away the most celebrated British man of letters of the last half century. Thomas Carlyle died this morning. … What he has done to mould the character of the youth of the English-speaking races during the past fifty years is incalculable … He has never been in sympathy with the spirit of democracy which is spreading throughout the world; and his "Strong Man theory of history" – in its absolute application – is rejected by the most original and energetic minds of the day. …" These words probably flowed from Robertson's pen; and among the young British men on whom Carlyle had an influence or impact between about 1875 and the late 1920s may be mentioned, in addition to Robertson, the Liberal David Lloyd George (in 1880), the anarchist Herbert Read, and the Conservative Enoch Powell. Of these three, Lloyd George was the only one who became a colleague of Robertson's; and had Robertson lived until about the end of 1936, instead of dying in January 1933, it seems unlikely that he would have been surprised to learn of the praise for Hitler as "a born leader" liberally bestowed by Lloyd George, whose sense of political Messianism and lust for personal power, with ruinous consequences for the Liberal Party, had already been roundly criticised by Robertson in *Mr. Lloyd George and Liberalism* (1923) following Lloyd George's downfall as Prime Minister.

Death of Disraeli

Meanwhile, in 1881, a former Prime Minister who hit the headlines was the Earl of Beaconsfield, otherwise known as Benjamin Disraeli, who died that year. As Conservative Prime Minister between 1874 and 1880 he was able to pursue policies upholding the monarchy, the British Empire, the Church of England, and a degree of social reform. A leader in the *Edinburgh Evening News* for 19 April 1881 included an obituary that was rather more sympathetic in tone than might have been expected, declaring: "Lord Beaconsfield died at half-past four this morning … It is a significant coincidence that the two foremost British party leaders of recent years have arrived at their position by transition from the extreme opposite attitude in politics. Lord Beaconsfield may be held to have changed his views with as much conscientiousness as Mr. Gladstone." The journalist added that the Conservatives had found their leader in "the caustic debater and sparkling – or rather glittering – novelist … Infinite finesse, wit, tact, audacity, and persistence – all these he had, and with these weapons he conquered for his party. The most old-fashioned of its members are now disposed to admit gracefully that he "educated" them. … His novels are the measure of his emotional nature, and they show him deficient in wide human sympathies. … They are the productions of a polished intellect …"

Courting Darwin

When on 20 March 1881 Dr. Edward Aveling was unable to lecture to the Scottish Secular Union in Edinburgh because of illness (to the great disappointment of the large audiences), his place was taken in the morning by W.E. Snell (who spoke on Bradlaugh's Parliamentary position), in the afternoon by Thomas Carlaw Martin (lecturing on William Godwin), and in the evening by John Robertson (who reviewed a paper on atheistic Liberals by the pro-Catholic polemicist W.H. Mallock). This last-named polemicist has become a forgotten figure, but Robertson was justified in devoting a lecture to him as in his late Victorian and Edwardian heyday Mallock seemed to be one of the most vigorous sworn enemies of liberal causes, whether in religion or politics, in Britain, although Robertson may have become partly indebted to Mallock's *Critical Examination of Socialism* (1908), which J.M.R. noticed in *Courses of Study* (for Mallock see Anthony Quinton in *The Twentieth-Century Mind*, ed. C.B. Cox and A.E. Dyson, 1972, pp. 114-5, and Chris Tame in *J.M. Robertson*, 1987, pp. 115, 119, 121).

Aveling, a fine science teacher and popularizer, had written to Charles Darwin the previous October requesting permission to dedicate his handbook *The Student's Darwin* to him. In his reply by return, dated 13 October 1880, Darwin declined to give permission, apparently as he did not wish to hurt the religious feelings of members of his family. *The Student's Darwin* was duly published and printed in 1881 by Robertson's friends Annie Besant and Charles Bradlaugh (who both addressed public meetings in Edinburgh during the first six months of that year) under the imprint of the Freethought Publishing Company, 28 Stonecutter Street, E.C., London. Aveling's handbook, which was not dedicated to anyone, included fulsome praise of Darwin in the undated introduction (but it did not mention Marx or Engels); and it became a set book in the qualification course to receive a diploma as a National Secular Society certificated lecturer.[107]

According to the British freethought historian Edward Royle, one of the philosophical writers instrumental in introducing or disseminating Darwinian ideas among nineteenth century British secularists was the German Ludwig Büchner, with whom Robertson stayed at his home in Darmstadt during the winter of 1887. During the Scotsman's stay – at least in part to improve his knowledge and command of the German language and literature – Büchner quite probably mentioned the Austrian Marxist Karl Kautsky to Robertson; and when the latter moved on by early 1888 from Darmstadt to Vienna (more than 300 miles to the east), he may have thought of Kautsky when he (J.M.R.) sat smoking cheap Austrian cigarettes "in a warm attic in frivolous Vienna" – as Kautsky, like Robertson, was conscious of his debt to Darwin, Büchner and H.T. Buckle (see: Royle, 1980, p. 171; J.M.R.'s letter of 8.11.1887 to Patrick Geddes; J.M.R. in *NR*, 5.2.1888, pp. 82-3; and Gary P. Steenson, 1991 ed., pp. 24-30, 52, etc.).

Decades later – long after Aveling, his lover Eleanor Marx (who assisted him from April 1883 onwards with the editorship of the secularist periodical *Progress*, to which Robertson contributed articles), Marx himself, Engels, Darwin, Büchner, and Bradlaugh had all died, save Robertson – the Soviet Government, using the Moscow-based Marx-Engels Institute, which was in the throes of a Stalinist purge, ordered or sanctioned the commission in 1931 of documentary fraud (a deliberate Russian manipulation of Darwin's letter of 13 October 1880) to make it appear that Karl Marx, and not Aveling, had written to Darwin about the proposed dedication, and that Marx was the recipient of Darwin's letter of reply. This myth that Marx wanted to dedicate the second volume of *Das Kapital* to Darwin was apparently devised to foster the impression that Marxism was much more scientific, convincing and palatable than arguably it was.[108] This manoeuvre took place after the Soviet Politburo had ordered its State Security agency OGPU on 30 January 1930 to step up its intelligence gathering in Britain. This, in turn, resulted in OGPU's cultivation and use of a cipher clerk in the Foreign Office's Communications Department called Ernest Oldham, who in 1929 had offered to sell British secrets to the Russians; and their master-spy Dmitri Bystrolyotov visited Oldham a number of times at his London home, 31 Pembroke Gardens,

W.8, between September 1931 and Christmas 1932, while, ironically, Robertson lived only half a dozen doors away at 24 Pembroke Gardens. Between 1904 and 1932 Robertson commended books by the Russian revolutionary Stepniak, but was outspoken between at least 1925 and 1932 in his condemnation of the Soviet régime, its Marxist supporters and fellow-travellers.[109]

Supporting Bradlaugh

At the end of March 1881, and again at the end of April as on other occasions, Robertson's hero Bradlaugh (who had found it easier to communicate in a reasonably friendly way with Darwin than with Marx) held great public meetings in Northampton, where enthusiastic audiences thundered their pledge of support for him in his struggle to take his seat in Parliament, and they responded with a new hurricane of cheers when he asked them, "Will you stand by me in this fight?" On each of these two occasions, for example, a report of the meeting appeared in the *Edinburgh Evening News* the next working day (1 April and 2 May, respectively). These two meetings in Bradlaugh's constituency were separated by his re-election as an M.P. for Northampton on 9 April, although in that by-election his majority was actually slimmer than in the general election a year earlier.

In Edinburgh the secularists, following his new victory, appeared to be in the front rank of Bradlaugh's national army of supporters with their dedication and assiduousness in pressing petitions and resolutions defending Bradlaugh. On 15 May, in the context of the Sunday lectures, 125 people signed a petition at 3 Chambers Street, under the auspices of the Scottish Secular Union, in favour of Bradlaugh being admitted to the House of Commons; and the petition was similarly available the following Sunday. On 29 May, when Edward Aveling gave the S.S.U. three lectures, a resolution was unanimously adopted condemning Bradlaugh's exclusion from the House and approving his conduct regarding the oath. After initially attempting to affirm, Bradlaugh was willing to take the oath of allegiance, but (in the telling words of a commentator a century later) "as an atheist he was prevented from doing so by every trick of the law and parliamentary procedure".[110]

Robertson may be assumed to have participated as energetically as he could in such activities and agitation, certainly in Edinburgh, in support of Bradlaugh, who returned to the Scottish capital to address an audience of over 2,000 people on 11 June as part of his national campaign highlighting the crucial issue, as he saw it, of constitutional rights. The crowded and lively meeting was chaired by the net and twine manufacturer John Lees, and it was reported in the *Edinburgh Evening News* (almost certainly by Robertson) for the next working day. Years later – in his detailed and, in some respects, unique account (1894) of Bradlaugh's Parliamentary struggle, politics and teachings – Robertson would recall that at this meeting the body of the hall was filled with respectable church-going shopkeepers and middle-class citizens who had arrived hostile to Bradlaugh's atheistic propaganda and "notoriety", while in the gallery sat some initially rowdy Tory students. But Bradlaugh's voice rose easily above the students' din, and his quick repartee turned the laugh against them and soon silenced their interruptions, as the lion-hearted tribune of Northampton impressed and swayed his audience with the force of his personality, the passion and sincerity of his eloquence, the justice of his cause. At the close he made his usual call for a show of hands in favour of his taking his seat, and, as one of the promoters of the meeting, Robertson was interested to observe that Bradlaugh received a majority vote, with only about a dozen or so voting "on the contrary".[111]

Sympathy for Robertson Smith

The current flowing from Bradlaugh's struggle swelled a perceived tide of freethought, iconoclasm and heterodoxy which secular or ecclesiastical authorities in England and Scotland tried to block or stem at this time through exclusion shading into suppression of critics of the established order. Not only was Bradlaugh in effect excluded from due participation in the proceedings of the Westminster Parliament. As has been noted, in Edinburgh a leading secularist and Bradlaugh supporter, Alexander Orr, was turned out of the Waverley Market because of his success in disseminating freethought literature from his book-stall there. Also ejected was Professor William Robertson Smith, who was dismissed on account of his heterodoxy from his chair of Hebrew studies at the Free Church College in Aberdeen in May 1881. From 1876 onwards his case provided Victorian Scotland with its best known prosecution for heresy. The prosecution grew out of ominous rumblings of discontent – degenerating into a virtual vendetta against an unrepentant Robertson Smith – over his article "Bible" (1875) in the *Encyclopaedia Britannica*, where he rejected Mosaic authorship of Deuteronomy and presented the Bible as a collection of "edited versions" of documents on ancient religion in the Middle East. An investigation by a committee of his Church concluded that his opinions expressed in the article were hardly compatible with his rôle and status as a teacher of the Church's candidates for the ministry, but fell short – at least technically – of furnishing sufficient grounds for a formal charge of heresy. He was accordingly acquitted at the Free Church's 1880 General Assembly, albeit by a slender majority of just seven votes (299 to 292).

There then appeared a further volume of the *Encyclopaedia Britannica* with a contribution by Robertson Smith which aroused concerns similar to those already expressed; and the 1881 General Assembly decisively passed a vote of no confidence in him which was swiftly followed by his summary dismissal from his chair on the grounds of his alleged "insensitivity to his responsibilities as a theological professor and culpable lack of sympathy with the reasonable anxieties of the Church", without any specific "errors" in his teaching being identified and condemned. A leading article (probably penned by John Robertson) in the *Edinburgh Evening News* for 25 May 1881 commented: "It is difficult to realise all that is meant by the vote in the Free Church Assembly last night … All in the majority feel that Professor Smith is heterodox … the Church has disregarded its constitutional system of procedure; and its leaders, as its law-adviser showed, have repudiated its law, in order to settle the minds of weaker brethren. … there is a growing opinion among thoughtful men that such settlements are simply tending to settle the fate of the Church in an entirely disastrous sense." In such terms the *Edinburgh Evening News* extended to Robertson Smith a measure of sympathy and appreciation later amplified by John Robertson when the latter described the former as "a very remarkable man", "the ablest Biblical scholar in his own country" and "a scholar with rare gifts for humanist science remaining to the end in the formal faith in which he was nurtured, while all his scientific work went to destroy its historic foundations". John Robertson may also have been present when, in Edinburgh in 1881, Robertson Smith lectured at the Philosophical Institution (in January) and was publicly presented with an esteemed gift of Arabic manuscripts and books as a mark of support for him in facing the ordeal forced on him by his Church.[112] William Robertson Smith's work, and then his premature death in 1894 at the age of 47, may have encouraged John Robertson to pursue, and persevere with, his own studies of Christianity and mythology and of pagan Christs.

Listening to the Positivist Creed

Another speaker from outside Edinburgh whom Robertson probably heard lecture at about this time was Malcolm Quin of Newcastle-upon-Tyne, who was associated with the Positivist Church in that great Northern English city. In July 1881 Quin gave some lectures to the Scottish Secular Union in the hall at 3 Chambers Street, Edinburgh, where his chosen topics included what W.E. Snell called "an admirable account" of the politics of Positivism's French founder, Auguste Comte. However, John Robertson – later, if not in 1881 – was more critical of Comte, of whom he declared: "I did study Comte with the greatest interest, though I found his historical explanations too often verbalist. In his narrative we were asked to ascribe causation to abstract forces: chivalry did one thing; the church another; woman did a third; and so forth. I venture to think that the metaphysical method, which he repudiated, lingered into Comte's system."[113]

Decades later, in 1924, Malcolm Quin published a somewhat sardonic account of his own contact with, and lectures to, secularists in Edinburgh as from 1881: "The Secularists whom I found there were of a type much superior to most of those whom I had known elsewhere. Their active and guiding spirits were young men of thought and reading. One of them was T.C. [Thomas Carlaw] Martin, who then held some responsible position in connection with the Post Office, but was besides a musical and dramatic critic for one of the Edinburgh papers [*Edinburgh Evening News*]. At a later date he … was among the first journalists to be knighted. When I gave my "Secularist" lectures under his chairmanship, in the Chambers Street Hall in Edinburgh, we were, I dare say, far from anticipating this particular kind of distinction for him. I should like to think that he did nothing to deserve it." Quin continued: "Another of the bright-witted and capable Edinburgh Secularists whom I then met for the first time was a dark-haired, dark-eyed, soft-spoken young man from the North named J.M. Robertson. He was then assistant-editor [sic] of the *Edinburgh Evening News*, and was already as alert in mind, and as remorselessly keen in speech, if not quite as omniscient, as he has since proved himself to be to a wide public. We always had a free discussion after my lectures, as after others; and if Robertson had any share in it – as I think he must have had – I am sure I must have suffered much from the dexterous spear-thrusts which then, as ever afterwards, he could give to his opponents, either in print or on the platform." If Quin was struck by Robertson's verbal thrusts in 1881, immediately after the visitor's July lectures W.E. Snell noted the somewhat aggressive platform manner apparently adopted by the Newcastle Positivist: "Mr. Quin has given us six lectures of great interest, and has shown remarkable readiness and incisiveness in his replies to opposition." In his 1924 account – with half an eye still on what he had just written about Thomas Carlaw Martin – Quin added regarding Robertson: "He has, so far, not risen, or sunk, to a knighthood, but he has been a member of Parliament, a member of the Government …" and so on.[114] However, he refrained from pointing out that a number of his own friends, relations or acquaintances in the Newcastle area may well have lived or worked in Robertson's constituency for up to twelve consecutive years until 1918, and that at least some of them probably appreciated his services.

Ejecting Bradlaugh from Parliament

In the meantime there occurred an event imbued with great drama and symbolic significance concerning the exercise of establishment power and public determination to resist it: Bradlaugh's physical exclusion from the precincts of the House of Commons on 3 August 1881. On that day he came to the Palace of Westminster at the head of a huge crowd of supporters in an attempt to take his seat in Parliament in accordance with the mandate of his constituents; but, on being refused permission to enter the House, he became involved in a violent confrontation in which he was ejected from the members' lobby into Westminster Hall, and then flung into Palace Yard, by ten policemen, assisted by messengers or ushers – not to mention Tory M.P.s – in a brutal struggle. At one stage it looked as though Bradlaugh's supporters could have stormed the House of Commons had he not, through Annie Besant, restrained them.[115] Robertson, it seems, was unable to be present, but Edward Aveling, Bradlaugh's daughters Alice and Hypatia, and the poet James Thomson ('B.V.') – as well as Mrs. Besant – were there.

Four days later, on 7 August, the Scottish Secular Union held a Sunday evening meeting at 3 Chambers Street, Edinburgh, where an unusually large audience heard T.C. Martin read "a very spirited and interesting paper" on "Wilkes and Bradlaugh – an historic parallel". The audience unanimously passed a resolution that it "deeply regrets the course adopted by the House of Commons in the case of Mr. Bradlaugh, considering that according to the teaching of history it must inevitably lead to the degradation of the House and thereby to the discredit of representative institutions". (In that perspective the action by the House was rather counter-productive, suggesting a victory in prospect for the victimised.) Then, on 17 August, an impending by-election in Edinburgh gave impetus to the formation by Bradlaugh supporters, assembled in the Chambers Street Hall, of the Edinburgh Branch of the League for the Defence of Constitutional Rights. (The League had no publicly chosen president – but the vice-presidents included Annie Besant, Aveling, G.W. Foote and Charles Drysdale.) The *Edinburgh Evening News* reported that John Lees presided at this Edinburgh meeting, which passed a resolution that it "regrets the course adopted by the House of Commons, and is of opinion that during Mr. Bradlaugh's forcible exclusion from Parliament no candidate deserves support who will not pledge himself to make an effort for the restoration of the constitutional rights of the electors of Northampton". In the ensuing days members of the League's Edinburgh Branch fiercely cross-examined, or heckled, the by-election candidates at every possible public meeting through raising the issue of Charles Bradlaugh's rights, and this Branch's members arranged three electors' meetings in the run-up to the by-election. These steps by the new Branch's members were reported by W.E. Snell, who – after candidates in the election had dropped out (possibly encouraged to do so by the Edinburgh Branch's activist tactics) – added that Edinburgh's new M.P., Thomas Buchanan (returned unopposed), felt regarding Bradlaugh that "no obstacle should be put in his way in discharging the duties committed to him in the

House of Commons".[116] Decades later Buchanan and John Robertson – both bibliophiles of note – adorned the Liberal benches on the Government side of the House of Commons for some four consecutive years until about the end of 1909. During the early 1880s both Buchanan and Robertson – not to mention Bradlaugh – were almost certainly very familiar with what a British freethinker later fondly remembered as "the magnificent bookshops of Edinburgh … where the contents rivalled the finest bookshops of the Metropolis itself, and the proprietors were educated gentlemen who knew the contents of the volumes they handled".[117]

With the Scottish Secular Union

On 25 September 1881 – a remarkably fine day – Robertson was elected President of the Scottish Secular Union at its annual meeting held in Edinburgh at 3 Chambers Street. Also elected on that occasion were Charles Nicholson as Treasurer, Alexander Orr as Financial Secretary, and W.E. Snell as Correspondence Secretary, with three others becoming members of the Executive. The year's accounts showed an income very marginally greater than the expenditure. In the evening Charles Watts (who lectured in the afternoon on "Secular Propaganda") lectured on "Bible Theology" to a very large audience, which included Dr. Robert Lewins, author of the little treatise *Life and Mind*.

Robertson apparently followed up this success with an article on " 'Popular Educator' Theology" in Charles Watts's *Secular Review* for 15 October 1881, and, the day after the article appeared, with a lecture to the Scottish Secular Union in Edinburgh on "The Truth about Vaccination", "against which"

– according to Snell – "he made a strong case. His only critic was a medical man, who objected to compulsion." (In Britain compulsory or officially recommended vaccination, especially of children, would continue to arouse opposition or non-compliance for very many years, although smallpox, for example, would be eradicated by 1980.) Encouraged by journals like the *National Reformer* and, during the 1870s, the *Secular Chronicle*, most British freethinkers in the 1880s seem to have opposed compulsory vaccination; and even one of the relatively few British secularists who is known to have supported vaccination, Dr. Charles Drysdale, acknowledged that it could be made safer to administer. Robertson's lecture on the subject bore the same title as that of Dr. Ernest Hart's pro-vaccination pamphlet, which Robertson read with great care soon after it was published in 1880. On spotting that Hart's pamphlet contained information that apparently undermined the author's own argument, Robertson drew this to Drysdale's attention and also to the notice of the editor of *Health*, Dr. Andrew Wilson; but neither Drysdale nor Wilson gave any publicity to Robertson's point. In 1898 Robertson's critical stance regarding vaccination in general and Ernest Hart in particular would in effect be endorsed by the great naturalist Alfred Russel Wallace (arguably Darwin's undervalued fellow proponent of evolution by natural selection).[118]

William Archer – and W.E. Henley

Health issues also featured in the correspondence between Robertson and his dear friend William Archer at this time. On 21 October 1881 Archer wrote to Robertson, informing him he was about to leave England for the winter, mainly for health reasons, and would probably go to Rome. Robertson replied two days later: "You have given me a distressing surprise. I have told you the last two times you have been down that you weren't looking quite satisfactory, though I thought you better lately; but I didn't think you would need to change your climate to come round. … Really, you are rather to be envied than otherwise. "Liver dyspepsia", I trust, doesn't take long to cure … and who wouldn't get well in Italy! My best wishes go with you, my dear fellow. I shall often think of you, going about in Genoa and Venice – of course you'll see Venice – and Florence and Naples and Rome! Living in the past without any liver complaint, and in the present, by consequence, in a state of progressive convalescence …"

Then Robertson mentioned his own very recently established contact with the journalist W.E. Henley, the new editor of the *Magazine of Art*. "I met, the other evening, the man who has just been made editor – Henley, a pleasant, brilliant fellow, who goes with a crutch. He says he's going to introduce a new régime. But I have a notion he'll ruin the *Magazine* in six months, if he doesn't get sacked in three. He is considerably too good for the place, I should say … The E.N. [*Edinburgh Evening News*] staff express sincere concern about your health …" W.E. Henley was destined to become one of the prominent literary personalities of the late Victorian age. Robertson as a young man was, in his own words, "at feud with Henley on many points" and later maintained that "Henley, with his Disraelian pose and his music-hall sentimentalism, is about as good an authority on the serious issues of national life as Scott was on metaphysics or Dickens on the nebular hypothesis". Yet Robertson regarded Henley as "a journalist of genius" and considered his best poetic output was to be found in his highly realistic Hospital Poems (which Henley seems to have worked on while a tuberculosis patient under Joseph Lister at the Old Edinburgh Infirmary between 1873 and 1875).[119]

In an article in the *Secular Review* for 5 November 1881 Robertson berated the Bishop of Manchester for misrepresenting a letter the churchman had received from the Edinburgh secularist W.E. Snell, with the Bishop taking Snell's comment in this letter "Of course, Secularists repudiate the sacredness of marriage" to mean that Snell advocated free love – whereas, Robertson pointed out, Snell was simply suggesting that secularists regarded marriage as a civil contract. A week later, on 13 November, Robertson delivered "a carefully prepared and powerful lecture" (in Alexander Orr's words) to the Scottish Secular Union in Edinburgh. When Robertson awoke that Sunday he doubtless awoke to a city of silence, with the peace of the Presbyterian Sabbath broken later by the doleful clanging of church bells summoning the faithful and by the occasional rattle of horse-drawn cabs whose passengers, in breaking the Sabbath, were both paying double fares and imperilling their souls. As he went on his way to give his lecture in the Chambers Street Hall, Robertson almost certainly mused on "Christianity and Civilisation" (which was the title of his address) and on civilisation's supposed debt to Christianity (this discourse attracted "some lively opposition").[120] At about the same time William Archer, reserving his first letter from Italy for Robertson, enthused to his Edinburgh friend about his regenerating walk along the Riviera from Cannes towards Italy during a week of blazing sunshine, adding: "There have actually been several moments of every day when I should have liked to possess Joshua's power of bidding the sun to stand still. ... I don't know why any one lives anywhere else but on the Riviera. ..."[121] (As it happened, years later, after much research, Robertson surmised that Joshua was originally a sun-god and ascribed to him a central position in his mythological theory of Christian origins.)

Robertson's November lecture on "Christianity and Civilisation" was probably influenced by a study of the work of the British historian Henry Thomas Buckle, whom he first read – in Robertson's words to a friend some two decades later – "when I was young!" Robertson later, if not already in 1881, accepted, and defended, Buckle's master-ideas of the role of climate, soil and food, the growth of knowledge, the cross-fertilization of ideas, and the struggle between reason and superstition in history. He was much more critical of Buckle's near-contemporary, the Positivist Auguste Comte, whose devoted follower Malcolm Quin of Newcastle-upon-Tyne was billed to lecture on 11 December to the Scottish Secular Union in Edinburgh on "Science and Life" and, in the evening, on "Humanity" (which probably related to Comte's "religion of humanity"). In words indicating few illusions about human beings, Robertson would note that Comte "sets up for positive worship the abstraction of Humanity. When I used to argue the point, in youth, with my Comtist friends, I remember they fell back on the plea that Humanity is not an abstraction but an aggregate. Now just try to hypostatize, as an object of ethical and emotional worship, the aggregate of mankind … try to think of all that vast pell-mell of egoism and evil, cruelty and folly, cemented with a little good and bequeathing a little beauty to the human bee-hive of to-day …" [122] However, many years later the Rationalist Peace Society (of which Robertson would serve as President between 1910 and 1921) would appeal to Positivists, among others, for support.[123]

Meanwhile, in the week before Christmas 1881, Robertson rounded off his lectures for the year by returning to Glasgow to address the secularists there on *The Unseen Universe* (a controversial book published anonymously in 1875 by its two authors, Professors Balfour Stewart and P.G. Tait, both Scottish physicists) and "The Orthodoxy of Women" (which he, apparently convincingly, traced to female subjection).

Whereas the arrival of the New Year might have suggested not only hope and a degree of optimism, but also goodwill and a sense of tolerance, religious orthodoxy reared its ugly head in Edinburgh when, in early January 1882, the city's Presbytery abruptly cancelled a publicly advertised series of free lectures on Sunday evenings at the Old Greyfriars Church on religious, historical and scientific subjects. One of the suppressed lecturers was Dr. Andrew Wilson; and Robertson may have wryly noted the irony that Wilson, an advocate of vaccination who as editor of *Health* refused to publish Robertson's communication to him which was critical of vaccination, had himself fallen victim to a form of censorship wielded by orthodoxy.[124]

Moreover, in Edinburgh no profane music, no singing of secular songs, no whistling, no laughter from the streets, no sound of trams, carts or children at play, would have disturbed Robertson's thoughts on Sunday, 15 January as he prepared to set out to give his lecture to the Scottish Secular Union at 3 Chambers Street on "Five Portraits of Christ", portraits put in the public domain by five contemporary or near contemporary Western European writers: Seeley, Renan, Strauss, Cardinal Newman, and William Renton (of whom the last-named had lectured to the Edinburgh secularists in January 1880). It seems Robertson was rather shaken when, after his lecture, he was challenged by a friend of more mature years: "Why do you take it for granted that there was a Jesus at all?" His immediate response was, as he later confessed, to dismiss his friend's scepticism with a superior smile and declare: "That is an extravagance." The friend was quite probably John Lees, who was about seventeen years his senior and who regarded Christ as "an imaginary saviour". Indeed, Robertson was to discard his belief in the historicity of Jesus only after years of careful thought and investigation. Some seven years after his lecture, Robertson maintained in the *National Reformer* that "the fictional Gospel Jesus ... corresponds to one of those composite photographs in which the printing of many faces over each other yields a certain countenance that belongs to no actual person, but which may look quite as credible as an inferior portrait of a single person".[125] There seems to have been a sense in which Robertson's January 1882 lecture on Christ did much to pave the way for the scholarly groundwork that made Robertson, in his lifetime, the foremost British exponent of the Mythicist view of Christian origins, of which he would give a magnificent conspectus in half a dozen volumes published between 1900 and 1931; rather as his lecture in February 1882 on Carlyle may well have been taken into account in Robertson's *Modern Humanists* (1891), which included Carlyle.

These two lectures – on Christ and on Carlyle, respectively – were initially delivered (with free admission) to the Scottish Secular Union in Edinburgh, but were repeated in Glasgow on 21 May (in accordance with what seems to have been Robertson's practice regarding his lectures at that time). For the Edinburgh secularists on 19 February "Mr. Robertson read an able and deeply interesting paper dealing with Carlyle's dogmatism and inconsistency". For a pseudonymous freethinker attached to the Glasgow Eclectic and Secular Institute members in the Ramshorn Assembly Rooms at 16 Ingram Street on 21 May, "Mr. Robertson submitted one of the greatest estimates of Carlyle's religious and ethical philosophy it has ever been our good fortune to hear". In a different secularist journal that same freethinker declared of Robertson's lectures delivered in Glasgow on that date: "Treating of Carlyle's religion and ethics in the morning, he demonstrated how vague the first was, and how grotesque and arbitrary the latter were. Taking into account the evil influences some portions of Carlyle's philosophy had exerted on British thought, Mr. Robertson was still disposed to give Carlyle credit for having done good service to the cause of human progress. The evening discourse, on the views taken by some great modern thinkers of the life and teachings of Christ, was surprisingly fine, and won for the lecturer the golden opinions of all who heard it."[126]

Robertson was also in Glasgow on 26 February, when he was due to lecture to a large and attentive audience on "Christianity and Civilisation". Not long before giving his lecture, Robertson may have recalled a letter William Archer had written to him on 8 January from Rome. Archer had walked from Cannes along the sun-drenched French Riviera many years before it became a popular international tourist resort. But when he got to Rome, Archer (as he confessed in his letter to Robertson) was "haunted at every turn by the feeling that every stone is speaking … You feel that the earth is impregnated with the whole history of the world, sacred and profane … The roof of Santa Maria Maggiore is gilded with the first gold sent by the Spanish adventurers from Peru. A common walk of mine is past a church from the steps of which Augustine departed to convert Britain, while Gregory the Great solemnly blessed him. The sight of them brings back to you the whole of British history down to the Bradlaugh struggle."[127] In fact, on 26 February, while Robertson was in Glasgow for his lecture, Edinburgh secularists, under the auspices of the Scottish Secular Union at the Chambers Street Hall, unanimously adopted a resolution protesting against Bradlaugh's exclusion from Parliament as "not only a gross injustice to his constituency and to himself, but also an insult to every elector in the kingdom" and calling upon all the electors of Northampton "to unite heartily for the purpose of securing Mr. Bradlaugh's triumphant return".

Honouring Ibsen and Burns

In his letter of 8 January 1882 to Robertson from Rome, William Archer went on to describe his contact there with the Norwegian dramatist Henrik Ibsen. "Many thanks for the magazine [containing W.A.'s article on Henrik Ibsen], which is at present in the hands of the mighty Ibsen himself. I see that great man almost every day at a café which he and I both frequent for an afternoon glass of vermouth, and I have a yarn with him occasionally. He has just published a play called *Ghosts* … Remember me to everyone – Wilson, Martin, and all your godless crew at the 'E.N.'"[128] It may be taken as read that Robertson passed on Archer's news and best wishes to John Wilson, Thomas Carlaw Martin and others who worked for the *Edinburgh Evening News*. This was before Marx's daughter Eleanor became known as a promoter of Ibsen. Certainly in 1886 – itself three years before Ibsen achieved his first real success on the English stage – Robertson would call Ibsen's dramas "the strongest body of dramatic work of modern times", containing "a distinct element of romanticism … in addition to much subtle analysis and faithful observation". (Robertson's comments, just quoted, are to be found in a brilliant extended essay – published in Annie Besant's *Our Corner* – where he traced the evolution of drama, from primitive man to Henrik Ibsen, as a changing product of interacting social, political and economic forces.)[129]

While the Norwegian dramatist was still little known in Britain in 1882, on 6 April that year an immense and enthusiastic crowd in the old Scottish town of Dumfries, where Robert Burns had died, witnessed Lord Rosebery's unveiling of a woman sculptor's graceful marble statue of the man regarded as Scotland's national poet. It was almost certainly Rosebery's speech on that occasion that Robertson had in mind when, years later, J.M.R. described the address at the unveiling by "a distinguished living statesman" as "a brilliant address, witty, intelligent, broad in view, and finished in phrase" which roused his audience when Rosebery suddenly referred to them as "a nation alight with disinterested moral enthusiasm, with a towering indignation against the oppressor, and a glowing sympathy with the oppressed" (J.M.R.'s *Essays in Ethics*, 1903, pp. 139-40). The gifted if flowery secularist writer William Stewart Ross – recently appointed co-editor of the *Secular Review* – was awarded a gold medal for the prize poem on Burns, of whom a leader writer (evidently Robertson) who had clearly attended the unveiling ceremony declared the next day in the *Edinburgh Evening News*: "From how much of hard self-righteousness, gloomy hypocrisy, and sour fanaticism he has saved his countrymen they can now surmise, though they cannot even yet fully estimate." This observation would resurface a couple of years later in Robertson's article "The Art of Burns", where the claim would be made that "his influence among the English-speaking nations has been mighty for democracy".

Death of Darwin

Then, on 19 April 1882, died, at the age of 73, a great British scientist who had received part of his education at Edinburgh and whose ground-breaking work had been greeted with outbursts of fanatical hostility in much of the English-speaking world. Two days after the death of Darwin at his rural Kentish retreat where he had lived and worked for forty years (Down House), the *Edinburgh Evening News* commented in a perceptive, eulogistic leading article almost certainly penned by Robertson: "Among those who recognise the greatness of Charles Darwin, a peculiar significance will be felt in the fact that he had been dead twenty-four hours before the news became public. … He dies as he has lived, out of the eye of the public; and just as his work has been done in absolute disregard of contemporary popularity, so it is certain that the mass of men have at present little or no conception of the validity of his title to enduring fame. … When all his vast labours are reviewed, when his unhasting, unresting ardour in his search for truth is contrasted with the long bray of vituperation from a thousand pulpits, and the shrieks of silly sentimentalists, which have formed the commonest criticism of his theories, the simple magnanimity of the man creates a feeling that does not fall short of reverence. … He is the ideal naturalist. … The clergy of to-day are beginning to accept with more or less of compromise the theory which those of thirty years ago execrated. Carlyle, who passed a scandalously hasty and foolish criticism on it before even attempting to understand it, lived to acknowledge that Darwin was personally one of the most charming of men. It is needless to say that every year must add to the general appreciation of his work. The form of the exposition may have to be recast, and its relation to the evolution theory as expounded by Spencer will have to be more and more clearly brought out, but the complete body of Darwin's work is a monument that will keep his name eminent for many a century to come."

In mid June 1873 Karl Marx had sent Darwin - and also, it

seems, Herbert Spencer - a copy of a German edition of *Das Kapital*. Three and a half months later Darwin responded with a very brief letter of acknowledgement which seemed to imply he did not wish to discuss Marx's book or welcome any further contact from the author. Equally no indisputable evidence has emerged that Marx ever tried to dedicate any of his work to Darwin. Marx apparently believed that capitalism could not survive through adaptation and, in Robertson's words, "puts a catastrophic and finally static theory of social destiny under a pseudo-evolutionary form".[130]

By the time of Darwin's death British secularists were becoming increasingly conscious that Darwinian evolutionism dealt Christianity a well nigh fatal blow. Darwin had been a Vice-President of the Sunday Lecture Society and, although generally reluctant to attack religious orthodoxy directly, had doubted whether there had ever been a Revelation and had declared that the Bible, which attributed to God the feelings of a revengeful tyrant, was no more to be trusted than the sacred books of the Hindus and Muslims. In 1876 he admitted that disbelief had crept over him; in 1879 he indicated that generally the term Agnostic would correctly describe his state of mind; and by 13 October 1880 he regarded himself as "a strong advocate for free thought on all subjects". Little wonder that Robertson criticised the fact that Darwin was buried in Westminster Abbey a week after his death; and he attended the opening of Down House to the public in June 1929.[131]

On Sunday, 30 April 1882, Robertson was billed to give a lecture to the Scottish Secular Union in Edinburgh on "Apocryphal Books and Sacred Canons" in the evening; while in the morning the National Secular Society Edinburgh Branch appointed him (apparently with regard to his position as President of the S.S.U.) and John Lees (President of the Branch) as delegates to the impending N.S.S. Annual Conference, to be held in Edinburgh. The N.S.S. Edinburgh Branch also elected Robertson as its delegate to the national demonstration in Trafalgar Square, London, in support of Bradlaugh which would take place on 10 May, the first anniversary of a House of Commons resolution debarring the mighty orator and agitator from entering the House. Robertson duly attended the London demonstration and protest meeting – organised by the League for the Defence of Constitutional Rights, attended by delegates from more than a hundred towns, and addressed by Bradlaugh – which unanimously carried, amid the most passionate enthusiasm, a resolution upholding Bradlaugh's right to take his seat. Referring to this mass meeting in London "last night", the *Edinburgh Evening News* on 11 May recorded in an editorial that "between one and two thousand persons took part in what was a very orderly demonstration"; and, just three days after the editorial appeared, Robertson reported back to the Edinburgh secularists direct on the Trafalgar Square meeting[132] (which had apparently provided the rationale for his first visit to London).

N.S.S. Annual Conference in Edinburgh

Such agitation and mobilisation reached a crescendo on 28 May (Whit Sunday) 1882, when the National Secular Society held its Annual Conference for the first, and, in Robertson's lifetime, only, time in Edinburgh, no doubt in recognition of the sustained work for freethought and secularism undertaken in the Athens of the North by Robertson and his friends. For many N.S.S. branches in the South of England the distance involved was prohibitive, but more than forty towns throughout

Britain managed to send a total of over sixty delegates, in addition to several hundred freethinkers from Edinburgh and elsewhere in Scotland. A few well-known figures in the movement such as Edward Aveling (who was apparently ill) and James Thomson ("B.V." – the Scottish-born author of the bleakly pessimistic poem *The City of Dreadful Night* – who died prematurely on 3 June in London) were not recorded as being in attendance. But Robertson, who seems to have helped out unobtrusively and behind the scenes at the Conference, would become one of the first British men of letters to express a critical appreciation of Thomson's work when in 1892 he edited and introduced *Poems, Essays and Fragments* by Thomson, published by Bradlaugh's daughter Hypatia. And the Conference itself buzzed with excitement, commitment and fervour. The venue, the Chambers Street Hall, had been gaily decorated and seemed as bright inside as the weather outside. On the wall behind the President's chair hung a well-executed monogram N.S.S., in Bradlaugh's Northampton election colours of green, white and mauve, surmounted by "We seek for truth" (the motto of the N.S.S.) and "Thorough" (Bradlaugh's own motto). The *Freethinker* concluded: "The Edinburgh friends exerted themselves to give all the visitors to their noble city a right hearty welcome. And they thoroughly succeeded. Their hospitality and attention were beyond all praise: Messrs. Lees, Wilson, Robertson, Nicholson, and Henry deserve especial mention." (W.A. Wilson was John Lees's business partner; Alexander Henry was an agnostic grocer; and Charles Nicholson, as John Lees said a decade later, "was everything to the Edinburgh Branch of the National Secular Society – Secretary, Treasurer, Hallkeeper, and Bookseller, and as active and intelligent in such work as he was in Radical politics and the Temperance cause". Nicholson died a fortnight after Bradlaugh.)[133]

The N.S.S. Annual Report, read out by Bradlaugh, referred to attempts by Christian Tory M.P.s to induce the Government to prosecute Foote's *Freethinker* and to have the higher education classes closed down at the Society's Hall of Science in London. The Report also pointed out that "in England, Wales, and Ireland a person with no religious belief may affirm as a witness, but cannot legally affirm as a juryman, or as a member of Parliament. In Scotland such a person not only cannot affirm in either capacity, but is not even competent, under any circumstances, to give evidence." In this climate of religious intolerance, dominated by Bradlaugh's protracted Parliamentary struggle, "1,304 new members have joined the Society since our last Conference and twelve new branches have been established. The last of these is one at Christ Church, New Zealand …" (Christchurch would be a hotbed of secularism, freethought and progressive politics for at least three decades from 1881 onwards.) A resolution was passed unanimously that an invitation to lecture in Britain should be extended to the great American freethought orator Colonel Robert Ingersoll, whose humorous *Mistakes of Moses* apparently enjoyed quite a wide sale in 1881 when published in Britain at 3d., though Robertson was to maintain: "I can remember the day when you could get Ingersoll's *Mistakes of Moses* for a penny; and a very good pennyworth it was."[134]

In the wake of an official report in February on plans for a Channel Tunnel, which had prompted the aristocratic republican and rationalist Algernon Swinburne to write a poem on the subject in April, a South London delegate suggested that the N.S.S. Conference should support the scheme for a Channel Tunnel, as "tending to the spread of freedom of thought and the general advancement of the peoples by breaking down the race hatreds, the result of past centuries of misrepresentation and misunderstanding". But although there was insufficient time to discuss this at the Conference, five years later Bradlaugh would issue what Robertson would call "a weighty little pamphlet: *The Channel Tunnel: Ought the Democracy to Oppose or Support It?* which was widely circulated as the strongest possible popular plea for the undertaking".[135] The Channel Tunnel would become a reality a century or so later.

After the South London delegate's contribution, Bradlaugh's studious daughter Hypatia came forward to read her first public paper, on "Education an Aid to Freethought Propaganda", which was well received. Then, after forceful and eloquent speeches from Mrs. Besant, G.W. Foote (whose election as an N.S.S. Vice-President formalised his reconciliation with Bradlaugh after a period of estrangement), George Standring (the young editor of *The Republican*), and others, Bradlaugh rose, to prolonged cheering, to deliver the closing address. Pinpointing Scotland, he declared: "One speaker has referred to Scotland as a land of bigotry. Perhaps that is so; but let us not forget that the land of bigotry is also the land of earnestness, and I almost prefer bigoted earnestness to hypocritical indifference. There is hope of winning the one; there is little use in the other. But Scotland has higher attractions to freethinkers than that of earnestness. Freethought owes enormously to Scotch thought, whether it be for or against itself. Some of the closest reasoners bear Scottish names. ... Scotland, above the other English countries, has done most to destroy the hope of bigotry by its universities throwing open the highest education to the children of the poor. Scotch, too, is that Chambers' literature which has done so much for education, without serving one sect more than another. ... Sixty, nay, fifty, years ago men and women went to gaol in Edinburgh for holding the opinions with which we are identified to-night. There was no society to stand by them then; no organisation to aid them then. We should be as weak as they, were it not for the public opinion made by the organised propaganda we keep up. ... Each who links himself to our Society makes us stronger to meet the powerful organisations against us, and in some measure repays the debt he owes to the Freethinkers of the past." Bradlaugh concluded his speech with a proud and defiant reference to his own struggle, proclaiming: "I have been reproached for lack of education; one word certainly I have never learned: Defeat, and I am too old to begin to learn it now."[136]

Before and after the Conference some of the assembled freethinkers strolled along Princes Street to admire the fine shops on one side, the well-kept gardens on the other, and towering over them the mighty castle-rock. Some enjoyed the fine panorama of land and water from the summit of the nearby extinct volcano known as Arthur's Seat. Others took a trip by steamer in the Firth of Forth, with the sun glowing gloriously in the azure sky and a refreshing breeze dancing over the waves. With Bradlaugh's resounding words still virtually ringing in their ears, at least some of those who had attended the Conference or were sympathetic to the freethought cause would have seen the unsigned factual report, almost certainly penned by Robertson, who had been present as a delegate, describing the Conference's proceedings in the *Edinburgh Evening News* the day after it was held. The reporter explained: "The executive desired to urge upon all freethinkers the necessity and duty of claiming to give evidence on affirmation; and stated their readiness, in all cases where evidence is illegally refused, to fight the question in the higher courts. They trust that the oath question will not now be allowed to rest without some clear legislative settlement ... Since last conference the circulation of the society's leaflets had nearly doubled." (In Edinburgh in October of 1881 Alexander Orr of 8 North Pitt Street printed and circulated, at his own expense, five thousand neat handbills announcing that he was selling Bradlaugh's *National Reformer*.) The reporter continued: "The progress of the society had aroused fierce opposition in the Christian ranks, and a more persecuting spirit was manifested than had been seen for some years."[137]

The May 1882 Conference rather seems to have galvanised N.S.S. members in Edinburgh – and Bradlaugh's invocation of the historic debt contemporary freethinkers owed to their predecessors would have appealed to Robertson. On 11 June the Edinburgh Branch of the N.S.S. held a business meeting at which "votes of thanks were passed to Messrs. Fisher, Banner, Chamberlain, Warden, Stewart, Orr, and others for their service during the Conference. Mr. John Robertson was elected member of the N.S.S. Council for the year 1882-83, and Alex. Henry Treasurer and Secretary, for the year … Fourteen members have joined the branch since the Conference."[138]

Remembering 'B.V.' and Garibaldi

It seems it was not possible for the *Edinburgh Evening News* to carry its own obituary of the freethinking writer James Thomson ("B.V.") – who was virtually notorious in some quarters – as soon as it became known he had died on 3 June. Thomson and Bradlaugh had become friends in the early 1850s, and for years Thomson was accepted as a member of the Bradlaugh household, where his company and friendship were much appreciated by Bradlaugh's daughters Alice and

Hypatia, with Thomson's most memorable poem, *The City of Dreadful Night*, first appearing in Bradlaugh's *National Reformer* in 1874. Robertson later declared that "Thomson's ill-starred life, joined with the burden of his tragic poem, could keep him in the odour of unpopularity inseparable from the *National Reformer* in its day". Thomson's melancholic and unstable personality, scarred by alcoholism, led to increasing strain, and the Knowlton prosecution of 1877 occasioned a serious breach between Thomson and Bradlaugh, with Robertson claiming in a private letter (written in 1931) that it was G.W. Foote "who, in early days, set James Thomson (a dipsomaniac, poor devil) against Bradlaugh, who had housed and helped Thomson like a brother for long years."[139] Thomson's early biographers, such as Henry Salt of the Humanitarian League, appear to have been unaware of Robertson's unsettling information about Foote, which was presumably based, at least in part, on extensive personal knowledge of some of the personalities involved. Ironically, by 1879 Foote had also broken with Thomson, who during the last year or so of his life may have been edging towards a form of reconciliation with Bradlaugh: on 6 March 1881 both Bradlaugh and Thomson, but apparently not Foote, attended the ceremony marking the opening of the Leicester Secular Hall.

One death which did not go unnoticed in the *Edinburgh Evening News* was that of the Italian nationalist, military liberator and atheist Giuseppe Garibaldi, whose cause had enjoyed much enthusiastic support among British radicals and freethinkers. (These included Charles Bradlaugh, who at some personal risk during a visit to Italy in 1861, and subsequently, gave Italian nationalists much needed and useful practical assistance as a contact man and message-bearer from London and in other ways.[140]) The day after Garibaldi died in

Italy on 2 June, a leader writer – almost certainly Robertson – in the *Edinburgh Evening News* paid him a glowing tribute, declaring: "Garibaldi's career was of a kind that conquers admiration. Among the men who have helped to make modern European history he stands absolutely unique in his individuality. … in what Whitman calls "the small theatre of the antique" there is none of the breadth and intensity of interest that belongs to the wonderful drama of Garibaldi's life." (Two years later, in 1884, Robertson published in Edinburgh his book *Walt Whitman, Poet and Democrat*.) The leader writer continued: "everywhere and always he is a figure of heroic mould, absolutely incomparable in his age. … Such a genius as his for attack in soldiership there has probably not been since Napoleon" (Garibaldi's military failure to free Rome from papal control in 1862 and 1867 appears to have been occasioned by a combination of factors). The Edinburgh journalist added: "in his last years, when his sword was hung up for ever, the hero turned his unresting brain to the oft-contemplated but never accomplished task of reclaiming the great Roman Campagna. … Only the heart of his nation, in which Garibaldi's name is enshrined, can speak his epitaph" (the article could also have thrown into relief Garibaldi's support of democratic reforms).

Empire and Humanity

It is not known whether Robertson commented on Austria's historic imperial presence in Italy when he gave a lecture on "Empire and Humanity" to the Glasgow Eclectic and Secular Institute in the Ramshorn Assembly Rooms at 16 Ingram Street on 18 June 1882. His lecture "provoked some discussion"; and later, on 9 July, he returned to the Glasgow secularists at the same location to read the second part of his paper on his chosen subject, following which there was "a lengthy discussion". No copy of Robertson's script or notes for that two-part lecture, or of any newspaper account of its content, has come to light. Accordingly the extent, if any, to which his lecture focused on the British Empire is not known. But the title of his lecture could suggest that at some level he saw the interests of humanity as at odds with those of empire-builders, particularly perhaps as in *The Truth about the War* (1902) – his Open Letter to Arthur Conan Doyle – he would attack that chauvinistic writer "in the name … of the ideals of justice and humanity which you have shamed and defied" over the war between the imperialist British Government and the Boers in South Africa from 1899 to 1902. Certainly Robertson's two-part lecture was given before the publication of Sir John Seeley's *The Expansion of England* (1883) imprinted itself on Victorian public consciousness, at a time when there were no courses or lectures on British imperial history at Oxford University and virtually none at Cambridge University, British public school debates on colonial questions were generally thinly attended, and in British public schools an ethos of service and duty nurtured by Dr. Thomas Arnold of Rugby in the 1830s had not yet been drowned out by a sharper, more strident imperialist and militaristic emphasis on control as the British empire expanded.[141] Robertson would develop his critique of imperialism, notably in *Patriotism and Empire* (1899) and *The Evolution of States* (1912).

An Unconventional Brotherhood

In Glasgow Robertson's lecture of 18 June on imperialism was deemed "excellent" by a secularist cloaked in a pseudonym.

Certainly the Glaswegian James Pinkerton Gilmour, who had come to rationalism through Darwin, Colenso and the *National Reformer*, came to regard Robertson as *primus inter* pares in a remarkable group of five clever and enthusiastic young men who infused new life and prestige into the freethought movement in the "east-windy, west-endy" city of Edinburgh, a bastion of orthodoxy. Gilmour would identify these five as comprising Robertson, Thomas Carlaw Martin, W.E. Snell, Joseph Mazzini Wheeler, and, not least, John Lees, "a man of a most chivalrous nature" who delighted in gathering scholarly, able and idealistic young men around him. Dr. Charles Drysdale would benevolently describe these Edinburgh freethinkers to Bradlaugh's daughters Alice and Hypatia as "five such fine young men, and never a vice between them!" Gilmour may not have realised that Wheeler's contribution in Edinburgh had been somewhat limited as he had left in 1881 to settle in London: although, arguably, his place was taken to some extent by Charles Nicholson. Of "the Edinburgh five" (so to speak) Gilmour would recall: "It was one of the conventions of the members of this unconventional brotherhood to wear hyacinthine locks, to have whiskers and a beard, and, for the platform, to sport a brown or black velvet jacket. These 'insignia' were very becoming for 'J.M.R.', who had then, as to the end of his life, a fine manly presence; and later, when as a lecturer he 'invaded' England, he was described as 'the handsome Scotsman'." Gilmour would provide a similarly detailed account of Robertson's physique: "He was then under thirty years of age, tall, with a well-knit, athletic frame, a capacious cranium, highly developed in the frontal region, keen expressive eyes, and a mobile countenance. He was a personable and picturesque figure." The first meeting between Gilmour and Robertson may have taken place when the latter lectured to secularists in Glasgow on 17 October 1880. But the two probably first met on 20 November

1881, when, at the close of what seems to have been the first lecture Gilmour gave to the Scottish Secular Union in Edinburgh, Robertson (according to Gilmour's recollection) "uttered some words of approbation and encouragement that served as an inspiration to me, not only then, but for many years after. That was the beginning of a friendship which has subsisted between us ever since."[142]

Having apparently contributed during the summer of 1882 to Bradlaugh's fund, advertised in the *National Reformer*, to fight the bigots, Robertson was probably present on 6 August that year at one or both of the lectures given to the N.S.S. Edinburgh Branch by the N.S.S. national secretary (since 1877) Robert Forder, who had met Bradlaugh in 1862 at a London rally in support of Garibaldi, and whose own August 1882 visit to Edinburgh Forder himself promptly reported in the *National Reformer*: "At Edinburgh, where I have lectured twice this year, the branch is doing exceedingly well. I am greatly indebted to the kindness of many friends there – especially to Messrs. Orr, Lees, Robertson, and Henry – for making my stay in their city a pleasant one."[143] Forder was regarded by Robertson as an abler lecturer than Charles Watts, for example.

During the summer and autumn of 1882 Robertson apparently addressed secularists in Edinburgh on the future of freethought, the recently deceased American ethical thinker Emerson, Britain's fairly recently formed Salvation Army, and the fairly recently published treatise *Progress and Poverty* by the American political economist Henry George. (Emerson – of whom Robertson considered himself an "ex-pupil" – had lectured at the Philosophical Institution in Edinburgh many years earlier.[144]) Robertson's approach may have included criticism of George's views on the population question which would soon be hammered by Robertson in his pamphlet *Socialism and Malthusianism* (1885). Indeed, Robertson would regard Henry George's criticism of Malthus as "an argument chasing its tail", adding: "Again and again George surrenders the case ... The pretence that over-population was not recognised before Malthus is the last word of historical ignorance, uttered in the face of the records of infanticide, migrations of peoples, and the practice and debates of antiquity."[145]

Meanwhile Robertson was apparently a member of a group involved in framing a new statement of principles and objects for the Edinburgh Secular Society. He would later recall that "two Socialist members, good men both, seceded on the ground that we did not insert in the program a declaration of Socialism. Yet neither seceder, so far as I am aware, ever proposed that any Socialist Society of which he was a member should insert in its program a declaration of Rationalism."[146] (The two seceders may have been the Edinburgh socialists Robert Banner and, possibly, his mentor Andreas Scheu, who, like Edward Aveling and Marx's daughter Eleanor, both joined H.M. Hyndman's (Social) Democratic Federation in the early 1880s and then the breakaway Socialist League in the London area. Scheu had given a lecture, which Robertson may have heard, on 24 August 1879 to the Scottish Secular Union in Edinburgh on "Socialism versus Capitalism"; and in August 1884 Scheu was an (S.) D.F. delegate from Edinburgh.[147]) In May 1882 Robertson and Thomas Carlaw Martin were listed among those who renewed their membership of the National Secular Society in the Edinburgh Branch. Then, on 1 October that year, the N.S.S. Edinburgh Branch held its first, and very well attended, annual meeting, at which John Lees was elected Chairman and Secretary, and Charles Nicholson Treasurer, for the ensuing year. At this same meeting, where it was revealed that the Branch had doubled its membership since the previous year, John Robertson moved the following resolution, which was passed unanimously: "That this meeting records its protest against the injustice to the constituency of Northampton, and to every elector in the Kingdom, by the illegal exclusion of Mr. Bradlaugh, a duly-elected member, from his seat in the House of Commons." A week earlier, under the auspices of the N.S.S. Edinburgh Branch and to a very large audience, John Lees gave his first public lecture in aid of the Freethinkers' Benevolent Fund (for which he raised a tidy sum), taking as his subject "Charles Bradlaugh, his life and work".

This was followed by John Robertson presiding at a meeting held in the Chambers Street Hall on Sunday, 29 October to consider what action Edinburgh secularists should take regarding the representation of the city in the light of the impending by-election there. Some 400 people at the meeting heard W.E. Snell suggest that, as neither of the two candidates in the field was prepared to support Bradlaugh taking his seat in the House as he was legally entitled to, secularists should withhold their votes. A resolution to this effect was being put to the meeting when, as reported in the *Edinburgh Evening News* but not in the *National Reformer* at the time, it was objected to on the basis that the Bradlaugh question was not the only important issue that would be brought before Parliament. In the event the meeting adopted, with three dissentients, a pro-Bradlaugh resolution referring to "the supreme importance of the constitutional rights of electors"; and Snell proposed that some of those in the hall should go on to ask pro-Bradlaugh questions at election meetings addressed by both aspiring Parliamentary candidates. A week later Bradlaugh himself declared in the *National Reformer*: "I thank the Edinburgh Freethinkers for their active and useful work in fully raising the constitutional grievance of Northampton as part of the pending election-struggle. The special meeting, so well attended, and the wide delivery of my address "To the Electors", of which 15,000 were circulated, prevent the enemy from ignoring the question."[148]

Then, on 5 November 1882, Robertson gave his first known freethought lectures in "Bonnie Dundee", a fishing port by the "silvery" Tay (where local secularists had cancelled Bradlaugh's lectures some five years earlier). In the morning the young Scot addressed the Dundee Secular Society in the Upper Hall, Lindsay Street, on "The Orthodoxy of Women", which may well have partly explained the relative under-representation of women in the British freethought and secularist movement, certainly among the rank and file, and which lecture he had already delivered to the Scottish Secular Union in Edinburgh on 26 June 1881 and to the Glasgow Eclectic and Secular Institute and Branch of the N.S.S. on 18 December of that same year. This lecture, in which Robertson traced the orthodoxy of women to female subjection by men, appears to have provided the basis for his article with the same title that would appear in the journal *Progress* in May 1884.

Also on 5 November 1882 he spoke, during the afternoon, to the Dundee Branch of the N.S.S., Albert Hall, 15 Murraygate, on "The Dishonesty of Clergymen" – a lecture which he had given to secularists in Edinburgh in March and would be advertised to deliver in Glasgow in early December – and the Dundee Branch secretary commented: "The way in which the lecturer treated his subject left nothing to be desired." In the evening, while fires springing from Christian sectarianism blazed across the United Kingdom, Robertson, on his return to the Dundee Secular Society, rather boldly "gave a sketch of 'How the Bible was compiled', to a good audience".[149]

Promoting Republicanism

As the year 1882 drew to a close, an Edinburgh Branch of the potentially vigorous Republican League was formed in the Chambers Street Hall on 8 November, when twenty-two people, "including several of the local secularists", expressed an interest in joining, with an unanimous decision "to conduct the work of the League quite independently of anti-theological propaganda". At this gathering a key part was played by George Standring, a young secularist from Hackney in London; and a week later the Edinburgh Branch chose its officers, with Robertson's friend John Lees as chairman, though Robertson himself was not among the principal office-bearers. On 15 November – according to the Branch secretary as reported in the *National Reformer* for 26 November – "about thirty members" were enrolled; while according to George Standring, writing as editor, in *The Republican* for December 1882, "the result of the gathering was that the members' roll reached 62". An esteemed historian of nineteenth century British freethought may have erred, at least regarding the republican branch in Edinburgh which that historian specifically mentioned, when he declared in that context that "although such republican activities were nominally independent of freethought, they were in fact entirely dependent on Secularists"[150] (certainly the secretary and treasurer of the Republican League's Edinburgh Branch do not appear to have been known as prominent Bradlaughite secularists in Edinburgh at this time). However, Annie Besant and Charles Bradlaugh were enthusiastically received when they addressed a large audience at a meeting (almost certainly attended by Robertson) of the Edinburgh Republican League on 5 January 1883.

Mrs. Besant's speech on 5 January in the Chambers Street Hall was reported the following day by the *Edinburgh Evening News*, which drew attention to the fact that in the course of calling for a more equitable taxation system she referred to "the cost of the royal family and the army and navy". Then, on 14 January, the Edinburgh Branch of the N.S.S. appointed delegates to attend the demonstration in London on 15 February in support of Bradlaugh and constitutional rights, and noted: "The Republican League Branch are also to send delegates." Resolutions relating to Bradlaugh's exclusion from Parliament were expected to be moved at the meeting of the Edinburgh Branch of the Republican League on 7 February, when John Robertson was due to address that Branch on "The case against Republicanism" (although no account of what he would have said on that occasion has come to hand). Certainly the *Edinburgh Evening News* on 15 February gave coverage to a meeting of the Edinburgh Republican League the previous day, when that Branch adopted a resolution expressing deep concern at "the infringement of constitutional rights in the continued exclusion of Mr. Bradlaugh from the House of Commons". Moreover, Robertson may have been among Edinburgh delegates who managed to attend the pro-Bradlaugh demonstration in Trafalgar Square, London, on 15 February, when up to 20,000 Bradlaugh supporters were present, despite railway companies cancelling excursion tickets to London.[151]

During the early months of 1883 Robertson seemed as active as ever. On 14 January he read a "clever" paper to the Edinburgh Secular Society on the alleged religious tone of Shakespeare's plays. Then, on 18 February, Robertson presumably returned to the hall at 3 Chambers Street to address the Society on "The Future of the Working Classes", on which he had been advertised to lecture there on that date. Although no record of what he would have said has been traced in newspapers and journals of the period, he may have thought or suggested that the working class could well become better educated, more questioning of or less reliant on religious belief, and more engaged and informed as a body of citizens able to use the vote to effect change in Britain.

Enter Patrick Geddes

In the meantime, on 22 January, from his rented accommodation at 17 London Street, Robertson wrote for help to Patrick Geddes, apparently a fairly new friend whom he had met at meetings of the Edinburgh Secular Society. Since 1880 Geddes had been attached to Edinburgh University as a zoology lecturer with wide-ranging interests (he would be credited with coining the term "conurbation", for example). He was a slightly built but immensely energetic, voluble and stimulating young man with copious hair parted in the middle and a thick reddish beard. In his "confabulations" with Robertson he apparently formulated ideas relating to civics, sociology and town planning, for which he was to become famous, and praised John Ruskin, who much influenced him – in Robertson's words – "with a warmth of sympathy and respect which any prophet might be proud to elicit". Geddes's work won praise from Charles Darwin and Albert Einstein, not to mention the American urban theorist Lewis Mumford, who said Geddes "for me is the most prodigious thinker in the modern world"; and his influence extended from Bombay in India to Jerusalem and Tel Aviv in Palestine. Robertson seems to have had a consistently high regard for Geddes's work (though, rather curiously, town planning and accordingly Geddes's *Cities in Evolution* were not included in Robertson's generally impressive compendium published in 1932 as the third edition of *Courses of Study*). Geddes, for his part, ranked Robertson as a freethinker with Bradlaugh.[152] Both Robertson and Geddes were quite happy crossing boundaries that could restrict the relationship between disciplines; both men encouraged people "to think outside the box" and to think for themselves; both would become prominent supporters of organisations like the Sociological Society, South Place Ethical Society and the Rationalist Press Association; and they kept in touch with each other partly through correspondence, mainly, it seems, in the 1880s.

In his letter to Geddes of 22 January 1883 Robertson asked for a copy of Geddes's paper on the classification of statistics (which dated from 1881) for his economist friend Joseph Hiam Levy, and also whether Geddes could help find suitable employment for another friend of Robertson's, Joseph Mazzini Wheeler. Although Wheeler seems to have been based in Edinburgh until about September 1881, he and Geddes do not appear to have known each other as Robertson's letter provided biographical information about Wheeler, whose praises he sang, without in any way focusing on Wheeler working as sub-editor of G.W. Foote's *Freethinker* (for a pound a week). While Geddes does not seem to have been able to help Wheeler on that occasion, the freethought and secularist cause in Edinburgh appeared to be making headway. Towards the end of February 1883, at 332 Lawnmarket, Alexander Orr opened a new freethought bookshop (no doubt visited and supported by Robertson) and circulated ten thousand handbills announcing his new venture; and at the beginning of March Annie Besant hailed as "a ray of light" the very recent purchase by John Lees and his business partner W.A. Wilson (a fellow N.S.S. member) of a property in Edinburgh for adaptation and use as a secular hall, in view of the exorbitantly high rent Edinburgh secularists were being made to pay for their current hall.[153]

Prosecuted for Blasphemy

Then, on 5 March, the day after Mrs. Besant's glowing public reference to "a ray of light", the British freethought and secularist movement appeared to receive a severe blow which, ironically, gave it a new and reinvigorating sense of martyrdom, mission and militancy and, in the longer term, a kind of victory for the vanquished. During the summer of 1882 attempts were made, notably by the Christian Tory M.P. Sir Henry Tyler, to ensure that the *Freethinker* would be prosecuted for blasphemy. Such attempts resulted in the establishment of a *Freethinker* Defence Fund, to which, in November that year, Robertson apparently contributed one shilling (which may have been about as much as he felt he could spare at that time). Thereafter it was not long before G.W. Foote, William James Ramsey and Henry Kemp, as the editor, publisher and shopman respectively of the *Freethinker*, went on trial before Mr. Justice North at the Old Bailey for blasphemy involving the Christmas 1882 number.

This Christmas number included a provocative cartoon of "Moses Getting a Back View", which was inspired by Exodus 33:23 ("And I will take away mine hand, and thou shalt see my back parts"), and which portrayed a diminutive Moses gazing at the Almighty's bottom, clad in torn check or tartan trousers, with what looked a little like a tatter or tail hanging down behind, though it seems no less possible that there was an intention to depict, or hint at, the Almighty breaking wind or even defecating. Nearly fifty years later, in private correspondence, Robertson maintained that, in a first edition of the *Freethinker*'s Christmas number, the cartoon showed the Deity 'farting'. "Some, I remember, argued that the woodcut exhibited a tail. But common sense knew what it was meant for." Robertson claimed that Bradlaugh and "all my set of N.S.S. friends at Edinburgh" had seen the 'fart' form of the cartoon: "the 'obscene' cartoon appeared only in the first edition. You might fairly suggest that it was freak of the 'artist', not of Foote's planning, though he let it pass. But I certainly received an early copy, with the 'obscene' detail because I happened to be a contributor to the number. And I perfectly remember my shock of disgust, and my letter of protest to Foote, who simply answered that to catch the crowd you had to go to their level." Quite independently of Robertson, his Positivist acquaintance Malcolm Quin of Newcastle found the cartoons in the *Freethinker* so flagrant that, at about the same time, he wrote to Foote to remonstrate with him about them and to announce his discontinuation of contributions to the subject-matter of Foote's journals.[154] It seems Foote wanted to share the crown of freethought or the thorns of martyrdom with Bradlaugh, and to be convicted of blasphemy, but not of obscenity.

Robertson went on to declare: "Obviously, the moment Foote knew the police were on his track – which would be early – he would destroy the whole remainder of his first impression." Robertson also claimed that "most decent freethinkers would destroy their copies", and that the cartoon may well have been altered to delete representation of a 'fart': "wood blocks can be altered; but it is quite possible that a new one was made." (Almost certainly unbeknown to Robertson, in the run-up to Christmas 1882 Sir Thomas Nelson of the City of London, who had seen the Christmas issue of the *Freethinker*, had asked the Government whether the cartoon with the caption "Moses Getting a Back View" could be prosecuted under the Obscene Publications Act.) The Scottish secularist suggested that Sir William Harcourt was not unjustified as Home Secretary when, in the House of Commons in the summer of 1883, he described the Christmas number as "in the most strict sense of the word an obscene libel … a scandalous outrage upon public decency". No public attempt was made by Bradlaugh, Robertson and other freethinkers to refute Harcourt's accusation of obscenity: Robertson maintained that "the whole matter had to be fogged in public debate, because nobody could get up and talk about 'a fart' ". He added that, in private discussion among freethinkers, at least some admitted that, in terms of the dictionary definition, the visual representation of 'a fart' was obscene. He indicated that the cartoon's original form accounted for an allegation that the prosecuted Christmas number depicted a man "openly committing a nuisance": "the real point of the word 'obscene', as of 'nuisance', is against publicity … Of course, to exhibit the deity as farting was to combine blasphemy with obscenity." (In July 1884 Foote would publicly reveal that a man had written to him to claim that his brother-in-law had informed him that "our prosecuted Christmas Number contained a picture of a man openly committing a nuisance", which Foote denied was true.)[155]

If the accusation of obscenity levelled against Foote's original cartoon was, as Robertson put it, "technically supportable", the technicality of the alleged obscenity, combined with considerations relating to Victorian prudishness in scatological matters as well as a desire to attack militant atheism and discredit Bradlaugh's freethought supporters and associates, may help to explain why Foote was charged with blasphemy, and not obscenity. On trial at the Old Bailey, where he conducted his own defence, recognised by Robertson as "very able", Foote pointed out that J.S. Mill, Huxley, Buckle, Matthew Arnold, and Strauss had shocked Christian sensibilities without being prosecuted (and he quoted from Charles Gill's very recently published work *The Evolution of Christianity,* justifiably described by Robertson as "a powerful freethinking polemic"). Once Foote and his two comrades had been found guilty, Mr Justice North sentenced Foote, Ramsey and Kemp to twelve, nine and three months' imprisonment respectively on 5 March. The Catholic judge castigated Foote for having "chosen to prostitute his talents to the work of the Devil".[156] Yet he himself received a magisterial rebuke when Foote declared: "I thank you, my lord, your sentence is worthy of your creed" – arguably the noblest and most heroic moment in Foote's life.

The next day the prosecution and sentence were roundly criticised in a leader in the *Edinburgh Evening News* symptomatic of Robertson's fire and eloquence: "… the trial, regarded as an attempt to support religion, is one of those blunders which are worse than crimes … By this sentence the freethinkers of the working class are simply led to believe that Christianity has to make use of the dungeon in order to maintain itself against sceptical attacks; and their hostility to the reigning creed is intensified by the sense of persecution. … all resorts to force in modern religious disputes strengthen the coerced side. … The Society for the Suppression of Blasphemous Literature has proclaimed its intention of prosecuting, as its funds allow, the publishers of the works of Mill and Strauss, Professors Huxley and Tyndall, Mr. Spencer, Mr. Swinburne, Mr. Leslie Stephen, Mr. John Morley, … and the theistic author of *Supernatural Religion*. All reasonable people will say this is senseless fanaticism … All these writers have assuredly been guilty of blasphemy as the law stands. Mr. Arnold has said one or two things as blasphemous as anything in Paine. There is no drawing of the line possible. Either complete toleration must be accorded to freethought literature, or we must establish a Holy Office." The leader writer also declared that arguably "the offence for which Mr. Foote and his companions were punished was essentially one against public decency", which would seem to suggest that he had obscenity rather than blasphemy in mind; and in that context he was careful in his choice of words not to specify the offence of which Foote and his comrades had been guilty. (Four decades later Robertson would express regret that he himself had never been prosecuted for blasphemy.)[157]

Within days of the prison sentences being imposed at the Old Bailey on 5 March and the highly critical leader in the *Edinburgh Evening News* on 6 March, secularists and no doubt others in Edinburgh rallied to the cause. On Sunday, 11 March two protest meetings – both convened or supported by the Edinburgh Secular Society – were held in the hall at 3 Chambers Street, and both were reported in the evening paper the next day. At the morning meeting, attended by about a hundred freethinkers, John Lees, who presided, declared to applause that "though he did not sympathise with everything in the *Freethinker*, yet he considered it their duty to defend it when it was assailed by proceedings which involved the liberty of the press"; and at his suggestion resolutions were framed for submission to the evening meeting (this could suggest that the secularists felt they had to tread carefully in weighing considerations relating to obscenity and to blasphemy). At the public meeting in the evening some 500 protesters heard Robertson, W.E. Snell, Lees and Charles Nicholson speak to two resolutions. Indeed, in its own terms this second meeting seems to have constituted not only a great success for Edinburgh freethinkers as a group, but also an early triumph for Robertson as a public speaker, debater and champion of contemporary freethought in the political arena. The account in the *Edinburgh Evening News* recorded that in the evening in the crowded hall "a resolution was unanimously adopted to the effect that while expressing no opinion as to the contents of the *Freethinker*, the meeting condemned the prosecution as a dangerous revival of laws framed in a spirit of persecution, and now out of harmony with enlightened opinion; and resolved to take all lawful means to obtain a repeal of these laws." The second resolution, carried overwhelmingly to loud cheering, supported a proposed memorial to the Home Secretary for a remission of the sentences on Foote, Ramsey and Kemp. Distinguished figures in science and literature endorsing the memorial included Herbert Spencer, Leslie Stephen, T.H. Huxley, John Tyndall and Henry Maudsley, with Bradlaugh writing an open letter denouncing Mr. Justice North.[158] But Sir William Harcourt refused to budge.

Foote had left his closest friend Joseph Mazzini Wheeler in charge of his two journals the *Freethinker* and *Progress* (for which a secularist manufacturer in Leicester, Josiah Gimson – father of Robertson's future friend Sydney Gimson – had apparently provided substantial capital[159]), but without access to funds to cover the immediate costs of paper and printing. The weight of this responsibility and the strain imposed by Foote's imprisonment proved too much for Wheeler, who within a fortnight of Foote entering upon his prison sentence had become temporarily insane and was placed in a private asylum where he spent several months before recovering. On his discharge Wheeler, still brooding on Foote's imprisonment, took a sea trip to Scotland, where he may have met his friend

John Robertson, who had already renewed contact with him during a brief visit that Robertson made to the Greater London area in early July 1882, when the two of them spent an enjoyable day rambling with Foote through the countryside around Kew and Richmond.[160] (Some seventy years later the famous archaeologist Sir Mortimer Wheeler would write of his own father, formerly of Edinburgh: "He was a failure by all standards save his own. … He … became, incidentally, an advanced freethinker of the militant type of the early 'eighties. … For a time my father, with a young wife, was caught up in a circle which included (Sir) Carlaw Martin, later Director of the Royal Scottish Museum, and J.M. Robertson, later a persistent M.P. …"[161]) For his part, Foote seemed to feel that he 'owned' the vulnerable Joe Wheeler, of whom he would write in 1901: "he would have gone into the Pass of Thermopylae with me whenever I beckoned him"[162]; and thirty years after Foote's claim, Robertson would maintain in private correspondence: "Once [probably in the summer of 1884], when Joe was invited by Mrs. Besant to contribute to her *Our Corner*, and did so to earn a few guineas, Foote formally informed him by letter that he (F.) could not permit those 'of his entourage' to contribute to a rival magazine."[163]

With Foote in prison, Edward Aveling took over as editor of the *Freethinker* and *Progress*. The secularist propagandist Joseph Symes felt that Aveling "diddled" him out of the editorship of the *Freethinker* ; while Robertson himself was one of the unpaid contributors to *Progress*, which Foote had launched as recently as January 1883 as a refined (if now struggling) monthly, where Robertson's first essay – in the March issue – was on the social philosopher Herbert Spencer, rather as the young Scot's earlier letter of 14 May 1882 in Bradlaugh's *National Reformer* was partly devoted to Spencer.

Although the *Edinburgh Evening News* carried only a brief notice – reprinted from the *Newcastle Chronicle* – of Karl Marx's death on 14 March 1883, it was apparently relatively soon after Marx's death that when Robertson asked socialist friends, "How are you going to get the scheme to work in this point and that point?" they replied: "We are seeking to cross a river. We cannot tell how we shall act until we get over. Let us cross the river first and then discuss how we shall get on." To this Robertson retorted: "You are proposing to cross an ocean instead of a river … to go into a new state of things without knowing how it will work – that for me is nonsense." A century or so later the Communist historian Eric Hobsbawm would make virtually the same point using a similar metaphor: "socialists, Marxist or otherwise, before 1917 had been too busy opposing capitalism to give much thought to the nature of the economy that would replace it, and after October Lenin himself, dipping, as he himself put it, one foot into the deep waters of socialism, made no attempt to dive into the unknown."[164]

Meanwhile, in 1883, Aveling was successful in getting a number of Marxian socialists and Communists, such as Marx's daughter Eleanor and Marx's lifelong collaborator Friedrich Engels, to contribute in various ways to the continued (if relatively short-term) survival of *Progress*. Another contributor to the monthly, under the *nom de plume* of "Norman Britton", was Robertson's friend William Archer, who much admired Foote and felt outraged by the use of the criminal law against him in an attack on free speech, though Archer also disapproved strongly of the offending matter in the *Freethinker* prosecution.

Many years later, long after Robertson, Archer, Foote and Aveling were all dead, Dr. H. George Farmer, who passed for a friend of Foote's, would claim that in the book *William Archer as Rationalist* (1925) – published less than a full year after Archer's death – Robertson, the editor, totally ignored the "ten" articles contributed by Archer, under his pseudonym, to *Progress* from early 1883 onwards, because Robertson resented Foote's success as editor of the *Freethinker*, President of the N.S.S. and founder of the Secular Society Ltd.[165] (Archer's biographer Peter Whitebrook would maintain in 1993 that Archer published fifteen articles in *Progress* during 1883-84.) Although Robertson came to regard Foote as dishonourable, no evidence has come to hand to support Farmer's actual allegations about Robertson's attitude to Foote; and, regarding the *Freethinker*, Robertson would declare that Foote came out to find that "the sale of his journal was greatly extended" during the 1883-84 period.[166] Moreover, Foote was publicly described after his death as "a man of good culture and literary capacity, with debating and oratorical powers adequate to all his occasions" by Robertson, who also declared the establishment of the Secular Society Ltd. to have been "one of Mr. Foote's services to his cause".[167] *William Archer as Rationalist* had a sub-title, *A Collection of His Heterodox Writings*, which was perfectly accurate: it did not purport to be comprehensive. As it was published by Watts & Co., which was closely associated with the Rationalist Press Association, it seems understandable that the collection should focus on Archer's contributions to publications associated with them.

Bright, Browning, and Buckle

Without doubt in 1883 "there were giants in the earth in those days", when Robertson was busy assessing some of the eminent Victorians such as John Bright in politics and Robert Browning in literature. On 22 March the young Scot was in Glasgow for the Rectorial address reported in next day's *Edinburgh Evening News* and delivered at the University by the veteran Free Trade orator and Liberal reformer John Bright, a Quaker who had steadfastly opposed Britain's participation in the Crimean War, sharply criticised British rule in India, and supported Bradlaugh in his Parliamentary struggle. Bright later recorded that he spoke "with ease and freedom", and his speech might have encouraged Robertson's adherence to the principle of Free Trade – but Robertson seems to have been disappointed by Bright's address. As Robertson would explain six years later in referring to "what I venture to call the temperamental snare of the Liberal – the belief that the reforms he wants will settle the question for good. The most dramatic exhibition of that illusion which I can call to mind is a speech which I heard Mr. Bright deliver in Glasgow on the occasion of his Rectorial visit – a speech in which he intimated that all the great questions of political strife not yet settled were evidently approaching settlement, and that very soon there would be nothing to quarrel about."[168] (More than a century later, through his book *The End of History and the Last Man* (1992), which posited the triumph of Western liberal democracy as the end point of humanity's ideological evolution, the American political scientist Francis Fukuyama would seem to be in danger of falling into a trap similar to the one that, in Robertson's estimation, caught John Bright.)

In April 1883 Robertson published his second article in *Progress*. Entitled "Mr. Browning's 'Jocoseria'", this reflected his general enthusiasm for the work of the poet Robert Browning, of whom he asked rhetorically: "What poet has given us such a manifold creation; such hours of intellectual exaltation; such moments of strange perception, as of gazers on new seas?" Eight years later, less than eighteen months after Browning's death in December 1889, Robertson would admit: "I too am a Browningite – on this side idolatry. Browning has given me, by his manifold psychologising, a larger number of hours of vivid interest than any other poet, excepting Shakspere, Dante, and Homer. He is comparatively seldom musically delightful; but he is in general splendidly alive. And yet … his world-philosophy represents simply the vivacious empiricism of an egoist of literary genius …"[169] Robertson's interest in Browning would find renewed expression in his *Browning and Tennyson as Teachers* (1903), which provided a detailed comparative study of these Victorian poets from a humanist angle.

Both Browning and Henry Thomas Buckle appeared to be theists, and both were admired by Robertson, albeit essentially for different reasons, the former for his literary art and the latter for his insightful contribution to the study of history and sociology. Of Buckle Robertson would declare: "From his *Introduction to the History of Civilization in England* you will learn … that the welter of historic events, which looks like a great chaos or measureless sea, has its laws, its intelligible sequences, as truly as any department of nature."[170] (More than a century later Buckle's emphasis on the major role that climate has played in history would resonate in an age acutely aware of the potentially catastrophic effects of climate change.) Robertson's *Buckle and His Critics* (1895) – itself a notable contribution to sociology and the science of history – was a powerful defence of the dead historian against the misrepresentations of his detractors, though Robertson also exposed or attempted to correct many of Buckle's undoubted errors and exaggerations. For decades it was the only full-scale book in English to give a fair yet sympathetic assessment of Buckle's work. It impressed a number of twentieth century English-speaking historians, including George Peabody Gooch and Bernard Semmel. (Gooch, who, like Robertson, sat as a Liberal M.P. between 1906 and 1910, regarded Robertson as an excellent speaker, energy incarnate, and one of the keenest intellects he had ever known.[171]) Robertson's monumental book still provided in the twenty-first century a reference point and source material for further reading on Buckle; and it may have partly originated as a lecture – described at the time as "able" – Robertson gave on "Buckle and the Scotch" to the Edinburgh Secular Society at 3 Chambers Street on 29 April 1883. This lecture of 1883 on Buckle appears to have been Robertson's earliest lecture on that brilliantly promising but short-lived heterodox Victorian historian, whom he would call "my early master" and whose *Introduction to the History of Civilization in England* he would thoroughly edit in 1904; rather as Robertson would publicly hail Herbert Spencer as "spiritual Father and honoured Master … the greatest herald of the new age".[172]

Women leading the way

No doubt a new age seemed to dawn for Robertson and his friends when, on Sunday, 27 May 1883, Mrs. Besant opened the Roxburgh Hall, which had been purchased so that the Edinburgh Branch of the N.S.S. would have its own premises, free from exorbitant rent or sectarian ban. Destined to be the scene of some of young Robertson's successes as a public speaker in Scotland, this small building in Drummond Street was tastefully painted, with an interior gallery running round three sides, and thick glass windows softly tinged with yellow. The next day in the Hall, after a tea attended by nearly one hundred people, Mrs. Besant (who had given the inaugural lecture there on the Sunday) proposed a hearty vote of thanks, seconded by W.E. Snell, to the high-minded manufacturer John Lees for his part in securing the building for the Branch.

Two weeks earlier John Lees had featured quite prominently at the N.S.S. Annual Conference in Manchester, where he and his sister were Edinburgh delegates and he was elected an N.S.S. Vice-President for the first time (together with Bradlaugh's daughter Hypatia): in his case this was surely a mark of appreciation and thanks for his work in securing the Roxburgh Hall. He told the Conference that "he had been a Freethinker for many years, but beyond working hard in his business and enjoying himself with a book or walk on Sunday, he had not recognised his duty"; and he had felt shamed and galvanized into action in 1878 when "Edinburgh disgraced itself by breaking a contract made with Mr. Bradlaugh for a hall". He added: "After 1800 years of Christianity the world has still to be redeemed. Not from ... the wrath of an imaginary god by an imaginary savior [*sic*], but it needed to be redeemed from disease, dirt, crime, ignorance and folly, and every man and every woman can help to be a savior."[173] (There seemed to be some illustration of this when, at about the time of the Conference, Mrs. Besant and Bradlaugh's elder daughter Alice were refused admission to the practical botany class at University College in London.) No doubt to the regret of both Scotsmen, John Lees's words were not heard by John Robertson, who was not at the Conference as he was lined up to lecture on 13 May 1883 to the Glasgow Eclectic and Secular Institute on "The Religion of Shakespeare" (in the morning) and on Henry George's *Progress and Poverty* (in the evening). Robertson's evening lecture was described in the *Secular Review* as "a criticism" of Henry George (at a time when British freethinkers were beginning to subject the American's ideas to a frontal attack or searching scrutiny).[174]

While for some one door remained closed, for Robertson, at least, a new door opened: in May his first signed article in Mrs. Besant's *Our Corner* appeared. His article was an agreeably erudite contribution entitled "Some Plagiarisms", which would be reprinted in his *Criticisms* (second volume) in 1903; and Annie Besant's *Our Corner* was a promising, high-class monthly launched by her in January, the selfsame month as Foote's *Progress*, with some contributors, including Robertson, writing for both journals. However, *Progress* would feature fewer pieces by Robertson than *Our Corner* (which would last a year longer – until December 1888 – than *Progress*). Both journals attracted socialist writers, though *Progress* may have presented a greater number of the undeniably Marxist variety, which was rather ironic as Foote was consistently somewhat hostile to socialism whereas Annie Besant would become a convert to it. Unlike some contributors to *Progress*, Robertson, who was an advanced radical, seems to have sent in money (towards the end of April 1883) to the *Freethinker* Prisoners' Aid Fund set up to support the families of the imprisoned martyrs Foote, Ramsey and Kemp, who, Bradlaugh told the N.S.S. Conference in May, "can write no letters save once in three months, can see no visitors save at the same interval and have to pick oakum in their solitary confinement, not being allowed to hold the smallest communication with each other". Yet the martyrdom of Foote and his two comrades may have done as much, if not more, to further the cause of freethought and secularism in Britain as any remission of their sentences would have done. The prosecution in their case both activated and increased the membership of the N.S.S., which, in terms of estimated numbers of new members, seems to have reached its peak soon afterwards; and Robertson would maintain that on his release Foote – who was an N.S.S. Vice-President – "came out to find a larger audience than ever as a lecturer".[175]

In an era when secularists and freethinkers were among the leading champions of the republican cause in Britain, Robertson apparently addressed the Edinburgh Branch of the Republican League on 6 June, in the new Roxburgh Hall, on "Reasons against Home Rule" (of which no recorded exposition has come to hand). However, during the summer Robertson devoted much of his attention to literary matters rather than to political or public policy issues. For example, the June issue of *Progress* carried the first of three articles by him, appearing in consecutive months, on the recently deceased Victorian novelist Marian Evans, better known as George Eliot. In the first article his comments on the Brontë sisters Emily and Charlotte seem more thought-provoking and arresting than those on George Eliot herself, with Robertson observing towards the end of this article that *Wuthering Heights* was "unquestionably a more extraordinary book than any of her sister's. Charlotte Brontë will live in the memory of all of us as a brave and fiery soul, a keen and true observer, and a fine artist; but besides the elemental force and daring superiority to convention in Emily's work, Charlotte's resolute propriety, as well as her emphatic little philosophy, suggest very decidedly the gifted governess. … Emily Brontë's mind, marvellously powerful as it was, came short of perfect sanity. …"

There was perhaps at least a hint of the mentality of a gifted governess of resolute propriety in Bradlaugh's daughter Hypatia, who in early June travelled north on a crowded train bound for Edinburgh to fulfil lecturing engagements there, her first to the Edinburgh Branch of the N.S.S. Her third such lecture was on the Elizabethan writers Lyly, Sidney and Marlowe; and it seems to have been about this time that she began to get to know Robertson, with whom she would form a lifelong friendship. On that occasion they probably met by the Firth of Forth at the Portobello house of John Lees and his sister Isabella, with whom she was staying; and Hypatia's meeting with Robertson was, in her words, "punctuated with a clash – the clash of ignorance against knowledge. At that time I was newly a student of Elizabethan literature, and, of course, I thought I knew a great deal about it. … My little difficulty was merely a disagreement over the name of one of the Elizabethan writers. Then there was Marlowe. In my young days Marlowe had a great fascination for me. I even loved the rant and bombast of his Tamburlaine 'threatening the world in high astounding terms'. I was somehow convinced that Mr Robertson's appreciation of Marlowe did not reach to the level that I thought it ought to have done, and I think I was a little jealous on Marlowe's account." Many years later, though in Hypatia's lifetime, Robertson would in effect pay her a kind of compliment when the evolution of his thinking resulted in his attributing to Marlowe some of the work commonly considered to be Shakespeare's. He also came to believe that Marlowe, in *Tamburlaine*, was not above stealing a phrase from Edmund Spenser (as indeed Robertson's friend the poet, dramatist and critic T.S. Eliot would point out in an essay of 1932 on Marlowe), rather as Robertson had declared in his article of May 1883 on "Some Plagiarisms" that Milton "borrowed frequently from Spenser".[176]

Tennyson, Wordsworth – and Pepys

In the meantime, on 24 June 1883, the day after a sun-burnt Hypatia Bradlaugh left Edinburgh with regret for Newcastle, Robertson gave a lecture – admission being free – to the Edinburgh Secular Society on "The Theology of Tennyson", who was the current Poet Laureate of whom Robertson later wrote: "On religion his utterances are either platitudes or fallacies … All through life he was obsessed by the craving for future life." Although no transcript of his lecture has come to light, Robertson's paper was described as "able" by a secularist who presumably heard it read; and it may be assumed that it was taken into account in Robertson's composition of *Browning and Tennyson as Teachers* (1903), where he maintained: "Tennyson's effort has gone to what is most special to his art, melodious expression, beauty of cadence, golden speech."[177] Decades after its publication, this book would still be noticed by writers on Tennyson.

At about the time of Robertson's lecture on Tennyson William Nimmo and Co. of Edinburgh published Robertson's *Winnowings from Wordsworth*, which was the Scot's first work to appear in book form. He may have felt encouraged to study Wordsworth by his Edinburgh friend William Archer, who had read the English poet with appreciation for a college essay. Be that as it may, Robertson's firstling received little attention in 1883, although this miniature book bound in blue with an attractive gilt decoration may have been on sale in Alexander Orr's new freethought bookshop in Edinburgh, and Robertson himself would acknowledge his paternity of *Winnowings from Wordsworth* almost ten years later (in the *National Reformer* for 10 April 1892, which did not mention his supposed authorship of a novel said, after his death, to have been serialized in a provincial newspaper in his youth).

Robertson's anonymous publication was an anthology with an unsigned twenty-one page preface which was critical of Matthew Arnold's views on Wordsworth, and which incidentally referred to Thomas Carlaw Martin's article on "Wordsworth as a Teacher" in *Progress* for January 1883. In this preface (later described as "sprightly" by his friend Gilmour) Robertson appeared to attribute Wordsworth's "amazing lapses into triviality and doggerel" to "the injurious influence of his solitary life" and to his submitting his abundant verse to "no harder test than the edgeless criticism of an admiring domestic circle". Although Robertson believed that Wordsworth tended to confuse simplicity with banality, and although his judgement that *Michael* was a poor poem because of its "almost uniformly leaden" style may seem excessively harsh, he also recognised that Wordsworth's "felicity of style when at his best was the complement of his intensity of feeling … it is no small achievement to have produced so much fine work as is here winnowed out … he has given us poetry which, by its exquisiteness of style and depth of clarified emotion, charms us as we are seldom charmed by other verse of his own or previous generations."

Possibly stimulated by Wordsworth's initial enthusiasm for the French Revolution or by Thomas Carlyle's work on that momentous event, Robertson wrote a poem *On the Anniversary of the Fall of the Bastille* which was published in the July issue of *Our Corner*, together with his article "On Diary-Keeping". This thought-provoking article in effect opened with some striking observations on the famous seventeenth century English diarist Samuel Pepys (whose diary was composed in a form of shorthand which was only deciphered after Pepys's death and only fully published in English a century or so after Robertson's essay). Declared Robertson: "The side-lights thrown by his eager gossip on the life of his time undoubtedly give his book a special value for students of history; but its charm, its distinctive quality as a book, is its incomparable naïveté of self-portraiture. And here comes up the psychological problem underlying all diary-keeping: What induces men and women to write down deliberately in their diaries … not only much that they would be horrified to have published, but much that can only give them discomfort in the after-reading? … To be sure, there is the class of religious diarist, who notes his aberrations from the path of pietistic righteousness with a sense of supplementing the ritual he assists at in church … Then we are all conscious of having at times ministered to our own amour-propre by confessing to certain weaknesses, having all the while a secret feeling that by the candor [sic] of our acknowledgment we place ourselves above even our own reproaches … Diary-keeping – so might the generalisation be worded – is only one outcome of the innate impulse to self-expression … It is extremely dubious whether any woman ever was delivered of a series of aphorisms even distantly resembling those presented as extracts from Ottilie's diary in Goethe's *Wahlverwandschaften*. …"

The vaccination controversy

Very few in Britain in 1883 would have heard of, let alone been familiar with, Goethe's challenging novel Die *Wahlverwandschaften (Elective Affinities)*; but virtually everyone would have been aware of the controversy surrounding compulsory vaccination, to which the opposition was so strong that the British Government and, indeed, the Cabinet became alarmed by it in June. Less than four weeks later, on 15 July, Robertson lectured on "The Vaccination Myth" to the Edinburgh Secular Society in Roxburgh Hall, Drummond Street. Referring to Robertson's attack on an M.P. who was a prominent figure in Parliament on the pro-vaccination side, the secularist "S." (probably W.E. Snell) reported that in his lecture Robertson had contended that Sir Lyon Playfair's own figures refuted his own argument. Six months earlier, on 27 January, an Edinburgh newspaper, the *Evening Express*, carried a nasty personal attack on Snell when it allowed a pseudonymous columnist sarcastically to pronounce that he had been "immortalised … as a disciple of Bradlaugh" and then ask rhetorically with mock caution: "Can it be possible that this is the W.E. Snell who, a few weeks ago, was convicted and punished by the Sheriff for wilful failure to comply with the Vaccination Act, and who, under the able control of the Queen's Remembrancer, Mr. John James Reid, … officiates … as a third-class clerk … Surely the Queen's Remembrancer, who is an old friend of Mr. Waddy [the junior Liberal M.P. for Edinburgh], might make some trifling effort to prevent this Government clerk from harassing the junior member, or making a public scandal of a Government office."

A different tone was adopted by the *National Reformer* in its brief report of Snell's case only a few days after it came to court in Edinburgh in late October 1882. Bradlaugh's paper pointed out that the presiding Sheriff "quite believed that Mr. Snell's objections were conscientious" in his failing to have his baby daughter vaccinated, for which he was fined, with a larger sum for costs (or three days' imprisonment as the alternative penalty). According to Robertson's own recollection (in 1897) of this, or a very similar, case he had covered as a journalist, "the magistrate said the law gave him no choice. This struck me as a monstrous tyranny, which could never have been contemplated by the parliaments which made vaccination compulsory. … To my surprise, my editor objected to any comment on the case I have mentioned, urging that we ought to do nothing to bring vaccination into discredit. This, to me, unsatisfactory position set me upon fully investigating the subject, and I spent many weeks upon it, reading all the literature I could obtain on both sides. Some of the attacks on vaccination, in particular the pamphlet by Mr.

P.A. Taylor, struck me as extremely weighty." The successful experiment in 1881 by the French chemist and bacteriologist Louis Pasteur in administering an anthrax vaccine (which owed much, though Pasteur did not acknowledge it, to the pioneering work of the contemporary French scientist Toussaint) may have encouraged vaccination. Although the practice of vaccination would become refined and extended in the fight against disease, Robertson would refer in 1932 to "the vexed question of vaccination". Between 1937 and 1958 slightly more than one third of the children born in England and Wales were vaccinated for smallpox, and, of those so vaccinated, 91 were apparently killed by vaccination, whereas only two children under five died of smallpox; and in 1974 there were some indications that vaccination could cause brain damage.[178]

An N.S.S. outing

But the Edinburgh secularists of the 1880s occasionally allowed themselves to take a more relaxed approach to the serious business of life. When, on Sunday 29 July 1883, the Edinburgh Branch of the N.S.S. held its first picnic, eighty-eight members left the Roxburgh Hall at nine o'clock in the morning and drove seventeen miles across rich farmland by the coast, and past large houses set in grounds adorned by birds, to Gullane Moor, with magnificent views of the sandy beaches of the Firth of Forth, haunted by waders and wild-fowl and overlooked by the Lammermuir Hills. The weather was perfect; and Robertson was among those active all the way in dropping freethought leaflets – scattering seeds of thought as they went – which were largely picked up by all classes of people. The secularist cavalcade, openly engaged in breaking the Sabbath, attracted cheers and handkerchief-waving from sympathetic couples and small groups by the wayside, and sour looks from the 'unco guid', the latter embodying what the historian H.T. Buckle some twenty years earlier had characterized as "a sour and fanatical spirit, an aversion to innocent gaiety, a disposition to limit the enjoyments of others, and ... gloomy and austere to the last degree, a creed which is full of forebodings and threats and horrors of every sort ... " (near the conclusion of Buckle's famous *Introduction*). Camping out all day and reaching home at eight o'clock at night, the freethinkers had taken care to provide refreshment for themselves and their horses, but the refusal of two innkeepers to water their horses was "an unlooked for brutality that caused some trouble". The presiding genius, and kindly tea-maker, of the day was revealed (apparently by John Lees) to have been Charles Nicholson, who had conceived of and managed the outing. Nicholson's friend Chamberlain had actively participated with Robertson and others in distributing the secularist leaflets; and both Nicholson and Chamberlain had recently been publicly thanked by their comrades for their work in connection with the opening of the new Roxburgh Hall. (Nicholson's son-in-law George Berry became secretary to the Edinburgh Sunday Society.)[179]

Enter Alice Bradlaugh

Although Sunday outings appeared to be quite a regular and popular feature of the programmes of secularist societies during the 1880s, this particular excursion seems to have been somewhat experimental for the Edinburgh freethinkers at this time; and the sense of innovation was continued a fortnight later when Bradlaugh's elder daughter Alice gave her first lecture in Edinburgh, to a large and appreciative local secularist audience that most probably included Robertson. Her subject, "Mind considered physiologically", no doubt provided a basis for her little penny tract which she issued in 1884 under a very similar title, and which would constitute her sole written memorial as a science teacher, as Robertson would indicate after her tragically premature death in 1888 at the age of 32 from typhoid complicated by meningitis. Almost exactly the same age as Robertson, this intelligent, cheerful, attractive and fine young woman may well have met him at John Lees's house at Portobello and gone boating with Robertson in the vicinity, as her sister Hypatia sometimes did, "much to the scandal of the holy neighbourhood" (in Hypatia's words), when Robertson visited Portobello on a Sunday.[180] Alice and Robertson had a number of shared interests, apart from freethought, secularism and materialism: aspects of science, music and the French language, for example (a talented science and singing teacher, she was also a good pianist with a pleasant mezzo-soprano voice); and it might be speculated that had she lived longer Robertson may have wanted to marry her. Some years after her death he would record that "she was her father's daughter in her high spirit, in her generosity, in her energy, and in the thoroughness of her work as a student and teacher of biology"; and several decades later he would remember her in his *History of Freethought in the Nineteenth Century*.

During the weeks immediately following Alice Bradlaugh's Edinburgh lecture on 12 August in 1883, Robertson would address the question of female potential and achievements in various fields. But during the month that lecture was given, Robertson's concluding article on "George Eliot" appeared in *Progress*, in which he showered praise on the gifted woman novelist who had already reached the peak of her literary reputation with the Victorians: "It is not merely that she, so cosmopolitan in her thinking, can get inside the narrowest personalities and touch all their nerve centres without a hint of contempt; or that, being a trained and convinced agnostic, she yet projected the finest ideals of emotional religious life, and treated every phase of superstition with equal gentleness. The crowning grace of all is the all-maternal love which includes alike the sinner and the sinned against, making all life seem kindred in the glow of a boundless pity." These perceptions merit comparison with the conclusions reached by the literary critic Walter Allen just over eighty years later regarding George Eliot and her later novels: "These novels are distinguished by a psychological realism unknown before in English fiction except, perhaps, in Fielding's *Amelia* and Jane Austen's *Emma*. Character has become destiny, and character is subjected to intense critical scrutiny. ... for all her profound reverence, she is never a religious novelist; and the reality of sexual passion is also foreign to her. Her view of life was unswervingly and all the time a moral view, and nothing that existed outside the moral view, that could not be netted by it, existed for her."[181] In 1929, in his *History of Freethought in the Nineteenth Century*, Robertson indicated that George Eliot vitiated her art as a novelist by constantly stressing "moral doctrine".

On the theatre and Edinburgh literary life

Having focused on a renowned British novelist, Robertson in 1883 turned his attention to drama; and on 26 August that year he read a paper, briefly and tantalisingly noticed as "embodying much acute criticism", on "The Theatre – as it is and as it ought to be" to a large secularist audience in the Roxburgh Hall. This was followed on 10 September by a leading article in the *Edinburgh Evening News*, almost certainly by Robertson, reviewing William Archer's very recently published *Henry Irving, Actor and Manager*, which was, the leader said, "a dispassionate but close examination of the art of Mr. Irving and the bases on which his popularity rests … Mr. Archer not only subjects to coolly merciless criticism Mr. Irving's defects of elocution and deportment, but sums him up as an artist possessing intellect without inspiration. … The writer is thoroughly at home in his subject, and treats it with an acumen and literary finish which make the book a most enjoyable piece of reading; but … it would require to be explained to those who hold, with Lamb and Diderot, that a great actor is above his emotions, where the line is to be drawn between intellect and inspiration. Mr. Archer allows Mr. Irving "intensity", and the distinction is not clear. …"[182] These words would have been read by theatre-goers and, quite probably, Irving himself, as, on the very day the review appeared, the opening of the new Royal Lyceum Theatre in Edinburgh was celebrated with a performance of Shakespeare's *Much Ado about Nothing*, starring Irving as Benedick (reported in the *Edinburgh Evening News* next day), and with Robertson probably in the audience.

It was at this time when William Archer was no longer based in Edinburgh or indeed Scotland that a leader writer in the *Edinburgh Evening News* – again almost certainly Robertson – paused to take stock of the state of literary life in Edinburgh, declaring on 11 September: "There are no widely celebrated literary men resident in the city at present; but the standard of literary reputation is higher in these days than fifty years ago; and in any case there is less "provincialism" – in the sense of narrow-mindedness – in Edinburgh now than ever … and the general level of education and liberality of thought is incomparably above what it was in the first half of the century." It is not entirely clear how far the leader writer intended his observations to apply not only to Edinburgh but also to the situation in Scotland or the United Kingdom generally; though it may be presumed that he took account of the fact that Robert Burns had died in 1796 and Walter Scott in 1832. Moreover, it was only after 1883 that both Robert Louis Stevenson and W.E. Henley, for example, achieved literary prominence (the latter was not a Scot, although for some time both men were residents of Edinburgh).

A remarkable feminist leader

Then, on 24 September 1883, a rather remarkable contribution to public education and debate regarding the social roles and advance of women in modern Britain was made in the form of a leading article – almost certainly from Robertson's pen – in the *Edinburgh Evening News*. Four months later the feminist leader Millicent Garrett Fawcett, whose political views were somewhat similar to a number of Robertson's, publicly announced that the Liberal Association in Edinburgh had adopted a resolution supporting the principle of women's suffrage. But the leader writer was much bolder, striking a note that was prophetic as well as visionary. (The writer's style and reference to the character Dinah Morris in George Eliot's novel *Adam Bede* suggest that he was Robertson, whose assessment of George Eliot published in *Progress* won the admiration of William Archer.)[183]

The writer noted that women were increasingly found in "occupations hitherto reserved exclusively for the lords of creation" (one case in point was that of the female sculptor of the Burns statue unveiled in Dumfries in 1882). He added that female doctors, for example, were "fast taking root in this country, and it is quite within the bounds of probability that in the perhaps not distant future some fair girl advocate may make an irresistible appeal to a British jury. Who knows whether, as a result of the relaxation in doctrine and practice, about which so much is heard nowadays, the pulpit itself, hitherto held sacred from female intrusion, may not in years to come be invaded, and be flooded with fair enthusiasts holding forth with all the unction and all the fascination of a Dinah Morris?" (Indeed, Millicent Garrett Fawcett's sister – before she was known as Elizabeth Garrett Anderson on her marriage – had become the first woman (accepted as such) to qualify and work as a physician in Britain, in 1865; while the first woman to qualify as a barrister in England did so in May 1922 (when Robertson was turned sixty-five); and the first woman was ordained as a Church of England priest in 1994, more than a century after the leading article appeared in the *Edinburgh Evening News*.)

The leader writer then surmised, almost exactly a century before the event, that "female politicians may yet follow some lady premier into the division lobby. … When such ideas are propounded there is apt to be an expression of alarm and even resentment on the score that there are already so many men who have a difficulty in finding employment. … there can be no hesitation in saying that the argument from the existence of unemployed men should have no weight against the movement for furthering the employment of women. … So long as the population is not actually increased in comparison with the resources of the country, the utilisation of labour power of any kind which has hitherto been idle must tend, so far from increasing poverty, to increase wealth." The argument here which Robertson rejected found a kind of echo or parallel at Oxford and Cambridge, where a prejudice lurked and lingered that University places should be offered to middle class, even lower middle class, young men rather than to women (although both Girton and Newnham – the latter co-founded by Millicent Garrett Fawcett – were functioning in the Cambridge area by 1880 as colleges for women, they only became fully fledged institutions of Cambridge University after the Second World War). [184] In contrast to many Oxbridge academics of his generation Robertson was a lifelong advocate of women's rights – a cause staunchly espoused by adherents of the British freethought movement, whose ranks included such gifted women as Annie Besant, Harriet Law, and Bradlaugh's daughters Alice and Hypatia, all of whom addressed secularist audiences in Edinburgh during Robertson's time there, with the torch of freethought also proudly held by progressive local female residents like William Marshall's common-law wife Eliza and John Lees's sister Isabella. Moreover, a statue of Millicent Garrett Fawcett would finally be unveiled in Parliament Square in April 2018.

As a leader writer in Edinburgh Robertson would be remembered both for his distinction and for his notable personal characteristics as perceived by his fellow Scot and journalist colleague Robert Donald, whose career included more than one stint as a newspaper editor. For Donald: "The characteristics of the *Evening News* were due, in large measure, to Mr. John M. Robertson. When I joined the paper as a junior reporter in the eighties, Mr. Robertson was leader writer. His articles were remarkable for their terseness, brevity, argumentative power and stern independence. He was against nearly everyone and everything except Mr. Bradlaugh and rationalism. His predecessor was Mr. William Archer, who was more restrained. ... No popular newspaper ever printed so much philosophy in its leading columns. Mr. Robertson was a rationalist of an advanced and aggressive type … The paper … stood for Radicalism … and it exercised an influence from the Tweed to the Tay. The late Mr. John Wilson was nominally editor of the paper, but no leader writer ever had more latitude … than had Robertson …" When the *Edinburgh Evening News* celebrated its golden jubilee in 1923, Robert Donald declared in his message to the newspaper: "In my time Mr. John M. Robertson, a man of wide knowledge and very decided opinions, was the chief leader writer. He combined terseness with lucidity and wrote up to the intelligence of his readers. The *Evening News* was then, and still is, a distinct force in Scottish and national journalism."[185] There seems little doubt, from the general testimony of Donald's biographer added to Donald's personal recollections, that Donald's observation of Robertson's work at close quarters provided him with valuable training.

Irish Home Rule

George Standring, editor of *The Republican*, may have had Robertson in mind when, in April 1883, he called the *Edinburgh Evening News* "a Radical journal, conducted with marked ability". But there was little doubt about his appreciation of his Scottish colleague's intellectual capacity when he described as "brilliant" Robertson's article, "Thoughts on Home Rule", which appeared in Mrs. Besant's *Our Corner* for 1 October that year.[186] This was the first of two articles by Robertson which were published under that title in successive issues of *Our Corner*, where he critically examined the idea of Home Rule for Ireland, at a time when violent unrest there culminating in the assassination of a new Chief Secretary for Ireland, combined with intense verbal harrying at Westminster of the murdered Minister's successor by the Irish Home Rule leader Parnell, would have lodged in the minds of Robertson's readers.

Declared Robertson: "No one pretends that every district of Ireland is in favour of Home Rule … On what ground is it argued that the Catholic South has a right to impose Home Rule on the unwilling Protestant North?" He then referred to "the ordinary English argument against Home Rule – that the preponderating weight of England must determine the constitution of Ireland. It is idle to repeat that Ireland is a distinct community. That is precisely the point in dispute. Is it asserted that *a priori* justice is a matter of land and water boundary … that within Ireland a southern majority can justly coerce a northern minority; but that a majority east of St. George's Channel cannot justly coerce a minority west of it? … There is surely grave reason to fear that any measure of Home Rule would plunge Ireland into harmful turmoil … The prejudices which stand between Englishmen and Scotchmen, nay, between Englishmen and many Irishmen, are weak beside those which divide Orangemen from Catholics. Now, is there any hope that an Irish Parliament, however constituted, would not instantly strive for the endowment of Catholicism? … The most conspicuous defect in almost every statement of the case for Home Rule is a failure to define the constitution it is proposed to confer on Ireland. … Where would the limit of Irish independence of England and Scotland be drawn? To pronounce for Home Rule without answering that, is to urge a leap blindfold on ground untrodden and unscanned."

Robertson's words would have a familiar ring decades later. In 1883 his attitude may have been influenced, perhaps unconsciously, by the fact that Ulster had been "planted" largely by Scottish Protestants. Despite a suspicion that

Home Rule would mean Rome Rule, he may have given insufficient weight to the fact that some prominent Irish advocates of Irish Home Rule or of Irish nationalism like Isaac Butt, Charles Parnell and, later, Erskine Childers were Protestants. Moreover, towards the end of his article he did indicate that in the imperial Parliament proposed by "Home Rulers" for Ireland, England and Scotland, "Ireland would be the mere satellite of England. Will any one say that is a role to which Irishmen would take kindly?"[187] Even so, Robertson may have underestimated the strength of hatred long felt by Irish people on account of Oliver Cromwell's massacre at Drogheda and at Wexford and their associated extended experience of colonial oppression and bloody coercion at the hands of the English. Equally he did not go into the option of a political partition of Ireland between north and south: such a partition did not appear to be on the cards in 1883.

It would not be easy to assess how far the mass of British secularists in 1883 shared Robertson's views as expressed in his October article, published more than two years before Gladstone introduced his first Home Rule Bill. Mrs. Besant referred in the *National Reformer* to Robertson's "very able" article which "should be carefully read … its arguments deserve to be well weighed". On the other hand, Bradlaugh, who had seen Ireland as a British soldier, had favoured a Home Rule solution, encompassing federation but not separation for Ireland, in a lecture in New York in 1873.

In his concluding article on Home Rule (in the November 1883 issue of *Our Corner*, which was possibly drawn to Gladstone's attention in his capacity as Prime Minister and M.P. for the Scottish seat of Midlothian) Robertson continued his search for a just and peaceful solution to the Irish problem. While suggesting that the United States constitution could provide

support for "the feasibility of an Anglo-Irish confederation …
[and] the strongest argument which can be urged in defence
of the Home Rule position", he entered a caveat: "With the
stupendous stain of the American Civil War still crimson on the
page of history; with its scars still discernible in men's bodies
and women's hearts, who will say that if once Ireland, with
her heritage of unforgotten wrong and wasted possibilities,
were constituted a separate community, the grisly spectre of
war might not rise on us too in some murky hour, and shake
her serpent hair?" Arguably for a young man not yet twenty-
seven, who was essentially based in Scotland, with limited
spending power, and who had not yet visited America, J.M.R.
showed rather remarkable perspicacity with his comments
relating to the trauma caused by the American Civil War.
Certainly his premonition of the prospect of war, and indeed
civil war, in Ireland would be tragically fulfilled. Meanwhile, in
his article, Robertson attempted to answer his own question
by asserting: "The wise way, the only way, to appease the
people of Ireland is not to repeal the Act of Union, but to build
up an actual and cordial union. There must be the most
unreserved recognition of Irish rights to the fullest equality
with Englishmen and Scotchmen in all matters of legislation
and administration."[188]

Events were to force Robertson to recognise, reluctantly, that
"the majority of Englishmen are not capable of taking a truly
unitary view of the interests of the whole State"; and by 1897
he would become an advocate of "a Federal constitution for
England, Ireland, Scotland, and Wales, giving each province
a Parliament for its separate affairs and vesting the joint
interests of all in a Central Parliament".[189] In large measure
this would materialize more than a century later, with the
main exception being Ireland viewed as a whole, as most of
Ireland emerged as a separate, new state under the Anglo-

Irish Treaty of December 1921. It was the case that the Act of Union between Great Britain and Ireland came into effect (1801) almost a century after a similar Act uniting England and Scotland to form Great Britain; and that there was essentially a land boundary between England and Scotland, whereas the border between England, or Scotland, and Victorian Ireland was a sea boundary. Marx - who had died in March 1883 - did not envisage Ireland ravaged by war apart from class war.

Luther and the Reformation

Religious differences between Protestants and Catholics clearly played a part in the Irish troubles. Such differences had also become prominent between about 1517 and about 1648 in a Europe convulsed by the Protestant Reformation, Counter-Reformation and associated religious wars. When, on 10 November 1883, Protestants worldwide commemorated the quatercentenary of the birth of Martin Luther, seen as the most powerful agent of the Reformation, the *Edinburgh Evening News* made notable comment in a leading article, almost certainly by Robertson, referring to the liberal-inclined British historian Henry Hallam: "Hallam, at all events, protests that Luther no more recognised freedom of opinion than did the Pope; and that his opinions, taken all over, were not more rational than those of the Catholic Church. On the other hand … Luther's own act wrought an enormous work for intellectual freedom, even though he might not desire to effect all he did. That he too had his amazing superstitions and his fierce intolerances is but one of a thousand proofs that progress cannot be otherwise than gradual." The leader writer concluded that Luther was "a great assailant of a great spiritual tyranny". Robertson, however, would years later condemn Luther's "brutal" attitude towards the German Peasants' Revolt (not mentioned in the *News* leader): "in the massacres to which Luther gave his eager approval a hundred thousand men were destroyed." These peasants had been among his earlier supporters, but Luther then supported the nobles in their campaign against the peasants out of his concern to ensure the Lutheran movement's political success through the military force supplied by the nobles (and other rulers) against the Catholic Church. Robertson would point to the nobles' mercenary, materialistic and opportunistic motives in plundering Church estates and assets as an example of the power of sectarian economic interest in history, which he would often emphasize. He concluded that "Luther and Calvin alike did but set up an infallible book and a local tyranny against an infallible pope and a tyranny centring at Rome". Perhaps J.M.R. remembered Brutus's lines on Julius Caesar: "The abuse of greatness is when it disjoins / Remorse from power ... scorning the base degrees / By which he did ascend" (Shakespeare, Act II, Scene I).[190]

Indian self-rule and Jewish advance

However, Robertson's intellectual interests and political concerns were not confined to the continent of Europe. At a time when India was economically at a low ebb and Bradlaugh publicly espoused India's "fullest right of self-government, in course of time", Robertson attacked the British acquisition of India as a "great national theft" and contemplated "with tranquillity the ultimate surrender of India to native management, and the writing of 'Finis' to the story of British Oriental Empire". Moreover, Robertson was not loth to criticise George Eliot's glorification of national sentiment in general and support of Jewish nationalism in particular. He was also at pains to stress that he was not anti-Semitic, "has not animus against the Jews, but is glad to profit by whatever gifts they bring to the common store". He seemed to support the concept of "a modern Jewish community in the East, influencing Eastern civilisation for good", but not that of a theocratic Jewish state. J.M.R.'s comments were originally made at a time in Victorian Britain when leading novelists – even including Dickens and Thackeray – and a host of lesser writers had already depicted Jews in a distinctly or deliberately negative light. (Moreover, in 1891 – years before the advent of Einstein or even Freud – Robertson would predict that "rationalist Jews will in future be distinguished in science as they have already been distinguished in art".)[191]

Farewell to Joseph Symes

Meanwhile, in Edinburgh on 9 September 1883, John Robertson was appointed to the Edinburgh Secular Society's General Committee, together with John Lees, Thomas Carlaw Martin, W.E. Snell, William and Eliza Mackenzie Marshall and others, at the Society's Annual Meeting. Almost certainly most of these General Committee members, including Robertson, would have attended one or more of the three farewell lectures delivered in Roxburgh Hall on Sunday, 4 November by a vigorous middle-aged secularist and platform propagandist who had decided to emigrate to Australia: this was Joseph Symes, whose Mythicist views on the Jesus question might have contributed, at a sub-conscious level, to the development of Robertson's interpretation of Christian origins. With Symes as their guest of honour, the Edinburgh freethinkers and secularists then held a farewell soirée for him on 9 November, when Mrs. Besant presided at the tea and ensuing entertainment of songs, recitations, instrumental music, and dancing. Robertson was doubtless present at this soirée, at which none would have known that within a year another notable secularist tea and reunion, likewise graced by the presence of Mrs. Besant in Roxburgh Hall, would be held to mark a memorable departure for a southern destination.[192]

T. H. Huxley

On 18 November Robertson was apparently in Glasgow to lecture to the Eclectic and Secular Institute at 122 Ingram Street on "Agnostic morality and Christian conscience", on which he had addressed a large and enthusiastic audience provided by the Edinburgh Secular Society in Roxburgh Hall on 14 October. Although no summary of Robertson's lecture has come to light, he certainly soon focused on aspects of the thinking of the scientist who in 1869 had coined the term "agnostic": Thomas Henry Huxley. On 9 December the *National Reformer* published what appears to have been Robertson's first signed article in that journal, "Professor Huxley as a Logician", in which he expressed his suspicion that this eminent doubting Thomas was anxious to show himself "above the weakness of sharing in democratic enthusiasms", and that his recent observations on Agnosticism were "dictated by a desire to figure as superior to those unbelievers who are in earnest in attacking superstition". Robertson would later maintain that Huxley was "seriously lamed as a thinker by an inveterate habit of superficial pragmatism", and that academic Victorian freethinkers like "Spencer, Morley, Stephen, Arnold, even Huxley, were visibly open to criticism in the various accommodations they made to the religious positions which confronted them".[193]

Sympathy for Bradlaugh's enemy

Early in the New Year the Edinburgh secularists were addressed by a campaigner and platform speaker whose credentials as an atheist and militant unbeliever were not in doubt. This was none other than Charles Bradlaugh, who gave the secularists a lecture on 12 January, a Saturday, with Robertson most probably in the audience. Since the late 1870s, Bradlaugh had got to know, trust and, indeed on occasion, confide in Robertson, who would recall, after Bradlaugh's death, that the iconoclast had expressed, in his hearing, a real regret that his Parliamentary foe, the Tory M.P. C.N. Newdegate, had to sell some of his best timber to pay his legal costs imposed by Lord Chief Justice Coleridge in April 1883 in a case that Bradlaugh won. Robertson would add: "Newdegate's express object had been to make Mr. Bradlaugh bankrupt; but when the tables were thus turned the latter felt a generous and chivalrous sympathy. Perhaps there was in it some of the warrior's respect for a determined foe."[194]

Thomas Paine

Less than three weeks after the Bradlaugh meeting in Edinburgh, the freethinkers there met in honour of another remarkable iconoclastic and republican activist who had been born in England about a century before Bradlaugh, on whom he seems to have exercised a degree of influence. On

29 January 1884, the anniversary of Thomas Paine's birth, they held a soirée, concert and ball (presided over by Charles Nicholson) in Roxburgh Hall, where Robertson gave an address on "Thomas Paine". After Paine's death in America in 1809, his ideas had been disseminated in Scotland by the weaver and Radical journalist Alexander Rodger, amongst others; and on 29 January 1821, a few friends of freedom had met in Edinburgh in remembrance of Paine's birth. While this birthday seems to have been commemorated fairly regularly by Victorian Radicals and secularists in England from about 1863 onwards – quite often involving sharing a meal – a formal address or lecture on Paine delivered on his birthday before members and friends of a Scottish branch of the National Secular Society may not have been a common feature of the period 1866-86.[195] The delivery of Robertson's address virtually coincided with the formation in the United States of the Thomas Paine Historical Association on 29 January 1884 (albeit in a different time zone) in New York. Some two decades later the Association would elect as its President Moncure D. Conway, credited with having written the first comprehensive *Life of Thomas Paine* (1892), in which Conway recorded a debt to his relatively new friend Robertson, author of a vindicatory *Thomas Paine: An Investigation* (1888), which may, in turn, have grown out of his 1884 discourse.

Christian cruelty

Both Paine and G.W. Foote suffered imprisonment on account of their beliefs; and on 2 March 1884 the Edinburgh Secular Society held a public meeting (almost certainly attended by Robertson) which unanimously adopted a congratulatory resolution to be forwarded to Foote following his release from prison in London on 25 February. Not long afterwards Roxburgh Hall became the scene of a terrible incident also associated with intolerance or cruelty. The hall managers, Mr. and Mrs. Chamberlain, had a fourteen year old daughter, somewhat mentally retarded, who accidentally fell from a window at the secular hall onto some spiked railings at street level and became transfixed, with three spikes having pierced her body. The girl's distraught mother rushed downstairs and tried to lift the child off. But she was a small woman, and the girl was very big and heavy; again and again she half raised the child, but was powerless to prevent her falling back onto the spikes. A crowd gathered, and she appealed to the bystanders to help save her daughter. Not one responded: they all stood gazing at the writhing child and the agonised mother, while one man, who was standing close to them, actually said: "It serves the atheist right." At last a young female freethinker, a Miss Reid, came by, immediately gave assistance, and the child was lifted off, but died the next day. (In early June Miss Reid was presented with a bracelet by the ladies of the Edinburgh Branch for her humane conduct.) Mrs. Besant had apparently lectured in Roxburgh Hall only about a week or so before the tragic accident and virulent anti-secularist reaction it produced in the crowd, which she promptly reported in the *National Reformer* at the end of March, referring to "the proof it gives of the brutality caused by centuries of Christian teaching", adding: "Such is Christianity in the capital of Scotland in the year 1884." Robertson, who from early manhood onwards had detested cruelty, may have borne this contemporary brutality in mind when he lectured in Roxburgh Hall on 13 April on "Who are the Scotch?" (his projected opening address on Scottish history).[196]

Enjoying Shakespeare

But the theatre, at least, offered Robertson a form of catharsis. In early April he saw the mighty Italian actor Tommaso Salvini play Othello at the Royal Lyceum Theatre in Edinburgh; he was immensely impressed by the actor's performance; and, as the newspaper's drama critic, he wrote a highly eulogistic review for the *Edinburgh Evening News*. A couple of days later, on 10 April, he saw Salvini at the same theatre, but this time as Shakespeare's King Lear. In his review for the *News* next day he said that much of Salvini's acting in this part had been "moving in the extreme", the organ-voiced tragedian having sustained "his majesty of mien and mastery of passion and pathos all through". The critic felt, however, that even so great an actor, who had played the king so magnificently in the opening scenes, inevitably failed to attain the imaginable effect in the terrific contest of soliloquy and storm: the reason being, Robertson suggested, that "the backgrounding of the tempest of Lear's soul with a tempest in nature is a psychological master-stroke which defies concrete representation". Salvini's success and failure in this performance of *King Lear* would remain a vivid memory for Robertson for the rest of his life. After the Scotsman's death, his friend Harold Laski of the L.S.E. declared that although he remembered Robertson as a thinker, scholar and fighter, "I like to think of him as I saw him last, reciting some lines from *Lear* with an ecstatic enjoyment of their beauty which I cannot paint in words".[197] Moreover, Robertson was not alone among theatre-goers outside Italy in the late nineteenth century who placed on record their debt of gratitude to Salvini and admiration of his dramatic art and interpretation of major Shakespearean roles: another such admirer was the Russian actor and theatre director Konstantin Stanislavski, who while in Moscow saw Salvini play Othello, and whose teaching would, in part, later be credited with leading to the "method" style of acting in America.

For and Against Socialism

Meanwhile in London on 17 April 1884 an air of immanent drama hung over the iconic St. James's Hall as it filled up with those anxious to hear the debate there between H.M. Hyndman of the Democratic (later Social Democratic) Federation and Charles Bradlaugh on "Will Socialism Benefit the English People?" The debaters proved to be fairly evenly matched, although Hyndman admitted that, according to the reaction of most of the audience and press, Bradlaugh got the better of him. Hyndman attacked the injustices of capitalism rather than explained the benefits of socialism and the organisation of a socialist society. Whereas Bradlaugh laid some stress on working class investment in the preservation of capitalism, Hyndman pointed to the inadequacy of Bradlaugh's individualism as an answer to social problems. Whereas Bradlaugh was emphatic in his rejection of violent revolution, Hyndman's attitude towards the use of force seemed somewhat ambiguous. Bradlaugh's claim that socialism would destroy freedom and individuality was countered by Hyndman's assertion that capitalism itself stunted real individuality. Bradlaugh thought "the hope of private gain" a human trait incompatible with socialist theory. Hyndman replied – questionably – that no great thing had ever been done for direct personal gain.

The Hyndman-Bradlaugh encounter sparked off a fierce debate on socialism in the secularist movement at a time when socialism as an organised body of opinion was beginning to make itself felt in the Britain of the 1880s (the attraction of socialism led to a haemorrhaging of support for secularism, resulting in the demise in 1884 of the British Secular Union, which had been formed in 1877 to oppose Bradlaugh). In his contribution to this debate Robertson attempted – notably in an address to the Edinburgh Branch of the Democratic Federation on 13 May and then in an article in the June issue of *Progress* – to reconcile the views of the two contestants, as "one who, on the one hand, regards Socialism as the ultimate and ideal state of society, and, on the other, has the heartiest regard for Mr. Bradlaugh, having fought in his party in the past and hoping to do so always". According to the Democratic Federation's journal *Justice* in its report of Robertson's 13 May address, "Mr. Robertson admitted the cogency and eloquence of Mr. Hyndman's speech, but considered that Mr. Bradlaugh's objections were unanswerable. The lecturer said … he believed that Socialism is only possible in the far distant future; and that in the meantime the restriction of population and political reform were the most feasible and would prove most serviceable reforms." According to George Standring, who chaired the Edinburgh meeting, his friend Robertson "declared himself a Socialist theoretically". A concern for individual rights and liberties pervaded Robertson's life-work; and privately he may have mused on the irony that Bradlaugh the great individualist should have founded and promoted a national Society to accomplish social change. Publicly the young Scot maintained that "there is no real opposition between the Radical and the Socialist – except, indeed, in so far as Socialists propose the introduction of a Socialist regime en bloc".[198] That Robertson would continue to take an interest in Hyndman's work and career is indicated not only by the references to Hyndman in Robertson's *The Meaning of Liberalism*, but also by the fact that as late as November 1932

Robertson's *Courses of Study* would suggest that Hyndman's *Commercial Crises of the Nineteenth Century* (1892) was still worthy of some attention.

In his funeral oration at Marx's graveside in 1883, his long-standing comrade Friedrich Engels maintained that Marx had discovered the law of development in human history, just as Darwin had discovered the law of development of organic nature. A year later, Robertson linked socialism with a "rise above the condition of internecine struggle for existence", declaring in words that may have resonated to some extent with Hyndman (who was indebted to Marx, but who also stood as a candidate in elections within the British political system): "To spread the Socialist idea is to spread the concept of evolution in its most important form; each reform will in turn become proportionately easier when men conceive all reform as a simple process of continued growth."[199]

Female Religiosity

One phenomenon that for Robertson as a student of history seemed to withstand evolutionary change was female religiosity; and his article on "The Orthodoxy of Women" in *Progress* for May 1884 attempted to explain why, throughout the ages, women generally appeared to be more religious than men. He postulated that in primitive society "everything tended to make women worship strength – the first condition necessary for the growth of belief in gods; and when any religion had gained a footing, everything tended to make the woman more superstitious than the man. … The man's active life made him comparatively fanciless; the woman, however great a drudge she might be under her husband's eye, had long spells of inactive and apprehensive loneliness. How could she be otherwise than imaginative, fanciful, superstitious? … In all stages of civilisation the condition of subjection is favourable to superstition." He went on to say of "the average woman": "Her physical, social and moral characteristics all co-relate with her piety. She is in subjection; dependent; under-educated; taught not to think; encouraged to cultivate timidity; excluded from a share in political life. Her physique at the best makes her specially liable to nervous disorder and religious excitation."[200]

With Bradlaugh and Burns

At the same time Robertson continued with his series of lectures to Edinburgh secularists on Scottish history, devoting his third such lecture at the end of June to medieval civilisation. He took a break from these absorbing intellectual pursuits to go to London to attend Bradlaugh's trial, commencing on 13 June 1884, before Lord Chief Justice Coleridge, Baron Huddleston and Justice Grove and a jury, relating to substantial financial penalties imposed on Bradlaugh for alleged illegal voting in the Commons, with Bradlaugh representing himself and Robertson taking notes of the proceedings as a reporter.[201] The freethinking Scotsman apparently found himself in London again on 26 July to see the prominent Liberal politician Lord Rosebery unveil in the Thames Embankment Gardens a statue of the Scottish poet Robert Burns. Despite the steady downpour of rain, the ceremony was witnessed by thousands of enthusiastic Scots and Burns admirers, with the poet Robert Browning and the secularist G.J. Holyoake among those present.

Two days later, on 28 July, a leading article, bearing the hallmark of Robertson's style and authorship, in the *Edinburgh Evening News* – devoted to an account and assessment of the unveiling – rebuked Lord Rosebery for some comments he made at the ceremony. The leader writer declared: "Better things might be expected of his lordship than ringing the changes on such sayings as Burns 'raised the conception of the peasant and gave honour and dignity to toil'. The reverse of this would have been nearer the truth. … Taking Burns as a whole it will be found that he was not impressed with the honour and dignity of peasant toil, but rather with the dishonour, hardships, and degradation of labour. The poet realised too vividly man's inhumanity to man to delude himself into depicting poetic scenes of Arcadian beauty in which toil was a pleasure and poverty a glorious privilege. …" With his interest in Scottish matters, Lord Rosebery may well have read these words in the *Edinburgh Evening News*. Be that as it may, the leading article was followed quite quickly by the publication of Robertson's article on "The Art of Burns" in Mrs. Besant's *Our Corner* for 1 September. (As a writer, Robertson towards the end of his life would return to Burns with a two-part essay on "Burns and His Race" in the literary magazine *Criterion*, founded and edited by T.S. Eliot.) In "The Art of Burns" – republished in 1897 – Robertson indicated that Burns's satirical poems possessed "a pith and pungency not excelled by Butler, Swift, Pope, or Dryden", but also that "Tennyson's songs are almost invariably of a perfect finish, while Burns' are so very seldom; and this is so, in the main, because Tennyson has been able to give his whole life to his art, while Burns could only give the spare hours of a life whose toil began in boyhood and lasted till death. And it will be found that every great poet of whose life we have any knowledge was so because he was able to give his best hours to the cultivation of his genius."[202] This observation would be elaborated by Robertson in his 1898 essay "The Economics of Genius", where he advanced the socialistic thesis that genius generally seemed to require for its efflorescence leisure and culture opportunities which had historically been the prerogative of the ruling class.

Keats

Robertson's interest in late eighteenth and early nineteenth century literature, particularly poetry, in Britain had, indeed, most recently been in evidence in his two-part article on "The Art of Keats" in *Our Corner* for July and August 1884. In this article – republished thirteen years later – he contended that "Keen, fitful gusts are whispering here and there" was Keats's finest sonnet: "It has the crowning grace of an entire, a divine simplicity, beside which the Chapman sonnet savours of artificiality." Moreover, Keats's *Ode to a Nightingale* was, according to Robertson, "one of the most beautiful poems in any language", and the poet's *On Melancholy* merited comparison with it. Although little noticed at the time in its original form, Robertson's essay would attract attention from American critics a quarter of a century and more after it first appeared. In 1908 the American academic Albert Elmer Hancock would query his assertion that *Hyperion* lacks "the intense Dantean vibration of inward life"; and some two decades after Hancock, Clarence Dewitt Thorpe – again from across the Atlantic – would challenge Robertson's suggestion of faulty logic or ambiguity in a stanza from *Ode to a Nightingale*. Robertson concluded that "Keats was a great poet, prematurely cut off ... had he not carried in him the seeds of disease, we probably should not have had from him such precocious work, we yet constantly feel that had he tried he would have produced poetry which would have superseded all his early productions … He had a true heart, great sympathies, noble aspirations …"[203] Many years later Robertson would admit that, metaphorically speaking, he always kept a shrine for the failed medical student turned artist who had declared: "sure a poet is a sage; A humanist, physician to all men."

Diderot

If John Keats was a grandson, prematurely cut off, of the eighteenth century, the French savant Denis Diderot was one of its mature sons. The publication of the closing part of Robertson's article on "The Art of Keats" virtually coincided, in August 1884, with that of his essay "Carlyle on Diderot", which was the young Scotsman's first such article to appear in *Progress* since his critique in June of the Bradlaugh-Hyndman debate. At this time the centenary of Diderot's death and the unveiling in Paris of a statue of him were marked in France; but the great Encyclopedist was still not very well known in England, though perhaps rather better known in Scotland, where in 1781 Diderot had been elected an honorary member of the Society of Antiquaries in Edinburgh and where in 1766 an obscure teacher of French, with a school in Edinburgh, had dedicated a book by him to "Monsieur Diderot, auteur de l'Encyclopédie".

In "Carlyle on Diderot" Robertson defended Diderot against Carlyle's criticism of him and declared: "To us to-day the memory of Diderot is that of a brave man of letters who, whatever his faults and follies, spent his life ungrudgingly in ill-requited labour for the general good … We see in him one of the forerunners of the Revolution, but one of those who would have made the Revolution impossible had not their rulers done everything possible to silence their voices. Above all, we recognise in Diderot one of the band who, putting their faith in ideas, made determined war on the great enemy of ideas and of light – the Church."[204] These warm words may bear comparison with the following tribute to Diderot in the Marxist treatise *Ludwig Feuerbach*, which Friedrich Engels published under his own name in 1888 in a revised form containing a number of editorial changes made by him: "If ever anybody dedicated his whole life to the 'enthusiasm for truth and justice' – using this phrase in the good sense – it was Diderot." Moreover, Engels and his comrade Eleanor Marx had taken more than a passing interest in *Progress*, certainly during 1883-84 when in various ways they helped her friend, and later cohabitee, Edward Aveling to manage his editorship of the magazine while G.W. Foote languished in prison for a year.

Replacing Dr. Aveling

At this time Robertson's star was rising in the secularist firmament. Annie Besant, for example, already admired his scholarly, thought-provoking articles in freethought journals, including her own; and she had no doubt heard golden opinions of his lectures in Scotland when she visited freethinking groups there, most recently in Edinburgh in July 1884 for her lecture on the need for social reform, not socialism. She and Bradlaugh were also looking for a suitable replacement for the morally disreputable and politically unreliable Dr. Edward Aveling on the staff of the *National Reformer*, and they believed they found the man they wanted in John Robertson.

Although Robertson had recently declared himself a socialist, it was clear that this was at a theoretical level, while his loyalty to Bradlaugh and the latter's brand of advanced Radicalism was very great. Aveling's situation seemed distinctly different: in July he confessed to Bradlaugh that he was going to live with Marx's daughter Eleanor; and in addition to considering Aveling's unsavoury reputation where the handling of money, if not of women, was concerned, Bradlaugh probably felt disconcerted that Aveling – an eloquent public speaker and gifted science teacher who had become quite a prominent member of the National Secular Society leadership – could consolidate or formalize his relationship with a devoted daughter of the Communist leader with whom he, Bradlaugh, had long been at daggers drawn ideologically. Bradlaugh and Mrs. Besant, his business partner, undoubtedly had ample opportunity to discuss Robertson's advancement and Aveling's eclipse during a break the two partners took in August by Loch Long, in accommodation arranged by John Lees, while Aveling and Eleanor Marx were in Derbyshire.[205] Bradlaugh and Besant may have concluded that their ability to persuade Robertson to join them on the staff of their paper, and the associated prospects of a new, closer relationship with him, could be enhanced by their relative geographical proximity to him in Scotland – compared with the distance between Edinburgh and London – and by the fact that John Lees (who had defended individualism in the discussion on 13 May immediately following Robertson's Edinburgh address on socialism) was on friendly terms with the three of them.

Then, on 24 August, Mrs. Besant was able to announce in the *National Reformer* – appropriately enough in its "Daybreak" column – that Robertson (a single man) had joined the staff of the paper, to which he would be a regular contributor, and that the warmest congratulations she had received on his appointment had come from his individualist debating opponent 'D.' (The latter, J.H. Levy, had initiated their debate, on socialism, in the *National Reformer* for 15 June, praising his young fellow-secularist as "a writer who is always sincere" and going on to declare of Robertson: "One can enter the lists with the full confidence that, whoever wins, truth will not lose."[206])

More Accountable Government

Under threat of expulsion by Bradlaugh, Aveling promptly resigned from the N.S.S. – ostensibly at least because of his outstanding debts to members of the Society – following Annie Besant's announcement on 24 August in the *National Reformer*, where she appeared to commend Robertson's article in the same issue on "The Manners of Public Life". This recorded Robertson's reflections following a recent visit by him to the House of Commons, to observe its proceedings from the Strangers' Gallery. "You sit down, on your first visit, with your head and heart full of swelling memories, and with a sense as of shadowy presences of the great dead brooding about the halls you have traversed." This initial romanticism was rudely dispelled, first by the truculence of the usher, then by the "simply shocking" rowdyism evident in the Commons. "Many barbarous peoples are incapable of such unseemly conduct in public council as takes place daily in the assemblies of the chief self-governing nations of the world … Birth and breeding seem to count for nothing when men meet together in political debate … all through our public life there runs this strain of rowdyism … democratic government remains unhealthy while it is not carried on in all respects with dignity or at least with decency. … It is possible to hope too much from the coming enfranchisement of women; but it is impossible not to feel that in this respect of civilising public procedure it is bound to work immense good."

Readers of Robertson's article (under his own name) could scarcely have foreseen, though some may have guessed, that, within a generation or so, his contributions on the floor of the House would enhance the quality of debate and discussion in what was then the greatest elected legislative assembly in the world. He never seems to have lost faith in the Parliamentary system in a democracy; and by virtue of subjecting various state and government institutions and agencies to critical scrutiny, principally in the *National Reformer*, during the six weeks preceding the end of September 1884, he emerged as an advocate of more democratic and accountable government in late Victorian Britain.

In the *National Reformer* for 31 August 1884 Robertson drew on a recent proposal by Matthew Macfie to advance the challenging proposition that the Cabinet's collective responsibility should be superseded by each Minister and, through him, his Department being held directly answerable to Parliament. (With his interest in the evolution of religions, Robertson would also have been absorbed by Matthew Macfie's scholarly lecture to the Sunday Lecture Society in London in February 1879 on "Religious Parallelisms and Symbolisms, Ancient and Modern".) Declared Robertson: "The proper business of the head of a department is to manage that department as well as possible; and to make him one of a small tribunal which decides the most important questions of national policy is inevitably to lessen his efficiency in his own department. ... If each Minister were accountable to Parliament, that body, and not the Cabinet, would decide whether or not the nation should go to war." Thirteen years later, Robertson would still protest against "the vice in our Constitution which makes it possible to a Cabinet to enter into war without even pretending to consult the representatives of the people".[207] But Robertson did not apparently foresee that, with the growth of Prime Ministerial Government, a significant number of vitally important decisions would be taken without the British Cabinet, still less Parliament, being enlisted. Examples of this are understood to include moves towards a de facto military alliance with France during the decade before the First World War, as well as the later decisions to test the first British atom bomb and, during the Suez crisis, to prepare plans for an Anglo-French attack on Port Said. During this period extending over decades – marked by the generally increasing complexity of Britain's Government machinery – tension between the Cabinet and Government Departments would often seem unresolved, with demands for less Cabinet secrecy and more open Government. Such demands would resonate, for example, in *Let Us Try Democracy* (1970) by Air Vice Marshal Don Bennett – a former Liberal M.P. – and with the spread of Commons Select Committees on the work of specific Government Departments.

Robertson's essay (entitled "Government by Party") on the unaccountable power of the British Cabinet was immediately followed by his article "Why Have a Second Chamber?", which appeared in the September issue of *Progress*. In this contribution – which the *National Reformer* described as "very thoughtful" – he scrutinized the views of de Tocqueville, Montesquieu, J.S. Mill, and the *Pall Mall Gazette*; and he critically examined the idea of a representative or popularly selected Upper House, concluding that "to place a responsible House over the House of Commons is to make the latter careless and rash in experiment … All these proposals for semi-constitutional safeguards against constitutional

Government are comparable to the stipulation of an anxious mother that her children, in bathing, shall never attempt to float without keeping one toe on the bottom." During 1884-85 the question of abolition or reform of the House of Lords was very much a live issue for Radicals; and readers of Robertson's article may have gone on to read Bradlaugh's little pamphlet *How are we to abolish the Lords?* (1884) or to join the People's League for the Abolition of the Hereditary Legislative Chamber. Robertson's article would be reprinted, with additions, in 1894, when the House of Lords would still appear to be about as powerful as the House of Commons, having regard to the capacity of the Lords to reject, amend or delay measures accepted by the Commons.[208] Later as an M.P. he would champion the People against the Peers in the constitutional battle of 1910, and also participate in the subsequent wartime Parliamentary Conference on the future of the Upper House, during which he would recommend its reconstitution as an advisory body pure and simple. Robertson's experience and status as an M.P. and Minister invested his long-standing opposition to an unelected and hereditary Second Chamber with an authority virtually unequalled among leading British freethinkers of the late Victorian age and early years of the twentieth century.

"Even some men advanced enough to contemplate the abolition of the House of Lords are found to count on the perpetual survival of the institution of an 'emperor-king' … If the monarchy were abolished to-morrow we should still be but a sorry democracy, with our millions of snobs and dog-souled sycophants. These must be abolished first." Thus declared Robertson (who would use similar language years later in *Why Preserve the Monarchy?*) in his article "The Persistence of Royalism", which appeared in the *National Reformer* for 7 September 1884, soon after a visit to Scotland by the Prince of Wales (the future Edward VII), but also after the high-water mark had been reached of open hostility to the Victorian monarchy, whose increasing popularity apparently coincided with the growth of British imperialism. Robertson observed that "an enormous mass of the British population pays a despicable devotion to its royal family as such, bowing slave-like before the merest semblance of greatness, and bestowing a degraded worship on a grotesquely unworthy object". It was therefore not very surprising that in 1895, when British imperialism and all its works would seem triumphant across the globe, Robertson would predict "that, provided there be no great foreign war or domestic commotion, the English House of Lords will be abolished within half a century; that members of Parliament will be salaried within a quarter of a century; and that the monarchy will be abolished within one or two centuries ..."[209] Even if his caveat about Britain's involvement in a great war is excluded, events have suggested that Robertson's predictions pointed in the right direction: the House of Lords, though not abolished, would have its powers curtailed in 1911 and 1949; M.P.s would be paid within a few years of the Liberal victory in the 1906 general election; and although the British monarchy has hitherto survived in a modified form, it has lost much of the reverence and mystique previously attached to it.

Meanwhile speakers from outside Scotland who addressed the Edinburgh secularists during the summer of 1884, and whom Robertson probably heard at this time, featured the Rev. Stewart Headlam, Annie Besant and Arthur Moss. Founder (in 1877) of the Christian Socialist Guild of St. Matthew and, later, a well-known backer of the Land Law Reform League and the Association for the Repeal of the Blasphemy Laws, Headlam had heard Bradlaugh lecture in 1875 and had supported him thereafter, perhaps most notably in the Knowlton *Fruits of Philosophy* prosecution. On 31 August 1884 Headlam lectured twice to the Edinburgh Branch of the N.S.S. – in the morning on Christian Socialism, and in the evening on "Some popular mistakes about the Church's teaching". It was probably on the latter occasion that Robertson, as he himself would recall in 1888, "once opposed Mr. Headlam's religious doctrines (amicably, I am glad to say) on a Secular platform". Stewart Headlam delivered his lectures at a time when he was conscious of the secularist challenge to his theological position and was minded to promote the Guild's objects, of which one of the most striking was "to get rid, by every possible means, of the existing prejudices, especially on the part of the secularists, against the Church, her Sacraments and doctrines, and to endeavour to justify God to the people".[210]

Three weeks before Headlam the visiting lecturer was the secularist Arthur B. Moss. About a year older than Robertson, Moss was eighteen or so when he first saw and heard Bradlaugh; and he would later remember with gratitude both a "comprehensive and masterly" speech by Robertson toasting Bradlaugh's memory, to the Bradlaugh Fellowship in Shoreditch, and, moreover, Annie Besant's "splendid work" as an advocate of freethought and secularism. Moss also assisted the social investigator George Sims (author of the ballad "It is Christmas Day in the workhouse") in collecting material in London for his book *How the Poor Live* (1883); and any knowledge of this book may have encouraged Robertson to conduct his own investigation into how the poor lived in Edinburgh. Certainly Moss was among those delighted to learn that Robertson had joined the staff of the *National Reformer*, where he read Robertson's contributions with keen interest, no doubt including his article "Some Slumming", which appeared on 14 September 1884.[211]

Visiting the slums

In this article Robertson soberly recorded his findings and impressions following his recent eye-opening tour of the Edinburgh slums. He began by explaining: "I 'did' a considerable part of the Edinburgh slums with a guide who is nominally a missionary, but who is something much more beneficent, and who knows the entire ground as men know their own houses, and the people better than most clergymen know their congregations. Conducted by him, I saw scores of interiors into which I could hardly have penetrated otherwise." At a time when the economic prospects of the Scottish working class seemed particularly bleak, Robertson found that in one building "occupied by somewhere about 170 people, there is not one water-closet; and that in a densely populated Edinburgh 'close', looking down on Princes Street and only a few yards from the National Security Savings Bank and the Free Church College, most of the families are thus situated, and have to empty their sewage into the gutter of the 'close'. … It was not astonishing to find that tenements of wretched 'houses' – as single rooms and garrets are called in the Scotch slums - were owned and rack-rented by men in good positions and acting as elders in churches. Landlords of this kind, themselves living in West End houses, will exact an exorbitant rent for a den that is going to utter wreck, while refusing to repair a disintegrating door or plaster a crevice. … On the average of a large number of cases I calculated that the most miserable people in the city paid about twice as much for the cubic space of their hideous lairs, in the grimiest and most dilapidated buildings of the lowest slums, as I did for that of comfortably furnished lodgings in a good locality – though the cost of my lodgings covered attendance." (Robertson was concerned not only about environmental degradation clearly associated with dire poverty, but also about unseen or barely visible pollution which could directly and adversely affect the whole community, illustrated by his elsewhere deploring – while still a young man – the discharge of untreated sewage into the sea and rivers. In this latter sense Robertson was a comparatively early environmentalist pioneer in modern Britain.)

Concerning "the inhabitants of these regions", Robertson added: "They very rarely commit suicide. … I saw, in a 'house' which was made by boarding up part of a passage – which had no window, and in which it was necessary to burn an oil lamp all day, thus adding to the burden of the rent – a family of three, man, wife and child, whose lot was hardly of their own making. The man was tall and bronzed, but he was dying of heart disease; he could not do hard work, and he was too clumsy for light work; so he sat there, after his day's fruitless search, patiently nursing his miserable, scrofulous baby, in his dim and narrow den."

Robertson continued: "I witnessed one or two meetings of a committee formed to deal with the slum question, and was edified to find that the majority of the philanthropic members were chiefly intent on two things – preventing what is called 'immorality' among the lapsed, and closing as many public-houses as possible. Ladies and gentlemen, holding the moral philosophy of the middle ages, argued that the lapsed had free wills, and would be all right if they stopped drinking. Some of us had faintly hoped to establish in the slums sorely-needed public-houses of a beneficent sort, and a few such aids to free-will as recreation-rooms and washing-houses, but we went to the wall."[212] This committee may have been synonymous with the discussion group that Robertson's friend Patrick Geddes became involved with in Edinburgh, and that decided, towards the end of 1884, to reconstitute itself as a more focused and active group, in effect a new body, addressing the needs of the Edinburgh slum-dwellers. This group, which held a preliminary meeting on the new basis by November, became known as the Environment Society – to improve existing material conditions, in large part through decorating halls and schools and organising musical and other entertainment for the residents – and then as the Edinburgh Social Union. The E.S.U. would hold its inaugural meeting in early January 1885 in Patrick Geddes's flat, some three months after Robertson left Edinburgh, and under Geddes's leadership it would initiate a policy of adding bathrooms where feasible. In any event, Robertson's September 1884 record of his personal encounter with the Edinburgh slums added a useful snapshot to the apparent paucity of literature generated that year about them and may have helped to encourage the formulation and implementation of the type of organisational changes embarked upon by Geddes and his friends in late 1884 – early 1885.

Countering militarism

As a strikingly high proportion of British Army recruits came from working-class areas, including the slums, it scarcely seems surprising that, a fortnight after the *National Reformer* published "Some Slumming", Robertson turned his attention in its pages to "The Problem of the Army". In this article he suggested that the soldier surrendered his conscience to the State in exchange for economic security, and that "the average citizen is the accomplice of the soldier. He who hires another to kill is clearly in the same moral category as he who kills for hire." Although "to resort to sweeping denunciation of the military profession would be as injudicious as invidious … reformers should, as individuals, do everything in their power to bring the military profession, as such, into disrepute, and try to make the obtaining of recruits, of whatever grade, for the army more and more difficult. … the existence of standing armies – themselves morally indefensible institutions – is, in the present stage of civilisation, the chief encouragement to unjust wars." [213] Robertson's article did not appear to take account of Thoreau's attack (in 1847) on standing armies and the military as cannon-fodder of the State, or of implications of Bakunin's prophecy of total war. But some sixty years after his article, Robertson's point could be extended to include those wielding state power in Nazi Germany and Vichy France who had issued deadly orders victimising Jews.

While this article included a passing reference to the desirability of "promoting international disarmament", Robertson, in the previous week's issue of the *National Reformer* (for 21 September), had advanced the unsettling proposition that "the spirit which we are accustomed to term patriotism" was at the root of misunderstanding, great and small, between nations: a theme that a more seasoned Robertson would vividly elaborate in his pioneering study *Patriotism and Empire* (1899). In the meantime he virtually concluded his 21 September article on "International Amenities" with the affirmation that "the men of no church in all nations should make it their constant care to promote that goodwill among men which it is the empty boast of Christianity to have spread. They surely can see that the diseases and woes of any nation are the woes of humanity … and that the spirit which rejoices in the inferiority of another people to our own is the authentic 'mark of the beast'."[214] Indeed, over a period of many years he would establish himself as a consistent and quite prominent advocate of international arbitration and disarmament (for example, in 1908, in the interests of international law and arbitration, Robertson would present a paper in the German Reichstag during a Conference of the Inter-Parliamentary Union).

Shelley

In his younger days he had been attracted by Percy Bysshe Shelley's "passion for liberty and human brotherhood" and dazzled by the poet's use of language. But when his essay "Shelley and Poetry" first appeared in Annie Besant's *Our Corner* for 1 October 1884 he expressed a more detached and critical view of Shelley. Over a year before the formation of the Shelley Society in 1886 and at a time when speakers from the Radical, socialist and secularist camps could enthral working class audiences with recitations from Shelley (many of them, no doubt, drawn from his more overtly republican and atheistical work), Robertson advanced his assessment of Shelley that "at twenty-eight as at twenty his thinking is spasmodic, ill-digested, unsubstantial"; and he seemed to suspect that many of Shelley's admirers could be classified as lovers of the sentimental and mystical. (His essay appeared in instalments between October and December.)

Of individual poems by Shelley, Robertson slated *The Revolt of Islam* for its "bad rhyme, bad grammar, banal phrase, preposterous figure, fustian rhetoric, confused logic, meaningless collocations of words, extravagant comparisons, ideas thin-spun to puerility". *To A Skylark* was, as Robertson elaborated, "ruinously defective in point of technique". *Prometheus Unbound* contained eloquent blank-verse "embedded in a body of falsetto declamation and rhyming verbiage". *Adonais* suggested "an elaborate failure … where Milton's rhetoric is august and golden, Shelley's is shrill, hysterical, bombastic". *Epipsychidion* and *Lines written among the Euganean Hills* "stand alone among Shelley's poems of more than two hundred lines in respect of combined intensity and finish". Of Shelley's short poems, *The Cloud* was "a masterpiece of controlled fancy and delicate yet reposeful art, presenting a combination of exquisitely beautiful phrase, wealth of imagery, and music, such as had not appeared before in the language"; and the posthumously discovered fragment *To The Moon* was "one of Shelley's finest things".

More than forty years after its original publication Robertson himself would criticise "Shelley and Poetry" as "doubtless rather juvenile". Yet in 1976 the American academic Leo Storm, with his eye on Robertson's essay (as published in 1897), would suggest that Robertson had exerted an unacknowledged influence on both T.S. Eliot and F.R. Leavis, as literary men, regarding their critical attitude to Shelley. Storm declared: "Eliot attended to the technical defects of Shelley by employing a technique similar to Robertson's … Eliot's *Shelley and Keats* (so much of it as deals with Shelley) is basically warmed-over Robertson … we can find a striking similarity between Robertson's *Shelley and Poetry* and F.R. Leavis' *Shelley* – similar in point of assertiveness of manner and force of style in pursuit of Shelley's flaws in thought and technique." Even if the Cambridge don Leavis did refer to Robertson on at least one occasion (to a Cambridge student) as an "iron-clad rationalist", twenty years after Storm's thought-provoking contribution Leavis's son, L.R. Leavis, would testify that F.R. Leavis was quite familiar with Robertson's work as a literary critic.[215]

Walt Whitman

Meanwhile, by the 1880s in Victorian Britain, in lecture halls associated with popular culture, Shelley was known as the poet of democracy. Another such poet was, from the English-speaking world across the Atlantic, Walt Whitman, who was born during Shelley's short lifetime. Whitman was the subject of John Robertson's first work in book form that appeared under his own name. This was *Walt Whitman, Poet and Democrat*, published by William Brown of 26 Princes Street, Edinburgh, in the Round Table Series of studies of eminent modern authors, of which it was the fourth. Although it was published in November 1884, it was clearly at a very advanced stage of publication by early October, when Robertson left Edinburgh for a life in London. It is not known how he came to write this little book, but it may have been connected with knowledge of a threatened prosecution in 1882 of Whitman's then American publisher of *Leaves of Grass* for obscenity unless the work were amended or withdrawn from circulation (in his book Robertson pointed out that "the greatest living American author" was still regarded as a kind of literary "barbarian" in the United States). With his fifty or so pages of thoughtful, sympathetic and judicious appraisal, Robertson established himself as one of the comparatively few British literary critics to show keen appreciation of Whitman's work at a time when that American poet was not as widely known or esteemed in the British Isles as he deserved. Robertson did not have much time for some aspects of Whitman's early poetry on account of its "grotesque phraseology, the coined mongrel words, the abrupt transitions, the reckless collocations of parts of speech, the slang, the insupportable catalogues". Comparing Whitman boldly with William Blake, Robertson declared that "Blake, much of whose verse is so curiously like Whitman's, likewise gave overt signs of strong leanings to the primitive". The Victorian critic felt that Whitman's poetry would live, partly because "his message is the intense expression of his deepest passion".

On 17 December 1884 Whitman's English admirer and champion Anne Gilchrist wrote to him: "There seems a curious kind of ebb and flow about the recognition of you in England – just now there are signs of the flow – of a steadily gathering great wave, one indication of which is the little pamphlet just published in Edinburgh – one of the 'Round Table' Series – no doubt a copy has been sent you. If not and you would care to see it, I will send you one. On the whole I like it (barring one or two stupidities) – at any rate, as compared with what has hitherto been written." Gilchrist's letter did not explain what the "stupidities" were; but Whitman himself saw and apparently appreciated Robertson's book, for some seven years later the American poet offered, without any adverse comment, to mail a copy to one of his own friends. Although favourably if briefly reviewed in the *National Reformer* and *Our Corner*, Robertson's first "bund book" apparently earned him exactly 1s. 8d. But Robertson would no doubt have been gratified to know that, fifty years after its initial publication, a scholarly historian of Whitman's reception in England would maintain that Robertson's book "deserves a high place in Whitman literature" because of its balanced approach – and also that in 1969 the book would be reprinted, in the poet's homeland.[216]

W.D. Howells

Among literary men in America who took a keen interest in

Walt Whitman's work over many years was the realist novelist William Dean Howells, to whom Robertson devoted an article on "Mr. Howells' Novels" in the *Westminster Review* for October 1884. In this article Robertson compared Howells, whom he called "an accomplished writer", with Henry James (who was influenced by Howells), Jane Austen and George Eliot, although he also pointedly declared: "Tourguenief leaves us, as a rule, contemplating life in the light of his story, while Mr. Howells sets us considering his story in the light of life." (Turgenev had died a year earlier.) Six years later Robertson would pen an essay on Howells's more recent novels. Although no evidence has come to hand that Howells and Robertson ever met or corresponded with each other, at least one similarity and one or two indirect links between them may be noted: each as a boy had worked for a printer before becoming a reporter, writer and critic; Howells had a longstanding friendship with Mark Twain, who seems to have regarded Robertson as a friendly acquaintance during the Scotsman's years in London; and the American playwright Clyde Fitch, who corresponded with Howells on a friendly basis, was apparently introduced to Robertson through the latter's American wife. Part of Robertson's 1884 essay – though none of that dating from 1890 – on Howells's novels would feature in an anthology (published in the United States in 1962) of critics' reviews and assessments of Howells's works.[217]

Surveying the theatre and drama

In October 1884 Robertson also turned his attention to the state of British theatre. His article on "The Prospects of the Stage", in the *National Reformer* for 5 October, was prompted by a paper recently presented to the Social Science Congress by the actress Madge Kendal, whom he regarded at that time as "the greatest of living English actresses". He expressed agreement with her comment that "the progress and culture of a nation depended upon its diversion as well as upon its occupations". This he called "a compendious statement of the case for the drama" – and he would explore aspects of this insight in his brilliant and remarkable essay "Evolution in Drama", serialised during 1886 in *Our Corner*, where he would trace the evolution of drama from ancient Greece and Rome to the age of Henrik Ibsen, with particular emphasis on England and France, explaining that various social, economic and political forces were determinants of the state of the theatre. In the meantime, in "The Prospects of the Stage", Robertson noted with satisfaction "the remarkable advance in the social status of actors during the present generation" and attacked the persistent prejudice against their morals. "Society's moral judgments take no note of the infinite amount of swindling and lying chargeable to trade, of the rapacity and venality of lawyers, of the gambling of stockbrokers, of the non-moral position of the soldier, of the dissimulation of clergymen … It is probable that, number for number, there are fewer actors in prison than clergymen; it is certain that the lives of famous actors will on the whole compare well with those of famous poets and famous generals; and if profligacy, commonly so-called, be a lowering vice, the House of Lords must be in a rather worse way than the stage." Crude and vulgar plays were perpetuated and encouraged not so much by the playwrights and players as by the theatre-going public, "though we are always faced by the perplexity that the stage influences the public, and might conceivably help to educate it".[218]

Farewell to Edinburgh

On the very day that Robertson's article appeared in the *National Reformer* – Sunday, 5 October 1884 – he delivered his farewell lecture to the Edinburgh Branch of the National Secular Society in Roxburgh Hall, which was appropriately or ironically situated in Drummond Street as he took as his subject Henry Drummond's book *Natural Law in the Spiritual World* (1883). This book, which went through some thirty editions between 1883 and 1890 and was translated into several European languages, probably did much to reassure orthodox believers with its suggestion of a reconciliation between religion and science. Although at about the time of his lecture Robertson acknowledged that Drummond "has been welcomed as a lecturer at the Edinburgh Philosophical Institution on the strength of his book", Drummond was given short shrift by Robertson as a lecturer in whose hands (apparently according to John Lees) "the weakness of the book was thoroughly exposed and denounced. Mr. Robertson had quite an ovation at the close." Four years later Robertson would declare in the pages of the *National Reformer*: "What Freethinker does not know people who hold to an irrational and uncritical supernaturalism while imagining they have learned what science has to teach? The vogue of such a triumph of charlatanry as Mr. Drummond's *Natural Law in the Spiritual World* is one of the evidences. It is not true that to teach science makes people view things scientifically. Thousands do but prostitute knowledge to the service of dogma." These words might have been read by the contemporary British churchman and Biblical scholar F.J.A. Hort, who towards the end of his life attacked Drummond's work as "a quite singularly muddle-headed book", which, Robertson would record in 1932, "was never academically accepted" – a point endorsed by the ecclesiastical historian Canon Elliott-Binns in 1956. It is not known what Robertson thought of the fact, if he was aware of it, that in 1906 (the year he himself was first elected to Parliament) four Labour M.P.s named Henry Drummond as their favourite author or one of their favourite authors. But Robertson did regard the apparent popularity of Drummond's book as conveying "a grievous impression of the average standard of culture and intelligence in the nation".[219]

Ironically, as a schoolboy Robertson may have seen Drummond in Stirling, where they were both educated, at about the same time, apparently at the same school. It is also intriguing that for his farewell lecture Robertson's subject was the same as that of the publicist he had been chosen to replace, Dr. Edward Aveling, whose projected series of articles on Drummond's book had been abruptly, even brutally, dropped from the columns of the freethought periodicals controlled by Bradlaugh and Besant.

As Robertson left Edinburgh in early October 1884 to live in London, he was unable, before he left, to address issues raised by the Roman Catholic Monsignor George Dillon in lectures the churchman delivered in Edinburgh during that same month: Dillon suggested that, through Voltaire and atheistical ideologues of the Age of Reason, freemasons, such as those associated with the Grand Orient organisation, were able to manipulate various radical, liberal and republican revolutionary groups in Europe from the time of the French Revolution in a war against the Christian Church and Christian civilization. But although Bradlaugh the atheist was a freemason honoured by the Grand Orient in 1862 and 1884, he was consistently strongly opposed to revolutionary socialism.

It seems to have been during Robertson's last few weeks or days in Edinburgh that he saw a local public figure he held in high esteem. This was Dr. Alexander Whyte, the Edinburgh Free Church divine whose spirited defence of the harried heterodox Professor Robertson Smith would be acclaimed for "its courage and manly frankness" by two historians who in 1978 described Whyte as "a reasonable man always ready to listen to others". Whyte would also be remembered for his endeavour in lectures to the Philosophical Institution of Edinburgh during the winter of 1876-77 to make Dante known to the Scottish reading public. More than thirty years would pass before Robertson would see Whyte again, this time visiting the House of Commons in wartime as an old man. Later still, within five years of his own death, Robertson, touching on Whyte's benevolent impulses, would refer to the "strenuously toiling" Scottish people of the early nineteenth century with "their hearts trodden hard, as Dr. Alexander Whyte once put it, under the feet of preachers". [220]

Like H.T. Buckle before him and Hugh Trevor-Roper after him, Robertson would write critically of aspects of Scottish Protestantism and its culture; but unlike other British historians, Robertson engaged in a personal struggle with it before rejecting its theological dogmas and creed. As in many ways he epitomized qualities associated with the Protestant ethic, it seems likely that his life in Scotland was largely dominated by his work and studies (he later married and had two children); and it is not known what any of his relatives, understood to be religious and conventional, thought of his impending move to England.

It was presumably at about this time that Robertson said goodbye to the brethren of the Edinburgh Symposium, which largely seems to have combined the functions of a convivial social club with those of a philosophical society whose members read papers to one another. Apart from Robertson himself, one of the Symposium's leading lights appears to have been his vibrant and voluble friend Patrick Geddes, the pioneer town planner. It may be suggested that by this time Robertson was becoming relatively well known in Edinburgh, where, for example, two different publishers had become involved in handling some of his literary work, in each case on an English-speaking poet. (Similarities between Wordsworth and Whitman may have encouraged J.M.R. to progress from the former to the latter.)[221] Moreover, he left the *Edinburgh Evening News* and the Edinburgh secularists with what seems to have been sufficient notice and after sufficient time – six or more years – had elapsed for others to be able to step into his shoes. In a somewhat similar way Geddes may have helpfully put in a word for Robertson, as the former's study of John Ruskin was no. 3 in the Round Table Series in which Robertson's study of Walt Whitman immediately followed as no. 4 (also published in 1884) in the series.

On Friday, 10 October 1884, Edinburgh freethought and secularism bade farewell to John Robertson. Annie Besant, who had been delighted to accept the invitation to preside ("the Edinburgh Society has long had a niche in my heart"), travelled to Edinburgh specially for the occasion, when a large number of members and friends of the Edinburgh Secular Society gathered to present Robertson with a handsome testimonial – in Mrs. Besant's words – "as a recognition of his earnest and thorough work for the freethought cause". At 8 p.m. they sat down to a very attractively served tea in Roxburgh Hall, Robertson being seated on Mrs. Besant's right and John Lees on her left. After tea she apologised in a felicitous speech to the Edinburgh secularists for stealing one of their best men, and heartily welcomed Robertson in the name of their London friends. Then John Lees, an N.S.S. Vice-President, presented the testimonial – a beautiful ink-stand, stationery case, gold pen and pencil, and other requisites of a writing table – and made a short speech, admirable in phrase and feeling, in which his Scottish self-control was a little strained at the thought of parting from one of his closest friends. Young Robertson's reply deeply moved his audience, full as it was of emotion that at times almost broke his voice. Music, songs and dancing thereafter lightened the mood of the occasion, when none could scarcely have foreseen the tragic and untimely death of John Lees, who, twelve years later at the age of fifty-seven, would commit suicide by placing himself in front of an advancing train not far from his home.

As his train steamed south and the Scottish landscape slipped away, Robertson, no doubt accompanied by the charming Mrs. Besant, may well have been stirred by a multitude of hopes and dreams, by a sense of excitement tinged with nostalgia for Scotland. If his move to England was symptomatic of the erosion of Scottish culture on which he would comment so aptly a few years later, the intellectual life of London would be enriched by his insatiable curiosity allied to a panoramic vision of life. A new chapter in a remarkably dynamic and productive life was about to begin.[222]

REFERENCES AND NOTES

1 John Ferguson, *Jesus in the Tide of Time*, 1980, p. 158, quoted by Martin Page in *Britain's Unknown Genius (BRUG)*, 1984, p. 9; and for Francis Ambrose Ridley, see *BRUG*, p. 6.

2 For details see: *Britain's Unknown Genius (BRUG)*; the present writer's preceding articles in the *Freethinker* between 1968 and 1971 on Robertson; *J.M. Robertson*, 1987, ed. George Albert Wells; Odin Dekkers, *J.M. Robertson*, 1998; and Conrad Joseph Kaczkowski, S.M., *John Mackinnon Robertson: Freethinker and Radical*, 1964, although as a Ph.D. dissertation for St. Louis University in the U.S.A., the last-named may not be easily obtainable for readers in Britain.

3 J.M.R. in the *National Reformer (NR)*, 2.4.1893, p. 210 (last line); and J.P. Gilmour in the 1936 ed. of Robertson's *History of Freethought (HF)*, p. xii (on J.M.R.'s commitment to what he was wont to call "tested truth" see also pp. 478-9 of Homer W. Smith's *Man and His Gods*, 1953, a book that showered praise on Robertson and his life-work: Homer Smith's book was warmly commended by Albert Einstein, who contributed a foreword to it, and by another Nobel Prize winner, Thomas Mann).

4 See the foreword by the Earl of Oxford (ex-Prime Minister H.H. Asquith) to J.M.R.'s *The Meaning of Liberalism (ML)*,

1925 ed.; William Kent, *John Burns: Labour's Lost Leader*, 1950, p. 236; and J.P. Gilmour in J.M.R.'s *HF*, 1936 ed., p. ix.

5 J.A. Hobson's tribute to Robertson appeared in the *Literary Guide (LG)* for February 1933, p. 37. If, as Hobson later maintained, J.M.R. "was apt to pursue every detected falsehood or fallacy to its remotest origins", that "defect" could arguably be justified or forgiven in the light of Robertson's "clearance of intellectual 'slums'" as "his great life-work" (to quote Hobson's words).

6 See *Oxford Dictionary of National Biography*, 2004, pp. 247, 246 (from entry on W.B. Carpenter). For a statue to Robertson on Arran, see *Ardrossan and Saltcoats Herald*, 20.1.1933, p. 3. Thorbjorn Campbell's history of Arran (2013; 2023) does not mention J.M.R. once.

7 Hobson, *Confessions of an Economic Heretic*, 1938, p. 50. It seems incredible J.M.R. could have said he was "only four generations from a painted Pict".

8 See *Buckle and His Critics*, p. 253; information supplied by Macleod Yearsley through his family.

9 Information gleaned from: Robertson's parents' marriage certificate; James Robertson's birth certificate; the 1851 Census records for Low Glen Cloy (the last two words otherwise spelt as one), Arran; M. Macbride, *Arran of the Bens, the Glens and the Brave*, 1910, p. 81; V.A. Firsoff, *Arran with Camera and Sketchbook*, 1951, p. 47; Robert McLellan, *The Isle of Arran*, 1970, pp. 184-5; and James C. Inglis, *Brodick – Old and New*, n.d., p. 82. See also George Eyre Todd, *The Highland Clans of Scotland*, 1923, Vol. 2, p. 328.

10 See, inter alia, J.M.R.'s birth certificate and McLellan (op. cit., p. 184), apparently relying on Inglis, op.cit., p. 83.

11 See R. Angus Downie, *All About Arran*, 1933, pp. 8-9; J.P. Gilmour in *LG* for February 1933, p. 36, and then in *HF*, 1936, pp. xvii-xviii, etc.; and Dekkers, op.cit. 1998, p. 23 (quoting Arthur Moss in 1915).

12 The birth of Susan Robertson's third child – Jane – was registered in the Stirling area in September 1859.

13 J.M.R. in *NR*, 1.3.1885, p. 197. The preceding quote is from *NR*, 6.9.1891, p. 151.

14 See Inglis, *Brodick – Old and New*.

15 *Town and Country: a mutual concern for the community*, National Council of Social Service, 1968, p. 32.

16 The quotation concluding this paragraph comes from J.M.R.'s *Papers for the People*, No. 2 ("The People and Their Leaders"), n.d. (1896?), pp. 3-4.

17 *ML*, 1925 ed., p.27. See also J.M.R. in his *Essays in Ethics*, 1903, p. 116, and in *LG* for October 1911, p. 150.

18 Thomas Johnston, *The History of the Working Classes in Scotland*, 1946 (fourth ed.), p. 321.

19 See, inter alia, Robertson's *The Dynamics of Religion*, first published in 1897 under the pseudonym "M.W. Wiseman".

20 See J.M.R. in *LG* for January 1929, p. 2, and in his *Short History of Christianity*, 1931 ed., p. 229.

21 From J.M.R.'s *Papers for the People*, No. 1 ("The Priest and the Child"), n.d., p. 4.

22 See pp. xlv, 30 and 509 of the 2015 ed. by Mark Philp and Frederick Rosen of J.S. Mill's *On Liberty, Utilitarianism, and Other Essays*.

23 Gilmour in *The Reformer*, 15.12.1899, pp. 752-3.

24 Quoted in Lawrence James's *The Rise and Fall of the British Empire*, 1998 ed., 2000 reprint, pp. 191-2.

25 Geoffrey Andrews (who lived with Robertson and his family for about a year shortly before the First World War) in a letter (2.1.1972) to the present writer.

26 George S. Pryde, *Scotland from 1603 to the Present Day*, 1962, pp. 252-3.

27 Philip Viscount Snowden, *An Autobiography*, 1934, Vol. 1, p. 312. The 1861 Census and Duncan Robertson's birth certificate shed invaluable light on the Robertson family circumstances at this time, measured against George Pryde's aggregated information.

28 J.M.R.'s comments on the domineering he suffered in his childhood and on his father's rheumatism, respectively, were expressed to friends like Sydney Gimson and Hypatia Bradlaugh Bonner, most probably during the early 1890s. Also see J.M.R. in *NR*, 2.4.1893, p. 210.

29 The school-related information cited is provided by: S.L. Hunter, *The Scottish Educational System*, 1968, p. 9, and J.M. Reid, *Scotland Past and Present*, 1959, p. 95 (on the

percentage of Scottish children not attending school); Thomas Johnston, op.cit. 1946, p. 321 (on Glasgow children of school age working long hours in industry); and *Stirling Journal and Advertiser*, 12.1.1933, p. 4 (on J.M.R. educated at Stirling High School).

30 See A.F. Hutchison's authoritative *History of the High School of Stirling*, 1904 (e.g. pp. 190-91), and the much more compact *From Castle Rock to Torbrex* (1962) by Jessie M. Thomson and Charles Strachan (e.g. pp. 44-5).

31 J.M.R. in *NR*, 21.4.1889, p. 244.

32 *Manchester Guardian* obituary of J.M.R., 7.1.1933; Gilmour in *HF*, 1936, p. vii.

33 See William Jenkins's tribute to J.M.R. in *LG* for March 1933, p. 53; also *LG* for February 1933, p. 40; January 1927, p. 23; and September 1933, p. 168. In 1934 the R.P.A. received £1,000 as a bequest from "W. Jenkins".

34 J. Lascelles Graham, *"Old Boys" and their Stories of the High School of Stirling*, 1900, pp. 163, 206-7, and 223 (the last cited page being written by the editor of the *Stirling Journal and Advertiser* who may have heard of or even known J.M.R. as a fellow pupil at the School).

35 See J.M.R.'s *What To Read*, 1904, pp. 5-6, 10. Decades later the leading literary figures Albert Camus and André Malraux in effect tacitly endorsed Robertson's praise of *Robinson Crusoe*, but not F.R. Leavis's downgrading of Daniel Defoe (see John Gross's 1969 book, pp. 275 n.-276 n.).

36 J.M.R. in: *LG* for September 1905, p. 131; *NR*, 29.8.1886,

p. 133; and *The Historical Jesus*, 1916, p. 3.

37 See *LG* for January 1927, incorporating the text of a speech by J.M.R. marking his 70th birthday and autobiographical reminiscences.

38 Ibid.

39 Odin Dekkers, op.cit. 1998, pp. 46-7. The fact that Robertson died intestate during a period scarred by the Great Depression could suggest that he felt he had few liquid assets. If, indeed, J.M.R. was "hard up" by about 1932, this could shed light on the fact that, the day after Robertson's death in early January 1933, his latter-day friend Macleod Yearsley observed that Robertson's wife did not feed her husband well.

40 J.M.R. in *The Baconian Heresy*, 1913, p. 552 (on helping his father at work while he, J.M.R., was still at school), and in *The Political Economy of Free Trade*, 1928, p. 119 (on unemployed sugar-refiners). See also *Stirling Journal and Advertiser*, 12.1.1933, p. 4, and *Stirling Observer*, 10.1.1933, p. 6, on the Eagle Inn.

41 *NR*, 5.7.1891, p. 8, where the writer used the pseudonym Gigadibs Junior (which Robertson, the editor, is understood to have used in 1891 elsewhere in the newspaper: see Dekkers, p. 266), and where other information in the 5 July article was consistent with little known facts regarding J.M.R.'s life in Stirling during his youth. In 1885 J.M.R. used the pseudonym Arthur Gigadibs for a sister freethought publication. See also Marley Denwood's bibliography in *HF*, 1936, Vol. 2, p. 995.

42 From J.M.R.'s *Mr. Lloyd George and Liberalism*, 1923, pp.

15-6.

43 J.M.R., *The Baconian Heresy*, p. 552.

44 From a self-revelatory intervention in the House of Commons on 11 May 1906 (columns 91-2, on the Coal Mines Regulations Bill). See also reference note 57.

45 J.M.R. in his *Papers for the People*, No. 11 ("Railway Nationalisation"), n.d. (June 1897?), p. 3. In June 1886 Robertson proposed public ownership of the railways and tram systems among a batch of measures which, G.B. Shaw later admitted, anticipated much of the Fabian programme; and J.M.R. also advocated railway nationalisation in 1889 (*NR*, 6.10.89, p. 210).

46 See *The Post*, 4.2.1933, p. 98.

47 David Ross, *The North British Railway: A History*, 2014, p. 69; and see *Secular Chronicle (SC)* for 8.9.1878, p. 117, and 22.9.1878, p. 141.

48 Information from Geoffrey Andrews based on his personal friendship with J.M.R.; and Robertson in *NR*, 22.8.1886, p. 116, and in *The Monthly Criterion* for January 1928, p. 45.

49 See J.M.R. in *NR*, 19.10.1884, p. 259; and his comments in the *Secular Review*, 15.10.1881, p. 244.

50 J.M.R. in *NR*, 9.4.1893, p. 233.

51 For Robertson's religious orthodoxy in his youth see information supplied by "Viator" in the *Freethinker*, 22.1.1933, p. 61 (just after J.M.R.'s death); and by Robertson himself in

The Ethical World, 18.2.1899, p. 100 (specifically on his own experience of instruction in the Shorter Catechism).

52 "Macrobius" (most probably J.M.R.), *NR*, 22.2.1891, p. 119. Macrobius was a Roman pagan patrician who "makes one of the earliest attempts to resolve religion into solar myths" (Joseph McCabe, *A Rationalist Encyclopaedia*, 1948, p. 370).

53 J.M.R., *What To Read*, 1904, p. 10. (The fact that John Macfarlane, the founder of the Free Library and Museum in Stirling, had also been a liberal benefactor of the High School there and had only quite recently died, in late August 1868, while Robertson was still a pupil at the School, may have helped to encourage J.M.R. to access the Free Library and stimulate his love of learning.)

54 *Patriotism and Empire*, for instance pp. 87, 96-8, 130-31. For J.M.R. on Cornelius Nepos see *The Baconian Heresy*, p. 197n. See also Robertson's *What To Read*, 1904 – evidently aimed mainly at young people – for his suggestions on developing a sense of history and trying to understand issues relating to war and peace.

55 See Theodor Fontane, *Across the Tweed: Notes on travel in Scotland*, 1858, 1965 English ed., pp. 94-8, etc.; and J.M.R., *Letters on Reasoning*, second edition, 1905, p. 98.

56 *Letters on Reasoning*, 1905 ed., p. 98.

57 J.P. Gilmour's factual error concerning the date of Bradlaugh's Edinburgh lecture on Bruno appears in *HF*, 1936 ed., p. viii. He may similarly have been mistaken about the sequence of young Robertson's second and third jobs,

concerning which Gilmour, preparing the 1936 obituary of Robertson, was unable to consult William Jenkins, who died in 1933. Certainly Robertson's later indication in the House of Commons that his second job (at the age of 14) involved his working a "solid nine hours day" – "with short intervals for meals" – could well seem more applicable to "clerking in an insurance office" (to quote Gilmour's words) than to working for a lawyer in an Edinburgh law office, which could have entailed irregular hours and the lawyer, accompanied by Robertson on occasions, unavoidably or unexpectedly having to go to court.

58 J.M.R. in *The Reformer*, 15.3.1902, p. 172.

59 Ibid. For the North British Railway's insurance scheme see David Ross, *The North British Railway: A History*, 2014, p. 69.

60 For the length of time Robertson worked in a law office see O. Hood Phillips, *The Law Relating to Shakespeare, 1564 – 1964* (II), 1964, p. 423, and *LG* for January 1927, for example. As regards Laski's account of J.M.R.'s contact with, and intellectual debt to, Kingdon Clifford (1845-79) see the *Holmes – Laski Letters (The Correspondence of Mr. Justice Holmes and Harold J. Laski) 1916-35*, ed. DeWolfe Howe, Vol. 2, 1953, Laski to Holmes, 8.5.1932, p. 1383: the revelation was made only some eight months before Robertson's death.

61 Geoffrey Andrews's recollection concerning Robertson's damaged finger – apparently on his left hand – was tentatively conveyed by him in a letter (2.1.1972) to the present writer. Keir Hardie's boyhood reading is mentioned in G.M. Thomson's *A Short History of Scotland*, 1930, pp. 295-6. Timothy J. Madigan, *W.K. Clifford and "The Ethics*

of Belief", 2009, and M. Chisholm, *Such Silver Currents*, 2002, provide useful information about Kingdon Clifford (not to mention Einstein). For Clifford's Sunday Lecture Society lectures see his *Lectures and Essays* (ed. Leslie Stephen and Sir Frederick Pollock, 1901 ed., Vol. 1, e.g. p. 181). For J.M.R. on Clifford see, for example, Robertson's *A History of Freethought in the Nineteenth Century*, 1929, and his piece in *NR*, 2.11.1890, p. 275.

62 See J.M.R. in *LG* for January 1927.

63 J.M.R. in *NR*, 2.4.1893, pp. 210-11.

64 See Robertson in *What To Read*, 1904, p. 7: *Criticisms: First Faggot*, 1902 ("The Murder Novel"); and *'Hamlet' Once More*, 1923, p. 188.

65 J.M.R. in *The Baconian Heresy*, 1913, p. 197n., and in *War and Civilization*, second edition, September 1917, pp. 58-9, respectively.

66 For J.M.R. on Thomas Carlyle see Robertson's *Modern Humanists*, first edition July 1891, and his *Modern Humanists Reconsidered*, 1927. See also John Gross, *The Rise and Fall of the Man of Letters*, 1969, pp. 124 and 35 & n. on Carlyle, who may have led J.M.R. to study Goethe etc.

67 For "the turning of the balance" of opinion in Britain from about 1870 see J.M.R.'s *A History of Freethought in the Nineteenth Century*, 1929, Vol. 2, p. 391; also Warren Sylvester Smith, *The London Heretics 1870 – 1914*, 1967, and, more tersely, W. Warren Wagar, *Good Tidings*, 1972, pp. 26, 360.

68 See J.M.R. in *LG* for November 1902, pp. 163-4, and his *History of Freethought in the Nineteenth Century (HFNC)*.

69 For W.R. Cassels see – in addition to J.M.R. – F.J. Gould's *The Pioneers of Johnson's Court*, 1929, p. 40, and Joseph McCabe's *A Rationalist Encyclopaedia*, 1948, as well as Henry Coke's *Tracks of a Rolling Stone*, 1905. For J.M.R.'s "rib" story, see his account in *NR*, 17.5.1885, p. 372. For the Abraham and Isaac story see J.M.R. in *LG* for August 1928, p. 143. As regards his grappling with the concept of infinite personality, see J.M.R. in *The University Magazine and Free Review* for December 1897, pp. 264-5. See also Robertson's *The Historical Jesus*, 1916, p. xix.

70 J.M.R.'s reference to "the sensations of an Edinburgh law-clerk" is to be found in *N.R.*, 20.3.1887, p. 180. For Lord Shaw's legal ability see J.M.R. in *LG* for December 1928, p. 207. Like Robertson, Thomas Shaw was against the Boer War of 1899 – 1902 (see Richard Price, *An Imperial War and the British Working Class*, 1972, which, although it does not mention J.M.R. in the index, features *The Meaning of Liberalism*, 1912 ed., in the Bibliography).

71 J.M.R. in *NR*, 11.5.1890, pp. 293–4.

72 Information – regarding Robertson's solicitor introducing him to a glass of wine – from Geoffrey Andrews's letter of 2.1.1972 to the present writer. The nineteenth century thinkers and writers named by Robertson were mentioned in a context which suggested that their works were among those read or studied by him in his youth (see his *Letters on Reasoning*, second edition, 1905, p. 45 – and p. 41 for his early belief in the historicity of the Gospel Jesus – as well as *The Historical Jesus*, p. xix, for T.H. Huxley).

73 For J.M.R. on Charles Bradlaugh generally see the former's joint work with Hypatia Bradlaugh Bonner entitled *Charles Bradlaugh: A Record of His Life and Work* (1894), his monograph *Charles Bradlaugh* (1920), and *A History of Freethought in the Nineteenth Century* (1929). See also Robertson in *LG* for August 1919, p. 125 (on Bradlaugh's magnetism), and in *NR*, 8.2.1891, pp. 83-4 (on his first contact with Bradlaugh and the freethought movement), as well as Bradlaugh himself in *NR*, 18.3.1877, p. 161, on his Bruno lecture. Edward Royle indicates there were very few really active freethought societies in Scotland between, say, 1873 and 1876 (*Radicals, Secularists and Republicans*, 1980, pp. 341-2).

74 Bradlaugh's lecture on Bruno was summarized – quite probably by William Archer, who was a leader writer with the *Edinburgh Evening News* and a free spirit nurturing some heterodox opinions – in Edinburgh's evening newspaper on 3.3.1877, p. 2.

75 J.M.R. in *NR*, 8.2.1891; and also in a letter, 16.6.1931, to Edward Henry, referred to by Odin Dekkers, op. cit. 1998, p. 5.

76 J.M.R. in *HF*, 1936 ed., pp. 587-8. Robertson would not know that in 1995 the historian Diarmaid MacCulloch would declare of Bruno: "It has recently been shown that he was recruited as a spy by Walsingham and played a vital role in unmasking Francis Throckmorton's [Roman Catholic] plot" (*The History Today Companion to British History*, p. 110). If this became known or suspected at the Vatican during Bruno's lifetime, it could well have heightened the Church's animosity towards him.

77 See J.M.R. in Hypatia Bradlaugh Bonner's *The Reformer*, 15.10.1904, p. 632 (on the Rome Congress) and in *The University Magazine and Free Review* for November 1897, p. 128 (on the Knowlton prosecution's impact on Bradlaugh). In the latter case, Robertson, in his 1897 article, was careful not to attribute a general fall in the British birth rate solely to "the Neo-Malthusian propaganda" associated with the Knowlton prosecution. Much more recently, the historian Edward Royle concluded: "the one indisputable fact about the 1877 trial is that it did vastly increase the publicity given to birth-control arguments, which may have contributed to the falling birth rate among the lower classes" (Royle, op. cit. 1980, p. 256). Bradlaugh and George Drysdale had founded the Malthusian League in 1861, whereas Michael Rosen's 2017 book on Zola, which disregarded secularist journals, misleadingly indicated (chapter 8) the League was founded by Mrs. Besant in about 1877 during the Knowlton prosecution.

78 See *NR*, 23.9.1877, pp. 654-5 – also *NR*, 18.11.1877, p. 782 – and Royle, op. cit. 1980, p. 70, in the last case for the statement "it seems that the [Scottish Secular] Union was thought of as a Scottish equivalent to the N.S.S."

79 Mrs. Besant described her visit to Edinburgh in *NR*, 7.10.1877, pp. 682-3; and J.M.R. referred to the Jenny Geddes story in *NR*, 18.7.1886, p. 35n.

80 For William Archer's Edinburgh lodgings and landlady, see Charles Archer, *William Archer: Life, Work and Friendships*, 1931, pp. 67-8. For J.M.R. on his ripening contact with William Archer, see the former's Critical Notice, as editor, to *William Archer as Rationalist*, 1925, p. viii, etc. For Lowe's insurance company identified by Peter Whitebrook, see the latter's *William Archer: A Biography*, 1993, p. 22 (see also p. 26).

81 Decades after Archer's landlady disapproved of Archer and his friends playing card games on the Sabbath, R.H. Bruce Lockhart was familiar in his Scottish youth with "a Scottish Sabbath which was kept with the Presbyterian strictness of those days. Games of any kind were forbidden"; and in 1937 Bruce Lockhart would testify that his now aged and more relaxed father "has been known to play even cards on a Sunday, a form of amusement which he never tolerated during his fifty years as a schoolmaster" (R.H. Bruce Lockhart, *My Scottish Youth*, 1937, pp. 104, 106-7). For Robertson on Archer's devotion to Ibsen and *Peer Gynt*, see J.M.R.'s Critical Notice in *William Archer as Rationalist* and his review, in *LG* for August 1931, of Charles Archer's biography of his esteemed literary brother, for example.

82 See Robertson's Critical Notice, 1925, as cited. As regards William Archer's attitude to Spiritualism see especially p. xviii therein and Joseph McCabe's *A Rationalist Encyclopaedia*, 1948, p. 27.

83 In 1919 William Archer indicated that Robertson had also lived in an "attic" when both of them lived in the Scottish capital at the same time, but Archer gave no details regarding J.M.R.'s Edinburgh accommodation during 1877-8 (see *LG* for July 1919, p. 112). For their growing friendship in Edinburgh, see Robertson's Critical Notice, 1925, and Charles Archer's biography, 1931, cited. For J.M.R.'s encyclopaedic reading and knowledge, see seriatim: the *Ardrossan and Saltcoats Herald*, 13.1.1933, p. 3; John Gross, op. cit. 1969, p. 124; and *LG* for February 1933, p. 36. For Gilmour on J.M.R.'s novel etc., see *HF*, p. viii. For William Archer's 1923 recollections, see the *Edinburgh Evening News*, 26.5.1923 (jubilee edition).

84 See William Norrie, *Edinburgh Newspapers Past and*

Present, 1891, p. 22, on Edinburgh's "first successful daily evening newspaper". Further information on the *Edinburgh Evening News* from the *Newspaper Press Directory*, 1878, pp. 106, 197. For J.M.R. on a wage of £2 a week, see, for example, *HF*, p. xvi. (Some fifty years after Robertson became a journalist in Edinburgh, the painter Francis Bacon found as a young man that "three pounds a week was enough to live on" in London, according to Daniel Farson in his study of Bacon, 1994 ed., p. 20.)

85 For Hector Carsewell Macpherson (1851 – 1924) on J.M.R. see the former's letter in *The British Weekly*, 11.11.1920, p. 110. See also p. 9 of the 1925 memoir entitled *Hector Macpherson: The Man and His Work* by his son, also known as Hector Macpherson.

86 J.M.R. in *HFNC*, p. 221; J.P. Gilmour in *HF*, p. viii (Gilmour strongly implied that the editor of the *Edinburgh Evening News* in 1878 was "a disciple of Herbert Spencer", but no evidence has emerged that the then editor, John Wilson, was such a disciple); and T.S. Eliot in *The Monthly Criterion* for August 1927, p. 179, seriatim. (In *HF*, p. ix, Gilmour erroneously put "1894" for the politically significant "1895".)

87 For the emergence of the National Secular Society's Edinburgh Branch see, for example, *NR*, 8.9.1878, p. 157; 13.10.1878, p. 238; and 3.11.1878, p. 286. Also *The Secular Chronicle (SC)*, 20.10. 1878, p. 190. For Alexander Orr see, inter alia, his obituary in *LG* for December 1919, p. 189; while *LG* for August 1933, p. 159, gives useful information about Thomas Carlaw Martin. In the quotation (1877) from the *Free Sunday Advocate* the verb "discourse" is used in an archaic sense to mean "give forth (music etc.)" (*Reader's Digest Oxford Complete Wordfinder*, 1993 ed., p. 415).

88 *NR*, 3.11.1878, p. 286. See also G.H. Taylor, *A Chronology of British Secularism*, 1957, pp. 12-3.

89 J.M.R.'s *The Dynamics of Religion*, 1897, p. 280. Alfred Cox's recollection (of Robertson on Bradlaugh) appeared in *LG* for November 1933, p. 208.

90 Regarding the formation of the London Secular Choral Union, see Edward Royle, op. cit. 1980, p.140 (para. 2, where some wording clearly appears to be missing). For the Edinburgh choir, see, for example, *NR*, 10.11.1878, p. 301. Robertson seems to have submitted quite a few youthful and largely sentimental poems to Mrs. Besant's *Our Corner* under the initials "M.J.R." during his Edinburgh period. Charles Watts's assessment was published in *The Secular Review (SR)*, 22.2.1879, p. 115.

91 The main source of information regarding J.M. Wheeler has been Robertson's extensive obituary of him in *The Reformer*, 15.5.1898. See also *NR*, 12.1.1879, p. 29, and 9.3.1879, p. 158; and Royle, op. cit., pp. 105, 159, 171 and 176.

92 Information on at least some of the secularist speakers who would have been heard by Robertson and his friends in Edinburgh may be gleaned from his *HFNC*, the unpublished *Random Recollections* (Part 1, March 1932) of his Leicester friend Sydney Gimson, Edward Royle's work (op. cit. 1980), and *NR*, 12.10.1879, p. 669 (for a report on Dr. C.R. Drysdale), for example.

93 Also useful is Nigel Sinnott's typed and stencilled monograph entitled *Joseph Symes, the "flower of atheism"* (published by the Atheist Society of Australia, 1977, 30 pp.). In addition see: Joseph Symes in *NR*, 8.6.1879, p. 382;

Alexander Orr in *NR*, 18.5.1879, p. 334; and Stan Shipley, *Club Life and Socialism in Mid-Victorian London*, 1971, pp. 34-5. For the proposed Sunday science school and T.C. Martin, see the *Free Sunday Advocate* for December 1879, p. 47, and *Our Corner* for March 1884, p. 184.

94 Most of the information presented on the Edinburgh Philosophical Institution is derived from W. Addis Miller, *The "Philosophical"*, 1949, as well as from *The Jubilee Book of the Philosophical Institution*, 1897, J.M.R.'s *Letters on Reasoning*, second ed., 1905, p. 130, and John Sutherland Black and George Chrystal, *The Life of William Robertson Smith*, 1912, p. 82. As Addis Miller in 1949 was in a unique position, having been Secretary and Chief Librarian between 1903 and 1939, it seems a pity he did not try to give his readers a clearer idea of the types of people who used the Institution over the years, their tastes, their social position, economic circumstances and financial resources measured against social changes and the cost and benefits of membership.

95 Information from the *Edinburgh Evening News*, 26.5.1923 (jubilee edition), especially p. 8 (J.M.R.'s contribution). Apparently the *Edinburgh Evening News* continued to breed and use carrier homing pigeons until at least 1905 – twenty years or more after Robertson left the *News* to work in London – with the same occasional difficulties with their performance (as described by Bill Rae in 2013) that the *News* staff had experienced by about 1879. As Rae explained in the context of his grandfather's service, spanning four decades, with the *News*: "When a reporter went to a football match, he was accompanied by a boy carrying a wicker basket of pigeons. ... If the handler was careless and the pigeon was released with ruffled feathers, the upset bird was liable to fly to the nearest tree and preen itself, while the irate handler threw

stones in the hope of persuading the pigeon to take off for the newspaper office" (Ian Macdougall, *Voices of Scottish Journalists*, 2013, p. 329: also p. 322). In early May 2016 it was reported that the terrorist organisation Islamic State (Isil) was using homing pigeons in the Middle East to deliver messages to operatives outside its so-called caliphate.

96 Philip Magnus, *Gladstone*, 1963 ed., pp. 261, 263 (see also p. 265); and *Edinburgh Evening News*, 25.11.1879, pp. 2, 3, 29.11.1879, p. 2 (this stated inter alia: "Special editions of the *Evening News* will be published this afternoon containing full reports of Mr. Gladstone's speeches"), and 1.12.1879, p. 3.

97 The two quotations referring to Gladstone and then the one referring to the British Cabinet are drawn seriatim from Robertson in *The Reformer*, 15.4.1897, p. 38, in *Toryism and Barbarism*, 1885, p. 3, and then in *The Reformer* as cited, p. 38. Decades after Robertson favoured Parliamentary approval prior to the British Government embarking upon a war the idiosyncratic campaigner E.D. Morel adopted this position in *The Secret History of a Great Betrayal* (sixth edition, May 1925, p. 47). The question of abolition of the Cabinet was raised approvingly, if fleetingly, by Robertson in his pamphlet *The Future of Liberalism* (pp. 27-8; n.d., but probably 1897), which was published together with, or even as part of, his series of pamphlets entitled *Papers for the People*.

98 See the *Edinburgh Evening News*, 26.5.1923, p. 8, and 6.4.1880, p. 2. *The News* leader writer for 3.4.1880, p. 2 (probably J.M.R.), correctly predicted that Gladstone would defeat Lord Dalkeith in the election. For the Pope Pius IX and Queen Victoria quotations see E.R. Norman, *Anti-Catholicism in Victorian England*, 1968, and David Tribe, *President Charles Bradlaugh, M.P.*, 1971, respectively.

99 Gladstone's praise of "the disposing hand of God" in the 1880 election is cited in John Morley's *Life of Gladstone*, 1903, Vol. 2, p. 612. The comment by the *Edinburgh Evening News* leader writer (almost certainly J.M.R.) on 16.4.1880 that the atheist Bradlaugh had to contend with snobbery – as well as bigotry – found an echo some seven months later when Robertson was reported (in *The Edinburgh Courant*, 29.11.1880, p. 4) to have criticised the American clergyman Joseph Cook for being a snob.

100 For Morley, Arnold, Queen Victoria to Gladstone, and Lord Halifax to Sir Henry Ponsonby, see, for example: David Tribe, op. cit. 1971, p. 212; J.M.R. in *Modern Humanists*, 1891, p. 158, and in *Charles Bradlaugh: A Record*, 1894, Vol. 2, Part 2, p. 329; *LG* for November 1933, p. 196; and Arthur Ponsonby, *Henry Ponsonby: His Life from His Letters*, 1942, pp. 239-40. For J.H. Levy, A.B. Moss and Harriet Law generally, see Royle, op. cit. 1980. For Moss see also *The Malthusian* for July 1907, p. 50, and pieces in *LG*, e.g. for 1933, as well as his letter in the *Sunday Referee*, 1.1.1933, p. 9. For Harriet Law see also: David Tribe, op. cit. 1971; Malcolm Quin, *Memoirs of a Positivist*, 1924, p. 53; and 'Tatler' in *The North Briton*, 15.3.1879, p. 4. As editor of *The Secular Chronicle*, Mrs. Law published on 4.8.1878 an article by Karl Marx on the First International, for which see Henry Collins and Chimen Abramsky, *Karl Marx and the British Labour Movement*, 1965, pp. 110n. and 296. For Hyndman see, for example, Alex Callinicos, *The Revolutionary Ideas of Karl Marx*, 1995 ed., 2010 reprint, pp. 47-8. For aspects of the conflict between Marx and Engels on one side and Bakunin and his supporters on the other, Leslie R. Page's *Karl Marx and the Critical Examination of His Works*, in effect Part 1, 1987 (e.g. p. 78), may be consulted.

101 For Marx's criticism of Holyoake and Bradlaugh, see Edward Royle, op. cit., pp. 93, 122, and David Tribe, op. cit. 1971, pp. 124, 126, 346. Looking back, the Fabian Beatrice Webb would admit: "in the seventies and eighties it looked as if whole sections of the British proletariat – and these the élite – would be swept, like the corresponding class on the Continent, into a secularist movement" (quoted by Gertrude Himmelfarb, *Poverty and Compassion*, 1991, pp. 182, 428, from Webb's *My Apprenticeship*, 1971 ed., p. 147). The pro-Soviet Fabian intellectual G.D.H. Cole would acknowledge in *A Short History of the British Working-Class Movement 1789-1947* (1948 ed., p. 89) that secularism was one of two movements which "flourished greatly in the Victorian era"; while the Marxist (and Stalinist) historian A.L. Morton would declare that Bradlaugh's National Secular Society "became a noted centre of progressive politics" whose associated radical support base was "deeply rooted in the masses of workers and lower middle classes" (*The British Labour Movement 1770-1920*, 1956, p. 157). In March 1879 Watts's *Secular Review* published work by a nascent Marxian, Belfort Bax, whereas 'Tatler' belittled Harriet Law's "advanced Socialistic opinions" and "strong Cockney accent".

102 The quoted writer on Edinburgh was H. McGregor in *SR*, 3.7.1880, p. 14. See also the *Freethinker* for May 1881, p. 3. For the Affirmation Bill petition presented in mid 1880 see *NR* for that period, including its "Special Extra Number", p. 55. J.M.R.'s July S.S.U. lectures were reported in *SR* on 17.7.1880 and 24.7.1880. Holyoake's founding of *SR* is documented by Tribe in *100 Years of Freethought*, 1967, p. 154, and by Royle, op. cit., p. 12.

103 *SR*, 18.9.1880, p. 190, and *NR*, 19.9.1880, p. 237 (for the S.S.U. AGM); *The Malthusian* for November 1880, pp. 171-2;

SR, 6.11.1880, p. 303, and *The Malthusian* for January 1881, p. 191 (for the formation of the Malthusian League Edinburgh Branch); and J.M.R.'s extensive obituary of Eliza Marshall in *The Reformer*, 15.3.1902, pp. 188-9. On 15.8.1880 the *NR* (p. 158) advertised a lecture for that evening by William Marshall to the Edinburgh S.S.U. at 3 Chambers Street on "The Solar System" ("illustrated by models"). Their fellow freethinker W.E. Snell was billed to lecture to the Edinburgh S.S.U. on 18.1.1880, and his continuing devotion to freethought and Bradlaugh would appear to be indicated by the much appreciated lectures, particularly one on "Charles Bradlaugh: Atheist and Reformer", which "Mr. Snell" gave to secularists in Newcastle in early 1897 (see *The Reformer*, 15.4.1897, p. 47) – probably to audiences that a decade later would help to secure Robertson's election as Liberal M.P. for Tyneside.

104 For the Land Law Reform League and its formation, see J.M.R. in *Charles Bradlaugh: A Record*, 1894, Vol. 2, p. 180 et seq., Tribe in *100 Years of Freethought*, 1967, p. 92, and op. cit. 1971, p. 188, and Royle, op. cit., p. 196. For the Reform League Edinburgh meeting, see Bradlaugh in *NR*, 17.10.1880, p. 289, and comment in the *Edinburgh Evening News*, 7.10.1880, p. 2 (which referred to "an audience chiefly drawn from the artisan class"). For Robertson's debut as a lecturer in Glasgow, see, for example, *NR*, 17.10.1880, p. 302, and 24.10.1880, p. 318. For Harriet Martineau and her background, see, inter alia, J.M.R.'s *HFNC*, his *Modern Humanists* (p. 209), David Tribe, op. cit. 1971 (p. 55), the latter's *100 Years of Freethought* (p. 223), Royle, op. cit. 1980 (p. 171), and Joseph McCabe's *A Rationalist Encyclopaedia*, 1948 (p. 378).

105 *NR*, 5.12.1880, p. 409, and 30.4.1882, p. 348 (for Cook invited to debate with Bradlaugh); *The Edinburgh Courant*,

29.11.1880, p. 4; also *SR*, 4.12.1880, p. 366, and *NR*, 28.11.1880, p. 398.

106 See: *NR*, 6.2.1881, p. 93; Sydney Gimson, *Random Recollections of the Leicester Secular Society*, Part 1, March 1932 (unpublished typescript), pp. 10-11; J.M.R. in *NR*, 7.8.1892, p. 82 (on reading J.R. Green in 1881); *Courses of Study*, 1932 ed., p. 342; J.M.R.'s 1887 pamphlet on the religion of Shakespeare; J.M.R. in *The Reformer*, 15.9.1897, pp. 182-84, and in *LG* for February 1921, p. 26; and *HF*, 1936, pp. 551-5 (cf. McCabe, *A Rationalist Encyclopaedia*, pp. 539-40). See Curtis Brown Watson's book – which includes a passing reference to J.M.R. on *Hamlet – Shakespeare and the Renaissance Concept of Honor* (1960), G.F. Bradby in *About Shakespeare and His Plays*, 1926, pp. 73-4, and A.A. Smirnov in *Shakespeare: A Marxist Interpretation*, 1936, p. 92. As Shakespeare appeared to have a less than sycophantic or slavish political attitude towards the monarchist Establishment of Elizabethan England, it is at least conceivable that his views on religion also developed along bold or unorthodox lines. Despite his criticism of Green, Robertson would draw on the historian as one of his sources in substantial works like *The Saxon and the Celt* (1897), *The Dynamics of Religion* (1897 and 1926), and *The Evolution of States* (1912).

107 For Carlyle's influence on Lloyd George, see Emyr Price, *David Lloyd George*, 2006, p. 8, and Roy Hattersley's account with the same title, 2010, 2012 ed. p. 13. On 30.10.1939, only weeks after Britain declared war on Nazi Germany, Lloyd George in the Commons advised the British Government to consider carefully any peace terms offered by Hitler, only to be angrily accused by another M.P. of preaching surrender, with the former Prime Minister then leaving the Chamber looking "like a whipped pup" (Tim Bouverie, *Appeasing Hitler*,

2019, p. 387). Some two years later Lloyd George publicly advocated a negotiated peace between Britain and Hitler (Hattersley, p. 633); and in June 1946 – after Lloyd George's death – the Fascist leader Oswald Mosley provocatively quoted Lloyd George with apparent approval (on opposition to a war) on the title page of *My Answer*. For Carlyle's impact on Herbert Read, see Matthew Adams, *Kropotkin, Read, and the Intellectual History of British Anarchism*, 2015, p. 63; while Enoch Powell's debt to Carlyle may be gleaned from *The Listener*, 25.6.1970, p. 858, and Simon Heffer's *Like The Roman*, 1998. For Dr. Edward Aveling's failure to lecture on 20.3.1881, see *NR*, 27.3.1881, p. 221; and for his earlier letter to Darwin, see Leslie R. Page, *Marx and Darwin: The Unveiling of a Myth*, June 1983, pp. 1-4. See also Royle, p. 151.

108 See Leslie Page's *Marx and Darwin* as cited. But in *The Rise and Fall of Communism*, 2009, even a specialist in modern Communist politics like Professor Archie Brown– misled (pp. 38 and 627) by the Marx scholar David McLellan – perpetuated the myth that Marx wished to dedicate the second volume of *Das Kapital* to Darwin. Suspicions that the dedication story was a hoax which were articulated in 1959 (by the botanist Conway Zirkle) and more forcefully in 1967 (by the political scientist Shlomo Avineri) were followed by the discovery and presentation, in and after 1975, of definitive evidence of the hoax. In his last novel, *1984* (published in 1949), George Orwell dramatically presented aspects of the kind of falsification of history practised by the Soviet Communist regime, certainly in the 1930s. This practice arguably had a precedent in Karl Marx's treatment of cases drawn from Britain from the eighteenth century onwards which included: his calculated perversion and distortion of part of Gladstone's budget speech of April 1863 (to denigrate

the then Chancellor), and Marx's misrepresenting contents of Parliamentary Blue Books to suit the Communist's anti-capitalist agenda (see Leslie Page, *Karl Marx and the Critical Examination of His Works*, 1987, pp. 46-9, 59-60, 93-4).

109 See inter alia: Christopher Andrew and Vasili Mitrokhin, *The Mitrokhin Archive*, 2000 ed., pp. 55-64; Emil Draitser, *Stalin's Romeo Spy*, 2010; Nick Barratt, *The Forgotten Spy*, 2015 (concerning Oldham); and Christopher Andrew and Oleg Gordievsky, *KGB*, 1990, pp. 142-3, 179. Ironically, Robertson, an outspoken anti-Communist, and Oldham, a troubled spy for the Soviet regime, not only lived within a stone's throw of each other in the same street at the same time, but also both died at home, or very close to it, within nine months of each other in 1933.

110 For Bradlaugh's courteous if brief personal contact with Charles Darwin, see Hypatia Bradlaugh Bonner in *Charles Bradlaugh: A Record*, 1894, Vol. 2, Part 1, pp. 23-4; and for his hostile relationship with Karl Marx, see, for example, Tribe, op. cit. 1971, pp. 124, 126-7, 346. Royle (op. cit. 1980, p. 70) refers to "a strong Bradlaughite contingent" in Edinburgh at this time. For the pro-Bradlaugh petition and resolution there during the second half of May 1881, see *NR*, 22.5.1881, pp. 412 and 414, and 5.6.1881, p. 461. The quoted commentator is James R. Moore in *Religion in Victorian Britain*, Vol. 1: *Traditions* (ed. Gerald Parsons), 1988, p. 307.

111 Bradlaugh's 11.6.1881 meeting in Edinburgh was reported in the *Edinburgh Evening News* (p. 2) two days later and by Robertson in his part of *Charles Bradlaugh: A Record*, 1894, Vol. 2 (pp. 284-5). Well over a century later, in his account of this public meeting (in *Dare To Stand Alone*, 2010), Bryan Niblett – who in this context misspelt J.M.R.'s name and gave

his age incorrectly – claimed that Robertson chaired this meeting; whereas the *Edinburgh Evening News* (13.6.1881) said it was presided over by John Lees, and Robertson (1894) simply referred to himself as "one of the promoters of the meeting".

112 The strictures – probably penned by John Robertson – in the *Edinburgh Evening News* for 25.5.1881 regarding the way in which the Free Church authorities proceeded against William Robertson Smith were in effect endorsed over a century later when, independently of Robertson, David Christie-Murray declared in *A History of Heresy* (1989, p. 199) that the Free Church had dismissed Robertson Smith "illegally, from his post". (His dismissal on 26.5.1881 was also examined by T.C. Beidelman in 1974.) For the harassed Professor generally, see John Sutherland Black and George Chrystal, *The Life of William Robertson Smith*, 1912; and, more specifically for his unorthodox approach, see J.M.R.'s *HFNC* and also Alasdair Macintyre in *The Religious Significance of Atheism*, 1969, p. 55.

113 See *NR*, 17.7.1881, p. 78, for Malcolm Quin's July 1881 Edinburgh lectures, and J.M.R. (on 20.6.1904) in the Sociological Society's *Sociological Papers*, 1905, p. 215, for the Scottish atheist's study of Comte.

114 Malcolm Quin, *Memoirs of a Positivist*, 1924, pp. 66-7; *SR*, 23.7.1881, p. 63 (Snell).

115 Graphic accounts of Bradlaugh's ejection by physical brute force from the precincts of the House are to be found in *Charles Bradlaugh: A Record*, 1894, Vol. 2, Part 2 (by Robertson), pp. 285-8, and in David Tribe, op. cit. 1971, pp. 210-11. See also G.H. Taylor, *A Chronology of British*

Secularism, 1957, p. 13, and *Champion of Liberty*, 1933 (ed. J.P. Gilmour), pp. 44-6 (from appreciation of Bradlaugh by T.P. O'Connor, M.P.).

116 For Thomas Carlaw Martin's paper see *NR*, 14.8.1881, p. 174, and *SR*, 13.8.1881, p. 111. For the constitutional rights campaign, see the *Edinburgh Evening News (EEN)*, 18.8.1881, p. 2; Tribe, op. cit. 1971, pp. 205-6; *NR*, 28.8.1881, p. 222; and *SR*, 27.8.1881, p. 143, and 3.9.1881, p. 159.

117 *LG* for September 1920, p. 140: recollection by "Mimnermus" (John Smith).

118 For 25.9.1881 see Charles Watts as editor in *SR*, 1.10.1881, pp. 217-8, as well as W.E. Snell in the same issue, p. 222, and in *NR*, 9.10.1881, p. 317. For Robertson's 16.10.1881 lecture on vaccination, see Snell's account in *SR*, 22.10.1881, p. 271, and in *NR*, 23.10.1881, p. 346. For the longstanding vaccination controversy in Britain extending beyond the nineteenth century, see, inter alia: *Daily Mail*, 6.4.2017, p. 24; *The Times*, 20.2.2018, pp. 1-2; Edward Royle, op. cit. 1980, pp. 224-5; David Tribe, *100 Years of Freethought*, 1967, pp. 172-3; William J. Fishman, *East End 1888*, 1988, p. 255; and Alfred Russel Wallace, *The Wonderful Century*, 1898, pp. 226-37. In this last-cited work Wallace – later than Robertson, though almost certainly independently of him – castigated Ernest Hart (pp. 226-7) for "the monstrosity of his errors" in his pamphlet *The Truth about Vaccination* (1880). Wallace also revealed (p. 226) that when an "amazing and almost incredible misstatement" by Dr. W.B. Carpenter in the *Spectator* in April 1881 regarding the allegedly high smallpox mortality rate in eighteenth century London was pointed out to the pro-vaccination Dr. Carpenter, the latter's mistake was "acknowledged privately, but never withdrawn publicly!" This

would appear to indicate that the way a critic like Robertson was treated by one or two medical supporters of vaccination at this time was not limited to him. For J.M.R.'s contact with Charles R. Drysdale and with Andrew Wilson concerning Ernest Hart, see Robertson's letter in *NR*, 3.7.1887, p. 12, and his *Papers for the People*, No. 8 ("The Truth about Vaccination"), February 1897?, pp. 2-5.

119 See: Charles Archer, *William Archer: Life, Work and Friendships*, 1931, pp. 92-5; Robertson's "Burns and His Race II", *The Monthly Criterion*, February 1928, p. 154 et seq,; and the latter's *Criticisms: First Faggot*, 1902 ("Mr. W.E. Henley"), especially perhaps pp. 40-41, 48.

120 For J.M.R.'s 13.11.1881 lecture, see Alexander Orr in *SR*, 19.11.1881, p. 334. For Sundays in Edinburgh in the early 1880s, see Eleanor Sillar's remarkably vivid reminiscences in her *Edinburgh's Child*, 1961.

121 Charles Archer, *William Archer: Life, Work and Friendships*, 1931, p. 96.

122 The friend to whom Robertson addressed his comment about Buckle was the music critic Ernest Newman. For J.M.R.'s criticism of Auguste Comte see his *Spoken Essays*, 1925, pp. 202-9, and, to some extent, *The Economics of Progress*, 1918, pp. 14-5, for example.

123 See Royle, op. cit. 1980, p. 213.

124 The censorship was reported by Bradlaugh's daughters Alice and Hypatia in *NR*, 15.1.1882, p. 40.

125 For Sundays in Edinburgh, see *Edinburgh's Child*

by Eleanor Sillar (born 1869), and also the report in *NR*, 17.10.1880, p. 296, by Alice and Hypatia Bradlaugh of an Edinburgh meeting calling "to have gardens and galleries thrown open to the public" on Sundays. For Robertson's lecture on 15.1.1882, see *NR*, 15.1.82, p. 46, and *SR*, 21.1.1882, p. 46. For reaction to that lecture see J.M.R. in: *LG* for October 1911, p. 149; *Jesus and Judas*, 1927, p. vi; and *LG* for January 1911, p. 3. The quotation regarding "the fictional Gospel Jesus" is from the Scottish scholar's contribution in *NR*, 17.2.1889, p. 100.

126 Robertson's Edinburgh lecture on 19.2.1882 was reported by *SR*, 25.2.1882, p. 127, from which the quotation is drawn. As for his lecturing in Glasgow on 21.5.1882, the first cited "ZOSIMUS" quotation is from *NR*, 28.5.1882, p. 413, and the second from *SR*, 27.5.1882, p. 334.

127 Charles Archer, *William Archer: Life, Work and Friendships*, 1931, pp. 103-4 (from William Archer's letter of 8.1.1882 to Robertson).

128 For the pro-Bradlaugh S.S.U. resolution of 26.2.1882 in Edinburgh, see *NR*, 5.3.1882, p. 189 (and *NR*, 12.3.1882, p. 219). The Edinburgh contacts, mentioned by surname, that William Archer had in mind in his letter of 8.1.1882 are understood to have been Thomas Carlaw Martin and John Wilson of the *Edinburgh Evening News* (as distinct from John Lees's business partner, W.A. Wilson). For Ibsen's reputation and standing in England between 1880 (when he was only known to almost literally a handful of people there) and 1889 (when he "achieved his first real breakthrough on the English stage"), see: Michael Meyer, *Henrik Ibsen – The Top of a Cold Mountain, 1883-1906*, 1971, pp. 115-6, 174; Clarence R. Decker, *The Victorian Conscience*, 1952, pp. 117-20; and

Margot Peters, *Bernard Shaw and the Actresses*, 1980, p. 54.

129 Robertson's extended essay "Evolution in Drama" appeared in a number of issues of *Our Corner* for 1886, pp. 143-53, 225-31, 275-83, 333-41 (he commented on Ibsen in the last instalment). Arguably his essay did not receive the attention it deserved during his lifetime or for many years thereafter: for example, it was not referred to in the symposium entitled *J.M. Robertson (1856-1933)*, ed. G.A. Wells, 1987.

130 The 1882 unveiling of the Burns statue in Dumfries is described in *The World's Memorials of Robert Burns* (ed. Edward Goodwillie), 1911; and J.M.R.'s "The Art of Burns" appeared in *Our Corner* for September 1884. The different attitudes of Darwin and Herbert Spencer to the idea of progress are succinctly explored by Leslie R. Page (p. 132) in *Karl Marx and the Critical Examination of His Works*, 1987, which also explains Karl Marx's brief contact with Darwin, not to mention Spencer (p. 119). The appreciation by the April 1882 leader writer (almost certainly Robertson) of Darwin's enduring contribution may be contrasted with Tolstoy's claim twenty years later that Darwin was "beginning to be forgotten" (quoted by George Orwell, *Inside the Whale and Other Essays*, 1964 Penguin reprint, p. 104). The last J.M.R. quote comes from *HFNC*, p. 346.

131 See: David Tribe, *100 Years of Freethought*, 1967, p. 28, and Royle, op. cit. 1980, pp. 171, 176, 295 (on Darwin's impact); *Free Sunday Advocate* for November 1880, etc. (Darwin supporting the Sunday Lecture Society); "Darwin, Charles Robert" in Joseph McCabe's *A Rationalist Encyclopaedia*, 1948, pp. 133-4; *NR*, 16.12.1888, p. 390 (J.M.R.'s criticism of Darwin's Christian burial); and information supplied by Macleod Yearsley through his family (concerning Robertson's

attendance at Down House in June 1929). For Darwin's views on religion see his autobiography, as well as *The Life and Letters of Charles Darwin*, edited by his son Francis Darwin, Vol. 1, 1887, pp. 304, 307 and 309. Charles Darwin's reference to himself as "a strong advocate for free thought on all subjects" is to be found in his letter of 13 October 1880 to Edward Aveling, quoted by Margaret Fay in *Monthly Review*, New York, Vol. 31, no. 10, March 1980, pp. 42-3, and Francis Wheen's biography of Karl Marx, 2000 paperback edition, pp. 365-6, 418-9.

132 As regards J.M.R.'s agenda on 30.4.1882, see *SR*, 29.4.82, p. 271, and 6.5.82, p. 287; and concerning his activity on 10.5.1882, see *SR*, 20.5.82, p. 318, supplemented by Annie Besant's account in *NR*, 21.5.1882, pp. 386-7. The public acts of solidarity with Bradlaugh in London on 10.5.1882 were noticed by J.M.R. in his part of the 1894 biography of Bradlaugh; but rather surprisingly the mass demonstration and follow-up protest meeting were passed over by David Tribe, for example, in his 1971 biography.

133 The 1882 N.S.S. Annual Conference was reported in *NR*, 4.6.82, pp. 417-24 and 426-7; and in the *Freethinker*, same date, pp. 178-9. For Alexander Henry see *EEN*, 28.8.1882, p. 2. In mid February 1891 the *National Reformer*, in the early days of Robertson's editorship, offered John Lees a niche for his obituary of the stalwart Charles Nicholson.

134 Ingersoll was planning to visit Britain when he died in 1899 (Royle, op. cit. 1980, p. 80). For his *Mistakes of Moses* see J.M.R.'s seventieth birthday speech, reproduced in *LG* for January 1927.

135 Regarding Bradlaugh and the Channel Tunnel, see David

Tribe, op. cit. 1971, pp. 214, 358, and, for the Robertson quotation, J.M.R. in Charles *Bradlaugh: A Record*, 1894, Vol. 2, Part 2, p. 381.

136 Hypatia's paper was mentioned years later in the typescript "Life of Hypatia Bradlaugh Bonner", p. 38, by her husband Arthur Bonner, in a passage not reproduced in the condensed *Hypatia Bradlaugh Bonner: The Story of Her Life*, published in 1942, years after both had died. Bradlaugh's closing address was included in *Speeches by Charles Bradlaugh*, printed in 1890 by Arthur Bonner; and extracts from that address featured in *Champion of Liberty: Charles Bradlaugh* (ed. J.P. Gilmour), which appeared in September 1933 for the Bradlaugh centenary, during Hypatia's and Arthur's sunset years.

137 *EEN*, 29.5.1882, p. 2, and, for Alexander Orr's handbills, *NR*, 16.10.1881, p. 329.

138 *NR*, 18.6.1882, p. 460. Both Robertson and Thomas Carlaw Martin of the Edinburgh Branch had renewed their N.S.S. membership shortly before the Conference (*NR*, 14.5.1882, p. 377).

139 For J.M.R. on Thomson ("B.V."), following the latter's death, see: his edition (1892) of *Poems, Essays and Fragments* by James Thomson; his "Critical Chat" on "B.V." in *NR*, 15.1.1893, pp. 41-2; his *Charles Bradlaugh*, 1920, pp. 118-9; and his article on *The City of Dreadful Night* in *LG* for June 1932, pp. 99-101 – as well as *HFNC* for the general background to Thomson's relationship with Bradlaugh, Foote, etc. Robertson's letter on Thomson, Bradlaugh and Foote has been made available on a privileged basis.

140 For Bradlaugh at Leicester and in Italy, see Tribe, op. cit. 1971, pp. 186, 353, and 78-9, respectively. Specifically for the 1881 opening of the Leicester Secular Hall, see G.H. Taylor, *A Chronology of British Secularism*, 1957, p. 14, and Royle, op. cit. 1980, p. 56. On 1 March 1931 Robertson attended, and apparently spoke at, the Leicester Secular Hall celebrations to mark the fiftieth anniversary of the Hall's opening (see the report in the *Leicester Mercury*, 2.3.1931, p. 18).

141 The Garibaldi obituary appeared in *EEN*, 3.6.1882, p. 2. The fact that the obituarist referred to "his unresting brain" while, less than two months earlier, the *EEN* obituary-writer on Darwin had highlighted "his unhasting, unresting ardour" could well suggest that both obituaries were produced by the same person, and, together with the reference on 3.6.82 to Walt Whitman, appears to support a belief in the near certainty that person was Robertson. For imperialism and teaching about it at Oxford and Cambridge and at British public schools, see Bernard Porter, *The Absent-Minded Imperialists*, 2006 paperback ed., pp. 49-50, 53, 60-62, for example. J.M.R. delivered his lecture at about the time that a slight acquaintance of his, the Positivist Malcolm Quin of Newcastle, was developing an anti-imperialist critique (see Gregory Claeys, *Imperial Sceptics*, 2010, pp. 92-3, etc.). Robertson's two-part lecture was very briefly noticed in *NR*, 25.6.1882, p. 477, and 16.7.1882, p. 46. Between 1900 and 1907 Robertson would visit South Africa and Cromer's Egypt on the fringe of Britain's colonial empire and publicize and condemn outrages and injustices there. In 1951, when British influence was still discernible in both these territories on the African continent, Hannah Arendt would refer to "outstanding similarity between Rhodes's rule in South Africa and Cromer's domination of Egypt" (*The Burden of Our Time*, 1951, p. 212). For the views and experiences of a well-placed British official

who worked in the Middle East in the early twentieth century see *Orientations* (1937) by Sir Ronald Storrs.

142 For J.P. Gilmour's transition to rationalism, see F.J. Gould, *The Pioneers of Johnson's Court*, 1929, p. 134. For J.M. Wheeler's "translation" to London, see Edward Royle, op. cit. 1980, pp. 105, 159, and G.H.Taylor, *A Chronology of British Secularism*, 1957, pp. 13-4. For Robertson's named comrades in Edinburgh and for descriptions (mainly by Gilmour) of his physique and physical appearance at that time, see: Hypatia Bradlaugh Bonner's tribute to J.M.R. in the form of a freestanding leaflet reprinted from *LG* for July 1926; *LG* for January 1927 (p. 25), February 1933 (p. 36), and September 1938 (pp. 166-7); and *HF*, 1936 ed., pp. viii and xvii-xviii.

143 For Forder see Tribe, op. cit. 1971, p. 83, and Forder's notes in *NR*, 20.8.1882, p. 135. Robertson's high regard for the N.S.S. national secretary found expression in a letter of 13.9.1930 to the American freethinker Jack Benjamin.

144 For J.M.R.'s summer and autumn lectures in Edinburgh during 1882, see: *NR*, 2.7.82, p. 14 (on freethought); *NR*, 3.9.82, p. 173 (on Emerson); *SR*, 9.9.82, p. 175 (on the Salvation Army); and *NR*, 12.11.82, p. 334 (on *Progress and Poverty*). See also J.M.R. on Emerson in *Modern Humanists*, 1891, e.g. p. 121. Emerson lectured in England in 1847 (McCabe, *A Rationalist Encyclopaedia*, p. 183).

145 J.M.R., *The Economics of Progress*, 1918, p. 252.

146 Regarding the unsuccessful attempt by two socialist supporters in Edinburgh to turn their local secularist society (of which they were members) into one espousing socialism,

see J.M.R. in *The Reformer*, 1904, p. 637, and in *LG* for October 1931, p. 179, in the latter case from an article on "Scientific Humanism".

147 For the Austrian émigré Andreas Scheu, see: Willard Wolfe, *From Radicalism to Socialism*, 1975, pp. 106-7, 121n.; and John Quail, *The Slow Burning Fuse*, 1978, pp. 27-8, 31-4, 40 and 330-1, for example. For Robert Banner, see: Chushichi Tsuzuki, *The Life of Eleanor Marx, 1855-1898*, 1967, pp. 52, 224, 301n., etc.; Willard Wolfe, op. cit. above, pp. 121n., 302; Yvonne Kapp, *Eleanor Marx*, vol. 2: *The Crowded Years (1884-1898)*, 1976, p. 716n., etc.; John Quail, op. cit. above, pp. 32, 34-5; and Francis Wheen, *Karl Marx*, 2000 paperback ed., pp. 369, 419. Karl Marx knew of both Scheu and Banner. *Social Democracy in Britain*, 1935, by H.W. Lee and E. Archbold also provides some useful information in this context.

148 *NR*, 8.10.1882, p. 254, and 1.10.1882, p. 236; *EEN*, 30.10.1882, p. 2; and *NR*, 5.11.1882, pp. 305, 312 and 317.

149 *NR*, 5.11.1882, p. 318, and 12.11.1882, pp. 334 and 333, seriatim.

150 *The Republican* for December 1882, pp. 452, 454 (report by George Standring), and *NR*, 26.11.1882, p. 381. These two journals indicated that the elected Edinburgh republican branch chairman and secretary were John Lees and John L. McMahon, respectively. It is presumed that John L. McMahon was the same person as the "J.L. Mahon" described by Willard Wolfe as an "engineer … from Scottish Freethought" and as an early recruit to the S.D.F. (*From Radicalism to Socialism – a study of socialist ideas in England between 1881 and 1889* – p. 302.) It was not unknown for Victorian freethinkers or for

socialists on or after joining the S.D.F. to change, amend or hide their names. From about 1885 onwards "Mahon" found himself in the same North London branch of the Socialist League as Andreas Scheu, who had known, or been known to, the Edinburgh secularists since at least 1879. See John Quail, *The Slow Burning Fuse* (on British anarchists), 1978, pp. 40-1, 66. For the comments by an esteemed historian of British freethought see Edward Royle, op. cit. 1980, pp. 204-5, and *NR*, 14.1.1883, p. 29.

151 See: *EEN*, 6.1.1883, p. 2; *NR*, 21.1.1883, p. 45; *NR*, 4.2.1883, p. 78; *EEN*, 15.2.1883, p. 2 (with a fuller account submitted by "McM" in *NR*, 25.2.1883, p. 125); *Evening Express* (Edinburgh), 15.2.1883, p. 4 (on the 20,000 or so Bradlaugh supporters); and Tribe, op. cit. 1971, p. 222 (on cancelled railway tickets).

152 See *SR*, 20.1.1883, p. 46 (report by "S", probably W.E. Snell) and 17.2.1883, p. 111. The substance of Robertson's lecture advertised for 18.2.1883 may have provided leads years later for his *Papers for the People*, No. 2 ("The People and Their Leaders"). On the basis of *NR*, 10.9.1882, p. 187, Robertson's Edinburgh address was 17 London Street since at least that date. The only Robertson-Geddes letters believed to have survived are in the National Library of Scotland. For the information on Patrick Geddes various published sources have been consulted, including books by Philip Mairet (to whom Robertson's appreciative associate T.S. Eliot dedicated one of his own prose works) and Philip Boardman. For background to Geddes's praise of Ruskin, see J.M.R.'s *Modern Humanists Reconsidered*. For the Edinburgh secularist group linking Geddes and J.M.R., see *LG* for February 1933 and July 1926. For Geddes on J.M.R., see *LG* for April 1898.

153 *NR*, 2.10.1881, p. 302, referred to a lecture at that time to Glasgow secularists by "Mr. J.M. Wheeler, of Edinburgh". For Wheeler in late 1881, see G.H. Taylor, *A Chronology of British Secularism*, 1957, pp. 13-4 (the *Freethinker* was launched in May 1881). In the Edinburgh Branch of the N.S.S. a member whose initials were given as "M.P.G." in *NR*, 16.10.1881, may refer to Patrick Geddes (a person's initials were sometimes reproduced in *NR* in a misleading, unexpected or erroneous way, possibly in a few cases deliberately to obscure or conceal someone's identity). Robertson's "confabulations" with Geddes in Edinburgh – without any claim that J.M.R.'s scholarly friend Wheeler had also attended at some point on these occasions – were reported in *Sociological Papers*, 1905, p. 122. For Alexander Orr's bookshop, see *NR*, 25.2.1883, p. 121, and *Freethinker*, 4.3.1883, p. 69. For the acquisition of a secular hall in Edinburgh by John Lees and W.A. Wilson, see *NR* for 4.3.1883, p. 139, and 20.5.1883, p. 373 (in the latter case Lees mentioned it while addressing the N.S.S. Annual Conference in Manchester on 13.5.1883).

154 Sir Henry Tyler's efforts to secure prosecution of the *Freethinker* (in which he initially hoped to incriminate Bradlaugh) were subsequently described in detail by Robertson in *Charles Bradlaugh: A Record*, 1894, Vol. 2, Part 2, pp. 316-9 and 324-5, where, in Tyler's lifetime, J.M.R. openly branded as "malicious" aspects of the Tory grandee's anti-secularist mindset and behaviour. See also Tribe, op. cit. 1971, p. 219, and Royle, op. cit. 1980, pp. 272-3. For Robertson's financial contribution to the Defence Fund in late 1882, see *Freethinker*, 19.11.1882, p. 363. J.M.R.'s contribution to the Christmas 1882 number of the *Freethinker* was probably "A Talk with Mephistopheles" by "Macrobius" (a pseudonym Robertson is understood to have used), with the piece suggesting an acquaintance with the work of Heine,

Coleridge, Bunyan, Burns, Arnold, Goethe, and Byron. Soon afterwards Robertson's letter of protest to the *Freethinker* (regarding the cartoon in the Christmas number) prompted Foote to reply (according to J.M.R.'s recollection) that "to catch the crowd you had to go to their level". This recollection clearly appeared to be consistent with the obituarial comment on Foote by "Mimnermus" (John Smith) that "the popular style he used in writing and speaking was deliberately adopted in order to gain the greatest possible number of adherents for Freethought" (*LG* for December 1915, p. 189). For Quin's reaction to cartoons in the *Freethinker*, see his *Memoirs of a Positivist*, 1924, pp. 67-70.

155 Robertson's suggestion that the 'fart' cartoon may well have been altered and that accordingly production of the *Freethinker* at this time was liable to prove a less than smooth and straightforward operation appeared to receive some tentative, indirect support from G.H. Taylor, who, commenting on the printer for issues of the *Freethinker* during the summer of 1882, declared that "for July 23 he refuses to print at all, and continuity is saved by a few copies worked from a hand press at the last moment" (*A Chronology of British Secularism*, 1957, p. 15). For Sir Thomas Nelson, see Royle, op. cit. 1980, pp. 272-3, 291. When Harcourt gave the comments quoted, he prefaced them by making it clear he had seen the offending Christmas number of the *Freethinker* (see *NR*, 29.7.1883, p. 69, and *Freethinker*, 5.8.1883, p. 241). Robertson's quoted remarks featured in correspondence with a friend. For Foote's revelation, see his editorial in the *Freethinker*, 20.7.1884, p. 225.

156 For Foote's trials and tribulations, see: J.M.R.'s *HFNC*; the *Freethinker*, *NR* and *SR*, etc.; Jim Herrick, *Vision and Realism*, 1982, p. 12 (where, curiously, Herrick gives Henry

Arthur Kemp's name as William Kemp); and J.M.R. in *Charles Bradlaugh: A Record*, 1894, Vol. 2, Part 2, p. 325. Ramsey (who had run the bookstall at the Hall of Science and been manager of the Freethought Publishing Company set up by Bradlaugh and Besant) resigned as an N.S.S. member and Vice-President in 1886 after Bradlaugh had been pained to discover that he was responsible for a pirated version of Annie Besant's *The Law of Population*. In April 1892 Ramsey and Touzeau Parris were quite prominent freethought participants at a memorable London anarchist funeral attended by thousands (with Mrs. Besant taking temporary care of the deceased's little children): see, inter alia, Quail, *The Slow Burning Fuse*, 1978, pp. 127-8.

157 For Foote's rebuke of the judge ("your sentence is worthy of your creed"), see the *Freethinker*, 11.3.1883, p. 79. On J.M.R.'s regret that he had never been prosecuted for blasphemy, see his comment in *LG* for July 1922, p. 107; although he added in 1923: "I have been at times reminded that writings of mine were not unamenable to the Blasphemy Laws" (*'Hamlet' Once More*, 1923, p, 103n.).

158 The cause of popular education, seen as inseparable from the spirit of free enquiry and a free press, seemed to receive a boost from the fact that by the time of the two protest meetings on Sunday, 11.3.1883, in support of freedom of the press, "the offensive slums round Chambers Street" had been cleared away to make way for the Royal Scottish Museum (where Robertson's friend Thomas Carlaw Martin would become director) and a training institute (see T.C. Smout, *A Century of the Scottish People 1830-1950*, 1986, p. 47, and J. Brian Crossland, *Victorian Edinburgh*, 1966, p. 64). For coverage of the aforementioned two protest meetings, see *EEN*, 12.3.1883, p. 2. For the great and the

good supporting the memorial to Harcourt, see, for example, *Vision and Realism*, pp. 15-6; and for Bradlaugh's open letter to Mr. Justice North, see Robertson in *Charles Bradlaugh: A Record*, 1894, Vol. 2, Part 2, pp. 326-7.

159 See: Edward Royle, op. cit. 1980, p. 56; G.H. Taylor, op. cit. 1957, pp. 8-9; and Sydney Gimson, *Random Recollections of the Leicester Secular Society*, Part 1, March 1932 (unpublished typescript), p. 12.

160 For events relating to J.M. Wheeler's breakdown in 1883 see, inter alia: Annie Besant in *NR*, 18.3.1883, p. 186; J.M.R.'s extensive obituary of Wheeler in *The Reformer*, 15.5.1898; and Odin Dekkers, op. cit. 1998, p. 7.

161 Sir Mortimer Wheeler, *Still Digging*, 1955, pp. 13-5.

162 Foote in the *Freethinker*, 6.1.1901 (quoted in Victor B. Neuburg's Biographical Note in the 1931 Pioneer Press edition of Wheeler's *Footsteps of the Past*, p. v).

163 The quotation is from Robertson's letter of 9.10.1931 to Herbert Cutner (held at the London School of Economics).

164 For Symes feeling "diddled" by Aveling, see the former's article in the *Liberator*, Melbourne, Australia, 4.3.1888 (while Aveling was still alive). An article by Karl Marx (on a history of the International Working Men's Association) appeared in the *Secular Chronicle*, edited by the freethinker Harriet Law, for 4.8.1878, pp. 49-51. For Robertson's belief, held in the 1880s and later, that socialism was possible only in the distant future, see his article in *Progress* for June 1884 on the Bradlaugh-Hyndman debate of 17.4.1884 and also, a century later, *BRUG*, p. 75 et seq. The Eric Hobsbawm quotation comes

from his *Age of Extremes*, 1994, p. 377.

165 On William Archer's attitude to Foote and the prosecuted editor's work, see Charles Archer, *William Archer: Life, Work and Friendships*, 1931, pp. 119-20. For H.G. Farmer's claims regarding Robertson, Archer and Foote, see Farmer's article "William Archer as a Freethinker" in the *Freethinker*, 17.11.1961, p. 367.

166 Whitebrook's tally of fifteen articles – as opposed to Farmer's total of ten – by William Archer appearing in *Progress* during 1883-4 is to be found on pp. 45-6 of his 1993 biography of Archer. Certainly the care with which Farmer wrote his article is called into question by his statement that Foote received his twelve months' prison sentence in "April 1883" – whereas Foote received that sentence in early March, and in late April the prosecution dropped the charge against him in a separate court case. Farmer admitted: "Pretending that I did not know, I wrote Robertson concerning the identity of 'Norman Britton' [Archer's pseudonym]." Farmer claimed that Robertson replied that he was "not at liberty to disclose" that identity. As, Farmer admitted, Robertson "knew that I was friendly with Foote", Robertson may well have suspected, or even known, that Farmer's enquiry was disingenuous. The quotations conveying Robertson's praise of Foote are drawn from *HFNC*.

167 See J.M.R.'s *HFNC*, 1929, pp. 430 and 304 (as well as p. xxxii, for example).

168 For Bright on his Rectorial Address of 22.3.1883, see *The Diaries of John Bright*, 1930 ed., p. 495. The Robertson quotation comes from J.M.R.'s article "Our Drift" in *NR*, 19.5.1889, p. 308. According to Annie Swan, who was an

Edinburgh resident during the 1880s, Bright's sister Mrs. Priscilla Bright Maclaren was intellectually and, indeed, politically active in Edinburgh at about this time (for example, in a group working for votes for women: see Annie Swan, *My Life*, 1934, p. 52); and it seems perfectly possible that Robertson got to hear of Mrs. Bright Maclaren's feminist activity, particularly perhaps as Annie Swan knew not only Bright's sister, but also Robertson's friend Patrick Geddes.

169 J.M.R. in *Progress*, April 1883, p. 221; and in *NR*, 19.4.1891, p. 244.

170 J.M.R., *What To Read*, 1904, p. 11.

171 Information from G.P. Gooch in a face-to-face interview with the present writer.

172 For Robertson on Buckle, see *NR*, 6.5.1883, p. 350 (for brief report by "S." – probably W.E. Snell – on Robertson's lecture); *SR*, 28.4.1883, p. 271; and *What To Read*, p. 11. As regards J.M.R.'s encomium in honour of Herbert Spencer, see the conclusion of his essay on Spencer in *Modern Humanists*, 1891, p. 260. The actual choice of words in Robertson's acclamation of Spencer in 1891 countenanced a perception that J.M.R. did not regard Karl Marx, for example, in such glowing terms (although he would pay a fine yet balanced tribute to Marx in *Buckle and His Critics*, 1895, pp. 432-3). In and before 1891 reliable English translations of parts of *Das Kapital* that had been published were somewhat elusive in Britain. When Marx wrote in a letter in August 1866 that progress was not pure chance but a necessity, he was echoing words that Spencer had used in his *Social Statics* (1851); and in 1873 he apparently sent Spencer a copy of a recently published German edition of *Das Kapital*, Volume 1. "Spencer

foresaw ... that class divisions would become steadily less rigid. ... In this respect, his analysis was shrewder than that of Karl Marx, who expected the opposite to happen ..." (Ralph Blumenau, *Philosophy and Living*, 2002, p. 442).

173 *NR*, 3.6.1883, p. 407; 27.5.1883, p. 398; and 10.6.1883, p. 427 (all touching on Mrs. Besant's opening of the Roxburgh Hall). *NR*, 20.5.1883, pp. 375, 370, 372 (Lees's speech to N.S.S. Conference, Manchester, etc.).

174 J.M.R. in *Charles Bradlaugh: A Record*, 1894, Vol. 2, Part 2, p. 344, Nigel Sinnott, "Annie Besant as a Botanist" in the *Freethinker*, 19.10.1968, p. 332, and Tribe, op. cit. 1971, p. 226 (on Annie Besant and Alice Bradlaugh being refused admission to a botany class at University College, London – on top of other insulting and vindictive bans aimed at them by academically-oriented institutions). *SR*, 12.5.1883, p. 302 – see also p. 318 – and Royle, op. cit. 1980, p. 197 (on Henry George, etc.).

175 For Bradlaugh speaking on Foote, Ramsey and Kemp in May 1883, see *NR*, 20.5.1883, p. 370. For J.M.R. on Foote finding "a larger audience than ever as a lecturer" on his release from prison, see *HFNC*, 1929, p. 430.

176 For interaction between British republicanism and secularism from the late 1870s to at least the early 1880s, see, inter alia, Stan Shipley, *Club Life and Socialism in Mid-Victorian London*, 1971, pp. 34-5, and Edward Royle, op. cit. 1980, p. 20, etc. See also *NR*, 3.6.1883, p. 414, and Antony Taylor, *"Down with the Crown"*, 1999, for J.M.R. in 1887. The Robertson quotation on Emily and Charlotte Brontë appears in *Progress* for June 1883, p. 384. For Bradlaugh's daughter Hypatia see, for example: David Tribe, op. cit. 1971, p. 244

(for her public persona); her account in *NR*, 1.7.1883, p. 7 (for her train journey to Edinburgh); *NR*, 17.6.1883, p. 446, and 24.6.1883, p. 461 – the latter report by John Lees (for her lecture on three Elizabethan writers); and her tribute to Robertson in *LG* for July 1926, pp. 111-2 and *LG* for February 1933, p. 38. On 17.6.1883 Hypatia Bradlaugh's lecture on William Lloyd Garrison, Wendell Phillips and Charles Sumner – "three apostles of freedom", as she called them, who had all attended her father's first lecture on American soil, in New York, in 1873 – may have helped to stimulate Robertson's interest in the American Civil War. Like others, J.M.R. lacked the tools to explore economic experiences of American blacks on either side of the Mason-Dixon Line before and after slavery was formally abolished in 1865. For J.M.R. on Marlowe, etc., see his *Marlowe: A Conspectus*, 1931, and T.S.Eliot, "Christopher Marlowe", 1919, in *Selected Essays*, 1972, ed., p. 120; also *Our Corner* for May 1883, p. 278.

177 For J.M.R. (24.6.1883) on Tennyson, see *SR*, 30.6.1883, p. 414. By July 1887 William Archer seemed more critical of Tennyson and Browning as thinkers than J.M.R.

178 Just as T.C. Martin's January 1883 article on Wordsworth appeared in print before Robertson's *Winnowings from Wordsworth*; so, on 23 September 1883, Martin lectured to the Edinburgh Secular Society on Walt Whitman just over a year before Robertson's *Walt Whitman, Poet and Democrat* was published. Perhaps Thomas Carlaw Martin in some way encouraged or influenced J.M.R. to start, fashion or complete his own work on Wordsworth and on Whitman. (It may also seem a curious coincidence that Martin should lecture to the Scottish Secular Union on 30 May 1880 on "The Life and Works of the late Professor Clifford" – the only time Martin is known to have lectured on a scientist during the years

Robertson lived in Edinburgh – when Robertson was the only Edinburgh secularist of that time whose serious reading, to judge from Harold Laski's testimony, is understood to have been personally guided by W.K. Clifford less than a decade earlier.)   On the vaccination controversy in Britain from about 1882 onwards, see: Wemyss Reid (ed.), *Memoirs and Correspondence of Lyon Playfair*, 1899, p. 297 (opposition to compulsory vaccination in June 1883); *SR*, 14.7.1883, p. 31, and 21.7.1883, p. 46 (J.M.R.'s lecture of 15.7.1883); *Evening Express* (Edinburgh), 27.1. 1883, p. 2 (newspaper's direct personal attack on Government clerk W.E. Snell, a conscientious objector to compulsory vaccination); *NR*, 29.10. 1882, p. 296, and 4.2.1883, p. 74 (sympathetic coverage of Snell case); J.M.R., "The Truth about Vaccination", February 1897?, p. 2 ("my editor objected to any comment on the case": indeed, no reference to the Snell case has been found in *EEN* for the period of a week beginning 21.10.1882); J.M.R., *Courses of Study*, 1932 ed., p. 432 ("vexed question"); *The Observer*, 14.4.1974, p. 2.

179 For the Edinburgh secularists' excursion to Gullane Moor, see the account by "J.L." (taken to be John Lees) in *NR*, 5.8.1883, p. 92. For previous thanks to Nicholson and Chamberlain, see *NR*, 3.6.1883, p. 407 (regarding the opening of Roxburgh Hall). For George Berry's long association with Charles Nicholson, whose daughter Hannah he married, and also his acting as hon. secretary of the Edinburgh Sunday Society (still extant in 1902), see Berry's letter, 15.7.1902, to Hypatia Bradlaugh Bonner: item 2695, N.S.S. Bradlaugh Collection.

180 On Sunday outings by British freethinkers and secularists between about 1875 and about 1895, see Edward Royle, op. cit. 1980, p. 141 (although he does not notice such

excursions organised in Scotland). For Alice Bradlaugh, her Edinburgh lecture, and her work, interests, personality, etc., see *NR*, 19.8.1883, p. 125; Hypatia Bradlaugh Bonner's tribute to Robertson in *LG* for July 1926, later reprinted as a leaflet (regarding her sister Alice and "the scandal of the holy neighbourhood"); David Tribe, op. cit. 1971, p. 269; Royle, op. cit. 1980, pp. 140, 172, 317-9; and J.M.R. in *Charles Bradlaugh: A Record*, 1894, Vol. 2, Part 2, p. 401.

181 The Robertson quotation on George Eliot comes from *Progress* for August 1883, p. 118. Some eight months later his friend William Archer (using the pseudonym "N. Britton" in the same journal) praised J.M.R.'s contribution on George Eliot as follows: "We, of this generation, can sum up our obligations to her [Eliot] … An able effort in this direction, from the pen of Mr. J. Robertson, has already appeared in the pages of *Progress*, and I have no desire to do over again what he has already done so well." Archer's praise found expression in his piece "George Eliot's Essays" in *Progress* for April 1884, pp. 215-6. Yet, somewhat curiously, H. George Farmer would have readers believe that Robertson – presumably, at least in part, through a marked sense of modesty – deliberately ignored this article in which he was lavishly praised by a dear friend who was also an esteemed literary critic. "George Eliot's Essays" was specifically identified (by title) by Farmer as one of Archer's articles in *Progress* which Robertson, out of supposed pique at Foote's success, would allegedly intentionally, even arbitrarily, exclude from *William Archer as Rationalist*, published in 1925, ten years after Foote's death. (See reference note 165 and material relating to it in the present work.) For Walter Allen's critique see his *George Eliot*, 1965, pp. 180, 185.

182 See *HFNC*, p. 525, on George Eliot. For J.M.R.'s paper

on the theatre, read on 26.8.1883, see the notice by "S." (almost certainly W.E. Snell) in *NR*, 2.9.1883, p. 157; and for the review of William Archer's book on Henry Irving, see *EEN*, 10.9.1883, p. 2.

183 For Henry Irving as Benedick, and for the leader writer (almost certainly J.M.R.) on Edinburgh literary life in 1883, see *EEN*, 11.9.1883, p. 2. The striking feminist leading article is in *EEN*, 24.9.1883, p. 2. For William Archer's admiration, see reference note 181.

184 Britain's first female Prime Minister was also an Oxbridge graduate (Mrs. Thatcher, as she became, studied at Oxford during and immediately after the Second World War). In *The Absent-Minded Imperialists*, 2004, Bernard Porter seemed to suggest (pp. 296-8) that it may not have been entirely coincidence that the male-oriented British Empire finally collapsed under a female Premier, Margaret Thatcher, who took Britain in a more free market direction, and who "gave Britain's two last substantial colonies away" (pp. 303, 297) in the form of Rhodesia (Zimbabwe) and Hong Kong. But with both territories it had become increasingly clear, for some time before Thatcher entered Downing Street in 1979, that the duration of British colonial or white rule was distinctly limited. Moreover, Clement Attlee's Labour Government, which started a post-1945 process of decolonization, frowned upon free market economics, and, during her premiership and later, Thatcher's public image was more "macho" than that of many contemporary British male politicians.

185 For Robert Donald on J.M.R., see the former's contribution in *The British Weekly*, 4.11.1920, p. 91, and in *EEN*, 26.5.1923, p. 8 – as well as H.A. Taylor's biography, *Robert Donald*, 1934, p. 33. As Donald joined the *Edinburgh*

Evening News at least a couple of years after Archer left it, the basis for Donald's statement that William Archer "was more restrained" as leader writer than Robertson remains unclear.

186 Standring in *The Republican* for April 1883, p. 484, and for October 1883, p. 535.

187 For a different perspective see Paul Adelman in his *Victorian Radicalism*, 1984, p. 105. For J.M.R.'s article, see *Our Corner* for October 1883, pp. 213-8.

188 Annie Besant's comments appeared in *NR*, 14.10.1883, p. 247. The Joseph Chamberlain quotation relating to the American Civil War is drawn from Adelman's *Victorian Radicalism*, p. 106, citing J.L. Garvin's *Life of Joseph Chamberlain*, Vol. 1, 1932, p. 345. For J.M.R. see *Our Corner* for November 1883, pp. 274-81.

189 J.M.R. in *The Reformer*, 15.7.1897, p. 124. Already in 1892 (in *NR*, 3.4.1892, p. 212) Robertson critically reviewed his 1883 essay as follows: "as long ago as 1883 … I … sought to show reasons why the Radical ideal should not be Home Rule but true Union. The fundamental error of that essay, from the standpoint it took (which of course was far removed from that of Unionism so-called), was the failure to realise that it was already too late to argue so. I urged that Liberals ought for a generation back to have been conciliating Ireland by treating Irishmen as an integral part of the population …" He then added that Gladstone "did not attempt to govern Ireland through Irishmen, or to put Irishmen in his Cabinets. He imprisoned Mr. Parnell … and Sir William Harcourt carried through the worst Coercion Act on record, almost. … in 1883 … I argued that … the only union worth having was that signified by unity of law, of citizenship, of rights, of commerce,

of intercourse. That ideal has no place in Unionism ...The United States in 1861 *had* the Federal constitution for which Home Rulers are still contending: the Unionist policy is to *refuse* the constitution which the Northern States fought to maintain. ..." (Italics as per Robertson's original.)

190 For Luther see *EEN* leading article, 10.11.1883, p. 2 and J.M.R.'s *HF*, 1936, Vol. 1, p. 483 (the latter also for Calvin). Robertson's 1936 work sheds light on background factors relating to the German Peasants' Revolt, which he addressed directly, if quite briefly, in *The Germans*, 1916, pp. 150, 156-7, etc. See also J.M.R.'s *A Short History of Christianity,* 1913 ed.

191 For India economically at a low ebb in the 1880s, see David Tribe, op. cit. 1971, p. 255. The Bradlaugh quotation on India is drawn from his Northampton speech on 19.11.1883, reproduced in Arthur Bonner's edition of *Speeches by Charles Bradlaugh*, 1890, p. 45. The Robertson quotations on India, George Eliot and the Jews are taken from pp. 112-8 of J.M.R.'s essay "George Eliot on National Sentiment" (1883) in his *Essays in Sociology*, 1904, Vol. 2 (except for the 1891 quotation, from *NR*, 2.8.1891, p. 65). See also Josephine McDonagh, *George Eliot*, 1997, p.72, and Todd Endelman, *The Jews of Britain, 1656 to 2000*, 2002, pp. 151-2, 296. Robertson's sentence "There is no reasonable drawing of the line possible" on p. 107 of his "George Eliot on National Sentiment" – dated 1883 – stylistically added weight to the high probability that he wrote the militant leading article (on Foote's imprisonment) in the *Edinburgh Evening News* for 6 March 1883 which included the sentence "There is no drawing of the line possible". Information about H.H. Almond has been gleaned from *Imperialism and Popular Culture* (ed. John M. MacKenzie, 1986), which also mentions Robertson's

1899 book *Patriotism and Empire*; although no evidence has come to light that either J.M.R. or the headmaster of Loretto School (from 1862 to 1903) directly commented on the other.

192 See *NR*, 16.9.1883, p. 183, for the Edinburgh Secular Society Annual Meeting, and *NR*, 4.11.1883, p. 302, and 11.11.1883, pp. 317, 326, for the Joseph Symes farewell lectures and soirée. For more general information about Symes consult Edward Royle, op. cit. 1980, pp. 103, 123, etc., and Nigel Sinnott's 1977 study of the "flower of atheism".

193 For Robertson's lectures in Edinburgh and Glasgow in late 1883, see *NR*, 21.10.1883, p. 270, and 18.11.1883, p. 334, respectively. Criticism of aspects of T.H. Huxley's attitude to religion runs like a thread through the tapestry of J.M.R.'s literary work over many years. See, for example: *LG* for November 1923, p. 180; *LG* for September 1913, p. 134; *NR*, 25.6.1893, pp. 411-2; *The Dynamics of Religion*; *Modern Humanists* (pp. 146-7, 242-3) and *Modern Humanists Reconsidered*; *HFNC*. But perhaps Robertson's most extensive treatment of Huxley is to be found in his article "Huxley and Agnosticism" in the October 1895 issue (pp. 23-38) of *The Free Review*, which appeared very soon after Huxley's death. Huxley's *Hume* (1879) was consulted by Lenin, most probably at the British Museum Library, where Robertson may have been present or even noticed him while working on his 1908 (second) edition of *Courses of Study*, which assessed Huxley's *Hume*.

194 J.M.R. covered aspects of the litigation involving Bradlaugh and Newdegate in his Part 2 of *Charles Bradlaugh: A Record*, 1894, and in his 1920 life-story *Charles Bradlaugh*.

195 One of Bradlaugh's earliest works – dating from May

1850 – quoted from Paine (David Tribe, op. cit. 1971, p. 23). For the 29.1.1884 anniversary commemoration in Edinburgh see John Lees's report in *NR*, 10.2.1884, p. 93. Information regarding the 29.1.1821 celebration in Edinburgh of Paine's birth in 1737 derives from Richard Gimbel, *The Resurgence of Thomas Paine*, 1961; for English celebrations between 1863 and 1890 see Royle, op. cit. 1980, pp. 185, 140.

196 Robertson focused attention on Paine in his *History of Freethought* (various editions), his introduction in 1896 to *The Rights of Man* and, a some years later, to *The Age of Reason*, and in his article "The Rehabilitation of Paine" in the *R.P.A. Annual* for 1910, for example. For the Edinburgh Secular Society evening meeting on 2.3.1884, see *NR*, 9.3.1884, p. 174; and for the terrible incident which resulted in the death of the hall managers' daughter, see Annie Besant's report in *NR*, 30.3.1884, pp. 213-4 (and *NR*, 15.6.1884, p. 414, for the humane conduct presentation to "a young girl, a Freethinker", as Mrs. Besant had characterized her). That primitive superstition was still in evidence in Edinburgh some three and a half years later was indicated by the fact that the burning of Newsome's Circus in the city in early September 1887, very shortly before Bradlaugh was due to speak there, was regarded by a letter-writer in *EEN*, 14.9.1887, p. 2, as "a visitation from God caused by the impious action of the proprietor in letting the building to that arch-infidel and blasphemer, Charles Bradlaugh". This letter-writer's words were reproduced in *NR*, 25.9.1887, while Mrs Besant was still co-editor with Bradlaugh. J.M.R.'s longstanding detestation of cruelty was avowed, at the end of a lengthy, specially written contribution by him, in *NR*, 8.1.1893, p. 29; and his 13.4.1884 lecture was publicized in *NR*, 13.4.1884, p. 254, and 20.4.1884, p. 270 (in the latter case by John Lees, it seems).

197 In a letter published in *The British Weekly*, 11.11.1920, p. 110, the Scottish journalist Hector Carsewell Macpherson, who had worked on the *Edinburgh Evening News* for three decades, revealed that J.M.R. had been the *EEN*'s drama critic. But Macpherson had also been the newspaper's leader writer and drama critic during the 1880s (according to his son's *Memoir*, 1925, p. 10). As he was some five years older than Robertson, had joined the newspaper about a year earlier than J.M.R., and as neither Robertson nor William Archer seems to have mentioned that Robertson immediately became drama critic on joining the *News* in 1878, it may be presumed that Macpherson preceded J.M.R. in this role, and, indeed, as it turned out, that Robertson only became the paper's drama critic not more than about two years before he (J.M.R.) left the *News*. This suggested time-scale could help to explain the timing of the latter's 26.8.1883 lecture on the theatre and of the leader – believed to have been penned by Robertson – in *EEN*, 10.9.1883, reviewing Archer's book on the actor Henry Irving. For Salvini's impact on Robertson, see the latter's *The State of Shakespeare Study*, 1931, pp. 40-1, and *Elizabethan Literature*, 1914, p. 198. Laski's recollection of J.M.R.'s ecstatic recitation of lines from *King Lear* comes from his entry on Robertson in *D.N.B. 1931-1940*, 1949, p. 736.

198 For Salvini's impact, in the role of Othello, on Stanislavski, see the latter's *My Life in Art* in the Benedetti translation, 2008, pp. 142, 353, 356. For the British Secular Union and the attraction of socialism, see: G.H. Taylor, *A Chronology of British Secularism*, 1957, pp. 12, 16; David Tribe, *100 Years of Freethought*, 1967, p. 113, and op. cit. 1971, p. 248; Edward Royle, op. cit. 1980, pp. 18, 232-4. For J.M.R.'s response to the Bradlaugh-Hyndman debate see: *Progress* for June 1884, pp. 347-54; George Standring's *The Republican* for June

1884, p. 20; and the unsigned report in *Justice*, 24.5.1884, p. 6, which may have represented an early occasion when Henry Mayers Hyndman noticed Robertson and his spoken or written work.

199 For Robertson's attitude to socialism at this time, see his June 1884 article in *Progress* and also the exchanges in *NR* on socialism between him and the individualist 'D.' (Joseph Hiam Levy) which spanned the issues for 15.6.1884 (p. 402: Levy's initial article in this debate) and 27.7.1884 (p. 76: a letter of reply from J.M.R.), with an intervening letter of comment by J.M.R. (29.6.1884, p. 503) and a two-part article by Levy (6.7.1884, pp. 17-8, and 13.7.1884, pp. 33-5).

200 J.M.R., *Progress* for May 1884, pp. 295-6.

201   For Robertson's Scottish history lectures, see *NR*, 20.4.1884, p. 270, 25.5.1884, p. 366, and 6.7.1884, p. 30. For his reporting Bradlaugh's trial in London, see *Charles Bradlaugh: A Record*, 1894, Vol. 2, Part 2, p. 354 and footnote, and *EEN*, 13.6.1884, 14.6.1884 and 16.6.1884.

202 Accounts of the Burns statue unveiling in London appeared in *EEN*, 28.7.1884, p. 2, *The Times*, same date, p. 3, and Edward Goodwillie, *The World's Memorials of Robert Burns*, 1911, pp. 59-61. "The Art of Burns" was republished by J.M.R. in his *New Essays towards a Critical Method*, 1897; while his "Burns and His Race" appeared in *The Monthly Criterion* for January and February 1928.

203 "The Economics of Genius" resurfaced in J.M.R.'s *Essays in Sociology*, 1904, Vol. 2. "The Art of Keats" was republished in *New Essays towards a Critical Method*, where he modestly declared in his Preface (p. vii): "the essay on

Keats would hardly have been undertaken had Mr. [Sidney] Colvin's admirable monograph been in existence in 1884."

204 For Robertson's "shrine" for Keats, see J.P. Gilmour in *HF*, 1936, pp. xiv-xv. For the Diderot centenary and the unveiling of the Denis Diderot statue in Paris, see the *Freethinker*, 27.7.1884, p. 237, and *NR*, 10.8.1884, p. 104; and for awareness in Edinburgh of Diderot during his lifetime, see John Lough, *The Encyclopédie in Eighteenth-Century England and Other Studies*, 1970, pp. 14-5. The Robertson quotation about Diderot is drawn from p. 68 of "Carlyle on Diderot" in *Progress* for August 1884; and J.M.R.'s last, positive, word on the great Encyclopedist is to be found in *HF*, 1936.

205 As co-editor of *NR* at this time, Annie Besant would have been aware that in that journal for 6.7.1884 "J.L." (almost certainly John Lees) referred to Robertson's lecture a week earlier on medieval dimensions of Scottish history as "exceptionally interesting", and that in the *Freethinker* for 27.7.1884 "Sugar Plums" (presumably G.W. Foote, recently released from prison) described Robertson's article "Carlyle on Diderot" as "admirable". She gave her Edinburgh lecture on 6 July (when – as indicated by her biographer A.H. Nethercot – she was disconcertingly heckled by the socialist Andreas Scheu, who had thereby continued his heckling of her in London). For the Bradlaugh-Besant holiday break by Loch Long, see Bradlaugh's contribution "Fishing in the Western Highlands" in Mrs. Besant's *OC* for September 1884.

206 The date of J.M.R.'s address to the Democratic Federation's Edinburgh Branch is in *Justice*, 10.5.1884, p. 7. Bradlaugh described John Lees as "a very loyal and devoted Edinburgh friend" ("Fishing in the Western Highlands", *OC*

for September 1884, p. 138). Annie Besant's announcement of J.M.R.'s appointment appeared in *NR*, 24.8.1884, p. 135. The J.H. Levy quotation beginning "One can enter the lists" is to be found in *NR*, 6.7.1884, p. 17. For Robertson's letter of 1.11.1884 to Patrick Geddes, see Odin Dekkers, op. cit. 1998, p. 8 and n.

207 For Aveling's resignation see Tribe, op. cit. 1971, pp. 230, 360, and, to some extent, Royle, op. cit. 1980, pp. 106, 123-4. J.M.R.'s "The Manners of Public Life" was published in *NR*, 24.8.1884, pp. 130-1. This was followed a week later by his article "Government by Party" (*NR*, 31.8.1884, pp. 147-8), from which the quotations beginning "The proper business of the head of a department" are taken. The 1897 quotation regarding "the vice in our Constitution" is drawn from Robertson's article "The Power of Making War" in *The Reformer*, 15.4.1897, which indicated his awareness of the power British Prime Ministers had or thought they had. In terms suggesting he felt unable to be more explicit in public, Robertson wrote in that 1897 article of the then P.M. Lord Salisbury (on his third premiership): "I have trustworthy private information to the effect that during the Zanzibar difficulty with Germany he took up the position of declaring that a certain course on the German side would be regarded by the British Government as an act of hostility. That course was defiantly taken by the German Government; and Lord Salisbury pocketed the affront." A century later Salisbury's biographer Andrew Roberts acknowledged "another of his gaffes" relating to his latter-day Africa policy (p. 530 of Roberts's book). Moreover, in *The Reformer* (15.7.1897, p. 123) J.M.R. recognised that "the work of the House of Commons grows heavier from decade to decade"; and this clearly had implications for the machinery of Government. Robertson evidently hoped that the spread of more democratic

and accountable forms of government would help to reduce the chances of statesmen and politicians recklessly resorting to war.

208 J.M.R.'s "Why Have a Second Chamber?" was reprinted, with additions, in *The Free Review* for December 1894, edited by him. In December 1884 the N.S.S. resolved to affiliate with the People's League (*NR*, 7.12.84, p. 378: see also p. 371). David Tribe (op. cit. 1971, p. 243) and Edward Royle (op. cit. 1980, p. 206) give two different titles for the People's League, neither of which corresponds to the People's League for the Abolition of the Hereditary Legislative Chamber. Even decades later Chris Williams' *A Companion to Nineteenth Century Britain* (2004, p. 171) would refer to "the People's League for the Abolition of the Hereditary *Legislature*" (emphasis added by the present writer).

209 For declining hostility to the Victorian monarchy and the growth of British imperialism, see, for example, Royle, op. cit. 1980, p. 205, last para. "The Persistence of Royalism" appeared on pages 161-2 of *NR*, 7.9.1884. The final quotation incorporating Robertson's predictions in 1895 is to be found in his *Buckle and His Critics*, 1895, p. 313. Of the four belligerent empires swept away as a result of the First World War, all were based on a form of more or less autocratic monarchism.

210 Regarding Stewart Headlam, it may be noted that blasphemy laws were abolished in England and Wales in 2008, though not in Scotland, where, by that time, the last prosecution for blasphemy was in 1843. His Edinburgh lectures were advertised in *NR*, 31.8.1884, p. 159; and for Robertson's comments in 1888 see *NR*, 21.10.1888, p. 267. Details of Headlam's Guild are drawn from Chris Bryant's

Possible Dreams, 1996.

211 In *NR*, 17.8.1884, p. 125, John Lees declared: "EDINBURGH. – On Sunday Mr. Arthur B. Moss lectured here for the first time ..." This statement was almost certainly correct if it referred to Roxburgh Hall, but not if it referred – as it seemed – to Edinburgh as such: for Moss lectured twice in the Scottish capital, to the Scottish Secular Union, on 15.2.1880 (see *NR*, 22.2.1880, p. 126). For background information on Moss before he would have met Robertson, see the section headed "From Across the Tweed" in the present writer's narrative covering 1880, with associated reference note 100. See also, inter alia, J.P. Gilmour's article in *LG* for June 1929, p. 105, praising Moss, and the latter's contribution (on J.M.R.) in the *Freethinker*, 5.9.1915, pp. 570-1. By 1886 both Moss and Robertson were appointed approved N.S.S. lecturers (Royle, op. cit. 1980, p. 151); and, towards the end of their lives, both men became members of the General Committee formed to celebrate the centenary of Bradlaugh's birth.

212 "Some Slumming", from which the quotations are taken, covers pp. 178-9 in *NR*, 14.9.1884. By way of background Thomas Johnston's *The History of the Working Classes in Scotland*, 1946 ed., paints a vivid picture of the stark realities confronting poverty-stricken and downtrodden Victorians north of the Tweed. Robertson's interest in sanitation issues was indicated in his comments on a railway telegraph clerk's working life; and in his section of the 1894 biography of Bradlaugh he twice referred to the agitator's ultimately fruitful campaign for the pollution of Loch Long by Glasgow sewage to be stopped (pp. 380-1, 408). A doctor who had been a medical student in Edinburgh in the 1870s, and who published his reminiscences in 1918 under the pseudonym

"Alisma", recorded a visit he himself had made as a student to Edinburgh slums, but did not mention the sanitation aspects. In that respect J.M.R. seemed more in tune than the doctor with what a later generation would call health and safety concerns. Among the families both men met in the slums, "Alisma", crawling through a ramshackle doorway, found a breadwinner "in the last stage of tuberculosis", while, in a boarded up part of a passageway, Robertson met a man "dying of heart disease". "Alisma" noticed the incongruous proximity of slums, with all the misery and suffering they encapsulated, to an Edinburgh church with its hymns and praises to Almighty God; while J.M.R. pointed out that exploitative slum landlords were known to act as church elders. Moreover, Robertson no doubt had his Edinburgh experience in mind when in an 1886 lecture on "Equality" (printed in his *Essays in Ethics*, 1903) he declared, discreetly enough: "When, a year or two ago, I gave some time to the investigation of slum life in a large town, hardly anything – not even the grime and the ignominy – impressed me more than the extent to which moral gradations were recognised among those ill-starred multitudes."

213 A historian of modern Scotland, T.C. Smout, has pronounced Patrick Geddes "the most original [town] planner of the late nineteenth century" (*A Century of the Scottish People*, *1830-1950*, 1986, p. 56). Information on Geddes in 1884 and later may be gleaned from: Philip Boardman, *Patrick Geddes: Maker of the Future*, 1944, pp. 74-5, and, same author, *The Worlds of Patrick Geddes*, 1978, p. 73; and Philip Mairet, *Pioneer of Sociology: The Life and Letters of Patrick Geddes*, 1957, pp. 51, 68-9, inter alia. *Catastrophe: Europe Goes to War 1914* by Max Hastings, 2013, provides an indication (p. 208) that the authorities in Britain drew, or tried to draw, recruits for the British Army from the slums. J.M.R.'s "The Problem of the Army", from which the

quotations are taken, covers pp. 210-11 in *NR*, 28.9.1884. In what is believed to have been Robertson's contribution to the Christmas 1882 number of the *Freethinker* (see reference note 154), the conversationalist Mephistopheles called the army "a body of hired slayers, whose profession, from the point of view of a purely rational morality, is the most grossly immoral in existence" (p. 13, in language very similar to that used in "The Problem of the Army" by Robertson, who had lectured on "Rational Morality" to the Scottish Secular Union in Edinburgh on 2 March 1879).

214 Thoreau delivered his attack in 1847 in a lecture published in 1849 as *Resistance to Civil Government*. Robertson's *Modern Humanists*, 1891, would include a passing reference (p. 133) to the mutual influence flowing between Thoreau and Emerson during an era when the former "gave Emerson the right lead on the slavery question". Bakunin, who referred to "perpetually belligerent states", declared in *Statism and Anarchy*, 1873: "to exist, a state must become an invader of other states." A perusal of *NR* between 12.4.1885 and 3.5.1885 suggests that J.M.R. studied Bakunin at about the time of those two dates. J.M.R.'s "International Amenities", from which the quotations in the narrative are taken, covers pp. 196-7 in *NR*, 21.9.1884. In his later study *Patriotism and Empire*, Robertson summed up a key element in his own thinking when he quite wittily remarked (p. 138): "Patriotism, conventionally defined as love of country, now turns out rather obviously to stand for love of more country." The authorities and various leaders of opinion in European empires fighting on different sides in the First World War professed to be heavily indebted to Christian belief and principles.

215 Looking back in October 1893, J.M.R. – perhaps somewhat surprisingly – declared of *NR*, of which, between

1891 and 1893, he was the last editor: "it has fought … above all for Peace. I believe that no British journal, excepting those solely devoted to such advocacy, has more constantly wrought for International Peace than the *National Reformer*" (*NR*, 1.10.1893, p. 210). Robertson's role as a leading member of the British peace movement during a period of twenty years or more from the early 1890s to the onset of the First World War is detailed in Paul Laity's *The British Peace Movement 1870-1914*, 2001. J.M.R.'s years of service in this field included his involvement in London with such bodies as the South Place Ethical Society, the Rainbow Circle discussion group, the International Arbitration and Peace Association, the International Arbitration League (on which see G.A. Wells (ed.), *J.M. Robertson*, 1987, p. 52), and the Rationalist Peace Society (of which he was President between 1910 and 1921). For Shelley the left-wing poet see Stan Shipley, *Club Life and Socialism in Mid-Victorian London*, 1971, p. 28. J.M.R.'s "Shelley and Poetry" was reprinted, with amendments by him, in his book *New Essays towards a Critical Method*, 1897, where his 1884 essay "The Art of Keats" was also reprinted; and in 1933 T.S. Eliot devoted an essay to "Shelley and Keats". In his essay on Keats Robertson criticised one of the latter's poems for not marking "the intense Dantean vibration of inward life"; whereas T.S. Eliot discovered in 1950 that "Shelley's *The Triumph of Life* contained 'some of the greatest and most Dantesque lines in English'" (Stephen Spender, *T.S. Eliot*, 1976, p. 145). By 1932-33 both Robertson and Eliot had become more critical of Shelley than they had been in their youth (see also J.M.R. in *NR*, 31.7.1892, p. 66). Robertson's admission of his "doubtless rather juvenile" effort is located in his letter in *LG* for December 1928, p. 222. Leo Storm seems to have been the first literary critic or commentator to suggest that J.M.R. had exerted an influence on both T.S. Eliot and F.R. Leavis regarding Shelley (for which see Odin

Dekkers, op. cit. 1998, pp. 245-6, 273, and G.A. Wells (ed.), *J.M. Robertson*, 1987, p. 59). See also F.R. Leavis himself in his *Anna Karenina and Other Essays*, 1967, p. 182 ("T.S. Eliot as Critic").

216 The Robertson quotations expressing his thoughts about Whitman are drawn from the text (fifty or so pages) of J.M.R.'s 1884 book; but the reader may also care to consult Odin Dekkers, op. cit. 1998, pp. 246-50, 259. For Anne Gilchrist's involvement, see *The Letters of Anne Gilchrist and Walt Whitman*, ed. Thomas B. Harned. The claim that Robertson's book on Whitman "deserves a high place in Whitman literature" is made on p. 200 of Harold Blodgett's *Walt Whitman in England*, 1934.

217 "Mr. Howells' Novels" appeared unsigned in the *Westminster and Foreign Quarterly Review* for October 1884, pp. 347-75; but it would be reprinted in J.M.R.'s *Essays towards a Critical Method*, 1889, and in part by Edwin Cady and David Frazier in the U.S.A. in 1962. Comparing Howells disadvantageously with Tourguenief/Turgenev as a literary artist, as Robertson did, was rather ironic as in 1873 "imitation of Turgénieff's fidelity to life was set as a model of excellence for the realistic novel" by Howells himself (in the words of Elizabeth Brownson Stanton in her 1942 Doctor of Philosophy dissertation, p. 84, on William Dean Howells for the Ohio State University). In *Clyde Fitch and His Letters*, 1924, Montrose J. Moses and Virginia Gerson indicated that Robertson's future wife Maud, in her youth, had met Clyde Fitch by about 1886 - thereafter becoming friendly with him – and that, following her marriage to J.M.R. in 1893, her husband had met Fitch by September 1894 (if not earlier). Certainly on 1.9.1894, from his address in Chelsea, Clyde Fitch wrote of the Robertson couple: "Maud and John are

gone, and I miss them." (See Moses and Gerson, pp. 29, 36, 42, 45, 93, and, for Fitch-Howells correspondence, 257-9.) Fitch may have provided information enabling J.M.R. to refer (in *The Saxon and the Celt*, 1897, p. 122) to W.D. Howells as "privately one of the most amiable of men" – with that phrase in itself suggesting some personal knowledge of Howells or contact with someone who had.

218 See reference note 197 for presumed background to J.M.R.'s work as a drama critic. Regarding his early ambition to write plays and novels, see G.A. Wells (ed.), op. cit. 1987, p. 14, citing *LG* for January 1927.

219 For J.M.R. on Henry Drummond, see, inter alia: *NR*, 12.10.1884, p. 253; *NR*, 19.8.1888, p. 117; and *Courses of Study*, 1932 ed., p. 122. For F.J.A. Hort and Elliott-Binns on Drummond, see, respectively, Arthur Hort's edition of his father's *Life and Letters*, Vol. 2, 1896, p. 340 (letter of 22.2.1886) and Binns' *English Thought, 1860-1900*. For the Labour M.P.s, see J. Rose, *The Intellectual Life of the British Working Classes*, 2001, p. 42.

220 For the dropping of Aveling's articles on Drummond's *Natural Law in the Spiritual World*, see A.H. Nethercot, *The First Five Lives of Annie Besant*, 1961, p. 220. See also Royle, op. cit. 1980, p. 158. (For Drummond at Stirling High School, see the history of the School, 1904, p. 307, compiled by A.F. Hutchison, who knew Drummond personally.) For George Dillon's Edinburgh lectures, see his material, as published in a new edition in 1950, under the title *Grand Orient Freemasonry Unmasked*. The fullest accounts that have come to light regarding Bradlaugh's relations with freemasons of the Grand Orient are to be found in J.P. Gilmour (ed.), *Champion of Liberty: Charles Bradlaugh*, 1933, pp. 327-9, contribution

by Hypatia Bradlaugh Bonner, and pp. 203-6 of her part of the biography *Charles Bradlaugh: A Record*, 1894 (where, in his part, Robertson dealt with other aspects of Bradlaugh's life and work). The two historians who in 1978 acclaimed Alexander Whyte – in particular for his defence of William Robertson Smith – were Andrew Drummond and James Bulloch in *The Church in Late Victorian Scotland 1874-1900*, 1978, pp. 54-7. For J.M.R. on Whyte see *LG* for December 1927, p. 208, and *The Monthly Criterion* for February 1928, "Burns and His Race" (II), p. 162. For Whyte's pioneering work in Scotland on behalf of Dante – particularly during 1876-7 at the Edinburgh Philosophical Institution – see G.F. Barbour, *The Life of Alexander Whyte*, October 1925, pp. 177-8. Referring to Robertson's essay on "The Art of Keats", which was originally published in 1884, the academic A.E. Hancock (in *John Keats: A Literary Biography*, 1908, p. 123) would query his assertion that *Hyperion* lacks "the intense Dantean vibration of inward life". But as Robertson in his essay on Keats also quoted (*OC* for July 1884, p. 43) Carlyle on Dante, the possibility remains that J.M.R. came to Dante through Carlyle, whom he much studied, rather than – or at least as much as – through Whyte. In 1891 Robertson declared: "Browning has given me … a larger number of hours of vivid interest than any other poet, excepting Shakspere, Dante, and Homer" (*NR*, 19.4.1891, p. 244).

221 "The Art of Keats" (on p. 42) included quite an extensive and – for Robertson's known written work up to at least July 1884 – frank if relatively uncommon reference by him to "the sexual instincts". (See *BRUG*, p. 66, for another such reference dating from 1894.) In October 1884 J.M.R.'s "Shelley and Poetry" (*OC*, p. 346) alluded in passing to "a charm in Wordsworth's distillation of reflexion and feeling". The fact that Wordsworth wrote a poem about the island of

Arran might have provided an added attraction for Robertson. But reading Wordsworth does not seem to have had quite the dramatic impact on him that it had on John Stuart Mill as recorded in the latter's autobiography; and, unlike Thomas Carlaw Martin (on 20 August 1882), J.M.R. does not appear to have given a lecture on Wordsworth to Edinburgh secularists during the early 1880s, not to mention the late 1870s. Finally, a letter of 15.1.1885 from J.M.R. to Patrick Geddes mentioned the prospect of a Symposium discussion (see G.A. Wells (ed.), *J.M. Robertson*, 1987, p. 24). For the Edinburgh Symposium see also Robertson's letters of 1.11.1884 and 10.12.1926 to Geddes (in the National Library of Scotland). See also reference note 218 and, for Wordsworth-Whitman similarities, F.O. Matthiessen's *American Renaissance*, 1941, pp. 613-14.

222 For J.M.R.'s farewell to the Edinburgh secularists and freethinkers on 10.10.1884 see *NR*, 12.10.1884, p. 247 (Annie Besant's report). For particulars of John Lees's death on 12.12.1896, see his death certificate issued by the authorities in Scotland. The fact that he "was killed on the railway … near his home", in the words of his long-standing secularist colleague J.F. Dewar, was recorded in the *Freethinker*, 27.12.1896, p. 828. On his arrival in London Robertson occupied one of the extra rooms in Mrs. Besant's large house, where two women friends of hers were also lodgers (Gertrude M. Williams, *The Passionate Pilgrim: A Life of Annie Besant*, 1931, p. 152).

NOTES ON A SELECTION OF ROBERTSON'S WRITINGS

(arranged alphabetically according to the title, followed generally by the year of first publication in book form)

The Baconian Heresy (1913)

This monumental, path-breaking book all but destroyed the case for Francis Bacon's authorship of the plays attributed to Shakespeare. Robertson critically examined claims for Bacon's authorship relating to or based on legal allusions, legal phraseology, the alleged classical scholarship of the plays, coincidences of phrase in Shakespeare and Bacon, their prose style, their vocabularies, their intellectual interests, and aspects of their known lives and personalities. Almost as an aside Robertson referred (p. 531) to a "proof of Bacon's aloofness from the contemporary theatre". The freethinking journalist and lecturer S.K. Ratcliffe – for long associated, like J.M.R. himself, with London's South Place Ethical Society – said of Robertson's book: "Its erudition is marvellous. Alone it might, for other men of learning, have stood as the result of a life's study. Robertson produced it as a holiday task." Ratcliffe's distinctly positive attitude towards J.M.R.'s achievement was shared by the Shakespeare luminary Sir Sidney Lee (*A Life of William Shakespeare*, 1915 ed., pp. 656, 43n.). For J.P. Gilmour, Robertson succeeded in "effectively demolishing, especially in his monumental *Baconian Heresy*, the freakish ascription to Bacon of the authorship of the

[Shakespeare] sonnets and plays" (*HF*, 1936, p. xii). But in point of fact Robertson's book focused very much on the plays and devoted virtually no attention to Bacon's supposed authorship of the sonnets. Regrettably the present writer has already had reason, on several other occasions, to notice or strongly suspect instances where Gilmour's biographical account of J.M.R. in *HF*, 1936, clearly seems misleading or factually inaccurate.

In an aside in the conclusion of *The Baconian Heresy* Robertson declared: "Probably the whirligig of Time will cast up yet other fantasies in far greater numbers than rational contributions to Shakespeare study. I do not despair of seeing seriously advanced the theory that the Plays were written by Queen Elizabeth, who was a good classical scholar, and must have heard … a good deal about law" (p. 592). It seems redundant to point out that the value of Robertson's investigation far outweighs the somewhat amusing fact that this prophecy was fulfilled forty-three years later with the first detailed and apparently serious presentation of Elizabeth Tudor as William Shakespeare. As Professor G.W. Keeton (who had been associated with the R.P.A.) stated in 1967: "It has become very difficult indeed to establish a case for the Baconian authorship of the plays since the ruthless and exhaustive examination of the whole question by J.M. Robertson." Moreover, J.M.R.'s comment in *The Upshot of 'Hamlet'* (1885) that the theory that Bacon wrote the plays attributed to Shakespeare was unscientific may be thought to have anticipated *The Baconian Heresy*. Nearly a century after J.M.R.'s 1913 book was published, Scott McCrea relied on it quite markedly in *The Case for Shakespeare* (2005).

Bolingbroke and Walpole (1919)

Although modestly excluded by Robertson from mention in his own *Courses of Study* (1932 ed.), *Bolingbroke and Walpole* has been regarded by a number of historians as a useful contribution to an understanding of the first half of eighteenth century Britain. Referring to Sir Robert Walpole – commonly seen as Britain's first Prime Minister – G.R. Stirling Taylor declared in 1931 that since the dawn of the nineteenth century "there have been only two biographies in English that have treated him in a way that deserves very serious notice from the historical student. There is Mr John (afterwards Lord) Morley's small volume published in 1889. … The other important book is Mr. J.M. Robertson's … published in 1919. This also is by a Liberal politician who had held ministerial rank; for Walpole, as the supremely practical minister, naturally interests the professional. … It is the most scientific study of Walpole that has yet appeared, but, though profounder than Lord Morley's book, it is rather an economic and sociological analysis than a biography. An author who had read most of the history of Europe in every language could scarcely be expected to have examined very minutely the local literature which contains the immediate personal details necessary for a life of Walpole" (*Robert Walpole and His Age*, pp. 11-12). Echoing Stirling Taylor twenty years later, the *Bibliography of British History: The Eighteenth Century, 1714-1789* (1951, ed. Stanley Pargellis and D.J. Medley, p. 24) considered Robertson's book to be "a thoughtful work, primarily valuable for its social and economic analysis of the period, with little on Bolingbroke". Apparently regarding *Bolingbroke and Walpole* as a sequel to *The Evolution of States* (1912), Robertson was critical of Bolingbroke as a politician and thinker, whereas he thought that Walpole was a sagacious statesman making for political, social and intellectual progress, financial stability, prosperity, and attempts to avoid foreign wars. *Bolingbroke and Walpole* was noticed in H.T. Dickinson's 1970 study of Bolingbroke; and J.M.R.'s 1919 work provided a useful reference point for the commentators Chris Tame (whose premature death in 2006 marked a real loss to British cultural debate) and Dr. David Berman in their respective contributions to *J.M. Robertson* (ed. G.A. Wells, 1987).

In his 1919 book Robertson censured "Bolingbroke's intellectual duplicity" as a deist philosopher. But three years later J.M.R. presented a more benign or charitable picture of him (in the context of his alleged influence on Voltaire): "Bolingbroke is unduly disparaged as superficial and inexact in his critico-historical speculation, in an age in which hardly any rational inquiry had been made into Jewish and Christian religious history save on orthodox lines, and his talk may have been instructive" (*Voltaire*, 1922, p. 116). In his survey (2014) of the scores of British Prime Ministers – who never included Bolingbroke – from Walpole onwards, Dick Leonard, in his occasional comments on Bolingbroke (whom Walpole chose to regard as a political opponent who, at one point, was also a traitor), largely focused on Bolingbroke's influence, through his political thought and writings, on the Earl of Bute and George III.

In April 1942 the world-famous art critic and connoisseur Bernard Berenson – a resident of Italy seeking solace in a world riven by war – read *Bolingbroke and Walpole*, declaring of the early sections: "Robertson does not narrate at all, and, thinking you know the events and the characters, sets out to analyze and interpret them. This he does well enough, and happily with little partisan's Labourite spirit or dogmatism. What a many-sided writer poor J.M.R. was." On finishing reading the book, Berenson wrote: "Later chapters more narrative and descriptive of events and conditions", adding: "His picture of Walpole has many points of resemblance with Churchill's *Marlborough*" (*One Year's Reading for Fun (1942)*, 1960, pp. 55, 56). As Winston Churchill's *Marlborough* was published well over a decade after J.M.R.'s book, it would be more logical, and potentially more revealing, to say that Churchill's *Marlborough* bore many points of resemblance with Robertson's *Bolingbroke and Walpole*. By 1903 J.M.R. had come to regard Berenson as a friend; but although he praised and recommended a number of Berenson's works on art (most recently in the 1932 edition of *Courses of Study*), there is no indication that he was ever aware of, still less approved of, Berenson's hidden financially profitable and personally rewarding conflict of interest associated with his attributions and evaluation of various works of art.

Browning and Tennyson as Teachers (1903)

This proffered a detailed comparative study of these prominent Victorian poets from an atheistic viewpoint (see Martin Page's *BRUG*, 1984, pp. 58-9, for further information). Evidently with Robertson's 1903 book in mind, a friend and admirer, the poet and novelist Eden Phillpotts, wrote to him, most probably on 7.4.1931: "I thought your 'Tennyson' and 'Browning' about the best thing ever written on them. … My kindest and best good wishes to Mrs. Robertson and yourself; and don't work too hard I pray you" (*Eden Phillpotts (1862-1960) Selected Letters*, ed. James Dayananda, 1984, pp. 107-8). It may be speculated that reading J.M.R.'s literary criticism may have had some impact on Phillpotts's writing of poetry. In any event, Robertson's long essay on "The Teaching of

Tennyson", which constituted a substantial part of *Browning and Tennyson as Teachers*, was used by the Dutch literary critic Odin Dekkers in his 1998 book on Robertson as the basis for his general discussion (pp. 250-54) of Robertson on Tennyson.

Buckle and His Critics (1895)

"There is only one book dealing with Buckle as an historian: *Buckle and his Critics*, by J.M. Robertson." Thus declared – more than sixty years after Robertson's book had appeared – Giles St. Aubyn in *A Victorian Eminence* (1958, p. 197), which itself would be hailed in 1998 as the most recent account of Buckle's life (Odin Dekkers, *J.M. Robertson*, p. 78n.). Little wonder, therefore, that St. Aubyn was able to quote (on p. 165) Robertson's declaration in *Buckle and His Critics* (1895, p. 36): "Nothing indeed has struck me so much in the investigation of the criticism passed on Buckle as the sheer ignorance of his book on the part of most of his assailants." In the same vein in the same book (p. 21) Robertson – again quoted by St. Aubyn (p. 185) – had just criticised the *parti pris* exhibited by what a later generation would arguably consider part of the Establishment: "At this moment, with all the affectation of having buried Buckle that prevails in the literary world, there are hundreds of non-literary men who can testify how he has taught them to regard history in an enlightened and reflective fashion." Indeed, *Buckle and His Critics* was a powerful defence of the dead historian against the misrepresentations of his detractors, though J.M.R. also exposed or attempted to correct many of Buckle's undoubted errors and exaggerations. Hailing Buckle as a great pioneer in helping to establish the writing of history as a science, Robertson accepted his predecessor's master-ideas of the role of climate, soil and food, the growth of knowledge, the cross-fertilization of ideas, and the struggle between reason and superstition in history. Arguably adopting more of a materialist approach, Robertson, however, tended to emphasize cross-fertilization of cultures rather than that of ideas (see, for example, J.M.R. in his *Courses of Study*, 1932 ed., p. 213). Given that his 1895 book constituted "a study in sociology" (its subtitle), it was understandable that in it Robertson, as the iconoclastic campaigner Chris Tame would point out, subjected racialist "explanations" to critical scrutiny and adverse comment (*J.M. Robertson*, ed. G.A. Wells, 1987, p. 98).

Neither Buckle nor Robertson envisaged the prospect of global warming or of climate change on a global scale: Buckle died seventy years before Robertson, who in turn not only wrote *Buckle and His Critics*, but also died, years before explicit warnings about global climate change were beginning to be noticed, heard and understood (see Nathaniel Rich, *Losing Earth*, 2019, pp. 21-3, 48-9, etc.). But they were on the right track. Buckle showed some awareness of what he called "the average loss to agricultural industry caused by changes in the weather" in some areas (*Introduction to the History of Civilization in England*, ed. Robertson, 1904, p. 24 n. 5); and Robertson pointed out that "Buckle had expressly shown how excessive heat and moisture were deterrent to civilisation" (*Buckle and His Critics*, p. 207). Moreover, in his 1895 book Robertson declared: "The Scotch sociologists of last century had already gone too far in suggesting that the civilised man could adapt himself to any climate. We now know that, racially speaking, he cannot" (op. cit. 1895, p. 54). *Buckle and His Critics*, which marked Robertson's first major contribution to sociology and the science of history, had reached book form – "nearly finished" – by 15 January 1893 (J.M.R. in *NR* of that date, p. 41); although he indicated that its antecedents were traceable to his two-part article, bearing the same title as the book, of late October 1886 in *NR*. In that article – as in his monumental study almost ten years later – he defended Buckle against the Victorian critics Grant Allen and Leslie Stephen, albeit Robertson believed that Buckle's style was one of his weak points (which was sometimes the case with J.M.R. himself, arguably hindering his influence). He felt that while Buckle's concept of history was deficient inasmuch as it did not fully embrace the theory of evolution, "he connected climatic phaenomena with conditions of food production, these with economic law, and the whole with religious development, in a way that really helps us to comprehend history". Whereas Buckle's impact may have been blunted or overshadowed by Darwin's earthquake – there is no entry for Buckle in the *Macmillan Encyclopedia* (1995 ed.) or *Cambridge Biographical Encyclopedia* (1998 ed.), for example – the sociologist Professor Stanislav Andreski paid Robertson's book a handsome compliment almost a century after its appearance when he declared: "up to now no other history of sociology has been written which is both equally thorough and equally sophisticated" (*J.M. Robertson*, ed. G.A. Wells, p. 76).

In 1993 Bernard Semmel, an esteemed American historian who had himself written on H.T. Buckle and the science of history, declared: "For Buckle's life, see G. St. Aubyn, *A Victorian Eminence* ... the best treatment of his ideas is J.M. Robertson, *Buckle and His Critics* ..." (*The Liberal Ideal and the Demons of Empire*, p. 200, n. 26). The enduring value of J.M.R.'s 1895 book was indicated by the fact that it was specifically noticed, commended or referred to in a long succession of published works such as: *Introduction to the Study of History* (1898, Charles Langlois of the Sorbonne in Paris); *English Political Thought in the Nineteenth Century*

(1933, Crane Brinton); "The Critics of Buckle" (1956, G.A. Wells, *Past and Present*, 9); *Evolution and Society* (1966, John Burrow); *The Evolution of British Historiography* (1967, ed. J.R. Hale); *The Transformation of Intellectual Life in Victorian England* (1982, Thomas William Heyck, who would also contribute the entry on Buckle in the 2004 *Oxford Dictionary of National Biography*); *The English Historical Tradition since 1850* (1990, Christopher Parker); *Encyclopaedia of Nineteenth-Century Thought* (2005, Gregory Claeys); and *The Science of History in Victorian Britain* (2011, Ian Hesketh). In a notice of *Buckle and His Critics* in *Mind* (1896, Vol. V, pp. 266-9) the reviewer suggested that J.M.R. was not always measured or proportionate in his criticisms of the Victorian agnostic Leslie Stephen; although Noel Annan indicated in his study of Stephen (1984, p. 387) that the latter admitted that Robertson "may have found a blot or two" in his, Stephen's, attack on Buckle.

At his death in 1933 Robertson's library was about as large as that of his hero Buckle with about 20,000 volumes (Hesketh, p. 170, note 12; cf. Gilmour in *HF*, 1936, p. xvi). Sir Thomas Phillipps left about 40,000 books.

In 1945 the British Communist J.T. Murphy wrote that while the young Stalin was a theological student in the Georgian capital Tiflis, an illegal group of Russian Marxists introduced him to works by Marx, Engels, Kautsky, Ricardo, Feuerbach, Buckle, Charles Letourneau, and others (*Stalin*, p. 19). Of these, Buckle was a theist who stressed the role of material factors in human history, and Letourneau was believed to be an atheist and materialist. The contribution of these two writers was commended by Robertson; and while Murphy may have been misinformed, it seems unlikely that Murphy, as a devoted Stalinist, in a book published in Stalin's lifetime, would have concocted his statement that Stalin was introduced to works by Buckle and Letourneau when neither was exactly a household name in Britain. It is faintly possible that Buckle was mentioned to young Stalin by someone like Noah Zhordaniya, who perhaps also heard about J.M.R.'s work.

Chamberlain: A Study (1905)

In Britain in 1905 politically aware people, already familiar with the battle between Free Traders and tariff reformers, would have realised that the Chamberlain referred to in the title of this work was Joseph Chamberlain, the former Colonial Secretary (who over the previous two decades had coloured much of Britain's political life, as reflected in Parliament and in Government). Joseph Chamberlain at the age of 50 had abandoned the Liberal Party over Irish Home Rule to join the Tories and thereafter campaigned for tariff reform, thereby becoming responsible for a split or rift in each of the two main parties.

In his book (pp. 51, 58) Robertson accused Chamberlain of "unscrupulous self-seeking" and of being "the most hopelessly discredited statesman of modern times". (Gladstone had called Chamberlain "a most dangerous man, restless, ambitious, unscrupulous"; and more recently, in August 1903, the anti-imperialist Wilfrid Scawen Blunt had told H.M. Hyndman that Chamberlain was "just the clever unscrupulous fool to run the imperial motor to an imperial smash": William L. Strauss, *Joseph Chamberlain and the Theory of Imperialism*, U.S.A., 1942, p. 130; Lord Lytton, *Wilfrid Scawen Blunt*, 1961, pp. 115-6.) Robertson's book referred to Chamberlain as "the swaggering wrecker of the two Boer Republics" in the recent Anglo-Boer War (J.M.R. quoted by Jim Herrick in *J.M. Robertson*, ed. G.A. Wells, 1987, p. 39). This aspect of Robertson's attack on Chamberlain included the broadside: "What lies especially at his door is the responsibility for the sins of the new movement of vulgar and vicious 'Imperialism', which dates broadly from the time of his appearance as a Tory minister" (J.M.R. quoted by Strauss, op. cit. 1942, p. 123, from p. 51 of the 1905 book). Robertson also declared: "Chamberlain's moral inadequacy connects with intellectual limitation. … public life, action, power, were to him as the breath of his nostrils. After his years of pride of place, the prospect of exclusion from office for many years seems to have progressively maddened him" (p. 39). These strictures resemble those previously expressed by Theophilus Scholes in his *Chamberlain and Chamberlainism* (1903), published under the pseudonym Bartholomew Smith, when he asserted that "politically Mr. Chamberlain is without depth of conviction … his judgment is defective … he lacks high moral principles" (p. 42, etc.).

Robertson's attack on Joseph Chamberlain, not least for his latter-day promotion of Protectionism, has been designated "a vial of *ad hominem* vitriol" (by Jim Herrick, op. cit. 1987, ed. G.A. Wells, p. 39). However, this judgement is not uniformly true of J.M.R.'s book as a whole. In a fairly early section Robertson devoted a number of pages to quite a calm and balanced exploration of Chamberlain's secession from Gladstone's policy in 1886, with the Scottish Radical inclined to believe (p. 35) that "the first step in the severance of Chamberlain from the Liberal party was made on his side in good faith". While adding (p. 58) that "no man can say what depth of failure he may reach", Robertson rounded off his psychologically quite penetrating study on a humane, even compassionate, note: "The best close to his career that charity could wish him would be an evening of life passed in retirement, far from the turmoil which warped his character, unseated his judgment, and frustrated all the better aims of his better days" (p. 64). A matter of months later Chamberlain suffered a disabling stroke and withdrew from many aspects of public life.

Robertson also showed a chivalrous side when in 1904 – a year before political tensions were heightened through the selection of hundreds of Parliamentary candidates – he drew attention, in a neutral way, in *Courses of Study* to Joseph Chamberlain's *Home Rule and the Irish Question*. This last-named book was issued by Swan Sonnenschein and Co., which for well over a decade from 1887 onwards published work by Joseph Chamberlain, J.M. Robertson himself – and Beatrice Potter (Mrs. Beatrice Webb), who was close to the leading Fabians with whom Robertson (not a Fabian) was on friendly terms, although his periodic written criticism of them seemed to date from at least November 1887. Beatrice Potter, as she then was, had met Chamberlain in the early 1880s, fallen in love with him and had an intense affair with him which lasted several years and which she resurrected in her manuscript diaries between 1899 and 1902: "she retained for him a somewhat reluctant admiration" (Bernard Porter, *Critics of Empire*, 1968, pp. 118-19).

Chamberlain and Beatrice Webb came from similar middle-class backgrounds. In early November 1903 Chamberlain (well aware of her standing as one of the founders of the London School of Economics) wrote that the School "has done so much good work" (Rolf Dahrendorf, *LSE*, 1995, pp. 69, 525). She was a freethinker, whereas Chamberlain declared at one point: "I have always had a grudge against religion for absorbing the passion in men's nature" (David

Tribe, *100 Years of Freethought*, 1967, pp. 98, 97). Moreover, the Fabians appeared to bend before a Chamberlainite wind with their pro-imperialist manifesto *Fabianism and the Empire* (1900) and their equivocal tract on free trade and the fiscal question (1904). Arguably Chamberlain and the Fabians shared an interest in non-aristocratic élites reflecting the worlds of industry, business, education and training, and large-scale administration.

Characteristics of Men, Manners, Opinions, Times, etc. (Shaftesbury, ed. J.M.R. 1900)

If Joseph Chamberlain founded a political dynasty, Anthony Ashley Cooper, the third Earl of Shaftesbury, became an exemplar of a kind of dynasty dedicated to human betterment and human rights with an emphasis initially on intellectual freedom and philosophical debate, and subsequently on social reform (as with the well documented achievements of the philanthropic seventh Earl in the field of employment, industry and housing in mid nineteenth century Britain). The third Earl is remembered as the author of *Characteristics of Men, Manners, Opinions, Times, etc.* (1711), which Robertson edited in two volumes – an edition (1900) described in 1987 as "valuable" by the University lecturer Ian MacKillop, author of *The British Ethical Societies* (see *J.M. Robertson*, ed. G.A. Wells, p. 59). In fact, Robertson's edition would remain unsurpassed for generations, commended by the non-Marxist Italian philosopher Benedetto Croce in his *Shaftesbury in Italy* (1924) and also relied upon by the British Marxist literary critic Terry Eagleton in *Sweet Violence* (2003).

In a study of the deism of Shaftesbury's contemporary Bolingbroke, Walter Merrill, in discussing Shaftesbury's alleged influence on Bolingbroke, pointed out that the commentator C.A. Moore "entirely accepts Robertson's explanation of Bolingbroke's failure to give Shaftesbury credit", whereas he, Merrill, was unconvinced by Robertson's "explanation" in his edition for Bolingbroke's apparent reticence to acknowledge Shaftesbury's philosophical influence upon him (*From Statesman To Philosopher*, 1949, New York, pp. 101-3, 110). Later the American historians Will and Ariel Durant (in *The Age of Voltaire*, 1965, pp. 172, 817) seemed inclined to accept Robertson's account of Shaftesbury's influence on Bolingbroke. Perhaps somewhat similarly, a late twentieth century biographer of George III pooh-poohed the claim that Bolingbroke influenced that future monarch's political ideas (see *The History Today Companion to British History*, 1995, pp. 671-2).

In *Bolingbroke and His Circle* (1968: Harvard University Press), Isaac Kramnick correctly referenced *Bolingbroke and Walpole* (1919) by J.M. Robertson on p. 270, but on p. 273, and again on p. 285, presented "J.M. Robinson" (sic) as the 1900 editor of Shaftesbury's *Characteristics*. Steven Shapin's *A Social History of Truth* (1994) and Thomas Mautner's *The Penguin Dictionary of Philosophy* (1997 ed.) refer to a 1960s American (Indianapolis) version of Robertson's edition.

Robertson said that his edition set forth the view that Shaftesbury's ethic was "substantially derived from Spinoza" (*Courses of Study*, 1904 ed., p. 112, and 1932 ed., p. 140). For Ralph Blumenau more recently, Shaftesbury "denied that revelation by itself could be the source of our morality. ... Shaftesbury believed that ... we have, irrespective of God, an innate faculty to perceive moral beauty and an innate sense of right and wrong ..." (*Philosophy and Living*, 2002, p. 303). See also J.M.R.'s *Pioneer Humanists* (1907).

Charles Bradlaugh (1894:co-author)

Despite the production of biographical studies of Bradlaugh since the Second World War, the two-volume biography of Bradlaugh in which Robertson collaborated with Bradlaugh's surviving and fiercely devoted daughter Hypatia Bradlaugh Bonner has never been completely superseded as a contribution to, and reference book on, nineteenth century British secularism. Since the book's appearance in 1894, the papers of relevant Tory leaders, of Gladstone, and of other important Victorian informants and witnesses have become available. So inevitably, less than four years after Bradlaugh's death, Robertson and Hypatia could not benefit from access to them. Hypatia and Robertson were concerned – understandably – to defend Bradlaugh and his character against the vicious machinations, hatred and lies of his enemies and detractors; and arguably the detailed and quite often vivid accounts by the two co-authors in this regard retain a certain value even today. As Walter Arnstein has remarked with considerable justification concerning Robertson's contribution to the joint study: "Not only did he sometimes fail to appreciate the subtle shadings of opinion among the actors in the drama, but he lacked the materials to give a multi-dimensional portrayal of the impact of the case upon the various political parties and personalities" (*The Bradlaugh Case*, 1965, p. 4).

Admittedly the devoted daughter and disciple were in many ways too close to Bradlaugh, emotionally and in time, to assess him and his career with greater objectivity (although – to take two examples – in the book Hypatia revealed that she and her sister had been whipped as children, and Robertson admitted that to the last Bradlaugh had in him "something of

Cromwell's Berserker temper": Vol. 1, p. 118, and Vol. 2, p. 427, respectively). None the less, they processed an enormous mass of facts with remarkable accuracy in the circumstances; and for many decades their work would remain the standard and authoritative biography, indeed the only full-length biography of Bradlaugh written by two people with close, not to say intimate, personal knowledge of their subject. The Roman Catholic writer G.K. Chesterton would declare that Bradlaugh's story was "admirably told by his daughter and Mr. John M. Robertson (a writer always splendidly trenchant and sincere)" (*Daily News*, 1.8.1906).

Most of the book was written by Hypatia (some 511 pages), with rather more than 300 pages written by J.M.R., who focused on Bradlaugh's philosophical orientation, political doctrines and work, and Parliamentary struggle. Of this, a reviewer, G.W. Foote, remarked that Robertson "has compiled an extremely able history of Bradlaugh's parliamentary struggle. This piece of work is of high merit and permanent value." Regarding Bradlaugh's legal cases, David Tribe declared that Robertson "made minor errors in processing the material and attributed to some of the judges a bias there is no evidence of " (*President Charles Bradlaugh, M.P.*, 1971, p. 355). As Tribe in that context did not name any of the judges or identify any of the cases involved, it is not clear which incidents he particularly had in mind. (Moreover, Tribe's book was not free from mistakes, such as two misleading or incorrect statements concerning the youthful Robertson on p. 242, last para.; and on p. 367, reference 163, Annie Besant should read Arthur Bonner.) W. Ivor Jennings, Reader in English Law at London University, pointed out two apparently minor legal mistakes in Hypatia's part of the work, but he did not mention any in Robertson's part (*Champion of Liberty*, 1933, pp. 314-16). In addition, Jennings in *Champion of Liberty* did not accuse him, regarding the 1894 biography, of unjustifiably imputing an anti-Bradlaugh bias to any of the judges. However, Jennings wrote of Bradlaugh: "He had no great Judge on his side" (p. 325); though it may be added that in December 1884 Robertson praised Mr. Justice Grove and also, if to a lesser extent, Lord Chief Justice Coleridge, before both of whom Bradlaugh appeared (*NR*, 14.12.84, p. 387).

One British judge who went out of his way to express his admiration for Bradlaugh was (Sir) Edward Parry, whose support for Bradlaugh, surfacing in a pseudonymous pamphlet in 1885, only became widely known in 1932 when, in his autobiography, Parry praised Bradlaugh as "one of the most honest, courageous and sensible politicians of the age in which I have lived" (*My Own Way*, p. 91, where Parry revealed that J.M.R. gave his 1885 pamphlet "a serious and kindly review"). Robertson and Parry became members of the Centenary Celebrations General Committee to commemorate Bradlaugh's birth in 1833. (In 1926 Lord Justice Ronan left the R.P.A. £100.)

Walter Arnstein believed that few factual errors may be found in the Bradlaugh Bonner-Robertson book, which was "written with great care". It was listed as important by Willard Wolfe (*From Radicalism to Socialism*, 1975, p. 318); it set Percy Redfern "afire" when he read it as a secularist youth before 1900 (*Journey to Understanding*, 1946, p. 24); and J.M.R.'s part of the book was consulted by Janet Courtney (*Freethinkers of the Nineteenth Century*, 1920) and Chapman Cohen (*Bradlaugh and Ingersoll*, 1933), for example, not to mention Michael Rectenwald in 2016.

Charles Bradlaugh (1920)

Robertson's compact little book bearing the above title (122 pages) was issued by the freethought publisher Watts & Co. as part of its series Life-Stories of Famous Men, of which Charles Bradlaugh was one of the first four (followed in 1921 by one on Darwin). In a Prefatory Note to *Charles Bradlaugh* Robertson indicated (as later did *The Cambridge Bibliography of English Literature*) that it took account of the 1894 two-volume Bradlaugh Bonner-Robertson biography, to which he referred the reader for "fuller details". In fact his "short sketch", as he called it, was distinctly more readable and digestible than its predecessor. Both works would be recommended on the first page of the main text of *Champion of Liberty: Charles Bradlaugh*, published in September 1933 on behalf of the British freethought movement to mark the centenary of the champion's birth. (In 2005 the only biography of Bradlaugh commended by Gregory Claeys in his entry on Bradlaugh in the *Encyclopedia of Nineteenth-Century Thought*, which he edited, was the 1894 Bradlaugh Bonner-Robertson joint study.)

In April 1922 the *Literary Guide* reported (p. 55) that the birth control advocate Marie Stopes had a sneering reference to Robertson's 1920 book in the *Cambridge Magazine*. Then on 27 June 1922 she wrote: "The fact that I will not bow the knee to Bradlaugh … is anathema to the Atheistical School …" (as quoted in *Marie Stopes*, 1977, p. 199, by Ruth Hall, who commented that "any laudatory reference to Bradlaugh and other pioneers infuriated her". Cf. Jim Herrick, *Vision and Realism*, 1982, pp. 61-2).

Stopes would not have known that Hypatia Bradlaugh Bonner,

in her 1894 biography (Vol. 2, p. 24), had deliberately given a clear yet false and disingenuous impression that Darwin would have made a favourable and no doubt persuasive witness for birth control – quite contrary to his social attitudes on contraception – if only his health had been sufficiently robust to permit his attendance at court. This manipulation related to a letter of 6 June 1877 from Darwin to Charles Bradlaugh regarding giving evidence at the Knowlton birth control trial. Mrs. Bradlaugh Bonner quoted from this letter in her biography, but used dots to indicate words she omitted from the letter. This omitted material comprised some 17 lines, including Darwin's declaration that "my judgment would be in the strongest opposition to yours" (see James Moore in *Religion in Victorian Britain*, Vol. 1: *Traditions*, ed. Gerald Parsons, 1988, pp. 306-7). Mrs. Bonner gave no date for Darwin's letter, which is not mentioned in Edward Royle's meticulous 1975 index to the N.S.S. Bradlaugh Papers or in her list of letters to her father from British notables between 1869 and 1889 which she exhibited at the Centenary Commemoration Dinner in 1933. Robertson's 1920 book referred only, and briefly (p. 60), to Darwin's courteous reply excusing himself from attending court on health grounds. There is no reason to suppose that Robertson ever knew about – still less, approved of – her manipulation of the letter (a letter from which Tribe's 1971 biography quotes fleetingly – pp. 181, 353 – only in its curtailed printed version).

Christianity and Mythology (1900; second edition, 1910)

J.M. Robertson was, in his lifetime, the foremost British exponent of the Mythicist view of Christian origins, of which – by any criteria – he gave a highly impressive conspectus in half a dozen volumes spanning thirty years from *Christianity and Mythology* to *A Short History of Christianity* (third edition, 1931). He combined a persuasive statement of the case for the non-historicity of Jesus with his often devastating replies to Christian opponents who distorted and misrepresented his views. He went beyond stressing the testimony of the Pauline Epistles to the divinity of Jesus and their lack of detail as to his life and teaching, or pointing to vital differences between the account in the Fourth Gospel and the narratives of the other three Gospels – as well as glaring discrepancies between the Synoptics themselves. Armed with immense knowledge secured by the progress of comparative mythology, Biblical criticism, archaeology, anthropology and sociology, he traced many challenging similarities between Christian and non-Christian myths, suggesting that Christianity assimilated and perpetuated many features of other religions. For example, in *Christianity and Mythology* (1910 edition, p. 34) he drew parallels with features of ancient religions, including use of the signs of the zodiac, to present Jesus as a Sun-God. (Little wonder, therefore, that the font in a thirteenth century Romney Marsh church bore the twelve signs of the zodiac!)

In his book the section on Christ and Krishna (issued separately in 1890) probably established Robertson as the first British rationalist scholar to refute the claim that Krishnaism had borrowed mythological and theological data from Christianity. On the other hand, "it becomes conceivable that certain parts of the Christian Birth-legend are derived from Krishnaism". Robertson's thesis, however, was distorted by Albert Schweitzer, who, in *The Quest of the Historical Jesus* (1910), represented Robertson as claiming that "the Christ-myth is merely a form of the Krishna-myth"! Schweitzer's blunder notwithstanding, his book received a fine tribute from Robertson on its publication in England.

Christianity and Mythology established its author as an early British freethinker to argue that many anecdotes in the Gospels are based on interpretation of pagan works of art. Elements of Robertson's theory were developed, more than thirty years later, by Naomi Mitchison, by Professor Toynbee in *A Study of History*, by J.B.S. Haldane, and by Robert Graves and Joshua Podro in *The Nazarene Gospel Restored*. G.B. Shaw apparently drew on *Christianity and Mythology* (second edition, 1910) when he drafted his essay *On the Prospects of Christianity* (1915); and half a century after the first appearance of Robertson's book, Adam Gowans Whyte (Literary Adviser of the R.P.A.) rightly said that it had "gained and retained an international reputation". In 1956, the Biblical critic A.D. Howell Smith declared the work to be "of great value to the well-trained investigator"; and, in the same year, Archibald Robertson pronounced it the greatest of his namesake's contributions to comparative hierology.

The German Mythicist Arthur Drews declared that Robertson "has traced the picture of Christ in the Gospels to a mixture of mythological elements in heathenism and Judaism" (*The Christ Myth*, 1910 English translation, pp. 7-8; see also Lenin, Collected Works, Moscow, Vol. 33, p. 231). In *Christianity and Mythology* Robertson indicated that the Lord's Prayer, the Sermon on the Mount, and the Didache reflected such Jewish influence.

Various British, American, French, Italian, Danish, German, Russian and Swiss writers – too numerous to list here – are known to have drawn upon *Christianity and Mythology* over the years. As the British philosopher C.E.M. Joad said of Robertson: "in *Christianity and Mythology* he startled his contemporaries." Three writers who acknowledged Robertson's contribution to freethought and, more specifically, their debt to his *Christianity and Mythology* were the Historicist Joseph McCabe in *The Sources of the Morality of the Gospels* (1914) and, in mainland Europe, the Danish Mythicist Georg Brandes in his book published in English as *Jesus: A Myth* (which, according to J.M.R.'s 1932 *Courses of Study*, appeared in 1927), and the Dutch scholar and well-respected historian Jan Romein, who was instrumental in encouraging and facilitating the publication of Anne Frank's Diary: see Romein's *The Watershed of Two Eras*, 1978 ed.; *The Diary of Anne Frank: The Critical Edition*, 1989 ed.; Melissa Müller, *Anne Frank*, 1999 ed. In his 1932 *Courses of Study* Robertson commended a work on the suffering of the Jews (J.M.R., p. 304: see also p. 219). McCabe's *Pagan Christs* (1920s) cited *Christianity and Mythology*, but not J.M.R.'s *Pagan Christs*.

The Church and Education (1903)

This work originally appeared as a two-part article in consecutive issues of Hypatia Bradlaugh Bonner's *The Reformer* during 1903 (15 June, pp. 328-38, and 15 July, pp. 400-17), in effect less than four years before the formation in Britain of the Secular Education League, which would be supported by Robertson. Although his essay was only some thirty pages long, within those limits it offered a reasonably comprehensive survey of the largely dismal record of the Christian Church in Europe relating to education and schooling from the early centuries of the Christian era until about 1902, with Robertson's main focus being on the Church of England. Giving his sources and references, he provided a mine of information from which a collection of gems could be extracted, such as the observation that the Churches in question "acted as all corporations whatever tend to act; and this in despite, it may be, of the enlightenment of their most thoughtful members. The common view of class interest will always determine class action; and the enlightened members of a hierarchy are practically powerless save when their view chimes with that interest" (p. 337). Robertson's study was reprinted as a pamphlet by his friends Arthur and Hypatia Bradlaugh Bonner; and in 1943 - ten years after Robertson's death – it was published in a modified and updated version by Adam Gowans Whyte acting on behalf of Watts & Co. Not long afterwards Watts & Co. published in the same series of cheap pamphlets – The Thinker's Forum – an abridged edition, probably also prepared by the dedicated Gowans Whyte, of J.M.R.'s *Rationalism* (1912) to appear in 1945, when a devastating recent outbreak of mass irrationality highlighted an urgent need for the voice of reason to be heard and heeded. By the time he died in 1950 Whyte had been a good and faithful servant of rationalism, the R.P.A. and Watts & Co. for fully fifty years.

Courses of Study (1904; second ed., 1908; third, 1932)

With his passion for promoting knowledge, culture and rational thought, J.M. Robertson's whole life may be said to have been devoted to the cause of education in the widest and deepest sense, certainly from the day when he was a young amateur librarian at the People's Palace in a deprived area of London to the day when, as a sick old man of seventy-six, he looked back at the publication of the third edition of *Courses of Study*. This was a massive bibliography of over 525 printed pages (including the indexes), which was appropriately his last book to be published in his lifetime. The undertaking began as a series of articles entitled "Courses of Study" compiled by Robertson for the *National Reformer* in the wake of Bradlaugh's death in 1891, in response to continual appeals to him as the new editor from readers anxious for advice on reading subjects that interested them; and in late 1932 the third edition of the book was completed after Robertson suffered "a touch of paresis" on delivering the indexes at the R.P.A. offices (information from Macleod Yearsley via his family; see also J.M.R. in *NR*, 1.10.1893, p. 211). The immense work involved in preparing the third edition almost certainly exhausted him. For whatever unexplained reason(s), J.M.R. as editor did not reveal the identity of any of the "trusted critics or the qualified experts who have so kindly assisted him" in the production of the much revised and updated *Courses of Study* (third ed., p. vii). Yet J.M.R. deservedly voiced his disapproval of the U.S. Government's record in its treatment of North American Red Indians, for example (see p. 387).

If Robertson did not have a completely free hand in compiling the third edition and with due allowance for limitations of space and time, it still seems surprising that the book omits Bakunin, Rosa Luxemburg, Plekhanov, Cassirer, Max Eastman, Mosca, Pareto, Spengler, Hitler, Kraepelin, Warlaam Tcherkesoff or Bukharin. Books about Lenin are listed, but none by him; though J.M.R. recognised (p. 308) the importance of Trotsky's history of the Russian Revolution. If the stunning Nazi victory in the German general election of 31 July 1932, making the Nazis the largest party in the German Parliament (Reichstag), came too late to be taken into account in Robertson's third edition, J.M.R. could have considered implications of the Nazi triumph in the Reichstag election of 14 September 1930, which made the Nazi party the second largest in the national Parliament, after the Socialists. This could have led Robertson to examine the rise of Nazism, as reflected in books by Harry Kessler (1923) and Stanley High (1925), N. Fairweather's article "Hitler and Hitlerism" in the *Atlantic Monthly* for March 1932, Dorothy Thompson's interview with Hitler recorded in *Cosmopolitan* for April 1932, or even *The German Crisis* by Hubert Knickerbocker or *Hitlerism* by Louis Snyder ("Nordicus"), both books being available in America in 1932 – none of them noticed in *Courses of Study*. Robertson had apparently received private "inside" information from quite highly placed Russian and Italian émigrés in the wake of the Bolshevik and Fascist Revolutions respectively. But he did not seem to have a similar source inside the Weimar Republic of post-war Germany. Be that as it may, J.M.R. deserved credit for his insistence in 1932 that "Since the World War, International Law has acquired a new importance" (p. 413).

In view of Robertson's abiding interest in education (illustrated by his article in *NR*, 2.4.1893, "Justice to Children", quoted in *BRUG*, pp. 66-7), it is surprising that in his 1932 book he does not notice work associated with Alfred Adler, Homer Lane's Little Commonwealth, Susan Isaacs' Malting House School, or the Modern School of the Spanish libertarian martyr Francisco Ferrer (whose "judicial murder" in 1909 J.M.R. consistently condemned). Robertson refers (p. 335) to his friend William Archer's "investigation of the case of Ferrer", but neither Archer's book nor Joseph McCabe's work on Ferrer is specified. However, Robertson notes (p. 263) McCabe's *Spain in Revolt* (1931) in the context of "the causation and significance of the Spanish Revolution of 1931". Only some nine months after J.M.R.'s death Einstein hid for three weeks in a hut in Cromer, Norfolk, under armed guard against Nazi assassins just before, from Kensington and later America, he supported fighting Nazism.

If Robertson was not as alert as he could or should have been to the rising tide of Hitlerism, arguably this was at least as true of a leading far-left cultural critic and historian like C.L.R. James, who admitted in the 1980s that he, and others, had unwittingly underestimated the gross evil posed by the Nazi danger, of which he declared: "we saw it late" (quoted by Priyamvada Gopal in her *Insurgent Empire*, 2019, p. 532, n. 156). There was a faint indirect link between James, who arrived in Britain by about April 1932, and Robertson, inasmuch as fairly soon after his arrival from the Caribbean James went to work for the cricket commentator Neville Cardus (who was one of J.M.R.'s admirers).

On the other hand, the third edition of *Courses of Study* gives no indication that Robertson was deceived or misled by the Piltdown Man fraud, or conceivably by the psychologist Cyril Burt, who later became mired in accusations of dishonest research findings. Whereas J.M.R. commended works by Burt's mentor William McDougall, he seems to have studiously avoided noticing any by Burt himself. Although his 1932 edition does not mention the path-breaking *On Growth and Form* (1917) by D'Arcy Thompson (who had been friendly with J.M.R.'s Edinburgh friend Patrick Geddes), in Robertson's *Courses of Study* Ronald Fisher's important work on genetics and evolution is tacitly acknowledged; and in the 1904 edition J.M.R. emerged as a relatively early supporter of pioneers of genetics through his recognition of the importance of Mendel and of Mendel's British advocate William Bateson (pp. 471-2), with Mendel's studies having been rediscovered in 1900 and Bateson's book on Mendel appearing in 1902. The 1908 edition of Robertson's book made a deep impression on two such different political figures as Harold Laski (at fifteen a self-styled "devout Robertsonian") and, at about the same time in distant Ceylon, the young (Sir) William Darling.

On some twenty occasions in his 1932 edition - only about three months before he died - J.M.R. commended works by Joseph McCabe. On the other hand, McCabe's slur in 1947 (*Eighty Years A Rebel*, p. 83) that J.M.R. had attacked him at a 1928 R.P.A. meeting - before the Great Depression erupted - for a fee trashed Bill Cooke's specific tribute, resting on false claims, to McCabe on p. 57 of his 2001 biography.

The Decadence (1929)

This is one of the more remarkable polemical and insightful works of Robertson's closing years. According to comments in the posthumously published (1936) edition of *A History of Freethought* edited by J.P. Gilmour, who made use of bibliographic information supplied by Robertson's old personal friend Marley Denwood and accepted as accurate by subsequent writers on Robertson and an official historian of the R.P.A., J.M.R. was the author of *The Decadence*, published under the pseudonym of L. Macaulay by Watts & Co. Moreover, stylistic tests, such as the nature of the language used in the main text, and the choice and treatment of the subject-matter (dominated by the author's commitment to Free Trade and hostility to Soviet tyranny), clearly suggest Robertson's authorship.

Written from the point of view of a future historian looking back on England's decline since World War I, Robertson's futuristic sketch, "dateable 1949" (as the title-page indicated), attacked Winston Churchill for what seemed to be political opportunism and erratic judgement. For example: "In 1929, Winston Churchill was writing that in 1918 England had reached the highest point in her history. He could not conceive, doubtless, that already the arc was on the downward turn, and that in 1948 this would be obvious to English as well as to alien eyes. Yet in the World War four empires had been smitten to fragments because their rulers had lacked vision" (p. 24). J.M.R. added that Britain's wealth had been built up by Free Trade, to which, he critically noted, Churchill no longer appeared to be committed. Of the contemporary British statesmen who figured most prominently in Robertson's book – men like Lloyd George and Baldwin – Winston Churchill was perhaps the one most vividly sketched. J.M.R. seemed to respond to Churchill as if he knew him very well and wrote about him as much in sorrow as in anger, bearing in mind that they had been fellow Ministers and Free Traders together in a Liberal Government. Robertson declared: "Always the Exchequer had been the goal of Churchill's ambition, short of a very doubtfully possible premiership" (p. 30). Indeed, it took Churchill another eleven years to become Prime Minister, and then in exceptional wartime circumstances.

Conscious that empires nurtured seeds of their own decay, Robertson suggested that Britain, like other great states, had been weakened in various ways by the huge loss of its younger males in the First World War. This, he believed, was at least a factor in Britain's decline from a first-rate to a third-rate power, with successful democratic, self-governing industrial states requiring "adequate knowledge and judgment" on the part of the majority of their electors. He felt that an intelligent public spirit of this kind was lacking in Britain on account of the influence of "sinister interests" and economic ignorance, which encouraged tariff reformers and Communists alike, with mounting unemployment, as a consequence of the erosion of Free Trade, fostering the "feverish" activities of Communists. Declaring that Marx's theory of value in *Das Kapital* was vitiated by his exclusion of the time factor (p. 55),

Robertson, perhaps with Lenin's New Economic Policy in mind, maintained that socialism, as applied in Soviet Russia, had produced "miserable social and industrial failure". He concluded: "Marxian Socialism, in short, was demonstrably a spurious equation, in which the really vital factors were falsified" – a pioneering verdict on the Soviet system (p. 55).

It was against this background that Robertson discussed the sale of honours and titles scandal that erupted in June 1922. As he explained: "It was in the years of the Coalition governments headed by Lloyd George that the 'traffic in honours' had become most notorious … The size of the fund thus amassed and controlled by Mr. George was a matter of common comment … It was said, and understood, that the Conservative section of the Coalition had received its due share of the so-called loot" (p. 10: the accuracy of these statements is confirmed by Nicholas Comfort, *The Politics Book*, 2005, p. 358).

In his book Robertson also shed some light on a significant development in modern British political history that would become buried and forgotten. He wrote: "It was in a stage of already far advanced demoralisation that men who had called themselves Liberals came forward to urge that their party should be merged in the Conservative" (p. 39). Indeed, Lloyd George and F.E. Smith (Lord Birkenhead) appeared to be key figures in proposing such an amalgamation in February 1920, as if a long-established Liberal movement were a plaything in their hands (see Maurice Cowling, *The Impact of Labour 1920-1924*, 1971, pp. 94-5, 112-3, etc., and Roy Hattersley, op cit.). They were keen to undermine the prospect of a Liberal revival under Asquith following his return to the House of Commons in a by-election.

In *The Decadence* the author's description of the Liberal Council as representative of Asquith's "steadfast remnant" (p. 23) suggested a familiarity with the Council that would be compatible with Robertson's authorship, as he was a Vice-President of the Liberal Council from its formal inception in 1927. He had also been President of the National Liberal Federation between 1920 and 1923; and he spoke at twenty or more meetings on Free Trade in the run-up to the general election in May 1929 (when *The Decadence* was published).

Although *The Decadence* focused mainly on British politics, it virtually closed with Robertson berating *The Times* for acclaiming Mussolini on account of "his deal with the Pope" (p. 106), with J.M.R. appearing to be alive to the Concordat's implicit significance, not just for Italy (where, it later transpired, the philosopher Piero Martinetti (1872-1943), understood to have been an atheist who refused to kowtow to Mussolini, took account of Robertson's *Christianity and Mythology* in his own *Jesus Christ and Christianity*).

The Dethronement of the Khedive (A.H. Beaman, ed. with introduction by J.M.R., 1929)

As Robertson explained in his Introduction: "This book was left in my charge for publication by its author, the late Ardern Hulme Beaman ... In this, his last book, written in 1927 and revised by him in 1928, he set himself to reveal a strange historical episode which has hitherto entirely escaped public knowledge. ... I knew him as an expert in all matters touching Egypt, where he served as an Intelligence Officer during and after the [First World] War." Beaman – J.M.R. continued – related "how Abbas II, accused of 'deserting his country' and 'adhering to the enemy', had, in fact, been arbitrarily prevented by the British authorities at Constantinople from returning to

Egypt when only partially convalescent from the dangerous wounds inflicted in the Turkish attempt to assassinate him … No official explanation has ever been offered of the grounds on which Abbas II was insulted, defamed, and deposed … with no shadow of proof that Abbas had been in communication with the enemy at all. … Nor has anyone ever told us what could have induced the Khedive to join the Central Powers. The victory of Germany would certainly have meant German annexation of Egypt …" Robertson added that had there been "any real adherence to the Central Powers, the pecuniary offers made later in Switzerland to Abbas II by the British authorities would never have been thought of. … They [the British] had actually decided to depose him without the semblance of a trial, at a time when he lay dangerously wounded … It was within my knowledge that Lord Kitchener, on imperialistic grounds, had aimed at the deposition of Abbas II before the War was dreamed of. … As Beaman says and shows, the notion that Cromer and Kitchener were straightforward 'plain-dealers' was an absurd delusion. Cromer practised forms of espionage of which, to my knowledge, some of his subordinates were ashamed. …" As recounted by Robertson (*Courses of Study*, 1932 ed., p. 228), early in 1932 the ex-Khedive, in legal action, won an apology and retraction from the London publishers of a book containing hostile material. In his memoirs, published in English in 1998, Abbas Hilmi II spoke highly of "our friend Mr. Robertson, Egypt's great friend" (p. 294). Earlier, in 1930, Abbas Hilmi II, on a dedication page, referred to J.M.R. as "an old and sincere supporter of Egyptian Constitutional freedom" (*A Few Words on the Anglo-Egyptian Settlement*). In *Orientations* (1937), which ignored Beaman and his book, Ronald Storrs was semi-sympathetic towards the Khedive (pp. 138-9, 158).

Did Shakespeare Write 'Titus Andronicus'? (1905)

Confronted by puzzling features associated with the plays attributed to Shakespeare, Robertson began to subject the texts to what he regarded as scientific tests of diction, vocabulary, metre, rhythm and dramatic construction. In the process of doing so, he detected in the plays the presence of various Elizabethan dramatists, with Shakespeare adapting or substantially revising plays by his predecessors and contemporaries, "by way of freshening their appeal to the public, or giving new opportunities to actors", in an age when composite authorship was accepted theatrical practice and writers were unprotected by copyright. Of all the extensive manifestations of J.M.R.'s 'disintegrationist' Group Theory, his trail-blazing case for George Peele's share in *Titus Andronicus* (with Shakespeare's contribution being a modest one) was perhaps the one of his that gained most support in literary and academic circles. In 1923 Professor C.H. Herford, describing J.M.R. as "a critic of remarkable learning, ingenuity, and resource", referred with evident approval to his "minute examination of diction and vocabulary" in *Titus Andronicus (A Sketch of Recent Shakespearean Investigation 1893-1923*, p. 23). Robertson had been assisted in his task by Ernest Newman, who on his behalf kept his eye open for certain words or phrases in reading through works of several of the lesser Elizabethan dramatists (*HF*, 1936, p. xxvi). J.M.R.'s Shakespeare sparring partner George Greenwood, in pointing out that Robertson cited the word "triumpher" as one of the words found in *Titus Andronicus* which are not found elsewhere in Shakespeare though found in Peele, upbraided J.M.R. for not noticing that the word "triumphing" appears in *The Rape of Lucrece* and in *Love's Labour's Lost*. Yet the fact remains that "triumpher" and "triumphing" are not identical, and in 1914 Robertson believed that *Love's Labour's Lost* "points to outside collaboration" (*Elizabethan Literature*, p. 179). Professor T.M. Parrott and W.W. Greg were among those who seemed most receptive to Robertson's line of argument.

In 1960 the critic Olive Wagner Driver commented on Robertson's "exhaustive study" of the play. In 1948 the Shakespearean scholar John Dover Wilson, who had clashed with J.M.R. on some literary points, felt able to declare: "I bring forward fresh evidence to support – I would claim, to demonstrate – the theory, which J.M. Robertson, though refusing to see the hand of Shakespeare anywhere, went some way towards proving, viz. that we must look to George Peele for the authorship, not only of Act I, but of most of the basic text upon which Shakespeare worked" (introduction to his edition of *Titus Andronicus*, p. xxv: in that sentence Dover Wilson seemed to criticise, if not contradict, himself regarding J.M.R.'s attitude to Shakespeare and *Titus Andronicus*). In 2002 Brian Vickers, who concluded that *Titus Andronicus* was co-written by Peele and Shakespeare, pointed out that of sixteen words and phrases characteristic of Peele or used uniquely by him, twelve were to be found in *Titus Andronicus* (*Shakespeare, Co-Author*, pp. 138, 60, 162). Some years later Bill Bryson declared: "George Peele is also mentioned often as a probable collaborator on *Titus Andronicus*" (*Shakespeare*, 2007, 2016 updated edition, p. 148).

In 1922 J.M.R. built on the 'disintegrationist' approach he indicated he had initiated with his 1905 work on *Titus Andronicus* by dissecting the origination of *Henry V* and of *Julius Caesar* and analysing the authorship of *Richard III*. His 1922 book became, in effect, the first part of a total of four parts (the last one being subdivided into two, making five volumes in all) explicitly focusing – up to 1932 – on different plays in the Shakespeare Canon, with his returning to the problem of *Titus Andronicus* in a separate work in 1924.

The Dynamics of Religion (1897; second ed., 1926)

This book was originally published by the very press which issued both Havelock Ellis's *Sexual Inversion* (included in an indictment in 1898 aimed at "obscene" publications) and two of Robertson's books, *The Saxon and the Celt*, and *Montaigne and Shakspere*, copies of which were seized in a London police raid in 1898 associated with the indictment. Neither the printer, who was Robertson's friend Arthur Bonner (married to Bradlaugh's daughter Hypatia), nor Robertson himself was ever charged; but in case prosecution was envisaged regarding *The Dynamics of Religion*, Robertson publicly revealed that he was the sole author of that historical work ostensibly by M.W. Wiseman (his pseudonym).

As early as 1886, in *The Perversion of Scotland: An Indictment of the Scottish Church*, Robertson had pointed to the importance of economic factors in sustaining religious movements and institutions. He developed this theme in *The Dynamics of Religion* and other writings which in large measure preceded the work of sociologists and social critics like Sombart, Troeltsch, Weber, Tawney and Hobson in exploring interactions between God and Mammon. It seems clear that these contributions by Robertson to sociology were made independently of such writers. (However, as Professor Stanislav Andreski claimed in 1979 and again in 1987 that there is no evidence that Robertson and Max Weber were acquainted with each other's writings, it seems necessary to put the qualification that in 1984 it was pointed out – in *BRUG*, pp. 36-7 – that there was a brief late reference in *Courses of Study*, 1932 ed., to a work by Weber.)

The Dynamics of Religion presents a careful critical survey of developments such as deism and scepticism in England since the Reformation and Henry VIII, with freethought up to the end of the nineteenth century having to struggle against priestly vested interests and "the prejudice of corporations living for themselves rather than for the common weal". The anonymous reviewer in Hypatia Bradlaugh Bonner's *The Reformer* for 15 October 1897 regretted Robertson did not give a fuller account of thinkers like Anthony Collins, Toland, Tindal, and Chubb, not to mention Mandeville; and he also regretted the absence of attention devoted to the Evangelical movement and to J.R. Seeley's *Ecce Homo*. In 1954 Roland Stromberg claimed that in *The Dynamics of Religion* "Robertson exaggerates the perils of free thought, and completely misunderstands the position of Locke and Newton, who were certainly not terrorized into orthodoxy" (*Religious Liberalism*, p. 7 & n.l). This contrasts with the comment of *The Reformer* reviewer, who invoked "the memory of those men who braved the real dangers of speaking out – dangers that men of assured position like Locke and Newton were afraid to face even for their relatively mild form of heresy" (p. 228). Moreover, Stromberg overlooked corrective material in J.M.R.'s 1936 ed. of *A History of Freethought* and the severe punishment in 1761 of Peter Annet, for example, for blasphemy.

The 1897 reviewer judged that J.M.R.'s book "is, in fact, nothing less than a far-reaching study in scientific sociology … and a permanent contribution to the rational history of modern thought" (p. 227). The unnamed reviewer displayed an evident familiarity with German, which in itself would rather tend to suggest that he was none other than Robertson's friend Ernest Newman, who had learnt German by this time and who had contributed an article on "Provincial Culture" under his adopted name to the 15 July 1897 issue of *The Reformer*.

In his 1926 Preface to his second edition – with his concluding section on "Modern Thought" focusing on developments within English Christianity – J.M.R. declared that ecclesiastical organizations "subsist by the exploitation of a persisting appetite" (p. vii). While arguably he may not always have appeared to take sufficient account of the appeal of religion as an emotional crutch, offering solace and comfort to troubled or vulnerable people at times of crisis in their lives, he did seem distinctly conscious of religionists able and willing to exploit and abuse those with apparently unmet emotional or psychological needs (illustrated more recently by an article entitled, on the cover, "How I Survived The Children of God Cult" in the *Sunday Times* magazine for 9 August 2020). In 1852 Marx had famously declared (in *The Eighteenth Brumaire of Louis Bonaparte*): "The tradition of all the dead generations weighs like a nightmare on the brain of the living" (quoted by Lewis Feuer, *Marx and Engels: Basic Writings*, 1969 ed., p. 360); and Robertson may have had these arresting words at the back of his mind when, towards the end of *The Dynamics of Religion*, he wrote that the Church was an endowed machinery "for the imposition of the dead hand of an ignorant past on the living present" (1926 ed., p. 243).

In his book Robertson did not focus on the extent to which the monarchy in modern times felt it needed to be seen as predicated on a close relationship with some particular form of religion in Western Europe; and he may have concluded that this raised issues somewhat outside his conception of the scope or main thrust of *The Dynamics of Religion*. Despite its references to various British monarchs (principally perhaps Henry VIII), "monarchism", "royalty" and "kingship" do not feature in the index to the work; and it may be instructive to record that the British gentleman scholar Gould Francis Leckie – whom J.M.R. did not mention – in his book *Essay on the Practice of the British Government* (some 175 pages, published in London in 1812) did not appear to assign any major supportive role to Christianity or to religion in his defence of a constitutional or responsive monarchy, also remarking for good measure: "the Commons have ceased to be tribunes of the people, from the moment that they are its governors" (p. 137).

The Economics of Progress (1918)

This work was noticed, soon after its publication in London, by Elisha Friedman, Statistician with the War Finance Corporation in America, in *International Commerce and Reconstruction* (1920, p. 418). Almost inevitably in the circumstances for a wartime production, Robertson's book, which was largely based on lectures he delivered in October-December 1917 to the Political and Economic Circle of the National Liberal Club in the British capital, included attacks on three German economists for their support of the German Government: Gustav Schmoller, Lujo Brentano, and Werner Sombart. Robertson denounced Sombart for his "dithyramb on the naturalness and the beneficence of war" in one work and for the fact that in another, *Händler und Helden* ("Traders and Heroes"), "the Professor discourses on the contemptible

British people" (p. 30). Almost as if they had read Robertson's remarks eight decades later, the historians John Horne and Alan Kramer declared in 2001: "The pamphlet by the noted sociologist, Werner Sombart, entitled *Händler und Helden* ('Merchants and Heroes'), which celebrated the warrior idealism of German spirituality over crass British materialism and hypocrisy, was only the most famous expression of convictions held by German intellectuals of different political persuasions" (*German Atrocities*, 1914, pp. 278-9).

But in his 1918 book – arguably the most wide-ranging of his works on economics – Robertson dealt with issues beyond those at the forefront of many minds in Britain during the First World War: in consecutive sections he examined the economics of education, labour, land, capital, commerce and population. He had no section on state health care (but see p. 119 and also *BRUG*, pp. 18-19, for J.M.R. in 1891, etc.). He favoured land nationalisation (pp. 149-50) and defended Ricardo, a massive extension of state-sponsored education (even to University level) - partly on the economic ground that a better educated workforce tends to be a more productive one – the mixed economy, and Free Trade. Whereas Marx addressed the falling rate of profit, J.M.R. seemed no less interested in productivity. While acknowledging the conceivable prospect of an exodus of capital from Britain – "the rate of profit per unit of production having undoubtedly decreased" (p. 109 et seq.) – Robertson advocated taxation of capital values combined with improved methods of production and labour-saving machinery including electrification of railways. He firmly declared: "If the electrification of railways should mean saving of engine-staff as well as of coal, it will have to be pursued" (p. 101). (By 1928 the Royal Mail/Post Office had developed an electrically powered underground railway – running beneath London's streets – to move mail quickly between different parts of the capital, with this rail facility operating for some seventy-five years.)

Robertson had already foreseen in 1893 that Britain's dominant commercial and industrial position, largely built on coal, would be overtaken by the United States, with its more extensive coalfields and other sources of fuel and conceivably offering "an opening for emigration" from Britain. At that time, decades before the widespread development of hydro-electric power, Robertson proposed the harnessing of "a new motive-power to be abundantly supplied by the transmutation of tidal or other inexhaustible force into electricity". In 1922 his rationalist colleague Adam Gowans Whyte advocated widespread expansion in the use of electric cars (*The All-Electric Age*, pp. 48-51). To reduce the pollution, Britain's last coal-fired power station at Port Talbot was closed down in 2024.

Robertson believed that "Syndicalism negates not only the solidarity of the State but the solidarity of labour" (p. 99). He also attacked Guild Socialists and their programme, of which he declared: "it would be difficult to plan a worse way of increasing output. … The demand is for the complete control of the workshops by labour … The means proposed tend directly to the curtailment of production, which means poverty for the worker as surely as for the employer" (p. 112). Even if this picture seemed overdrawn, J.M.R. still doubted – as indicated in his *Liberalism and Labour* (1921) – whether Guild Socialism would result in better or more efficient management of existing enterprises. While his criticism of Guild Socialism focused on economic factors, the political difficulties facing the Guild Socialist movement in Britain were such that it collapsed by August 1923, its demise largely triggered by post-war British Communists through their commitment to "work for the Communist Revolution", with their party "creating divisions in the Guild Socialist Movement and ... drawing from it key workers into its own ranks" (Walter Kendall, *The Revolutionary Movement in Britain 1900-21*, 1969, pp. 282-3). A somewhat similar development took place in the U.S.A. from at least January 1923 onwards (see Zygmund Dobbs, *Keynes at Harvard*, 1962 ed., p. 37).

Fully half of a century before the British Parliament brought in a register of members' interests for United Kingdom M.P.s, Robertson publicly and voluntarily declared in *The Economics of Progress*: "I have no shipping or any other shares, and no interest in any commercial concern" (p. 221).

The Eight Hours Question (1893)

In *The Economics of Progress* (1918) Robertson indicated that, as he saw it, progress involved not only "the lessening of toil for mere maintenance", but also a "rise in quantity and quality of pleasurable life", which, for him at least, included "mental life of all kinds" (pp. 120, 1, and 82). Such general humanistic principles had guided Robertson a quarter of a century earlier when he completed and published his socio-economic study *The Eight Hours Question*, in which he declared at the outset: "The ideal that guides or misguides my own constructive proposals is one of a state of things in which considerably less than eight hours should have to be worked per day in mechanical or toilsome employments. That the workers should have more leisure is assuredly one of the first conditions of social betterment" (p. 9). Already, from early 1889 onwards, as he would have been aware from the *National Reformer*, some Northumberland coal heavers feared that an Eight Hours Bill would increase their work hours to eight per day (see Edward Royle, op. cit. 1980, pp. 230, 243, n. 49). In 1887, for example, not all those who could be regarded as socialists in Britain appeared to favour an Eight Hour Labour Bill (see John Quail's *The Slow Burning Fuse*, 1978, p. 66). In his 1890 public debate with H.M. Hyndman Charles Bradlaugh expressed his opposition to an eight-hour working day enforced by legislation; and in 1971 Bradlaugh's biographer David Tribe would declare that "it was his opponents who often swam in naïve economics" (op. cit. pp. 273, 365, where Tom Mann is referred to). In 1891 Robertson criticised the concept of an eight hours law in his *Modern Humanists*.

Fabian Society propaganda favouring an Eight Hour Day reinforced pressure on the Liberals, and "in particular the carefully documented analysis of the problem by Sidney Webb and Harold Cox which appeared in 1891 … must have been very persuasive" (A.M. McBriar, *Fabian Socialism and English Politics 1884-1918*, 1962, p. 244). Yet the book by Webb and Cox was subjected to stringent criticism by Robertson, who pointed out in his 1893 study (pp. 36 and 37) that the two co-authors ended their joint work by admitting that a general eight hours law was impracticable. Robertson's book mounted a passionate attack on Fabians like Webb, Cox and Bernard Shaw, who, he charged, were misleading the workers, on whom they would force bitter disappointment as a result of their half-baked agitation unrealistically raising expectations: for an eight hours law would not help seasonal trades, correct trade fluctuations or prevent strikes, but it would ignore different conditions in different industries and would tend to reduce earnings, raise prices or limit employment. On paper a maximum eight hours working day was introduced in the Soviet Union, which was a state uncritically supported by leading Fabians. In 1956 a shortened workday for most Soviet workers (including those in the mining industry) to seven or six hours was promised to take effect by 1960 (Tony Cliff, *Russia: A Marxist Analysis*, n.d., 1964?, p. 293): the context seemed to imply problems associated with a general eight hours working day enforced by law or decree. J.M.R. criticised Fabian "drill-sergeants" (1928), and Kautsky (1904) branded them "supporters of bureaucratic centralism and enemies of democratic forms of organisation, particularly the Webbs" (Ken Eaton, 1973, I.L.P., p. 20).

Electoral Justice (1931)

On 15 January 1931 the National Liberal Club's Political Committee agreed to share (it seems with the author) the publication costs of Robertson's *Electoral Justice*. In this little book – subtitled *A Survey of the Theory and Practice of Political Representation* – he presented the case for Proportional Representation on the grounds of democracy and political justice as he saw it. His 1906 general election address – on which he was elected to Parliament – had included support for the provision of Proportional Representation; and he was associated with the Proportional Representation Society during his early years in Parliament. In July 1917 the *Edinburgh Review* featured a 23-page essay on Proportional Representation by J.M.R. (who in his conclusion suggested that a system of Proportional Representation in the United States might have averted the American Civil War, "has given to the political life of Belgium a stability that has endured the earthquake shock of the present war" and "would healthfully modify the opposition to compromise both in Ulster and in Nationalist Ireland"). After the Great War he reiterated that

Proportional Representation would safeguard the rights of minorities (*The Meaning of Liberalism*, 1925 ed., p. 109).

In 1932 Robertson's *Courses of Study* indicated that *Electoral Justice* – which he strangely enough, even amid thousands of titles mentioned, said (p. 184) was entitled *Political Justice* – provided a "summary sketch" of the slow development of serious opposition to the "maldistribution" of the franchise. The "first past the post" system of elections still existed in the UK decades later. (See also *BRUG*, p. 19, last para.)

Elizabethan Literature (1914)

With all due allowance for the mass of information and research that has accumulated in recent times concerning the literature of Elizabeth I's reign, and in particular notwithstanding the enormous growth of the Shakespeare industry since the First World War, Robertson's *Elizabethan Literature* (published in July 1914) was a compact yet reasonably comprehensive, graceful, lucid and readable introduction to its subject which may still repay attention today. For example, in his chapter on Shakespeare he unfavourably compared the descriptive power of "a great living master", the novelist and former seaman Joseph Conrad, in devoting pages to conjuring up the immense force and roar of a hurricane, with Shakespeare's dramatic work where "in *Pericles* the idea is put in a line and a half:

The seaman's whistle

Is as a whisper in the ear[s] of death,

Unheard.

This is the lion's claw: no other man could so strike with words"
(pp. 199-200: see *Pericles*, Act III, Scene I, Pericles's opening
words). In the same chapter J.M.R., exuding enthusiasm
and verve, developed his appreciation of Shakespeare's
Coriolanus, where "he builds another great artistic whole,
wherein nearly every character is limned with a masterly
power … Tragedy has here become … a whole aspect of
life" (pp. 188, 189: in 1923 J.M.R. repeated his tribute to
Coriolanus in *'Hamlet' Once More*, pp. 189-90).

Elizabethan Literature also has three fine chapters on
Elizabethan prose, in one of which Robertson referred
in passing to his conviction that the French freethinker
Montaigne "deeply stimulated both Bacon and Shakespeare:
it would have been astonishing if he had not" (p. 139). In
addition there are two chapters on poetry before and after
Spenser. In his chapter on "The Pre-Shakespearean Drama"
– which follows one specifically on Spenser – Robertson
declared that "the style is not Shakespeare's" (p. 105) in
the unsigned play *Edward III*, which he felt was conceivably
written by Robert Greene (three years later J.M.R. indicated in
Shakespeare and Chapman that *Edward III* contained traces
of Marlowe and Greene). This set Robertson at odds with the
Royal Shakespeare Company, which in 2002 produced and
presented *Edward III* as a play by William Shakespeare and
solely by him, though the RSC had to admit that "there is no
external evidence for the attribution". In *Elizabethan Literature*
J.M.R. maintained that it was "now substantially certain" that
Thomas Kyd wrote the anonymous play *Arden of Feversham*
(p. 100: a claim repeated by Robertson in *'Hamlet' Once More*,
p. 129). In the latter case Brian Vickers in 2008, and Darren
Freebury-Jones in 2018, in effect supported J.M.R.'s attitude

towards Kyd as the presumed author of *Arden of Feversham*. Robertson's useful Bibliographical Note was preceded by his final chapter ("The Later Dramatists"), which offers pertinent comment on Shakespeare's rival Ben Jonson and the latter's *Sejanus*.

J.M.R.'s book was noticed in Germany in 1928 by Eduard Eckhardt in his book (p. X, in German) on English drama in the Reformation and the Renaissance, and in the U.S.A. in 1968 by Leonard Ashley in *Authorship and Evidence* (p. 101 and note 2). In his 1914 book Robertson suggested that the play *The Troublesome Raigne of King John* "in the main, was probably the work of [Thomas] Lodge" (p. 181). By 1922, however, Robertson had modified his surmise to the extent of seeing "much of Peele in *The Troublesome Raigne of King John*" (*The Shakespeare Canon*, p. x). In *Elizabethan Literature* (p. 79) Robertson referred in passing to "Greene or Peele in *Locrine*"; and in 2020 Darren Freebury-Jones, a leading authorship attribution specialist, concluded that Robert Greene was the most likely author of *Locrine*.

Essays in Ethics (1903)

This is the only one of Robertson's many published books to feature the word "ethics" in the title (although almost two decades later he would publish *A Short History of Morals*, and what may be considered an ethical vein runs through the body of his work as a whole). His 1903 book comprises eight essays mostly originally delivered as lectures between 1885 and 1897. His essays touched on subjects such as "the ethics of propaganda", regeneration and compromise, "the pleasures of malignity", international ethics, equality, the role of emotion in history, and the ethics of vivisection. As the libertarian publicist Chris Tame maintained, "Robertson did not attempt to … construct a scientific ethical system. Nevertheless, in a variety of areas he made a number of extremely suggestive and penetrating observations" (*J.M. Robertson*, ed. G.A. Wells, 1987, p. 109). It may be taken as an example that Robertson highlighted a problem facing societies at varying stages of embodying democratic principles when he stated that "the ideal of civic life" was "the reconciliation of constant conflict in opinion with constant amenity in action and intercourse" (p. 66) – which, as Professor G.A. Wells would indicate (op. cit. 1987, p. 253), seemed to place Robertson's attitude on the same footing as the view expressed by the Basel theologian Franz Overbeck in an 1869 letter he wrote to the German thinker Treitschke (the latter being studied by Robertson during the late Victorian period, when, as here, "intercourse" meant social interaction).

J.M.R.'s essays/lectures were based on a form of humanistic utilitarianism as he saw it, although he was quick to point out that "John Stuart Mill, the utilitarian, supposed by many of his discerning contemporaries to advocate the constant subordination of the beautiful to the vulgarly useful" stood alone among English literary men in publicly protesting against a railway scheme whose implementation would have destroyed a lovely stretch of scenery on the way to Brighton (p. 177: from a lecture in 1886). Robertson also showed his awareness of environmental issues when he stated, at least in 1890, "the cleanest of us continue to allow our sewage to pollute the river and the sea-beach" (p. 94). Already, in September 1888, nearly eighty years before the Conservation Society was established in Britain (1966), J.M.R., in the *National Reformer*, deplored the threat of pollution posed by the discharge of untreated sewage into Britain's seas and rivers.

When Robertson declared – originally in 1897 – that "the relapse of German civilisation in and after the Thirty Years' War was a disaster without parallel since the Dark Ages" (p. 15), historical research published a century later indicated that was scarcely an exaggeration, if it was one at all, bearing in mind the military action, sacking, population loss, food shortages, bubonic plague and other epidemic diseases, etc. (see *The Thirty Years' War*, ed. Geoffrey Parker, second ed. 1997, pp. 188-9). J.M.R. asserted that those who suffered in the nineteenth century because of their unwillingness to compromise included the rebel British publisher Richard Carlile and the French Communards, "strenuously faithful to their convictions" (p. 63).

Equally some were ready to attack Turkey when it was supposed Turkey could hardly resist: "another unpleasing feature of our international ethics. We never talk of so attacking a military power believed to be strong, no matter how much we may sympathise with its victims – be it Austria tyrannising in Italy in the last generation, or Prussia coercing Denmark" (pp. 128-9). Robertson went on to express concern for the "myriads" of persecuted Jews driven out of Russia "a few years ago" (p. 130); and he disparagingly referred to the supposed racial stocks of "Aryan" and "non-Aryan" (which would taint life in Germany and elsewhere in Europe decades later). He concluded this lecture on "International Ethics" from 1897 by declaring: "the hopes of humanity in the future must centre on the growth of the spirit which seeks to solve all human problems in the light of human reason and human experience" (p. 141). This seems to bear some comparison with the development since 1945 of a humanistic rules-based international order. But perhaps above all, in an 1886 lecture at South Place Institute – with which he would be associated for almost half a century – he suggested that its members would witness "many contests of ideas - the contests on behalf of the freedom of women, of children, of the workers, of the lower races, of the masses of the higher races" (p. 164). In this way Robertson, conscious of Victorian conventional thought, language and prejudices, was reaching out towards a more modern, egalitarian approach. As Robertson explained in an editorial in the *National Reformer* (11 December 1892), he was also concerned to promote and encourage the more humane treatment of animals – an attitude that would be developed and taken forward by G.W. Foote and the National Secular Society.

Essays in Sociology (1904, 2 vols.)

Robertson concluded his *Essays in Ethics* with a balanced examination of the ethics of vivisection. Earlier in that volume, just before discussing the development in the United States of opposition to slavery, he posed a penetrating question that arguably related more to sociology than to ethics: "Are great historic changes the result of ideas deduced from earlier ideas; or are they rather the outcome of, as it were, spontaneous tides of feeling, which the ideas serve only to justify and express?" (p. 173). Such a question would have whetted the reader's appetite for an analysis of issues raised by his follow-up companion collection entitled *Essays in Sociology*, in which, looking ahead at an early stage, he maintained that it was "hardly conceivable that, if France and Germany were socialised, the war spirit would remain as before" (Vol. 1, pp. 13-14). Each of the two volumes in this companion collection contained some half a dozen previously published or composed essays. Of those in the first volume, "England before and since the French Revolution" concentrated not so much on visible landmarks or milestones in English social history as on the evolution and flow of rationalistic ideas such as those associated with the early English deists (Norman Torrey's classic *Voltaire and the English Deists*, 1930, contains more than a dozen references to J.M.R.'s work in this field). Of religion in Britain in his day Robertson wrote in his 1904 work: "The 'general mind' of the day, as distinguished from the intelligence of the studious minority, is either turning away from religion in simple apathy or turning blindly to the more exciting forms of religion" (Vol. 1, p. 49). This conclusion would strike a chord in Britain a century or so later, more especially perhaps as regards Protestant denominations. Three essays in Vol. 1 largely focused on aspects of sociology or culture; and a fourth considered "Machiavelli and Calvin", Robertson having written on Machiavelli at some length in *The Reformer* for 15 March 1901 and going on to present a study of him in *Pioneer Humanists* (1907).

Of those essays in the second volume, "The Economics of Genius" (originally 1898) and "George Eliot on National Sentiment" (originally 1883) have already been touched upon in the present writer's current work. "The Economics of Genius" appears to have been based, at least in part, on the Epilogue to his *Modern Humanists* (1891), where he declared: "Hitherto our best literature, science, and art have largely depended on the accidental possession of inherited income, or family advantages, by persons of genius" (p. 271: though Robertson referred there to a paper of his in *NR*, 5.5.1889); and his essay, particularly in any earlier form or version, preceded Thorstein Veblen's *The Theory of the Leisure Class* (1899), praised in *Courses of Study*. "The Economics of Genius" was much appreciated by the scholarly British socialist and freethought luminary Frank Ridley, part of whose contribution to modern thought was noticed by Priyamvada Gopal in 2019; and J.M.R.'s essay was highlighted by Ian MacKillop in *The British Ethical Societies* (1986, pp. 182-3: MacKillop would praise J.M.R. on A.H. Clough).

The second volume also included a brilliant essay (1897) on "Nietzsche's Sociology", composed during Friedrich Nietzsche's own lifetime, in which Robertson hailed this iconoclastic German writer as a "stricken man of genius" who was "so often the most stimulating of thinkers". More than twenty years before the birth of the Nazi Party, J.M.R. wrote of Nietzsche: "His assault on 'sympathy' is the rebuttal of his attacks on the anti-Semites, who may now claim to be applying his principles." Much later, barely five months before his own death and Hitler's accession to power, he explicitly noted that Nietzsche's thought had no affinity with Hitlerism. Robertson's long-standing friend Ernest Newman was largely instrumental in exposing the falsification of Nietzsche's work undertaken by his pro-Nazi sister Elisabeth Förster-Nietzsche.

The following essay, "Cromwell and the Historians", noted that Victorian historians extolled the religiously fanatical and imperialistic Oliver Cromwell, whose reputation Robertson strongly attacked in that essay on the tercentenary of his birth (1899). Another essay in Vol. 2 was devoted to "The Possibilities of Women", which Robertson updated in an optimistic spirit in 1931 in an essay with the same title appearing in *Woman's Coming of Age*, published in America and co-edited by his friend, or friendly contact, V.F. Calverton. David Caute, critical of Russian Communism and its Western supporters, placed Calverton among "leaders of the literary Left" in New York by 1932 (*The Fellow-Travellers*, 1973, p. 336). In October 1929 Great Britain's Judicial Committee of the Privy Council ruled that the definition of "persons" in the 1867 British North America Act (section 24) must include women, and therefore could not deny Canadian women full participation in their country's state and government structure. The fact that Robertson did not emphasize the importance of this case (brought by five Canadian women) was the more surprising as he had become a Privy Counsellor in 1915. Robertson concluded his updated essay with a question: "In science, last century had Mary Somerville: this has Madame Curie. Who shall say that there are not more to come?" (op. cit. 1931, p. 368). In 1897 Robertson had had cause to pen an essay "The Inertia of English Universities" – reproduced in his 1904 work, Vol. 2 - but with a situation largely transformed after the First World War, J.M.R. received an answer, at least in Britain, to his question with the later emergence of the women scientists Rosalind Franklin and Dorothy Hodgkin, not to mention the female astronomers Cecilia Payne and Vera C. Rubin, for example, in America. This befitted the secularist of whom Edward Royle wrote: "women's subjects received greater coverage in the *National Reformer* … under Robertson's editorship than in the 1880s under [Mrs.] Besant's … Robertson devoted a leader in 1893 to the advocacy of female suffrage" (op. cit. 1980, p. 247).

Essays towards a Critical Method (1889)

This book contains four essays - all on literary subjects – of which three had previously appeared in Besant's *Our Corner* or the *Westminster Review*: "The Fable of the Bees" (on the work by Bernard Mandeville), "The Art of Tennyson", and "Mr. Howells' Novels". In 1924 Robertson's essay on (de) Mandeville's *Fable of the Bees* would be perceived by F.B.

Kaye, editor of a major re-issue of that eighteenth century classic, as "among the best analyses of Mandeville". The remaining essay is probably best described by the literary critic Dekkers: "The 148-page treatise on 'Science in Criticism' ... represents Robertson's first major effort to come to terms with the problems involved in approaching literary criticism in a scientific manner." J.M.R. felt such an approach was possible, involving "connected steps of reasoning from verifiable data". In order to evaluate a work's "criticism of life", its intellectual importance and its artistic success, the literary critic needed to try to be consistent and conscientious, with a degree of detachment. Robertson's lack of close and even adequate definitions and his less than rigorous logic seemed to reflect difficulties inherent in his task. His wide-ranging and learned essay suggested a debt to Matthew Arnold and Sainte-Beuve. Dekkers concluded: "the structure of the essay remains relatively loose, and it admittedly bears ... a general lack of economy in the presentment of new ideas and concepts. However, in spite of these rough edges, the essay is on the whole remarkable for its breadth of ideas, historical scope, and insight into the processes underlying the formation of critical judgment" (Odin Dekkers, *J.M. Robertson*, 1998, p. 135). J.M.R.'s friend J.P. Gilmour pithily described the book as "a gallant attempt to introduce order into chaos" (*HF*, 1936, p. xi). Robertson's "The Art of Tennyson" was reproduced in its entirety in 1967 by Professor John Jump, who also provided a valuable introduction, in *Tennyson: The Critical Heritage*.

When Robertson's book appeared in 1889, he sent an inscribed copy to his friend Ernest Newman, who as a music critic influenced Neville Cardus, who in turn wrote, in his 1947 autobiography, concerning Robertson: "I owe much to him; his *Essays towards a Critical Method* and his *Evolution of States* were for long my constant bed-books" (p. 55). Bradlaugh had a copy of the 1889 book in his library.

Essays towards Peace (Various Hands; J.M.R.'s contribution, "Superstitions of Militarism"; 1913)

In 1913, virtually on the eve of the First World War, the Rationalist Peace Society (which had been founded in 1910, with J.M.R. as President) issued a little book in paperback form entitled *Essays towards Peace*. Amid concerns that rising international tensions could spark armed conflicts, the Society had been set up to ensure that the voice of reason and of secularism was heard and taken into account by those responding to calls or campaigns to promote international peace and understanding, and to oppose all manifestations of militarism. The Society declared: "It is not intended to act in any way antagonistically towards any existing Peace organizations; rather to co-operate with them, on the lines laid down, on every possible occasion" (unnumbered p. 94). The Society attracted broad support from leading figures in the British freethought movement and allied organizations on its fringes such as N.S.S. President G.W. Foote, the novelist Arnold Bennett, the ethicist F.J. Gould, the future Labour M.P. Harry Snell, the Positivist S.H. Swinny, and three of Robertson's friends, the writer Eden Phillpotts, Dr. Alfred Cox and Sydney Gimson. (J.M.R. had played with Gimson's two little sons who delighted in violently attacking him in his realistic imitation of a growling bear in a cave conveniently situated under Gimson's dining room table.)

Essays towards Peace (printed by Watts & Co.) presented four essays – by J.M.R., Professor Edvard Westermarck (a sociologist from Finland who, in *The Origin and Development of the Moral Ideas*, had noticed Robertson's *Patriotism and Empire* quite soon after its publication), Swinny, and the famous author of *The Great Illusion*, Norman Angell (whose adolescent Radicalism Robertson had fostered and whose writings he influenced). In his essay J.M.R. condemned the militarism of the German soldier von Moltke and of Lord Roberts, and he appeared to accept that the outcome of the Russo-Japanese War illustrated Angell's "war does not pay" thesis (see pp. 22, 25-7, 31). However, despite the rational advantage of a cost-benefit analysis, statesmen could still attack and invade other countries as a result of being blinded by emotional or ideological factors, greed, arrogance, miscalculation, over-reaction, or misleading or incorrect information. Robertson gave a novel emphasis (p. 24) when he declared: "it is arguable that *defeat*, in certain cases, has a wholesome effect on the vanquished – provided that he is not reduced to servitude" (a scenario possibly illustrated by West Germany since 1945).

The little book did not feature a designated editor, but it carried an introduction by Hypatia Bradlaugh Bonner, the Society's chairman. As Bill Cooke, historian of the R.P.A., has pointed out: "While the Rationalist Peace Society was opposed to militarism, it was not necessarily a pacifist organisation" (*The Blasphemy Depot*, 2003, p. 73); and following the outbreak of war in 1914 it condemned German aggression and Germany's invasion of Belgium (where the Kaiser's army committed undeniable atrocities). It is not known whether members of the Society ever discussed, even informally, the feasibility of recommending that a way should be found to limit any British involvement in the armed conflict to trying to help secure and safeguard Channel ports and Belgium's coastline and coastal towns, rather than the British Government deciding on 5 August 1914 that the British Expeditionary Force should go to France (see Max Hastings, 2013, p. 132; Hew Strachan, 2003, p. 52) – with the British Army soon getting bogged down in costly trench warfare. The Peace Society's message as conveyed in its 1913 book evidently made little impact; and although David Tribe was at least technically incorrect in suggesting that the Society "does not seem to have survived the first world war" (*100 Years of Freethought*, 1967, p. 236), it disbanded in 1921. *Essays towards Peace* was noticed by Professor Keith Robbins in *The Abolition of War* (1976).

The Evolution of States (1912)

Compared with his *Patriotism and Empire* (1899), Robertson's *The Evolution of States* contained a more systematic elaboration of the sociological interpretation of history which he had advanced in *Buckle and His Critics* (1895). The fruit of at least seven years' research and reflection, *The Evolution of States* displayed greater subtlety and richness of analysis than much Communist literature before or since, and offered explanations that were a real contribution towards understanding historical processes where others offered over-simplification, falsification or mystification. As a revised version of the substantial book that originally appeared in 1900 as *An Introduction to English Politics*, it was in many ways a masterly survey of West European political, economic and cultural development over two thousand years, from ancient Greece and Rome to the England of Queen Anne. Robertson's pithy description of the early Christian Church – in his chapter on ancient Rome – as "in itself a State within the State" (p. 169) was followed by a thought-provoking "General View of Decadence". Virtually as an aside in that Epilogue he noted that "the prospect of regeneration for Turkey has begun after the amputation of many of the provinces over which she maintained an alien rule" (p. 176). This was years before the final collapse of the Ottoman Empire and the rise to power of Atatürk in 1923 as the first President of Turkey as a secular state. (Atatürk's achievements included the adoption in 1926 of a slightly modified version of the Swiss Civil Code.)

While J.M.R.'s main focus was on Western Europe, it was one of the unsung merits of his 1912 work that he appeared, at the very least, to glimpse the importance and significance for world history of the epic struggle, lasting well over a decade, between Emperor Heraclius of the Eastern Roman Empire and Khusro II, the Shah of Persia, resulting, after stunning initial reverses, in a decisive victory for Heraclius that, in turn, would soon be overshadowed by the march and sweep of a third force: Islam. (The following year, 1913, Robertson touched on religious aspects of the Heraclius –"Chosroes" (also spelt "Khosrow") conflict in the second edition of *A Short History of Christianity*, pp. 149-51: cf. *The Evolution of States*, pp. 115-17.)

In *The Evolution of States* J.M.R. surveyed "The Laws of Socio-Political Development" (pp. 54-74), under which he discussed issues like the role of despotism and abundant food, cross-fertilization of ideas, stultifying religious dogma, crucial economic forces and class divisions, and "the instincts of attraction and repulsion in politics". He then went on to sketch "A General View of Decadence" (pp. 170-80), in which he noted an insatiable "appetite for extended dominion" in all States (p. 178), a "primary impulse to combat" and "inability to refrain from jealousy" among political leaders, and the creation of "buffer States" (p. 179). In *The Eighteenth Brumaire of Louis Bonaparte* (1852) Marx had indicated that all great world-historical facts tended to repeat themselves, "the first time as tragedy, the second as farce". Robertson seemed flexible and less dogmatic in his view of the sequence and interrelationship of tragedy and farce, suggesting an element of the "visibly farcical, as in the recent case of Russia in the Far East, and the earlier case of Britain with regard to Afghanistan" (p. 178): in Afghanistan tragedy would become intermixed with farce in August 2021.

At a time when the history of smaller states like Portugal, Switzerland, the Scandinavian countries and even, to some extent, Holland was little known in Britain, Robertson was a pioneering British historian in covering the field with such a wealth of learning and stimulation in a single volume. He referred very briefly to "a certain renewal of Danish empire" (p. 273), but he did not discuss the development of the Danish West Indies. Although he did not apparently take account of the work of Hanse historians like Ernst Daenell and Rudolf Häpke, J.M.R.'s chapter on the Hansa seems to have represented an early, if brief, attempt in England to acknowledge the Hansa's importance. Many years later the American sociologist Lewis Feuer noted that "J.M. Robertson's verdict on the Dutch trading companies had the sharp clarity of an English liberal" (*Spinoza and the Rise of Liberalism*, 1987 ed., p. 264).

On its publication *The Evolution of States* was noticed not only in Britain, but also in America, for example. In discussing sixteenth century European maritime commerce and colonial expansion, the French scholar Henri Sée declared: "Unfortunately, we have but few works on the economic and commercial activities of the Portuguese" (*Modern Capitalism*, 1928 ed., p. 192) – but he seemed unaware of Robertson's chapter on Portugal and, indeed, of his book, which established J.M.R. as one of the first British sociologists and historians to take an interest in the evolution of modern Brazil (independent of Portugal since 1822) and appreciate its enormous potential. J.M.R. incidentally pointed out that Brazil "was a colony, resorted to by men – many of them Jews – seeking freedom from the Inquisition" (p. 361). In more recent times the Jewish writer Stefan Zweig fled Nazism for sanctuary in London and later in Brazil (where he and his wife committed suicide). While Robertson's seven-page section – in the chapter devoted to Portugal – on the colonisation of Brazil seems relatively ample, given that the main focus is on Europe, the space he accorded the Portuguese in India was distinctly cursory and paltry; and in 1932 his *Courses of Study* commended (p. 332) four late Victorian commentaries relating to Portuguese activities in India that Robertson could have used to advantage in *The Evolution of States*, where he none the less showed a degree of initiative in applying Buckle's emphasis on climatic conditions to the early difficulties confronting the Portuguese in the sub-continent.

Towards the end of his chapter on Portugal (and Brazil) J.M.R. maintained: "Portugal, like Britain, began to accumulate a national debt in the period of chronic European war … All the while, the balance of productivity is more and more heavily on the side of Brazil. … When the English coal supply is exhausted, a vast debt, it is to be feared, may be left to a population ill-capable of sustaining it; and the apparently inevitable result will be such a drift of population from Britain to America or Australia as now goes from Portugal to Brazil" (p. 364). His friend J.A. Hobson (see the latter's *Work and Wealth*, 1914, p. 114) seemed to question the emphasis in *The Evolution of States* on environmental factors; but a century or so later Robertson appears to have been quite far-sighted when, earlier in his 1912 book, he stated: "When in the course of centuries the coalfields are exhausted, unless it should be found that the winds and tides can be made to yield electric power cheaply enough, our manufacturing population will probably dwindle. Either the United States will supersede us with their stores of coal, or … China may take the lead. The chief advantage left us would be the skill and efficiency of our industrial population" (p. 88).

He had just declared that "always men unite to oppose; always they must love to hate, fraternise to struggle" in developing his thesis of "the all-pervading biological forces or tendencies of attraction and repulsion in human affairs" (pp. 71, 70). By extension his thesis regarding the forces of attraction and repulsion could be applied to Britain's relations with European powers (as they became) like France, Germany and, to a lesser extent, Holland during the last few centuries.

Within a page of the words just quoted, Robertson went so far as to say: "A cessation of war is not only easily conceivable, but likely." These wildly optimistic words presaged the book's eloquent conclusion, which none the less expressed some doubts about humanity's prospects of sustained peace; whereas his Liberal colleague G.P. Gooch concluded his *History of Our Time* (1911; February 1914) in the expectation that "war between civilised nations will be considered as antiquated as the duel". Similarly, the Radical H.N. Brailsford believed early in 1914 that "there will be no more wars among the six Great Powers" (A.J.P. Taylor, *The Trouble Makers*, 1985 ed., p. 123).

There could be a semantic discussion as to why Robertson wrote "a cessation of war" rather than "the cessation of war" (he also somewhat qualified his words when he added on p. 71 that "evolution is now visibly towards an abandonment of brute strife among societies"). Moreover, it is true that he indicated no practical time-scale within which he thought a cessation of war would be secured; nor did he identify conditions on the ground in 1900 or up to 1912 that would specifically in that environment render likely, or even possible, the advent and consolidation of a sustained peace. Since the Second World War more serious efforts have been made, through international co-operation and arbitration, to secure a human future without recourse to war. As regards events in Europe leading up to, and during, the First World War, Emeritus Professor Alan Sharp remarked in 2014: "Europe experienced a number of crises in the new century, each of which was resolved peacefully, perhaps contributing to complacency ... each of the states entered a war that few had anticipated and whose magnitude and duration none had predicted" (*28 June*, pp. 3, 9).

Robertson saw science and freedom of thought and of trade as promoting cultural cross-fertilization and, by extension, as factors in human progress. Robertson was concerned to support self-government; and his defence of the status and potential of so-called small nations – as expounded in the first version (1900) of his book – was examined in 2007 by the academic Georgios Varouxakis, who declared: "Some of his arguments are bordering on the fallacious and sophistic" (in *Victorian Visions of Global Order*, ed. Duncan Bell, p. 152) – but without clearly specifying which ones he had in mind. The political scientist Professor Harold Laski regarded Robertson's book as "an invaluable authority on and guide for its subject". In an aside (p. 128) J.M.R. suggested that the intellectual development and potential of Australian aborigines had been thwarted by their physical environment.

In view of the Holocaust befalling European Jews only a decade or so after J.M.R.'s death, it seems fitting to recall that his 1912 book associated "contemporary anti-Semitism" with "pseudo-sociology" (p. 147).

Explorations (1923)

This collection of half a dozen previously published essays on literature and philosophy was pithily described in 1987 by the American scholar Peter Gay as containing "several severe and lucid critiques of religious thought", including two "highly convincing" papers on William James. In his 2003 history of the Rationalist Press Association Bill Cooke quoted with apparent approval from Robertson's essays in the collection on Herbert Spencer and William James. The collection also includes stimulating essays on the causes of the French Revolution, the prose of the English Bible, Tolstoy, and the meaning of materialism.

The Fallacy of Saving (1892)

On the basis of his writings between 1887 and 1892 (for which see *BRUG*, pp. 26-7) Robertson could arguably be regarded as one of the intellectual pioneers of the consumer and Keynesian revolutions of the twentieth century. His heterodox approach and analysis were elaborated in his 1892 book *The Fallacy of Saving*, which was – in Robertson's words – "a somewhat unfortunate title at best … the book is not at all a dissuasion to thrift, but a historical and critical study of the economic doctrine of saving for investment, from Turgot and [Adam] Smith onwards, leading up to a view of the economics of Consumption" (*The Economics of Progress*, 1918, p. vi). It is difficult to know how far Robertson may have taken into account G.A. Gaskell's *The Futility of Pecuniary Thrift as a Means to General Wellbeing*, published in 1890 by the freethought publisher Robert Forder. In his 1892 book (pp.

113-14) Robertson declared (as the academic Timo Särkkä from Finland would indicate in 2009): "it is not quantity but *kind* of consumption, the setting up a continuous demand which shall withdraw labour from the fatally easy fruitions of the mechanical manufacture of common necessaries, that will prevent chronic depression of trade." Särkkä added: "The merit of Robertson's argument lay in the fact that it carried economics into sociology" (*Hobson's Imperialism*, pp. 71, 72). But, bearing in mind that the subtitle of J.M.R.'s 1892 book was *A Study in Economics*, the reader may feel it would be more accurate to say that Robertson's argument carried sociology into economics (rather as, in commenting on the approach of his sociologist friend Patrick Geddes to civics, J.M.R. "stressed that the social conditions of cities were a political problem to the solution of which sociology could usefully contribute": see Stefan Collini, *Liberalism and Sociology*, 1979, p. 203).

Robertson preceded Keynes in delineating what was later called the "paradox of thrift", and was probably the first economist to do so explicitly, through his 1892 book (Robert Nash and William Gramm article in *History of Political Economy*, Vol. 1, No. 2, Fall 1969). Although in his *General Theory of Employment, Interest and Money* (1936), Keynes, in a footnote, dismissed (perhaps with a touch of sour grapes) *The Fallacy of Saving* as "not a book of much value or significance", Stanislav Andreski later praised J.M.R. and his book for "his discovery of the cornerstone of Keynes's theory of employment" (*J.M. Robertson*, ed. G.A. Wells, 1987, p. 68). This was high praise, not least as, virtually fifty years after J.M.R.'s death, Andreski hailed *The Evolution of States* as "Robertson's most important work". As Robert Nash and William Gramm declared from across the Atlantic in their 1969 article on Robertson: "Robertson felt that consumption was the most important factor in producing full employment. ... there is considerable similarity in the basic logic of Robertson's and Keynes's statements regarding the paradox of thrift. Robertson even appears to be using a liquidity preference demand for money assessment of transactions balances when he refutes Say's law [that "there can never be too much saving", in Andreski's words] ... Not only is the analysis of saving found in Robertson's work noticeably similar to that of Keynes [or rather vice versa! MP's note] ... conspicuous by its absence from Keynes's assessment [of J.M.R.'s 1892 book] is any reference to the explicit statement of the paradox of thrift found in *The Fallacy of Saving*. ... Keynes's analysis of saving was more theoretically complete and was fitted into a formal theory of employment, while Robertson's analysis was fragmented and submerged in a theory of overpopulation and underconsumption" (op. cit. Fall 1969, pp. 398-400). Having recently discovered the article by Nash and Gramm, the reader could be forgiven for thinking that Robertson's 1892 book was not the work belittled by Keynes in his *General Theory* as "entirely lacking in the penetrating intuitions of *The Physiology of Industry*" [by J.A. Hobson and A.F. Mummery].

In contrast to Keynes, Hobson was quick to pay tribute to J.M.R.'s "able analysis of the nature of 'paper savings'" in *The Fallacy of Saving (The Evolution of Modern Capitalism,* 1894, p. 187n.). In 1908 Herbert J. Davenport at the University of Chicago referred to "the problem of what has been termed the 'fallacy of saving' ... Ruskin, Robertson, Hobson, and Veblen seem to have done the best work here, not perhaps toward the solution of the problem, but to the development and definition of it" (*Value and Distribution*, p. 529: *Britain's Unknown Genius* was the first printed book devoted to Robertson explicitly to suggest he was a pioneer of Keynesianism).

Although it has been claimed that there is no direct evidence that Hobson was influenced by the Swiss economist and historian Sismondi, it may be one of the merits of *The Fallacy of Saving* that it summarised, albeit briefly, Sismondi's ideas associated with the theory of under-consumption. A number of twentieth century writers on economics (such as Nash and Gramm, John Cunningham Wood, and, more recently, Timo Särkkä) seemed to accept that a prototype of J.M.R.'s book may have largely preceded *The Physiology of Industry*. This last-named work, published in 1889 and written by Hobson in conjunction with A.F. Mummery, had in fact been preceded by some of Robertson's published economics articles in 1887 and 1888 – not to mention 1889 – pointing towards the same conclusion and conceivably seen by Hobson or Mummery. J.M.R. criticised the two co-authors for not linking "a rising demand for the higher products" with the need for birth control and a system of old age pensions; his weaving together these three strands into a coherent whole was probably one of the more original features of Robertson's book. There seems some reason to believe that his Fabian friend G.B. Shaw took some account of *The Fallacy of Saving* many years later in preparing his own *Intelligent Woman's Guide to Socialism*. Certainly "Shaw admitted that the Fabians gained some important ideas from J.M. Robertson's paper on taxation" at their June 1886 conference at South Place (A.M. McBriar, *Fabian Socialism and English Politics 1884-1918*, 1962, p. 24: see also p. 23).

The Fabians were associated, if not aligned, with Keynes, who grew up in an atmosphere of religious dissent, and who may have studied Robertson's *Modern Humanists* (1891), which preceded *The Fallacy of Saving*. (For Keynes and the Fabians see Zygmund Dobbs, *Keynes at Harvard*, 1962 ed., pp. 103, 45, etc.) In J.M.R.'s *Modern Humanists* his

Epilogue on Outlines of Social Reconstruction included socio-economic proposals for investment in public works, public utilities and housing and also the stimulation of consumption through the greater equalisation of incomes and wealth. Such proposals would be developed more than forty years later in Keynes' *General Theory* (see Roy F. Harrod's biography of Keynes, 1951, p. 461 etc.). In *Modern Humanists* the rôle of investment in Robertson's programme for social justice and reconstruction was not fully fleshed out – for example, regarding partnership or relations between private enterprise and state or municipal authorities, including issues associated with possible compensation to private companies by expanding public bodies – but he indicated awareness of the activity of "the class of investors generally" (p. 265, but see pp. 262-72). Both Robertson and Keynes saw a link between economic prosperity and cultural progress (for Keynes see *The History Today Companion to British History*, 1995, p. 447); and both men recognised the social importance of birth control.

Respect and regard for the eminent British economist Alfred Marshall (esteemed by the Fabians), or a good relationship with him, provided another link of sorts between Robertson and Keynes. Between about 1905 and 1915 the latter could be said to have become a protégé of Marshall, who supported Keynes intellectually and financially and influenced him (see Zygmund Dobbs, *Keynes at Harvard*, 1962 ed., pp. 42-5; see also p. 52). J.M.R.'s 1892 book included a number of balanced criticisms of Alfred Marshall's economic thought. In 1893 Robertson reported that he (J.M.R.) had attended an annual meeting of the British Economic Association at which Marshall spoke (see the *Free Review*, 1.10.1893, p. 5). Then, after J.M.R. entered Parliament in 1906, he (Robertson) wrote a summary of Alfred Marshall's

Memorandum – published as a Parliamentary Paper in 1908 – on what was termed the fiscal policy of international trade (see Conrad J. Kaczkowski, op. cit. 1964, pp. 475n., 639). This was followed by complimentary references to Marshall's books on economics in *Courses of Study* (1932 ed.). In the interim Robertson was somewhat more critical of Marshall in lectures (which Keynes as a civil servant in the Whitehall area may have attended) delivered by J.M.R. during October – December 1917 at the National Liberal Club (Keynes had declared himself a Liberal). These lectures formed the basis of Robertson's book *The Economics of Progress* (1918), in which, inter alia, he took Marshall to task for unnecessarily and unhelpfully highlighting the Jewish roots of the economist David Ricardo.

Some years later Marshall's pupil Keynes made remarks smacking of anti-Semitism in a published book about Soviet Russia, which Keynes visited a number of times, and Keynes went on to lavish praise on J.A. Hobson (admittedly as an economist) years after Hobson had himself made anti-Semitic comments in his published work. In 2009 the British historian Peter Clarke, in his study of Keynes (p. 153), declared that Hobson "had been closer to Keynes ideologically rather than academically"; and it may be wondered whether the lavishness and extent of Keynes' praise, in his *General Theory*, for Hobson were motivated by economic considerations alone.

Moreover, it is an inconvenient if possibly coincidental fact that on two occasions – in August 1933 and, again, towards the end of 1936 – Keynes made, authorized or condoned changes or additions (to win over a German audience) to the text in translation of two of his published writings, including his preface for the German edition of his *General Theory*, by way of gratuitous or unnecessary concessions to the

Nazis. The earlier, 1933 case involved an article of his that appeared in Nazi Germany at more or less the same time as *The Hitler Terror* appeared in London, where the latter work was published in September 1933 to alert the British public to the well-documented crimes of the Nazis since 1919. Joseph Schumpeter (hailed by Peter Clarke as a great economist) "drew a parallel between economic theory under the Nazis and the *General Theory* of Keynes" (in the words of Zygmund Dobbs, op. cit. 1962, p. 105).

Fiscal Fraud and Folly (1931)

This book – Robertson's last political work in book form – represented a bitter defence of Free Trade (of which he was a prominent champion in Britain) and attack on its opponents against quite a broad political background. Those attacked included Winston Churchill, Joseph Chamberlain, Lloyd George, John Maynard Keynes (at about the time the latter was beginning work on his *General Theory*), G.D.H. Cole, Philip Snowden, and Lord Beaverbrook (who wrote in his letter of 5 April 1931 to Sir Edward Nicholl: "There are immense forces against us in the Conservative Party who really believe in free imports, and who will do all they can to impede our progress").

Ostensibly J.M.R.'s main target (to judge from the book's subtitle), Beaverbrook was the founder (in 1929) and dynamo of the campaign for Empire Free Trade, which was intended, at least in part, to develop the power of the British Empire as a free trade bloc with external trade barriers, and which had even managed to get a candidate elected to Parliament in October 1930. In 1948 Oswald Mosley applied what seemed to be elements of an adapted version of his friend Beaverbrook's Empire plan to English-speaking territories in sub-Saharan Africa. The corporate state of Fascism seemed more compatible with a tariff system than with free trade. Moreover, in August 1936 Beaverbrook apparently enjoyed Hitler's hospitality at a social function in Berlin; the press baron was a friend of the pro-Nazi Edward VIII/Duke of Windsor; at an early stage of the Second World War Beaverbrook – like Lloyd George – favoured British negotiations (which could only be described as defeatist) for peace with Nazi Germany; and he would maintain a friendly relationship with Mosley until at least 1953. After lambasting Lord Beaverbrook's tariff campaign for promoting naked class interest and imposture, Robertson looked across the North Sea to view Germany, in his mind's eye, as hamstrung by Allied reparations, as if a nation on the brink of bankruptcy "could somehow pay the war debts of all the victors". Eight years later the Fabian Robert Dell would express similar condemnation of the reparations policy, with similar criticism of Lloyd George's responsibility in this matter (*The Geneva Racket*, pp. 16-7).

It seems J.M.R.'s book was based on a series of addresses with the same title that he gave at the National Liberal Club quite soon after late October 1930. At the second such address the Chairman and a section of the audience dissociated themselves from critical comments he made about Lloyd George. Thereafter officers from the Club examined J.M.R.'s remaining addresses and asked him to delete a number of passages relating to Lloyd George, which Robertson declined to do, or, indeed, to make any changes. Then at the National Liberal Club Political Committee meeting on 15 January 1931, it was agreed that the £100 grant towards publication costs of *Fiscal Fraud and Folly* be withdrawn, and that J.M.R.'s offer to release the Committee from their contract with him regarding the book be accepted.

During the campaigning for the December 1918 British general election Lloyd George had promised that defeated Germany would have to pay the Allies reparations or compensation "to the limit of its capacity", and he became one of the architects of the punitive Versailles Treaty, which imposed onerous reparations payments on Germany; whereas J.M.R. was an early and consistently forthright critic of the Allies' reparations policy (see *Fiscal Fraud and Folly*, p. 105, for example). The schedule of German reparations payments was relaxed in 1924 and 1929 and then abolished in mid 1932 – a matter of months before the Nazi accession to power in January 1933 – but "no other provisions of the Versailles Treaty poisoned the postwar period as much" in Germany, where between March 1930 and May 1932 Chancellor Brüning was willing to countenance mass unemployment to eradicate the reparations payments (Klaus Fischer, *Nazi Germany*, 1995, p. 64; Volker Ullrich, *Hitler*, Vol. 1, 2016 Eng. trans., p. 255). This in turn helped to fuel mass support for the Nazis, who within a decade precipitated the Second World War. Some of the damaging consequences of reparations payments were indicated (on pp. 104-5, etc.) in Robertson's book, which was published at about the same time as *The Way to Recovery* by the economist Sir George Paish with a broadly similar angle.

In J.M.R.'s book he declared: "in the way of collective tyranny the modern democracies have abundantly proved that they are 'sisters under the skins' with the autocracies and aristocracies of the past, and are as zealous to play the game of beggar-my-neighbour as were the trade guilds and monopolies of the Middle Ages" (p. 110). Robertson went on to criticise "the advanced section of the Labour Party" for advocating re-established trade relations with Russia: "Now, if there is sweated labour anywhere in Europe, by the tests of wages and the impotence of trade unions as such, it is in Russia. Yet trade with Russia will mean importation of nothing but goods and foods produced by sweated labour, in the trade union sense" (p. 130).   He blamed Protectionists and pro-Soviet ideologues for the prospect of Britain's "commercial suicide", adding: "If you ask for the deeds of Socialism, you have them in Soviet Russia. Look on that picture, and then look back on the record of Free Trade" (see p. 147 etc.). Robertson was perhaps particularly scathing about the Socialist intellectual G.D.H. Cole (concerning whom see *BRUG*, pp. 82-3 and, especially for his pro-Soviet and fanatical Stalinist views, Giles Udy, *Labour and the Gulag*, 2017, pp. 507-8, 513-15, 630-1, etc.). Robertson's contention during the 1921-31 period that Communists were active in the British Labour movement later received partial, if indirect, confirmation with the revelation that in 1926 British trade unions had 242 Communist delegates to Labour organisations and meetings, with 1,544 Communists as individual Labour Party members (David Burke, *The Lawn Road Flats*, 2014, p. 236). The pro-Soviet G.D.H. Cole may have influenced, as well as taught, the young Oxonian Harold Wilson, who was later suspected of serving Soviet interests through his failure to quell Ian Smith's white supremacist regime in "Rhodesia" or to send British troops to aid "South Vietnam", followed by Wilson's soft, protective attitude towards the Communist spy John Stonehouse, and Wilson's substantial loosening of restrictions on contacts between Labour M.P.s and notable Communists.

It may be speculated that Robertson's hostility to Soviet Russia had some influence on George Orwell, who shared many of J.M.R.'s values and aspirations and who drew on Robertson's introduction (published in 1927 and 1932) to an edition of Winwood Reade's *The Martyrdom of Man*. Orwell, who also worked in a Hampstead second-hand bookshop between 1934 and 1936, may well have perused or read other works by J.M.R. such as *The Meaning of Liberalism* and *Fiscal Fraud and Folly*, not to mention *The Decadence*, in which Robertson aired his anti-Soviet views. In *Fiscal Fraud and Folly* Robertson specifically exonerated the esteemed British Independent Labour Party leader James Maxton from "any complicity in the Labour imposture" that the pre-War Liberal Party had been merely a Free Trade party (the bookshop owners who employed Orwell were committed and active I.L.P. members, and their contacts "prompted him to think about social and economic problems": see D.J. Taylor, *Orwell*, 2004 ed., pp. 151-2). Moreover, Orwell's *1984* (1949) was partly inspired by his reading the dystopian novel *We* by Yevgeny Zamyatin, who just before his return to Russia at the time of the 1917 revolutionary upheaval there had worked as a naval engineer in Newcastle-upon-Tyne, where he would have mixed with people who lived or worked in Robertson's constituency and whence he could have carried respect for liberal values with him. In addition, during 1927-8 Orwell was friendly with an aspiring cultural commentator called Alan Clutton-Brock, whose father Arthur Clutton-Brock had been roundly criticised by Robertson in *'Hamlet' Once More* (1923).

The Future of Liberalism (n.d.: 1897?)

This pamphlet (of which the main text covered some 28 pages) was published by J.W. Gott of Bradford, an indefatigable and witty freethinker who helped to arrange some of J.M.R.'s lectures, with Robertson as a Minister privately approaching the Home Secretary, Reginald McKenna, in 1911 in mitigation of a prison sentence imposed on Gott for blasphemy.

(Robertson was also willing to take up the cudgels on behalf of James Rowney, a stalwart freethinker who delivered many hundreds of lectures in the public parks and yet appeared to have less of a high profile than J.W. Gott: as the *Literary Guide* explained in August 1909, Robertson appealed for funds to help Rowney in his old age.)

In his essay, penned towards the end of Gladstone's life, Robertson criticised the former Liberal Party leader and Prime Minister for having "always lived intellectually from hand to mouth. Hence he could never count on being steadily followed even by the electors" (p. 6). Gladstone "failed to educate the mass of the electorate up to a good and firm grasp of progressive Liberal principles" (p. 7).

As part of his recommended revision and enlargement of the Liberal Party's programme, Robertson proposed a commitment to introduce state old age pensions and "succour of the unemployed" – the latter delivered through public works, including "the reconstruction of the slum areas of cities" (p. 22) – so that the workers, a future majority of the electorate, would support the Liberals following their shattering defeat in the July 1895 general election (when the fairly recently formed Independent Labour Party failed to win any seats). Further measures "to promote equality of well-being and to restrict idle living" (p. 23) could well include nationalisation of the railways. He added: "The children of the masses can have no 'equality of opportunity' until they can pass freely from Board School to University if their capacity lie in the line of such culture; and it is clear that the masses will never be able to produce the leaders and teachers they need until their own best brains are thus given a fair chance of development" (p. 24). Arguably this education component of Robertson's vision for the future of British society would only come into its own a century later with the election of a Labour Government under Tony Blair.

In his essay Robertson went on to propose Proportional Representation, payment of M.P.s, and the abolition or at least curtailment and reform of "political anomalies" such as the House of Lords, the Cabinet system and the monarchy. As a pivotal figure in an age of transition to a more democratic society and greater awareness of human rights, Robertson in the 1880s and 1890s presented a package of proposals that, taken together, arguably constituted the most comprehensive, far-reaching and detailed radical programme for social and political reform – indeed, for a peaceful revolution – in Britain from anybody (as distinct from any body) with a non-Marxist perspective at that time. This was illustrated by his Epilogue on Social Reconstruction in his *Modern Humanists* (1891), his twelve *Papers for the People* (1896-7), and *The Future of Liberalism* (1897?). This achievement, for such it was, could be considered part of his genius. Be that as it may, his last-named essay virtually ended with his blaming the Tories in Britain for "their influence that has committed us to the besotted policy of chronic outlay on naval and military preparation in a state of panic. In this way the leading Naval States are playing the fool to the verge of bankruptcy, each egging on the other …" (p. 29). This was a theme to which he returned some twenty years later, in *The Future of Militarism*.

The Future of Liberalism was noticed in H.V. Emy's very useful study *Liberals, Radicals and Social Politics, 1892–1914* (1973), as was J.M.R.'s *The Fallacy of Saving*, in which, Emy said, Robertson "went further than Hobson and attacked the savings-investment link itself, seeing more clearly than Hobson the existence of what came to be called the savings paradox" (pp. 112, 113). Emy believed (p. 113) that *The*

Future of Liberalism was published in 1895, but although the bulk of this pamphlet could have been written in 1895 for a lecture, internal and ancillary evidence in its revisited and apparently expanded form as a pamphlet suggests that it was much more likely to date from 1897.

The Future of Militarism (1916)

It is widely accepted that J.M.R. was the pseudonymous author of this work (published by T. Fisher Unwin, who published other books of his). The subtitle of this wartime book is *An Examination of F. Scott Oliver's 'Ordeal by Battle'*, and in replying to Oliver's work Robertson, in an allusion to a French literary classic on a military conflict, adopted the pseudonym Roland to do so. The reactionary F.S. Oliver thought that conscription and large armies in peacetime were a sure way to avoid war. Militarists of Oliver's ilk – J.M.R. said – believed (in the latter's words) that "peace on earth is to be secured by all the nations of the earth being at all times armed to the utmost of their power" (p. 66). He added that supreme fitness for war "inevitably promotes the spirit of war" (p. 81). Robertson also indicated that a system of conscription by Britain could have led to an earlier war developing on a global scale (p. 48).

Robertson then claimed (p. 134): "Many Tories favour militarism because it makes in their opinion for the proper subordination of the masses", which could serve to nullify troublesome and vexatious demands for reform and social justice.

Robertson suggested that the capitulation of German

socialists to German militarism under Kaiser Wilhelm II illustrated this cast of mind, and that similarly "the enthusiastic acceptance of the war – invasion of Belgium and all – by the German people is plain evidence of the effect of militarism on the *mind* of a nation" (p. 153: his emphasis). In *The Germans* – also published in 1916 – J.M.R. seemed to imply (pp. 244-5) that one factor taken into account by the Kaiser and members of the élite around him was that a war would serve as a diversion to thwart the disturbing advance of the socialist party in Germany. On the basis of such an analysis the Great War reflected at least an element of class hatred as well as conflict between imperial powers. In June 1914, unbeknown to J.M.R., the Imperial German Chancellor Bethmann-Hollweg told a Ministerial colleague that "some in the Empire … believed that a war would have a healthy effect on domestic conditions in Germany, and would help the conservative cause" (quoted by Wolfgang Mommsen, *Imperial Germany 1867-1918*, Eng. trans. 1995, p. 280, n. 53). For F.S. Oliver – in Robertson's words – "the State has a right to call for unquestioning obedience from all its citizens" (p. 13); whereas for Robertson, "there would be small scope for criticism if the militarists were in political power" (p. 164). Indeed, in his book, as in the House of Commons, J.M.R. protested against ill-treatment of British conscientious objectors.

At the same time Robertson believed that "for *any* Power to seek to maintain the highest status at once on land and sea is simply the surest road to national bankruptcy. … Germany, before the war, was in such financial straits from this very cause that the strain counted for much in her precipitation of the land war, which she hoped would not involve a sea-war with Britain" (p. 111: J.M.R.'s emphasis). For Robertson: "the German ideal has materialized in the infernal machine which hewed Belgium as a carcass for hounds … while the Turkish ally, with German official endorsement, slaughtered half the population of Armenia, young and old" (p. 148). According to Nathaniel Weyl (*Karl Marx: Racist*, 1979, p. 129), the Turkish slaughter of the Armenians helped to convince Hitler that the annihilation of European Jewry was practicable. Thus J.M.R. condemned a systematic contempt for, and destruction of, human lives and human rights that a later generation would discover in Nazi militarism, totalitarianism and genocide. Robertson declared: "if a Europe exhausted by war is again to assume the burdens of militarism on the old scale, European civilization will simply be at the beginning of the end. … not for twenty years can the belligerent Powers recover from the drain that this war has made upon them" (p. 114). He would express similar sentiments, in similar terms, in his moving Parliamentary swan-song on 8 August 1918.

Believing that militarism was pervasive, Robertson proposed that the neutral powers in the world war should "enter into a common pact with the Allies for the maintenance of the peace of Europe by a machinery of arbitration which shall veto all aggression", with the Allies further resolving "to join in resisting any aggression upon any one of them" (p. 113). (Such views also found expression in his sixteen page pamphlet *Peace Organization after the War*, thought to have been written in 1918.) *The Future of Militarism* stands apart from other wartime works by J.M.R. on German militarism and aggression in so far as it provides a salutary reminder that militarism in his time was not confined to Germany or her allies.

The Genuine in Shakespeare: A Conspectus (1930)

In *'Hamlet' Once More* (1923) Robertson rather unexpectedly devoted some attention to *As You Like It* (attributed to Shakespeare) and, in particular, to a passage in the play revealing "a kind of touch that no one else has given us" such as that (in Act II, Scene 7, lines 109-12) where a chastened Orlando in beautiful language craves pardon, with J.M.R. commenting: "it is as if an enchanter had smitten the earth with his wand … The effect is quite alien to those of the well-made play … And that is but a minor kind of effect, for Shakespeare, belonging to his first period" (pp. 180-1). Robertson saw this charming touch as quite distinct from the realisation that Shakespeare "could on occasion make or adapt a well-calculated plot". Moreover, *As You Like It* had been based on Thomas Lodge's prose story *Rosalynde* (*Elizabethan Literature*, 1914, p. 182: a point reiterated in 2016 by Bill Bryson); and a sentence from Marlowe's *Hero and Leander* appeared unchanged in the Shakespearean play (see Bryson, *Shakespeare*, 2016 ed., pp. 99, 100; see also 112).

Shakespeare's contemporary dramatist Robert Greene accused the Bard of being "beautified by our feathers"; and the best part of 350 years later in *The Genuine in Shakespeare: A Conspectus* (1930) Robertson summarized many of his disintegrationist findings to date in other books of his on the Shakespeare Canon. Applying verse tests, he concluded that at least some of *The Comedy of Errors* was non-Shakespearean. Similarly, he discussed George Chapman's perceived contribution to *The Merry Wives of Windsor*, which he had sketched in the closing section of his Epilogue to his *Shakespeare and Chapman* (1917). In 1966 Professor

Geoffrey Bullough – perhaps rather peremptorily – dismissed J.M.R.'s contention that quite a bit of *Troilus and Cressida* was non-Shakespearean; although the Professor's conclusion that the play was "substantially" Shakespeare's because of its "unity of tone" sounded vague and subjective. (See Bullough's *Narrative and Dramatic Sources of Shakespeare*, Vol. VI.) The American critic Bernard Grebanier took account of J.M.R.'s comments on *Hamlet*. Robertson admired Shakespeare's "moral sanity" as a humanist.

In 1991 Grace Ioppolo, after stating that, according to Robertson, all of Shakespeare's plays except *A Midsummer Night's Dream* were adaptations of existing plays, declared: "Due to the lingering influence of F.G. Fleay and J.M. Robertson in the early twentieth century, critics such as John Dover Wilson continued to see pre-existing plays as the basis of many of Shakespeare's plays, and modern editors have agreed with Wilson in certain cases" (*Revising Shakespeare*, p. 86; see also pp. 105, 35. Cf. Bryson, p. 99, para. 1).

The Germans (1916)

The Germans consisted of two Parts: "The Teutonic Gospel of Race" and "The Old Germany and the New". In this ethnological and political study – in which, according to Professor L.T. Hobhouse, "the pseudo-scientific dogmas of race are torn to shreds" – Robertson continued his assault on "the Teutonic Gospel of Race" that he had begun before the First World War. In his book he wrote (p. 201) of "the 'rabies' of race-hatred and race-pride", and he added to criticism of the concept of an "Aryan race" (for which see his *Courses of Study*, 1932 ed., pp. 5-6). In *The Germans* (pp.

44, 106) J.M.R. referred to the racial cult that had developed in Germany around the scholarly French diplomat and writer Count Joseph Arthur de Gobineau (whose mid-nineteenth century admiration of the "Aryans" would be enthusiastically endorsed by the Nazis). *The Germans* was subsequently noticed in a 1935 Nazi bibliography on English propaganda in the World War, but it did not feature in Hermann Wanderscheck's associated, follow-up work entitled (in German) *English Lying Propaganda in the World War and Today* (1940): perhaps J.M.R.'s exclusion from the latter Nazi work was a kind of backhanded compliment to him! Both Robertson and the pro-Nazi publicist from England, Houston Stewart Chamberlain, quoted the same passage from H. d'Arbois de Jubainville's *Les Celtes* (1904) to the effect that "there is probably in Germany more Gallic blood than in France" – the point being made more cogently by J.M.R. than by his contemporary from Britain (*The Germans*, p. 103, note 1; *The Foundations of the Nineteenth Century*, 1911 English translation, Vol. 1, p. 499). In 1911 Robertson had critically reviewed Chamberlain's *Foundations*, for which see *BRUG*, p. 33.

The leading Nazi ideologue Alfred Rosenberg later placed H.S. Chamberlain and Paul de Lagarde among the four ancestors, named by him, of National Socialism (see Georg Lukacs, *The Destruction of Reason*, 1980 English ed., p. 715). In his 1916 book Robertson, in the same sentence, also linked Chamberlain and de Lagarde – albeit in a passing reference (p. 85). Hitler in *Mein Kampf* used de Lagarde as one of his unacknowledged sources (Karl Bracher, *The German Dictatorship*, 1973 Eng. trans. ed., p. 166; see also Volker Ullrich, *Hitler*, Vol. 1,2016 Eng. trans., pp. 176, 805). Indeed, as Professor F.L. Carsten wrote of de Lagarde and the Nazis: "Almost their whole programme can be found in his writings" (*The Rise of Fascism*, 1967, 1974 reprint, p. 26). Striking points of similarity between de Lagarde's proposals and Hitler's actions in Eastern Europe and Russia included: the Germanisation of countries bordering Germany and Austria in the east; the imperative to defeat Russia in war; the expulsion of Jews from their settled homelands in eastern Europe; and their destruction as what de Lagarde called "carriers of putrefaction" (ibid.). Yet de Lagarde has received scant or no attention from some historians of Nazism (Jan Romein, in Holland, referred to the views on Christianity of both J.M. Robertson and the orientalist Paul de Lagarde within six lines of each other on p. 485 of *The Watershed of Two Eras*). Professor Hans Günther - a prolific pro-Nazi ideologue with source material for *Mein Kampf* - was quite probably aware of the range of J.M.R.'s work on race.

Robertson did not analyse the anti-Semitic current in German political life; although the openly anti-Semitic political parties seemed to be in retreat by 1916: death had removed at least ten anti-Semitic leaders in Germany between 1903 and 1914 (see Richard S. Levy's 1975 book on the subject, p. 245 etc.), and many German Jews fought for the Kaiser in the World War. One such German Jew in the German army was Alfred Wiener, who in 1919 produced a pamphlet - *Prelude to pogroms?* - detailing numerous examples of German anti-Semitism (he later founded London's famous Wiener Library). The absence of discussion by Robertson of the German Society for Racial Hygiene, Navy League or Pan-German League seems surprising, with his book's focus on the development of German racialism and German state power in Europe over decades or a longer time-span, even if, as Professor Wolfgang Mommsen has maintained, the ideas promoted by these three bodies "were slow to percolate into the serious daily press" (*Imperial Germany 1867-1918,* 1995 ed., p. 191).

During the early years of the twentieth century Kaiser Wilhelm II's administration was not loath to approach and co-opt ostensibly independent scholars like the historian Karl Lamprecht to give it support (see Mommsen, op. cit., 1995 ed., pp. 194, 201, 279 n. 41). Lamprecht's 'on message' response evoked Robertson's forthright criticism of him in *The Germans* as in effect a cheer-leader for a shrill form of German nationalism (see pp. 97, 112); and sixteen years later J.M.R., in *Courses of Study*, was rather generous even in his somewhat guarded reference to Lamprecht's work as a historian. Both Lamprecht and Robertson drew attention with varying emphasis to the role of impersonal forces and social and economic conditions in history from a non-Marxist viewpoint.

In Part II of *The Germans* Robertson surveyed the evolution and growth of Germany and a perceived German national consciousness since the Middle Ages, Reformation and eighteenth century. He declared: "Even as the Prussian Diet [legislative assembly] has remained an illusory semblance of a constitutional government, in which class interests are supreme, so has the German Reichstag, the fruit of 1870, remained an 'unconstitutional' Parliament, in which the Kaiser's ministers are responsible to him, not to the representatives of the people. … the system had never been democratised" (p. 225). Or as Wolfgang Mommsen put it over seventy years later: in Wilhelmine Germany "progress towards constitutional democracy was kept in check" (op. cit., 1995 ed., p. 189: see also p. 31). Some fifty years before the German historian Karl Dietrich Bracher made a similar point, J.M.R. said: "the aggregate of the German people has reached State power without political education" (p. 226).

However, in 1982 Hugh MacDougall indicated that in *The Germans* Robertson "with considerable success … exposed many of the absurdities implicit in current racial interpretations of English and German history" (*Racial Myth in English History*, pp. 127, 141). *The Germans* also featured in the Bibliography of Ashley Montagu's *Man's Most Dangerous Myth: The Fallacy of Race* (fifth edition, 1974, p. 510).

One aspect that Robertson may have felt was not central to his task in *The Germans*, though it was arguably relevant, was the way the Kaiser's regime treated British prisoners of war between 1914 and 1918. Although *The Germans* was published some three months after J.M.R.'s *War and Civilization* in 1916, it did not focus on the Kaiser's appalling ill-treatment of captured British soldiers in the Great War. But *War and Civilization* did refer, albeit very briefly, to "reports by Dutch journalists of the brutalities and indignities inflicted by German officials on wounded British prisoners in transit" (p. 63) and to "highly attested accounts by British officers and soldiers of the killing of British wounded and prisoners" by Germans (p. 68). Liddell Hart and Hew Strachan, for example, gave scant attention to this aspect in their respective histories of the First World War (1930; 2003); and Joseph O'Neill's exposé and indictment of the Kaiser's record in this respect only appeared in *Military History Matters* for August/September 2021.

The Great Question: Free Trade or Tariff Reform? (1909)

Robertson was no stranger to debating face to face with an opponent on a public platform (for example, he debated the practicability of socialism with Harry Quelch, editor of *Justice*, in the Temperance Hall, Northampton, on 24 January 1908). But on the occasion under review the debate took a different form, described somewhat whimsically by his opponent Leo Amery, a Conservative politician who was not yet an M.P., still less Colonial Secretary. Amery explained that, shortly before starting a mountaineering holiday in the Canadian Rockies, he "had rashly promised Messrs. Pitman to write the protectionist half of a book which was to state both sides of the great tariff controversy, the other half to be written by J.M. Robertson, M.P. *The Great Question* had one amusing feature. In order that neither side should claim that its case was prejudiced by being stated last the book began at both ends. One reviewer described it as an amphisbaenic book, after a fabulous two-headed serpent [with a head at each end] … One cover was decorated with Britannia with trident and shield, prepared to meet a world at arms [Amery's]; the other Britannia, her weapons laid aside, open armed to welcome the doves of peaceful international trade [Robertson's]. My promise now had to be fulfilled somehow, so at intervals on board ship, on trains and in camp I managed to get it done. … I finished the wretched work between three-thirty and seven in the morning, and posted it back to a kind friend, Saxon Mills, to see it through the proof stage" (*My Political Life*, Vol. 1, 1953, pp. 339-40).

The precise circumstances under which Robertson presented his side of the argument in the controversy are not known. But available information from about this time suggests that his busy schedule in England and Scotland included attending Liberal Party rallies, freethought and sociology meetings, Parliament, and also (on 1 December 1908) a debate held by the Durham University Union Society on national defence, his opponent on that occasion being the anti-pacifist historian G.G. Coulton. J.M.R. would have had ready access to libraries, books, papers, etc.; and in 1910 Charles T. King recognised him as a powerful speaker against fiscal change (*The Asquith Parliament 1906-1909*, p. 335).

For his part, Leo Amery was a fervent believer in Britain's imperial mission and destiny, a protégé of Lord Milner in South Africa (where Amery grew up), and a devoted disciple of Joseph Chamberlain, who thought that the scattered British white settler colonies and Dominions of the Empire should be drawn into an integrated unit (partly through imperial tariffs) that would sustain Britain as a world power (see Stephen Dorril, *Blackshirt*, 2006, pp. 38, 572, and Martin Kitchen, *The British Empire and Commonwealth*, 1996 ed., pp. 57,71). By contrast, Free Trade (defended by Robertson) struck a more internationalist and less pugnacious note. As Colonial Secretary (1924-29), Amery wrote to Jan Smuts to express his concern that "the permanent maintenance of the white race against the black" in South Africa would turn out to be temporary (quoted by Will Podmore, *British Foreign Policy since 1870*, 2008, p. 53). In 1929 Robertson felt the need to comment directly on Amery when he declared that in the latter part of 1928 "two prominent if unimportant Ministers, Joynson-Hicks and Amery" proposed that the Tories should adopt a programme of "extended safeguarding" for the next election (*The Decadence*, p. 25). Although J.M.R. added that Amery had appeared "portentous", others seemed to look at this Minister in a slightly different way, for "it was said of him that he might have been Prime Minister if he had been half a head taller and his speeches half an hour shorter" (Michael Davie in a footnote in his edition of *The Diaries of Evelyn Waugh*, 1976, p. 647: entry for very early April 1946).

'Hamlet' Once More (1923)

Robertson believed and sought to show that admitted incongruities and perplexities in *Hamlet* had arisen because "Shakespeare was but transmuting an old play without reconstructing it … and he so irradiated it that to this day the play holds us spellbound" (*'Hamlet' Once More*, pp. 71-2). His theory of *Hamlet* owing quite a lot to Thomas Kyd found expression in *The Problem of 'Hamlet'* (1919) and its follow-up, companion volume *'Hamlet' Once More* (1923), of which the latter largely consisted of a rebuttal of the views of the British critic Arthur Clutton-Brock, who had taken exception to the earlier book. As Paul Gottschalk commented fifty years later: "Connoisseurs of literary mayhem will enjoy J.M. Robertson's rebuttal of Clutton-Brock" (*The Meaning of 'Hamlet'*, 1972, p. 170, n. 56).

However, Robertson was modest or honest enough to qualify or correct (op. cit. 1923, pp. 147n., 150n.) one or two of the statements he himself had made in *The Problem of 'Hamlet'*. He also acknowledged that only after that book was published in 1919 had he become aware of the existence of *The Genesis of 'Hamlet'* (1907) – by the American Professor Charlton M. Lewis of Yale University – which, J.M.R. had just discovered, had independently and substantially presented much the same analysis and solution as he did in 1919 (not to mention Robertson's essays on the subject in 1885 and 1895). After Robertson's death his 1923 book was noticed in the U.S.A. by Hubertis Cummings in a 1935 volume of essays by devoted pupils of Professor Thomas M. Parrott (who had himself appreciated J.M.R.'s work on Shakespeare and Chapman), by Bernard Grebanier in the 1960s and by Paul Gottschalk in the 1970s, for example. In 1936 the British scholar John

Dover Wilson, having named J.M.R. as one of three leaders of the "historical" school of Shakespearean critics, accused those leaders of "ignorance of history", "lack of historical curiosity" and groundless assumption "that the aesthetic sensibility of the Elizabethans as regards drama was crude", as well as "little or no attempt to study Shakespeare in the light of Elizabethan politics" (see introduction to his second edition of *Hamlet*). Yet J.M.R. in his 1923 book referred to Polonius as possibly "a skit on Lord Burleigh" (p. 132) and to "the mad Ophelia of the old play, who was actually a theme for laughter to the old audience" (p. 84). Moreover, Dover Wilson compared J.M.R. as a historian (apparently favourably) with Lord Acton (see *BRUG*, p. 39).

From time to time Robertson has been criticised, with some justification, for his style and the way in which he sometimes used the English language. But in *'Hamlet' Once More*, for example, his word-picture (pp. 111-12) of the finale to *Hamlet* was about as thrilling or as eloquent as his stylistically most appealing work: "the panting duellists, with every nerve and sinew alert and tense, fencing, it is to be supposed, as our actors do not now; the intent audience, knowing that there is death in the cup, poison on the foil, and two villains in the plot counting on one or other infallibly succeeding; and over all, at every hit by Hamlet, the boom of the "cannon", as it were the advancing stride of death: 'At each rap a blast/From the horns of hell', till the crashes of sound are swallowed up in the moral lightning-flash of fourfold doom."

The Historical Jesus (1916)

Looking back in 1929 on 1916, the humanist F.J. Gould

commented: "Robertson was aiding the dissolution of orthodoxy, Protestant and Catholic, by his *Historical Jesus*, a work which exhibited the figure of Jesus as entirely myth-made" (*The Pioneers of Johnson's Court*, p. 100). In this wartime work Robertson built on the investigations he had conducted in *Christianity and Mythology* (1900; 1910), *Pagan Christs* (1903; 1911), and *A Short History of Christianity* (1902; 1913); and he took account of development of the Myth Theory by the German Professor Arthur Drews and the American Professor William Benjamin Smith (Preamble, pp. xi-xii). When challenged by a learned Christian cleric to come up with a pagan story from ancient Greek literature that was as ethically impressive as that of the Good Samaritan, Robertson readily pointed to the story of Lycurgus, who, though blinded in one eye by Alcander, forgave him and through kindness turned him into a good citizen (*The Historical Jesus*, pp. 24-5: a story of redemption that Robertson had already recounted in his *Letters on Reasoning*, second ed. 1905, p. 252). In 1935 the Mythicist Gordon Rylands referred to *The Historical Jesus* (p. 163) as providing an example of the text in the Gospels being manipulated or reconstructed in modern times for ulterior religious motives.

In his book (pp. 190-1) Robertson engaged in some tentative, respectful criticism of the line of argument presented by the Marxist Karl Kautsky in *The Origin of Christianity* (1908). More recently Professor G.A. Wells wrote (in *J.M. Robertson*, 1987, p. 153) that Robertson in his book "censured Volney and Dupuis" for explaining Christian origins in terms of analogies with pagan elements; but "censured" seems rather harsh as Robertson, almost at the bottom of page 193, remarked that "their argument was both sound and important, so far as it went". Moreover, J.M.R. took Sir James Frazer to task for suggesting that religions seemed to require "great men" and "extraordinary minds" as founders.

In 1999 Professor Walter Weaver bracketed *The Historical Jesus* with the more extensive *Christianity and Mythology* and *Pagan Christs* with which he listed it as the kernel of J.M.R.'s work in this field (*The Historical Jesus in the Twentieth Century 1900-1950*, pp. 58, 421). However, his added comment (p. 62) that J.M.R.'s work generally was "lacking any interpretive power" was a travesty born, it is suggested, of religious prejudice. In 2000, also in the U.S.A., Robert Van Voorst added *A Short History of Christianity* and *The Jesus Problem* to this list, making five books in all which Van Voorst termed "Robertson's many books attacking Christianity by way of attacking the historicity of its founder" and "trying to discredit Christianity by showing that its savior was a myth" (*Jesus Outside the New Testament*, pp. 11-12, 229-30). But J.M.R. concluded that Jesus was a mythical figure after he had abandoned Christianity and only after a sustained period of painstaking scholarly research. Thoughtful writers who have taken account of Robertson's contribution in *The Historical Jesus* have included: Lynn Thorndike, a respected historian (1926), and Shirley Jackson Case (November 1928), in the United States; the Christian controversialist Herbert George Wood (1919) and the freethinkers Gordon Rylands (1935), Archibald Robertson (1946) and Herbert Cutner (1950) based in Britain; and Maurice Goguel (1950) in France. It seems incredible that a Christian Professor, Craig A. Evans, edited the massive *Encyclopedia of the Historical Jesus* (n.d.: 2009, main text 728 large pages) without noticing J.M.R.'s output. Plausibly J. M. Robertson's 1916 book overlooked the Rev. T.J. Thorburn's much shorter 1915 work bearing the same title, but with only a few, cursory references to J.M.R.

A History of Freethought Ancient and Modern to the Period of the French Revolution (1936)

This may be regarded as Robertson's greatest written work. It represented the fourth edition, considerably revised and expanded, of his *Short History of Freethought*, originally published in 1899. Completed shortly before his death in January 1933 (there is a reference to March 1930 on p. 241), it was published in 1936 by Watts & Co. in a fine two-volume edition (replete with references, sources, critical discussion, photogravures and half tones) whose appearance was in large measure facilitated by Robertson's old friend Marley Denwood, who, amid other services, found time to read all the proofs for press.

This monumental work profoundly impressed Professor Harold Laski of the L.S.E., who recorded a debt of gratitude to these two volumes as follows:

"They induce in me a feeling of helpless humility. Their range seems to stretch from China to Peru. The knowledge is sure; the precision is remarkable. With these volumes Rationalism acquires one of its fundamental classics, and the place of Robertson among the outstanding historians of our time is assured."

Decades later the American editor of *An Anthology of Atheism and Rationalism* (Gordon Stein, 1980) described Robertson's two volumes of this work as "unsurpassed monuments of scholarship" (pp. 67-8).

In his Preface Robertson declared: "To keep in view, everywhere, the conditioning and largely determinant influence of environment, situation, institutions, and culture, was always part of the author's plan, howsoever ill it may have been realized" (p. xxix). He went on virtually to conclude his Preface with the prescient comment (with the rise of Hitler, Stalin and the run-up to the Second World War) that "the world seems likely to pay, in a stadium of intellectual impoverishment, if not of decadence, for the awful holocaust of good minds in the [First] World War". He added that without hope of recovery "the survey of the past would be a sombre study. But the hope is perpetually generated by history, even as it is by the instinct of life" (p. xxxiii).

Towards the end of the twentieth century David Berman, an academic historian of British atheism, indicated that J.M.R. had not noticed the atheist pamphlet *An Investigation of the Essence of the Deity* by "Scepticus Britannicus", published in London in late 1797: a rare oversight, it may be added. However, Robertson's account of the eighteenth century English deists – if in an earlier (1915) version of his *History of Freethought* – was clearly taken into account by Norman Torrey in *Voltaire and the English Deists* (1930) and, to a lesser extent, by his fellow American James A. Herrick in *The Radical Rhetoric of the English Deists* (1997). In that context Herrick (pp. 213-14) quoted comments by Robertson in the second paragraph of page 717 of his *History* (indicating that English deism was quite widespread by 1710), but the American misleadingly omitted to acknowledge or include J.M.R.'s caveats presented at the beginning of that same paragraph on p. 717 of Robertson's 1936 work.

The 1936 edition is dedicated "To Sydney Ansell Gimson", but does not in any way make it clear whether this was simply because the previous 1914-15 edition had been dedicated to Robertson's longstanding Leicester secularist friend Gimson, or whether Robertson had given a definite indication that the much revised and expanded fourth (1936) edition was also to be dedicated to this friend (who outlived both J.M.R. and the publication date of the 1936 edition). Although technically that work was published by Watts & Co. and not by the Rationalist Press Association, Bill Cooke's 2003 history of the R.P.A., which is replete with references to Watts & Co., does not shed any light on the dedication in the 1936 edition, which that 2003 history barely mentions.

A History of Freethought in the Nineteenth Century (1929)

Robertson's *History of Freethought in the Nineteenth Century* first appeared in the early months of 1929 in thirteen fortnightly instalments issued by the Rationalist Press Association. The fruit of more than two years' unremitting labour, his *History* sought to trace the intellectual conflict between declining religion and advancing rationalism on a world scale. As F.J. Gould put it: "That history is an epic of encouragement to us. To the old theologies it is an elegy of sunset" (see *The Pioneers of Johnson's Court*, pp. 148,150).

At least part of Robertson's wartime two-volume *Short History of Freethought* (1914-15) would be covered by his *History of Freethought in the Nineteenth Century* (1929). In 1948 Joseph McCabe wrote of a hero of British law reform, Sir Samuel Romilly, whose most notable work was done after the French Revolution: "Robertson, who barely mentions him in his *Short History of Freethought*, wrongly says that it merely transpired after his death that he was a Deist (II, 448). The *Dictionary of National Biography* rightly says that 'he early lost all faith in Christianity but embraced with ardour the gospel of

Rousseau' "(*A Rationalist Encyclopaedia*, p. 508). But there was no necessary contradiction, or even a logical connection, between McCabe's two sentences relating to Robertson and the *DNB* respectively, not least as McCabe added that Rousseau "professed a high regard for 'pure Christianity'" (p. 510).

The scholar J.C.A. Gaskin in 1989 commended J.M.R.'s 1929 and 1936 histories as "invaluable mines of information" (*Varieties of Unbelief*, p. 232). Joel Wiener's *Radicalism and Freethought in Nineteenth-Century Britain* (1983) hailed J.M.R.'s 1929 *History* as "a work of impressive scholarship" (p. 275). That work of Robertson's, as Paul Cliteur indicated in 2010, notably articulated "one of the most severe criticisms of the father of liberal theology, [Friedrich] Schleiermacher" (*The Secular Outlook*, p. 19, note 22). Robertson discussed the teaching of Kierkegaard years before he was 'discovered' by the Existentialists (rather as Robertson had been among the select few in England in 1899 who appreciated Vico as a significant early eighteenth century Italian philosopher of history).

Yet in his 1929 work there were a number of rather surprising omissions (some regretted by Robertson) of individual freethinkers; there was next to nothing on Eastern European countries; the section on New Zealand and Australia was scanty even for the material at his disposal; and the American George E. Macdonald complained, regarding Robertson's "stately" *History*, that the United States only took up about "two score pages out of his more than six hundred" (*Fifty Years of Freethought*, Vol. 2, 1931, p. 626). Pressure of work or space may have inhibited Robertson, but his *History* covered a wider geographical area and seemed distinctly more scholarly than Fritz Mauthner's history of Western atheism, which appeared (in German) in four volumes between 1920 and 1923, and which took the story at least as far as Émile Zola. J.M.R. was a relatively early freethought historian in Britain to vindicate Richard Carlile, champion of a free press; and he praised Samuel Laing for his sterling work as a rationalist publicist in the 1880s and 1890s. Robertson seemed to have doubts (see pp. 321, 328) about the scientific reliability of Ernst Haeckel, who, in his lifetime and later, was accused of fraud and falsification. In the annals of German rationalism and atheism Haeckel's *The Riddle of the Universe* would occupy the same prominent position that during the second half of the nineteenth century was adorned by *Force and Matter (Kraft und Stoff)* by Ludwig Büchner, with whom Robertson stayed for some weeks in the late 1880s and whose German work later influenced Atatürk, the founder of modern Turkey (see M. Sükrü Hanioglu, *Atatürk*, 2011, pp. 52, 229, etc.).

Professor Kenneth Latourette at Yale University declared in 1959 that J.M.R.'s 1929 *History* was "based on extensive research" (*The Nineteenth Century in Europe*, p. 482). Also in the United States, Sidney Warren drew attention to the fact that in his 1929 *History* J.M.R. took the prominent American historian Charles Beard to task for not doing justice in 1927 to the theistic philosophy of the American thinker John Fiske (who had helped to popularize Herbert Spencer's work for audiences across the Atlantic). In his study *Matthew Arnold* – first published in 1939 – the distinguished American literary critic Lionel Trilling referred in his General Bibliography to a 1930 American edition of J.M.R.'s 1929 *History*. Laura Schwartz in her timely book *Infidel Feminism* (2013) noted Robertson's *History of Freethought in the Nineteenth Century* (where he took account of the contribution in the United States of the Anglo-American iconoclast Ernestine Rose, a brilliant lecturer).

In his 1929 *History* (p. 391) J.M.R. traced "the turning of the balance" of opinion in Britain against religious orthodoxy to about 1870 onwards; and the British humanist Colin Campbell indicated that the rationalist Alfred W. Benn "specifies 1877 as the year 'in which English rationalism reached its most intense expression'" (quoted by Campbell in *Towards a Sociology of Irreligion*, 1971, pp. 56, 149). 1877 was the year in which Robertson made his first direct personal contact with the contemporary British freethought movement.

Joseph McCabe, who struck up a friendship with the thinker Leslie Stephen, acknowledged that Robertson's criticisms of Stephen regarding the English deists were "for the most part justified" (*A Rationalist Encyclopaedia*, 1948, see pp. 142, 560, 10). Noel Annan, in his book on Leslie Stephen (1984, p. 391) referenced J.M.R.'s *History of Freethought in the Nineteenth Century*, as did Crane Brinton in 1933 and S. Maccoby in 1961. Robertson seemed to suggest that "the phenomenon of rationalism" could well become a force to be reckoned with among the subject races of Africa in the twentieth century. But although his admittedly rather guarded prophecy appeared to receive a measure of support, after J.M.R.'s death, from the Africanist Diedrich Westermann (*Africa and Christianity*, 1937, p. 131), Robertson seemed to be unduly optimistic in this respect. However, J.M.R. seemed mindful of Marx's debt to, and use of, the German atheist Ludwig Feuerbach when in his *History of Freethought in the Nineteenth Century* he noted (pp. 189-190) that "some of the most revolutionary" of post-Hegelian "movements of German thought – as those of … Feuerbach, and Marx – professedly founded on him [Hegel]". The Christian Sidney Dark and R.S. Essex (1937) appreciated and quoted J.M.R.'s work, including his comments (1929) about Hegel and Proudhon. In America Michael Rectenwald's *Nineteenth-Century British*

Secularism (2016) relied quite heavily on Robertson's 1929 *History*, and both that *History* and J.M.R.'s 1936 publication were commended in Frank Swancara's 1947 pamphlet (p. 15n.) on religion.

Introduction to the History of Civilization in England (by Henry Thomas Buckle: new and revised edition, with an introduction and annotations, by J.M.R., 1904)

Robertson edited and/or introduced a number of freethought and literary classics; and with "prefaces" taken to include "introductions", Professor Homer Smith in the U.S.A. declared twenty years after Robertson's death: "To each of these prefaces he contributed richly from the store of erudition and historical perspective with which he was himself so richly endowed by a lifetime of conscientious scholarship" (*Man and His Gods*, 1953, p. 478n.). These comments were eminently applicable to his unsurpassed one-volume edition (1904) of Buckle's historical work, with a substantial introduction and copious annotations and corrections, and with the benefit of all the proofs being read and checked by his music critic friend Ernest Newman (who went on to assist Robertson, in the latter's preparation of his 1905 book on *Titus Andronicus*, by looking out for patterns of word-usage by Elizabethan writers). Years later the noted American economist Jacob Viner used and commended J.M.R.'s "valuable editorial notes" in his 1904 work relating to Buckle (*Religious Thought and Economic Society*, 1978, p. 187n.). Rather curiously a fellow American, Lynn Thorndike, noticed Robertson's *The Historical Jesus* (1916) and *A Short History of Freethought* (1914-15) in this History Professor's *A Short History of Civilization* (1926), but not J.M.R.'s edition of Buckle's *Introduction to the History of Civilization in England*, which included a chapter (VI) – with thoughtful editorial notes by Robertson – specifically devoted to aspects of the Middle Ages, a period in which Thorndike tended to specialize.

In 1932 Robertson alerted readers who might not be familiar with Buckle's work that in his two-volume *Introduction* (1857 and 1861) Buckle had defended "the *laissez faire* theory". J.M.R. was more complimentary about Buckle's chapter (XV) on Spanish history, although even then he added that Buckle "is to be read under correction" (see *Courses of Study*, 1932 ed., pp. 186, 259, 261). Buckle's chapter on Spain followed a general survey of the influence of "mental and physical laws" and seven consecutive chapters on French history which included Buckle's brilliant, thought-provoking aphorism (p. 520) that "The hall of science is the temple of democracy". Buckle's Spanish chapter was in turn followed by five consecutive chapters on Scottish history, with Wales and Ireland in effect being excluded. Robertson's *An Introduction to English Politics* (1900) and, more particularly, its revised edition entitled *The Evolution of States* (1912) adopted a similar pattern to Buckle's. Robertson in 1900 and 1912 devoted less attention than Buckle to Scotland and France, or arguably even to Spain, with J.M.R. tending to view English history against a backcloth provided by political, economic and cultural forces in ancient times and by the Italian republics, Scandinavian peoples, the Hansa, Holland, Switzerland and Portugal much more recently.

In his edition of Buckle's *Introduction* Robertson graciously paid Buckle a great compliment: "Where Darwin definitely brought within the scope of scientific law the phenomena of biology ... Buckle began anew the most complicated and difficult task of all – the reduction to law of the phenomena of social evolution" (p. v). It may be instructive here to compare J.M.R.'s praise of Buckle and Darwin with Karl Kautsky's view of these two pioneers that the Austrian contributed to the new Marxian journal *Die Neue Zeit* in 1883 (the year in which this journal was founded with Kautsky as its long-serving editor, and the year in which J.M.R. in Scotland lectured on Buckle). Kautsky rated Marx above Buckle, but retained a high regard for the latter (see Kautsky's *The Materialist Conception of History*, 1988, edited by his grandson, pp. 147, 297). A commentator on the young Kautsky's contribution in this field (Gary P. Steenson, in 1978 and 1991) concluded that "his efforts to integrate Darwin and Marx sometimes resulted in a curious muddle of apparent contradiction" (see Steenson's 1991 reprint of *Karl Kautsky, 1854-1938*, p. 65). Moreover, whereas Kautsky argued (in Steenson's words) "some years before Darwin's theory emerged, Marx had placed history on a firmer basis" through emphasis on the class struggle, Robertson saw things rather differently, maintaining: "We have to remember that Marx came before Darwin, and that his converts, first and last, were men who had not learned to think in terms of the law of evolution" (*The Decadence*, p. 55). Robertson's edition of Buckle cited Darwin, but not Marx. Between 1885 and 1888, when Kautsky lived in London, he may have virtually come into contact, or come into fairly close personal contact, with Robertson, perhaps at the British Museum Library or through members of the Eleanor Marx-Edward Aveling circle. Certainly Kautsky and Robertson became aware of each other's work.

An Introduction to the Study of the Shakespeare Canon (1924)

Twenty years after Robertson's death, Professor Albert Feuillerat of Yale University, who had long taken a close interest in Elizabethan literature, wrote: "It must be recognised that Robertson had qualities which started him on the track of incontestable truths." Although the comment could be applied with equal justice to different facets of Robertson's works, the reference (in *The Composition of Shakespeare's Plays*, 1953) was specifically to his *Introduction to the Study of the Shakespeare Canon* (1924). This was a much expanded edition of his 1905 book entitled *Did Shakespeare Write 'Titus Andronicus'?* Applying what Robertson called "general tests of metrics, style, and treatment" (*The Shakespeare Canon*, 1922, p. xv), he rejected the concept of Shakespeare's supposed sole authorship of *Titus Andronicus*, which he believed was largely written by George Peele. (John Michell was quite wrong when in 1996 he declared in his *Who Wrote Shakespeare?*: "According to Robertson, Marlowe wrote *Titus Andronicus*", p. 228.)

Across the Channel J.M.R.'s 1924 book was apparently taken into account by the French-speaking academic Georges Connes in his *État présent des Études Shakespeariennes* (1932). In Britain Robertson's *Introduction* was noticed by the literary critics T.S. Eliot (in *Selected Essays*), William Empson (in *Essays on Shakespeare*), and E.K. Chambers (in *William Shakespeare: A Study of Facts and Problems*). Of these three notable commentators, Eliot (also a distinguished poet) was the most sympathetic to Robertson, and Chambers the most hostile. In 1941 the British literary critic George Sampson, in writing of Robertson as "a Shakespearean scholar with a view of his own", declared: "Robertson's greatest contribution to his subject is contained in *The Shakespeare Canon* (Part 1, 1922; Part II, 1923) and *An Introduction to the Study of the Shakespeare Canon* (1924 … he is not to be read without labour, though the labour is always worth while" (*The Concise Cambridge History of English Literature*, pp. 1031, 1032).

George Sampson also thought highly of J.M.R.'s *'Hamlet'*
Once More (1923), of which he wrote a glowing review.

Although he was not a rationalist, the critic George Wilson
Knight, with his "attention to the rhythm, imagery, and
poetic symbolism of Shakespeare's plays", may have owed
something to Robertson's approach (see Jason Harding, *The*
Criterion, 2002, p. 79; cf. K. Cooke, *A.C. Bradley and His*
Influence in Twentieth-Century Shakespeare Criticism, 1972,
p. 4).

Jesus and Judas (1927)

In his introduction to a re-issue in 1936 of *Christianity and*
Mythology, the British Historicist A.D. Howell Smith wrote
of its then dead author: "Equipped with a vast erudition and
unswerving love of truth, he devoted many years of study to
the question of Christian origins … In a series of carefully
documented works, of which *Christianity and Mythology*,
Pagan Christs, and *Jesus and Judas* were the most important,
Robertson not only dissected the mass of mythical data of
which he believed the Gospels to consist, adducing at the
same time a large number of Jewish and Pagan parallels,
but sought to explain how the story grew and how a cult of
sacramental salvation came to be based upon it. The measure
of his success will be variously estimated … Be that as it may,
the work of such men as John M. Robertson will not have
been in vain, since it serves as an ever needed challenge to
that unfruitful conservatism to which our mental laziness is so
prone." (Cf. Howell Smith's *Jesus Not A Myth*, 1942.)

In *Jesus and Judas* Robertson built on such work as his essays on "The Myth of Judas Iscariot" and "The Jesus Legend and the Myth of the Twelve Apostles", which dated from 1893 and 1894 respectively, and which were reproduced in his book *Studies in Religious Fallacy* (1900). J.M.R. suggested that the story of Judas was a late addition to the Gospels; and he was minded to reject the idea that "Iscariot" referred to the place from which Judas came, as S. Pearce Carey's 1931 book, also entitled *Jesus and Judas*, acknowledged (p. 16). Indeed, the implication appeared to be that "Iscariot" was used as an epithet meaning "the Deliverer". (See: J.M.R.'s 1927 book, pp. 50-51; Ahmed Osman, *The House of the Messiah*, 1992, pp. 81, 227, referring to those pages; and L. Gordon Rylands, *Did Jesus Ever Live?*, 1935, p. 24, etc. Moreover, the *Gospel of Judas* does not confirm that "Iscariot" relates to Judas' home town.) A close study of the Pauline Epistles, together with the ancient document known as the Didache, led Robertson as a young man to re-examine his belief in the historicity of Jesus. He concluded that the Didache was, in the words of his admirer Stanley Edgar Hyman, "a pre-Christian work with what he called 'Christist interpolations'" (*The Promised End*, 1963, p. 148) – and decades after Robertson articulated this conclusion the Historicist Joseph McCabe wrote that the first part of the Didache "is believed to be a Jewish document modified by Christians" (*A Rationalist Encyclopaedia*, 1948, p. 158). The Didache did not refer to the life, authority or personality of Jesus; and the approximately contemporaneous *Shepherd of Hermas* was equally silent about Jesus. When the early Christian Ignatius was asked for evidence to support his faith, he invoked only the Old Testament prophecies (see J.M.R.'s *Jesus and Judas*, pp. 122-3, and L. Gordon Rylands, *The Evolution of Christianity*, 1927, p. 225, referring to Robertson's argumentation).

The Mythicist exponent Herbert Cutner, who was friendly with

J.M. Robertson, defended him against a misrepresentation by the Historicist Archibald Robertson (not related to J.M.R.) of a passage in *Jesus and Judas* (1927) – just as Cutner sprang to J.M.R.'s defence regarding the latter's supposed unacknowledged debt to the pioneer Mythicist Robert Taylor as alleged by Joseph McCabe (see Cutner's 1950 *Jesus: God, Man or Myth?*).   Archibald Robertson's misrepresentation related to Cutner convicting him of an interpolation which in that context misleadingly suggested J.M.R. had conceded "A Galilean faith-healer named Jesus may have been offered as a human sacrifice" etc. (for details see Cutner's 1950 book, pp. 283-4; Archibald Robertson's *Jesus: Myth or History?* – 1946, second ed. 1949 – pp. 99-100; and *Jesus and Judas*, pp. 205-206).   Cutner's book was published in the U.S.A., as were works by Professors Shirley Jackson Case (1928), Chester Charlton McCown (1940) and G.A. Wells (1999) which all took account of J.M.R.'s *Jesus and Judas*.

The Jesus Problem (1917)

In America during the 1960s a well-known rationalist, Miriam Allen de Ford, hailed Robertson as "one of the great founders of what will be the generally accepted understanding of the origin and history of the Christian religion" and pointed to his *Christianity and Mythology*, *Pagan Christs*, *The Historical Jesus* and *The Jesus Problem* as "the cream and crown of his achievements".   The last work named by her was the second of two books on Christian origins that Robertson found time to write during the First World War, no doubt as a form of intellectual relaxation from more pressing matters. In *The Historical Jesus* (1916) he had critically examined the attitudes and claims of Historicist exponents such as

Flinders Petrie, Albert Schweitzer and the illustrious New Testament scholar Professor Alfred Loisy, devoting some four consecutive chapters to the last-named. Now, in *The Jesus Problem*, he presented "A restatement of the Myth Theory" (in the words of the subtitle of that book). But he virtually opened *The Jesus Problem* with a personal admission: "I began by assuming a historical Jesus, and sought historically to trace him, regarding the birth myth and the others as mere accretions" (p. 14). He went on, in *The Jesus Problem*, to mount a defence, both robust and modest, of the Myth Theory: "In the very nature of the case, the connections of the data must be speculative. It may well be that those here attempted – some of them modifications of previous theories – will have to be at various points reshaped … The complete establishment of a historical construction will be a long and difficult task. But in its least satisfying aspect the myth-theory is a scientific substitution for what is wholly *dis*satisfying – the entirely unhistorical construction furnished by the gospels" (p. 22: Robertson's emphasis). He had just pointed out (also with emphasis) that "a large portion of M. Loisy's own important critical performance consists precisely in explaining away as *inventions* a multitude of items in the gospel narrative" (p. 21).

In Britain *The Jesus Problem* was taken into account by Harry M. Paull in his *Literary Ethics* (1928), L. Gordon Rylands in *The Evolution of Christianity* (1927) – e.g. on the emergence of the Joshua/Jesus cult - and *Did Jesus Ever Live?* (1935), and Archibald Robertson in *Jesus: Myth or History?* (1946). Gordon Rylands highlighted the fact that in *The Jesus Problem* J.M.R. alluded to difficulties associated with the triumphal arrival of Jesus in Jerusalem being quickly followed by a clamour for his execution. In a section on literary forgeries in early Christianity Harry Paull declared: "In *The Jesus Problem*, Mr. J.M. Robertson warns us that it 'must be kept clearly and constantly in view that what we understand by a literary and historical conscience simply did not exist in the early Christian environment'." In *Jesus and Judas* (p. 57) J.M.R. pointed out the invidious position of the Church of England in 1927: "it would never do to admit that the gospel Jesus is merely a 'Cult-Hero', like Adonis or Attis. The British taxpayer will never consent to support a Christian State Church of which the accredited leaders avow that Jesus Christ never really existed." In *Jesus: Myth or History?* (second edition, 1949) Archibald Robertson – who suggested (p. 91) that in *The Jesus Problem* J.M.R. had understated issues associated with a prophecy attributed to the Jesus of the Synoptic Gospels - none the less presented a distinctly misleading example of J.M. Robertson's attitude towards the Gospel Jesus (see the previous entry for details). Archibald Robertson was the son of an Anglican Bishop of Exeter and had turned Communist before 1939, with Soviet Communists and Marxist ideologues perpetrating or supporting falsification, fabrication or mythology. In Archibald Robertson's Soviet Union I. Kryvelev, in *Christ: Myth or Reality?* (1987), also took account of J.M.R.'s 1917 book.

In 1932 J.M.R. declared that in *The Jesus Problem* he had replied "in detail" to F.C. Conybeare's *The Historical Christ* (1914), which in the course of attacking J.M.R. had condoned misrepresentation of Jesus as "the son of *Joseph and his wife* Mary" (*Courses of Study*, p 82: J.M.R.'s emphasis). Anyone reading J.M.R.'s witheringly fierce onslaught (e.g. in *The Historical Jesus*, pp. xvii-xviii, xxii-xxiii) on Conybeare's scholarship and then Bill Cooke's glowing tribute, decades later, to Conybeare's "rationalist scholarship at its best" (op. cit. 2003, p. 51) might conclude that Robertson and Cooke could not be referring to the same person.

In *Rationalism and Historical Criticism* (1919) H.G. Wood extended his previous criticism of *Pagan Christs* and *Christianity and Mythology* to include *The Jesus Problem*. The French scholars Maurice Goguel (1950) and Georges Ory (1968), and the American critics Shirley Jackson Case (1928) and Robert Van Voorst (2000), noticed *The Jesus Problem*, in each case together with *Christianity and Mythology* and *Pagan Christs*.

Letters from an Egyptian to an English Politician upon the Affairs of Egypt (with introduction by J.M.R., 1908)

Although the identity of the Egyptian author was not revealed, his published *Letters* were written in 1905, two years before Cromer's colonial rule in Egypt came to an end. Robertson described the author as "a travelled and enlightened Egyptian who has carefully compared notes with competent Europeans on the administration of his country as controlled by the British Agency"; and he added regarding the letters: "I am satisfied of their good faith, and of the competence of this writer to speak on Egyptian problems" (pp. iii, xii). The Egyptian author addressed such subjects as the administration of justice, legislation, tourism and bureaucracy, infant mortality, "faulty finance", urban reform, poor relief, and education. Looking back in 1932, Robertson, referring to this author, declared: "More pungent criticism was passed in some English books" (*Courses of Study*, p. 227). In his 1908 Introduction J.M.R. reported that many Egyptians believed, regarding the Suez Canal, that "the people whose labour constructed the canal, and through whose land it is made, have been manoeuvred out of all the profit it has brought" (p. vii). Robertson went on to address the attitude of a stereotypical British Liberal towards the Egyptians: "If he yields to the bare pretence that they are unfit for any measure of self-government, he is endorsing the formula that was used against every extension of the franchise in his own land" (p. xi). Probably because the Denshawai Affair (1906) occurred after the letters were written – though possibly also out of a sense of tact – Robertson, in his Introduction, did not focus on the Denshawai incident, when more than 20 Egyptians received draconian punishment for the apparently accidental death of one British officer, with Robertson signing a petition calling for the immediate release of the surviving imprisoned defendants (see C.H. Norman, *Essays and Letters on Public Affairs*, 1913, pp. 175-87). By early 1907 J.M.R., following a visit to Egypt, had become a firm believer in Egyptian self-government, and in 1971 Peter Mansfield, an authority on Egypt, paid tribute to his support for the growing nationalist pressure there before World War One (*The British in Egypt*, p. 145).

When Robertson left for Egypt in December 1906, the British Foreign Secretary, Sir Edward Grey, wrote to Lord Cromer: "I am glad Robertson has gone to Egypt. I can't say what view he will return with; but … I know him to be able, and believe him to be honest" (from letter of 21 December 1906 from Grey to Cromer: Public Record Office, F.O. 800/46, p. 203). Coincidentally Leslie Stephen seven years earlier had described J.M.R. in similar terms, writing of him: "I think that he is a very able and vigorous man as well as honest" (from letter of 2 June 1899 from Stephen to C.F. Adams: quoted by F.W. Maitland, *Life and Letters of Leslie Stephen*, 1906, p. 452). It may be added that with his trips to Germany, the United States, South Africa, Italy and Egypt, for example, Robertson was a much more widely travelled man than Grey the Foreign Secretary.

During his stay in Egypt the press there reported that "Mr. Robertson, M.P., who is so well-known to all the Egyptians", visited a variety of educational institutions, including the Cairo Police School, where he "was pleased to see its affairs all entrusted to capable native officials" (see *The Egyptian Gazette* for 5.1.1907, p. 3, and 11.1.1907, p. 3). Apart from Wilfrid Scawen Blunt, an activist in Britain who found Robertson's work concerning Egypt quite useful was the Communist journalist Theodore Rothstein, who, in his critical examination of British rule there entitled *Egypt's Ruin* (1910), referred to Robertson's awkward questions in Parliament, for example in 1907 on education in Egypt being conducted in English and not Arabic. (Ironically, specially selected native Egyptian police officers were sent to England in 1920 for training in 'anti-Bolshevik' surveillance techniques: Lawrence James, op. cit. 1998 ed., 2000 reprint, p. 373.) Contradicting his own Preface (p. xvi, para. 4), Ronald Storrs, in *Orientations* (1937, pp. 103-4), was highly aggressive towards Robertson as a visiting investigator, although even this imperialist bureaucrat disowned the Denshawai sentences.

Letters on Reasoning (1902; second ed., "revised, with additions", 1905)

This book was ostensibly written for J.M.R.'s two children, as part of their intellectual and moral education, to be read by them when they were "grown up". He indicated he was trying to encourage his children to question and reason, not present them with a rounded philosophy which they were free to develop for themselves (1905 ed., pp. 74, 217). His *Letters on Reasoning* made no original contribution to philosophy per se; Chris Tame maintained: "Robertson did not attempt to explore wider epistemological or metaphysical issues or to construct a scientific ethical system. Nevertheless, in a variety of areas he made a number of extremely suggestive and penetrating observations" (*J.M. Robertson*, ed, G.A. Wells, 1987, p. 109). In an abridged 1935 edition the rationalist Adam Gowans Whyte declared in the introduction: "No one can read its pages without feeling a lively stimulus to put his intellectual house in order" (p. vi). In his work Robertson emphasized the role of both reason and reciprocity, as later did the philosopher John Rawls, for instance. Robertson identified a number of causes, or snares, of bad reasoning or unreasoned judgment (1905, pp. 33-4); and he enthusiastically exposed the self-contradictions and fallacies of various thinkers and scholars and explored a range of philosophical and other issues such as those relating to "chance", "free will", and "determinism". In touching on some of these issues, Robertson paused to pay a tribute to Dostoyevsky (1905, p. 181), although J.M.R.'s *Criticisms* (Vol. 2,1903) offered a more extended focus on Russian fiction. In a sense J.M.R.'s critique of John Venn's work on "chance" was, in effect, taken up virtually two decades later by the American economist Frank H. Knight, who in his influential *Risk, Uncertainty and Profit* (1921) graciously acknowledged in closing his Preface that: "Professor Jacob Viner, of the University of Chicago, has kindly read the proof of the entire work" (p. xi). Jacob Viner praised J.M.R.'s edition of Buckle, which appeared at almost the same time as *Letters on Reasoning*.

Although occasionally his meaning was opaque and, as he himself admitted (pp. 34, 101), his writing was not necessarily free from error or illogicality, Robertson's book, leavened with some autobiographical asides, retained a power and charm in some ways reminiscent of a Diderot or Montaigne. From a different perspective the critic Odin Dekkers referred to the "strident rhetoric" of *Letters on Reasoning*, of which he added: "it is as fearless a piece of anti-religious polemics as any of his more openly controversial writings" (*J.M. Robertson*, 1998, p. 75). Yet in *Letters on Reasoning* J.M.R. painted a broader canvas than Dekkers' words could well suggest. Those he criticised included Kant, Hegel, Francis Herbert Bradley, Thomas Hill Green and the Idealists at a time (between 1890 and 1914) when Green's thinking, for example, was at its most influential in Britain (see Melvin Richter, *The Politics of Conscience*, 1964, pp. 293-4). In the 1904 edition (p. 96) of his *Courses of Study* Robertson alluded to his criticism of Green in his *Letters on Reasoning*; and later in the twentieth century Green's conceptual approach, or rather a popularized version of it, was criticised by the scholar Lord (Noel) Annan, who, in his study of Leslie Stephen, showed awareness of J.M.R.'s output: see also Annan's *Our Age*, 1991 ed., p. 208. Another target of Robertson's claymore was the distinctly cautious Victorian historian of rationalism, W.E.H. Lecky, who – Robertson indicated – proposed that false and foolish beliefs should not be openly attacked or challenged as they would "pass away 'silently'", with corrective criticism 'in the air' (1905 ed., pp. 92-3).

J.M.R. advised his children not to be browbeaten by those who claim that "to cultivate your reason is to lose the faculty for enjoying poetry, music, or any other art" (1905 ed., p. 13). His point would be reiterated by David Tribe six decades later (1967 book, pp. 195-6). Indeed, Robertson contributed to the arguably iconic *The Yellow Book* (1890s). Yet D.H. Lawrence once declared that Robertson "has called me a fool often enough in his damned *Letters on Reasoning* and such like" when there was no outward and visible sign of any reference to the freethinking Lawrence in any edition of *Letters on Reasoning* (see *The Collected Letters of D.H. Lawrence*, ed. Harry T. Moore, Vol. 1, 1962, p. 53: from letter of 8 May 1909 from Lawrence to Blanche Jennings). Also absent from *Letters on Reasoning* was an exploration by Robertson of possible links between emotional and intellectual factors in the development of "conscience", although in 1904 (*Courses of Study*) he commended as "very useful" Mrs. Besant's paper in *Our Corner* on the genesis of conscience.

Literary Detection: A Symposium on 'Macbeth' (1931)

On 8 December 1932, just a few weeks before he died, Robertson wrote to his friend Marley Denwood concerning a work he, J.M.R., had written but not yet published called *The Genesis of the 'Ancient Mariner': A Study in Literary Logic*: "To-day I have handed in the finally corrected copy to the publisher, I shall have to pay costs; but they won't be heavy; and it will probably pay its expenses – unless all serious book publishing is going to the devil" (*HF*, 1936, p. 1002: *The Genesis* would still be unpublished in 1936). A somewhat similar situation had been revealed by Robertson towards the end of 1931 when in the Preface to his *Literary Detection* on *Macbeth* he confessed that his work entitled *The Shakespeare Canon* "is in the financial sense a thoroughly unprofitable undertaking". These two events clearly seem to have put a degree of financial strain on the Robertson household during the last year or so of his life. He not surprisingly, therefore, resorted to what he regarded as "a more popular mode of inquiry" by presenting his thoughts on the authorship of *Macbeth* through an imagined literary conversation conducted by four Shakespeare buffs.

Long fascinated by *Macbeth*, Robertson suggested that it was based on a pre-Shakespearean play by Thomas Kyd which had become lost (this, he believed, had similarly been the case with *Hamlet*). Robertson had previously indicated that Montaigne's influence on Shakespeare could be discerned in *Macbeth*. Montaigne's humanistic *Essays* had been published in French from 1580 onwards and, if only by repute, could also have appealed to Kyd, who had been associated with Walter Raleigh's so-called "School of Atheism". Knowledge in England of Montaigne has been dated back to at least 1591, when Francis Bacon's brother Anthony (a key adviser to the Earl of Essex, Shakespeare's protector) "returned from twelve years in France and a personal acquaintance with Montaigne" (Hugh Grady, *Shakespeare, Machiavelli, and Montaigne*, 2002, p. 51: Kyd died in 1594). *Macbeth* as we know it has been dated to about 1605-06, but Robertson indicated in 1914 that "it is probable that both *Othello* and *Macbeth* were similarly [i.e. like *King Lear*] suggested by previous dramas" (*Elizabethan Literature*, p. 182): in this 1914 work J.M.R. devoted very little space to *Macbeth*, quite probably because it was seen as a product of the Jacobean rather than the Elizabethan age. As the literary critic Roy Walker pointed out in 1948, Robertson firmly declared in *Literary Detection* that Act IV, Scene 3, was "plainly non-Shakespearean in respect of its versification, as also of its diction" (p.6) – and J.M.R. was not alone in believing that Shakespeare was not solely responsible for the text of *Macbeth*. G.K. Hunter would quote, with apparent approval, the declaration by the respected literary critic G.B. Harrison in *Shakespeare's Tragedies* (1951) that *Macbeth* is "so full of blemishes that it is hard to believe that one man wrote it" (quoted by Hunter in *Aspects of 'Macbeth'*, 1977, p. 5: ed. K. Muir and P. Edwards). In *The Baconian Heresy* (1913) Robertson had suggested that *Macbeth* was among plays usually attributed to Shakespeare alone which were "either reconstructions of previous plays or works of collaboration" (p. 546); and in *Shakespeare and Chapman* (1917) he indicated that at least two scenes in *Macbeth* contained traces of George Chapman or his influence (p. 249). G.K. Hunter, in his essay just quoted, wrote of Robertson: "Middleton he found to have written the Witch-scenes, the Porter-scene ..." in *Macbeth*. But this was a distortion of what Robertson actually wrote, which was: "the Porter scene ... is definitely and confidently assigned to Middleton, whose special phraseology it embodies. That writer is, further, necessarily saddled with the contamination of most of the rhymed witch-scenes" (*Literary Detection*, 1931, Preface, p. 6).

For J.M.R. parts of *Macbeth* exemplified dramatic power and effect such as "Macbeth's 'Which of you have done this?' at the vision of the blood-boltered Banquo" (see Act III, Scene 4, and J.M.R.'s *'Hamlet' Once More*, 1923, p. 183). In January 1932 a reviewer of *Literary Detection* complimented J.M.R. on his "sound critical judgment", "accurate sense of verse rhythms", and "unrivalled knowledge of the Elizabethan drama" (quoted by Odin Dekkers, op. cit. 1998, p. 189). Robertson's *Literary Detection* (1931) was noticed by the eminent literary critic William Empson in his posthumously published *Essays on Shakespeare* (1986).

Literary Detection II: A Symposium on 'Troilus and Cressida' (unpublished MS in private hands)

This clearly appears to be a continuation, on a different Shakespearean play, of Robertson's *Literary Detection* on *Macbeth*, published in 1931. The unpublished work under consideration has been copied by hand (by a person shrouded in anonymity) from a typescript lent by Robertson's friend Marley Denwood, as a brief note on the inside front cover indicates. Immediately after the title page there is a handwritten copy of a letter dated 23 June 1932 "From J.M. Robertson to Marley Denwood" about his, J.M.R.'s, revisions to his composition of *Literary Detection II*. This is then followed by 113 handwritten pages providing a transcript of six sittings by several friends, apparently led by a man called Robinson, who have met to discuss the authorship of *Troilus and Cressida*. The friends, who rejoiced in the surnames Robinson (perhaps a thinly disguised Robertson), Brown, Jones and Smith, and their conversations are evidently imaginary, though most probably based on actual friends and conversations of Robertson's. The conversations, as recorded, are wide-ranging and, indeed, digressive, not only touching on various plays in the Shakespeare Canon, but also peppered with references to literary figures, many of more recent times, such as Lascelles Abercrombie, Francis Bacon, Churton Collins, Edward Dowden, Dryden, F.G. Fleay, Alfred W. Pollard, Arthur Quiller-Couch, Robert Louis Stevenson, Taine, Voltaire, and Zola.

The copyist's handwriting is often quite difficult to read, and "Robinson" and his friends discuss rather than clearly settle on unanimous agreement as to who wrote *Troilus and Cressida*; but Robertson's above-mentioned letter seems to indicate that he at least believed that it was based on a play by Dekker and Chettle. The discussions appear to lend credence to Robertson's view as expressed in *Elizabethan Literature* that *Troilus and Cressida* is "a baffling and disconcerting play" (p. 193), in which "the great orations … are magnificent pieces of writing inferably substituted for harangues by another hand" (*'Hamlet' Once More*, 1923, p. 119). On the basis of a clue in J.M.R.'s letter of 23 June 1932, some of the imagined conversations of the four friends reflected elements of Robertson's *The Genuine in Shakespeare* (1930), where he contended (p. 114 et seq.): "All that is broadly clear is that the opening matter [in *Troilus and Cressida*] is not originally Shakespeare's, even if touched by him; that Pandarus and Thersites are not creations of his; that the Thersites scurrility is from other hands; and that the huddle of events in the fifth act, and the poor finish, are also alien" (quoted by Professor Geoffrey Bullough, ed., *Narrative and Dramatic Sources of Shakespeare*, Vol. VI, 1966, p. 84). In June 1932 J.M.R. felt George Chapman contributed a script (pp. 31-33).

In his manuscript J.M.R. also commented that "Chaucer gave the theme of *Troylus and Criseyde* his fine handling" (p. 23); and this praise was accompanied by a claim (p. 88) that at one point Dekker, as initial draftsman, got his story from Chaucer's work as a source or model for *Troilus and Cressida*. Although Robertson was troubled by 1932 by the danger of a second world war, his unpublished manuscript did not dissect the extent to which *Troilus and Cressida* had an anti-war message. Chaucer the ex-soldier was pensioned under Richard II; whereas in about 1593-4 at the King's Lynn St. George's Guildhall, far from plague-ridden London, Shakespeare may have acted in or even produced his own *Richard II*, which presented English kings as murder victims. In 2005 Simon Barker maintained, somewhat airily, that Shakespeare "would have known" Chaucer's work bearing the same title (*Shakespeare's Problem Plays*, p. 19). However, in the same book of literary criticism Matthew Greenfield stated that the Shakespearean play does not allude specifically to Chaucer's *Troilus and Criseyde* (p. 203); and in 1917 Robertson had suggested (*Shakespeare and Chapman*, p. 281) that the Bard approached and treated Cressida in a very different way to Chaucer.

Marlowe: A Conspectus (1931)

Robertson's study of Marlowe reflected his concern to try to identify the extent, if any, of Marlowe's share and influence in the plays conventionally attributed to Shakespeare. As Gilbert Slater – described as an economist and social historian, but with a strong interest in the Shakespeare authorship question – explained: "No one has gone more thoroughly into the investigation of peculiarities of vocabulary, phrasing, versification, rhythm, and characteristics of outlook than Mr. J.M. Robertson. He maintains that *Richard III* is a Marlowe play, that the first act of *Richard II* is thoroughly Marlovian, that Marlowe was the principal author, with others, of *Henry V* … "(*Seven Shakespeares*, 1931, p. 127). Following in Gilbert Slater's footsteps, the critic R.C. Churchill declared that Robertson "believed that Marlowe was the principal author of *The Comedy of Errors* and *Henry V* and that he also contributed to *Romeo [and Juliet]* and *Julius Caesar*, including Antony's oration to the crowd" (*Shakespeare and His Betters*, 1958, pp. 48-9). Christopher Marlowe's biographer John Bakeless seemed prepared to concede that some alleged non-Shakespearean traces in *Julius Caesar* "are quite probably due to Marlowe" (*The Tragicall History of Christopher Marlowe*, Vol. 2, 1942, p. 255: he had just acknowledged that the Shakespearean plays where Marlowe's influence appeared to be important included *Henry VI, Richard II, Richard III,* and *Julius Caesar* – p. 217). The poetess Edith Sitwell agreed with J.M.R. that Marlowe's hand does seem to be detected in *King Henry VI (A Notebook on William Shakespeare*, 1948, pp. 159-60, etc.). From these attributions of Marlowe's influence in plays assigned to Shakespeare it would seem that quite a few manifestations of that influence occurred during Marlowe's lifetime. The poet T.S. Eliot pointed out that Robertson had "spotted" an instance where Marlowe had stolen (or borrowed) from Spenser (see *Selected Essays*, 1972 ed., p. 120). In view of unorthodox aspects of Marlowe's career and violent death, it could have been unwise for Shakespeare consciously to imitate Marlowe's work even if he had ever contemplated doing so.

Marlowe's reputed atheism led Joseph McCabe, in *A Rationalist Encyclopaedia* (1948, p. 375), to refer his readers to J.M.R.'s *Marlowe* (1931), a book which was noticed in passing by the extremely hostile S. Schoenbaum in *Internal Evidence and Elizabethan Dramatic Authorship* (1966). A quarter of a century later the more sympathetic James Shapiro declared: "J.M. Robertson was the first to claim that Marlowe (perhaps along with Kyd) wrote a Caesar play in three parts early in the 1590s. … William Wells and E.H.C. Oliphant would subsequently maintain the tradition that Shakespeare began with an 'old and apparently good Marlowe play'" (*Rival Playwrights: Marlowe, Jonson, Shakespeare*, 1991, pp. 185-6). In 1939 Frederick S. Boas, in very briefly referring to J.M.R.'s *Marlowe*, indicated that according to critics like Robertson "Shakspere's dramas are not the products of a genius in a continuous unbroken spell of activity. They are the result of successive revisions by Shakspere of his own earlier work or, as often as not, plays from some inferior hand. That this may be true in some instances need not be denied" (*Shakspere and His Predecessors*, 1940 ed., pp. xxi-xxii: an earlier edition of Boas's book had been noted in a neutral way by J.M.R. in *Courses of Study*, 1932 ed., where Robertson, like many authors, drew attention to his own work, in this case *Marlowe*). As Odin Dekkers later observed: "It is precisely this balance between character-creation and poetic invention which Robertson finds lacking in the playwright whom he ranked second after Shakespeare himself: Christopher Marlowe" (op. cit. 1998, p. 181).

While making no specific or direct reference to *Marlowe* (1931), the American theatre critic Calvin Hoffman, in *The Man Who Was Shakespeare* (1955, p. 147), described J.M.R. as "another Shakespeare conservative", going on promptly to allude to "the amusing, if ironic, spectacle of conservative Shakespearean scholarship, orthodox to the last, confirming Marlowe's authorship, sole or in part, in more than half the works of William Shakespeare, most of which were written after Marlowe's 'murder'". Any amusement or irony would more appositely be derived from the fact that the fourteen "Shakespeare" plays Hoffman had just listed as being ones that Robertson thought were influenced or contributed to by Marlowe comprised less than half the total of 37 plays (let alone poems) conventionally attributed to Shakespeare. Moreover, Hoffman appeared to overlook the point that Shakespeare could have adapted or altered pre-existing Marlowe material, and that J.M.R. was seen, certainly in his day, as far from "conservative" or "orthodox", being a leader of the "disintegrationist" school regarding Shakespeare.

The Meaning of Liberalism (1912; second ed., 1925)

This is one of Robertson's more important books. It is divided into three parts: "Liberalism as a Creed"; "Liberalism and Socialism" (with two sub-sections on, respectively, the economic and moral case for socialism); and "Capital, Brains and Labour". The whole work is enriched with much historical material, illustrated, for example, by his comment – almost an aside – that: "The Christian Church itself owned slaves as long as mediaeval slavery subsisted. Economic pressures alone sufficed to substitute, first, serfs" (1925 ed., p. 213: from Chapter VI in Part III on "The Ideal of Equality"). The book – which also included much criticism of Marx and Engels – seemed to be indebted to, if not partially derived from, Robertson's address on 20 January 1908 on "The Mission of Liberalism" (published as a pamphlet by the Young Liberals), in which he declared: "it is the business of Liberalism to seek to promote and guide rationally the interference of the State in the struggle for existence … if we are to limit idle living, … and therefore at the same time to make easier the lot of industrious living, one of the methods will certainly be a reform of taxation to those ends. … we should aim at public control of the industrial struggle wherever feasible" (p. 10 of pamphlet). To some at least it may have seemed scarcely surprising, in the context of the time, that in 1887 Robertson had referred to "some of us on the 'extreme left'" (*Essays in Sociology*, Vol. 1, p. 65: his quotation marks).

As Michael Freeden, an authority on early twentieth century British Liberalism, has stated: "In the generation after [John Stuart] Mill the commentaries of J.M. Robertson deserve closer scrutiny, and may serve as a test case in locating the more passionate aspects of liberalism. … in *The Meaning of Liberalism* (1912) Robertson employed an interesting turn of phrase – intellectual sympathy …" Freeden went on to point out that in *Letters on Reasoning* Robertson had already maintained that "The love of truth and rectitude *is* an emotion" (J.M.R.'s emphasis), and that "There can be no great 'movement' of an intellectual kind without its emotional side" (*Politics and Culture in Victorian Britain*, ed. Peter Ghosh and Lawrence Goldman, 2006, pp. 142, 143).

To this it may be added that in the first edition of *The Meaning of Liberalism* Robertson used another, and pioneering, interesting turn of phrase when he referred to "the growing demand of the mass for equity of treatment" against discrimination (1912, see pp. 24 et seq., 44; 1925, p. 36). How forward-looking Robertson was may be gauged from the fact that in 1912, in a leading legal text-book, it was strongly suggested that should a state treat any of its own subjects with pitiless cruelty there could be no intervention on grounds of international law alone, as well as from the fact that more than three decades – and two world wars – would pass before this demand for equity found expression in the Universal Declaration of Human Rights, not to mention the Charter of the United Nations (see Geoffrey Robertson – no relation to J.M.R.! – *Crimes Against Humanity*, 1999, 2002, ed., pp. 14-15, 538, 575, 599).

In *A Defence of Conservatism* (1927) the ideologue Anthony Ludovici, who espoused anti-Semitism, anti-feminism, monarchism and eugenics, indicated that the principle of equality associated with human rights bedevilled Liberal thinkers "from Locke and Rousseau to the Right Honourable J.M. Robertson" (pp. 63-4). Robertson in effect responded, by 1932, by declaring that Ludovici "threatens to become the professional champion of lost causes" (see Dan Stone, *Breeding Superman*, 2002, pp. 34-6, 147: Stone notices *The Meaning of Liberalism*, both editions). (Sixty years after its publication the first edition of *The Meaning of Liberalism* was also listed in the Bibliography of Richard Price's book about the second Boer War, *An Imperial War and the British Working Class*.) Michael Bentley would feature both editions of Robertson's book in the Bibliography of *The Liberal Mind 1914-1929* (1977).

Linking the nineteenth and the twentieth century, Robertson

was a great exponent of modern Liberalism, whose function he presented as one of mediation between the forces of stagnation and those of violent ideological change. He supported "a system of State interference which is democratically motived and scientifically planned with an eye not to the enrichment of classes but to the well-being of the entire community" (*The Meaning of Liberalism*, 1912 ed., p. 55; 1925 ed., p. 44). Sustained by such convictions from at least the 1880s onwards to the end of his life (see *BRUG*, 1984, p. 17 et seq. for details), Robertson may be regarded as one of the unsung prophets of the British Welfare State.

For Robertson, ability to forecast the shape of things to come was limited by the knowledge that historiography was not, and could not be, an exact science. He attacked the "fatalism" of Marx and Engels: "no prospective line of human action or revolution is rationally to be singled out as 'inevitable' when it depends upon choices not yet made, and events which have not yet happened" (1925 ed., p. 145). In his book's 1925 edition Robertson referred to the Russian "Bolshevik State, under which all semblance of political liberty has ceased to exist save for the governing oligarchy" (p. x). As later in *Fiscal Fraud and Folly* (1931), he focused his attack on Protectionists or Communists among the British Trades Union Congress controllers who eulogized the Bolshevik state, where "all political opposition is 'illegal', all printed censure of State action is impossible, and leaders of strikes are shot. … No worse tyranny has ever subsisted in Europe" (1925 ed., pp. x, 163). The Cheka's – later OGPU's – bloody suppression of workers and strikers in Russia is documented by Jay Sorenson (*The Life and Death of Trade Unionism in the USSR, 1917-1928*, 2010 ed., p. 177), Christopher Andrew and Oleg Gordievsky (*KGB*, 1990, pp. 41, 48-9, etc.), Martin Sixsmith (*Russia*, 2011, pp. 232-5), Andrew Smith (*I Was A*

Soviet Worker, 1937, p. 217), and others. Not one question was devoted to workers' organisations in industry in the forty-page section of "Questions on Russia" in *This Is Russia* (1943) by the pro-Soviet Hubert Griffith, who had travelled extensively in Russia during the 1930s. (Robertson did reply to Griffith – regarding Shakespeare: see *The Criterion* for July 1929.) J.M.R. showed more political wisdom than pro-Soviet rationalists like Harold Laski, Joseph McCabe and J.B.S. Haldane. In 1942-3 Laski's brother's household materially, even crucially, assisted the veteran Soviet spymaster "Agent Sonya", whose informants included J.B.S. Haldane (see Ben Macintyre's 2020 book, pp. 234-6). Moreover, Harold Laski, through family friendship, facilitated the admission of Michael Straight to the London School of Economics, where this future pro-Soviet spy studied while Laski taught there.

In his chapter on Liberalism and foreign policy Robertson declared: "Nor has France in Algiers played a better part than Holland in Java or England in India" (1925 ed., p. 113). In this way he highlighted three colonized territories as potential, if not actual, "flash-points" or "hotspots" for the imperial authorities. He gave an implicit note of warning when he commented (p. 117) that "the British Empire in India has endured thus far". In 1926 the Communists led a revolt in Java and elsewhere against Dutch rule. Within three to four decades of the publication of Robertson's 1925 book, colonial rule in the three territories named had effectively come to an end after centuries of Western imperialism. (Robertson referred – in a footnote on p. 116 – his readers to his paper on "The Rationale of Autonomy" which he presented in 1911 to an international congress on colonialism and subject races.)

Modern Humanists (1891)

Robertson was one of the first British men of letters to show keen appreciation of the work of Walt Whitman, Ibsen, Heinrich von Kleist, James Thomson ('B.V.'), Maupassant, Nietzsche and Zola, at a time when they were scorned or virtually unknown in England (Zola and Heinrich von Kleist were discussed in two of his essays collected in Vol. 2, published in 1903, of his *Criticisms*). Much better known in Britain were Carlyle, J.S. Mill, Emerson, Matthew Arnold, Ruskin, and Herbert Spencer, who were the subject of "sociological studies" in his *Modern Humanists* (1891). This book was regarded as "Robertson's first major work" by Conrad Kaczkowski (in his American University Ph.D. dissertation *John Mackinnon Robertson: Freethinker and Radical*, 1964, p. 354). Certainly Robertson's book reflected his interest in sociology from an early stage and appears to have been his first book-length work to feature the word "sociology" or "sociological" in its subtitle. It also gave expression to his belief that physical conditions may determine or at least influence mental processes – in this case relating to major Victorian prophets – with his stressing, often in quite an illuminating way, the importance of heredity and parental figures in moulding attitudes and personalities.

In 1900 Professor F.G. Peabody referred to Robertson's "unsparing criticism" of Carlyle and rather unsympathetic treatment of Ruskin in *Modern Humanists* (*Jesus Christ and the Social Question*, pp. 31-2). Robertson felt that John Ruskin and his friend Carlyle were united in their "hostility to modern developments" (p. 211). His paper on Carlyle featured in the Bibliography on that influential thinker in *The Cambridge History of English Literature* (1916: ed. by A.W. Ward and A.R. Waller). In the following essay J.M.R. praised

John Stuart Mill for advocating "for all men the possible maximum of liberty of action and of freedom of thought" (p. 111: this passage would be quoted by Charles Sprading in *Liberty and the Great Libertarians*, 1913, p. 37). J.M.R.'s *Modern Humanists* would also be noticed by Michael St. John Packe in his 1952 biography of J.S. Mill. (In his book *John Stuart Mill and the Pursuit of Virtue* (1984) the American academic Bernard Semmel also noticed J.M.R., but only his *Buckle and His Critics* in the Selected Bibliography.) J.M.R.'s paper on Emerson seems disappointing, not least because he did not directly elaborate as he could have done on his statement (p. 121) that he was "an ex-pupil" of Emerson's (the American's emphasis on sturdy self-reliance had also influenced Bradlaugh in his youth). Emerson was the only American in Robertson's study of six thinkers – none of whom had a sustained record as a militant atheist – and arguably Emerson's friend Henry Thoreau merited at least equal attention.

In 1969 the literary critic John Gross indicated that Matthew Arnold had proposed that Hyde Park rioters "ought to be flung from the nearest available equivalent to the Tarpeian Rock", and that J.M.R., in his essay on Arnold, could have reacted to Arnold's stance not so much with a sense of outrage, but rather "with a more polished sense of irony" (*The Rise and Fall of the Man of Letters*, pp. 126-7). It is by no means certain that so many readers in 2023, familiar with public figures being subjected to often fierce public scrutiny (e.g. on social media), would necessarily agree with Gross' preference for irony rather than outrage in this instance. Moreover, Robertson virtually concluded his paper – one of his more finely written essays – with a generous tribute to Matthew Arnold: "Against an occasional reinforcement of barbarism we have to set many a service to liberalism, to culture, to the very spirit of civilisation" (p. 182). This tribute would seem a sufficient rebuke to the self-avowed Christian, Vincent Buckley, who misleadingly referred in 1959 to "the scornful view of Arnold propagated by such men as J.M. Robertson" (*Poetry and Morality*, pp. 28, 217). In his essay Robertson wrote of Arnold: "his tastes and instincts led him from the first to appeal for justice for Ireland; and kept him almost to the last an advocate of equality, alive to what he termed the 'idolatrous work' in the social system built and conserved by our middle and upper classes" (p. 170).

His study of Matthew Arnold was noticed by George H. Ford in *Keats and the Victorians*, (1944, 1962 reprint, p. 61n.); and that of Ruskin was taken into account by John D. Rosenberg in *The Darkening Glass* (1961, p. 256). The 1891 essay on Ruskin has one passing reference (p. 188) to J.M.W. Turner, but Robertson, who was interested in art (it seems throughout his life), did not explore the fact that Ruskin not only admired Turner, but met him, became an executor of his estate and in 1856 began to sort and catalogue the 19,000 sketches Turner left to the nation (see James Dearden, *Facets of Ruskin*, 1970, pp. 12-13). Moreover, although Robertson pointed out that Ruskin "presents you with an execrable homily on the nobleness of true war" (p. 210), the young Scot did not dissect the pundit's 1865 lecture at the Royal Military Academy, Woolwich, on war and art in which Ruskin declared: "as peace is established or extended in Europe, the arts decline. … war is the foundation of all the arts, I mean also that it is the foundation of all the high virtues …" J.M.R.'s critique of Herbert Spencer seems reasonably balanced, if rather laborious.

His Epilogue entitled "Outlines of Social Reconstruction" was regarded by Kaczkowski (p. 354) as "Robertson's first significant attempt at influencing the program of the Liberal Party"; but it seems likely that he was casting his net more widely as a Radical. For Robertson – arguably in the Epilogue an unsung prophet of the consumer revolution – raising the worker's status seemed to entail accentuating the citizen's role as a consumer (pp. 268-9).

Praise for *Modern Humanists*, soon after its publication in July 1891, came from a rather unexpected quarter. *The Times* told its readers: "Mr. Robertson's style is excellent – nay, even brilliant – and his purely literary criticisms bear the mark of much acumen" (quoted at the back of the so-called second "edition", March 1895, on an unnumbered p. 278 devoted to press comments on books published by Swan Sonnenschein & Co.).

Modern Humanists Reconsidered (1927)

As the veteran British rationalist Nicolas Walter explained in America, Robertson in his books on "Humanists" used the term broadly in his titles to denote "writers who were not necessarily classical scholars or religious skeptics, but who were generally concerned with humanity" (*Humanism*, 1998, p. 64). *Modern Humanists* was followed almost four decades later by *Modern Humanists Reconsidered* (1927), which was much more a rewriting than a re-editing of the earlier book. The result was that each book contained information the other did not (for example, on Carlyle). As Robertson remarked in his 1927 book: "things are said in the older book entitled 'Modern Humanists' which are still to be taken into account; while some judgments, it may be, are partly corrected, and others are reiterated" (Preface, p. v). Of the six thinkers or Victorian prophets under review, in *Modern Humanists Reconsidered* quite a notable theme was their response to what Robertson called (p. 99) "the age of science" and "the spirit of science" in the light of their self-contradictions or equivocations. J.M.R. also indicated that Ruskin did "misstate the issues by crediting Turner with a moral passion for accuracy when he was exhibiting magnificence of imagination" (p. 83). Robertson's comment seems much more compatible than Ruskin's attitude (as cited) with Turner's apparent use of unsuspected or hidden figures of people, animals and objects to enrich his paintings with an additional dimension or layer of meaning. Stylistically *Modern Humanists Reconsidered* seems more free-flowing and somewhat lighter in tone than its predecessor.

However, the 1891 book occasionally gave vent to the power of prophecy, as when in the essay on Mill (who worked for the India Office) Robertson referred to prevalent English attitudes which "will hasten the inevitable separation of India from the British…just as a similar indifference, worsened by prejudice, has made inevitable the legislative separation of Ireland, and will one day make necessary the legislative separation of Scotland" (p. 89). "Legislative separation" did not necessarily mean "independence", though Robertson was, in effect, looking decades ahead. In the same work he contended that Mill's thoughts on socialism were "to the last in a perplexed state" and "tentative" – an issue he did not discuss in *Modern Humanists Reconsidered*, where he praised John Stuart Mill for "his rectitude, his candour, his humanity, his courage", although the latter had also unjustifiably blamed Gladstone for not stopping the Franco-Prussian War in 1870 (pp. 141, 155-6).

J.M.R. located Emerson's gifts in "calling men to higher thoughts and feelings than those of the pursuit of the dollar

… He is a poet without the singing voice, but with the singing soul" (1927, p. 70); although neither in 1891 nor in 1927 did he explore Emerson's "marked influence on Thoreau" (1891, p. 133). In an unsigned review in October 1927 T.S. Eliot praised Robertson's attack on Matthew Arnold's literary criticism and elements of Arnold's attitude to religion, but indicated that J.M.R.'s attack did not go far enough (*The Letters of T.S. Eliot*, ed. Valerie Eliot and J. Haffenden, Vol. 3, p. 733n.). Separately in 1927 T.S. Eliot drew attention to Arnold's inconsistency "painstakingly shown by Mr. J.M. Robertson" (*Selected Essays*, 1972 ed., p. 452). Criticising Spencer on religion, Robertson rebuked Ruskin for "always seeking to graft moral or religious issues upon aesthetic" (p. 82); and the reader may judge whether, in his updated essay on Emerson, Robertson made good on his confession in his June 1891 Preface of "an omission to dwell on valuable points in his teaching which I had formerly acknowledged".

In 1954 both *Modern Humanists* and *Modern Humanists Reconsidered* would feature in the Bibliography to Michael Packe's *Life of John Stuart Mill*, which also quoted from J.M.R.'s 1927 book. Packe's thorough and substantial work – which for decades would rank as a standard biography of J.S. Mill – also carried quite a short though suave Preface by the renowned and influential free market and "New Right" economist F.A. Hayek. Yet from the "Author's Acknowledgements" (p. xiv) it may be surmised that Packe owed far more to Hayek than to Robertson in preparing his biography. For almost exactly twenty years until 1950 Hayek was on the academic staff of the London School of Economics at the same time as Robertson's young friend and self-styled "devout Robertsonian" Professor Harold Laski, who had been initially influenced by Mill (though Robertson and Laski diverged sharply in their reaction to the Russian

Revolution: for Laski, a "Soviet enthusiast", see Giles Udy, *Labour and the Gulag*, 2017, p. 456, 601, 61, 456, 504-5, etc.). Arguably Robertson, with his belief in socially desirable and accountable state intervention and support, stood between Hayek and Laski (see *BRUG*, pp. 18, 22, for example).

Montaigne and Shakespeare (1909; originally published with slightly different title, 1897)

In a raid in 1898 on London business premises associated with alleged obscene publications, the police seized copies of Robertson's books entitled *Montaigne and Shakspere* and *The Saxon and the Celt*. These two scholarly books were published in 1897 by "The University Press", which that year also produced Robertson's *The Dynamics of Religion*, a survey of aspects of English culture history from the Reformation to virtually the twentieth century, highlighting economic, political and psychological factors sustaining religion (with a vigorous defence by him along the way of the thinker Anthony Collins, regarded by him and, much later, the respected British historian Roy Porter (*The Creation of the Modern World*, 2000, p. 520, note 110: cf. *BRUG*, p. 52 & n.) as a deist, not a dissembling atheist).

Among post-Reformation writers championed by J.M.R. were Montaigne and Shakespeare; and in 1983 the researcher Serena Jourdan in Salzburg, Austria, declared in her study of the Montaigne-Shakespeare relationship: "the inquiry begins in earnest in 1897 with the first edition of J.M. Robertson's *Montaigne and Shakespeare*. Robertson's analysis of verbal echoes of Montaigne in the plays is often reasonable … the objective of Robertson's work ultimately seems to be to challenge Shakespeare's learning and the integrity of his achievement, and in fact originated the disintegrationist school of Shakespeare criticism" (*The Sparrow and the Flea*, pp. 8-9). She added (p. 11) that the critic who "takes Robertson most tellingly to task" is Pierre Villey, who none the less "grants that the use of parallels can have value" even if he only "demolishes several of Robertson's examples".

Yet J.M.R.'s 1897 book on Montaigne and Shakespeare had been prefigured by his investigation *The Upshot of 'Hamlet'*, which was originally serialised in *Our Corner* between March and June 1885 and then issued very soon afterwards by Annie Besant and Charles Bradlaugh as a separate pamphlet. It was apparently Robertson's earliest essay to impress Bradlaugh's daughter Hypatia; and *The Upshot of 'Hamlet'* established J.M.R. as one of the first British scholars to suggest that "the extent of Shakspere's obligations to Montaigne is greater than is commonly supposed". In his 1885 essay, from which these words are taken, he pointed to quite a few echoes, in works attributed to Shakespeare, of Florio's translation of Montaigne; and he would develop this thesis in his 1897 book (which was enthusiastically commended by Hypatia Bradlaugh Bonner's *The Reformer*). In *The Baconian Heresy* (1913, pp. 207, 396) J.M.R. touched on echoes of Montaigne in *Hamlet*. As a literary critic put it in 2002: "Robertson argued for a profound, philosophical influence of Montaigne on Shakespeare, using both verbal and thematic parallels in support of his thesis" (Hugh Grady, *Shakespeare, Machiavelli, and Montaigne*, p. 50, n. 51).

Moreover, John Florio, who produced an English translation (1603) of Montaigne's *Essays*, had been a tutor to Shakespeare's patron the Earl of Southampton who was a devoted friend of the Earl of Essex, Shakespeare's protector.

(Robertson noted "the Essex conspiracy" in relation to a revival of *Richard II*, where the king expatiated tellingly on "sad stories of the death of kings": see *Elizabethan Literature*, pp. 115-16.) In 1923 Robertson remarked of Shakespeare: "There is reason to think that in the years between 1599 and 1604 he read much of Florio's translation of Montaigne, portions of which we know to have been passing from hand to hand some years before its publication", adding that Montaigne's influence was to be discerned in *Hamlet*, *Measure for Measure*, and *The Tempest* in particular (*'Hamlet' Once More*, pp. 113-4).

In his *Shakespeare's Debt to Montaigne* (1925) George C. Taylor concluded that "Shakspere [*sic*] was, beyond any doubt, profoundly and extensively influenced by Montaigne"; and he described J.M.R. as "the leading exponent in England of the theory of an extensive indebtedness of Shakspere to Montaigne" (see pp. 5, 4, 3 and v). The American academic also suggested that his compatriot Elizabeth Robbins Hooker was one of the very few scholars at that time who echoed or supported J.M.R.'s findings. The following year Robertson told Patrick Geddes: "at present I am revising, sentence by sentence, a new translation of Montaigne by a friend, for which I have written an introduction" (from letter of 10.12.1926, quoted in *J.M. Robertson*, ed. G.A. Wells, 1987, pp. 24-5). This Emil J. Trechmann translation/edition was apparently appreciated by the Marxian thinker Max Horkheimer or at least by some of his translators (see *Between Philosophy and Social Science*, 1993 ed.), and it was relied upon by the American historians Will and Ariel Durant in 1961. Robertson's 1909 book was noticed in Britain by the modernist Wyndham Lewis (1927) and by the rationalist Thomas Whittaker (1926); and Freud's disciple Ernest Jones noticed his 1897 book (*Modern Criticism: Theory and Practice*, ed. W. Sutton & R. Foster, 1963, p. 419), as did H.R.D. Anders (1904) and Susanne Türck (1930) in Berlin, as well as Robert Ellrodt (2011) in Paris. (Sutton and Foster reproduced, though not with complete fidelity regarding numbering, a section of Jones' *Hamlet and Oedipus*, 1949, pp. 45-6.) The scholars Frances A. Yates (1936), James Robinson Howe (1976) and R.T. Eriksen (1986) gave reasons for in effect rejecting Robertson's unduly firm belief that Giordano Bruno did not influence Shakespeare, as stated in *Montaigne and Shakespeare* (1909 ed., p. 132 et seq.; see Donna N. Murphy, *The Marlowe-Shakespeare Continuum*, 2013, pp. 230, 241). Ironically enough, the conclusion reached by the three scholars (just cited) in the twentieth century was compatible with Robertson's overall view of Shakespeare's sympathetic attitude towards scepticism and freethought.

During World War One the writer Rebecca West discussed Shakespeare and Montaigne with Robertson and William Archer over a meal at Westminster.

Mr. Lloyd George and Liberalism (1923)

In 1986 the scholar Michael Freeden, referring to British Liberalism in about 1921, described Robertson as "a liberal theorist of force and vigour" (*Liberalism Divided*, p. 61, n. 67). In 1923 J.M.R. turned his searchlight away from political theory to political practice illustrated by the subject of his book *Mr. Lloyd George and Liberalism*. While it is not one of his most impressive or major works, it was still an informative and readable, if rather neglected, contribution to British historiography of the 1906-23 period, in which Robertson was an active observer and participant in Liberal politics, not least as a Liberal M.P. from 1906 to 1918 and as an unsuccessful

Parliamentary candidate in Hendon in the 1923 general election.

He did not focus on Lloyd George's achievements in Government during the earlier part of this period, or even on his pro-Boer stance in the 1899-1902 South African War, but rather on Lloyd George's perceived treachery, misjudgements and slipperiness during and immediately after the First World War. J.M.R. believed that a post-war Liberal reunion of the Asquith and Lloyd George groups would sooner or later result in the latter (some ten years younger than Asquith) becoming Liberal Party leader, for which position he was deemed unsuitable. Robertson felt there was reason to suspect that Lloyd George, spurred by personal ambition, engineered the formation of the coalition War Cabinet under Asquith in 1915. (This suspicion was later substantiated by an admission by Lloyd George himself in his 1938 *War Memoirs*: see Roy Hattersley, *David Lloyd George*, 2012 ed., pp. 375, 673.) Moreover, Lloyd George had form: in 1910, artfully manipulating and sidelining Asquith, he tried to organise a coalition Government with the Tories, allegedly in the national interest (Hattersley, p. 280 etc.; Emmanuel Shinwell, *I've Lived Through It All*, 1973, p. 16). Then, in 1916, assisted by the Tories, he supplanted Asquith as Prime Minister in a coalition Government with them. Robertson did not endorse the claim that as wartime Prime Minister Lloyd George had introduced greater efficiency and order to Government decision-making in Britain. Indeed, J.M.R. criticised not only the Welshman's 1916 palace coup (which the leading Tory Stanley Baldwin clearly associated in 1922 with the fact, as he saw it, that "the Liberal Party has been smashed to pieces"). Robertson also criticised Lloyd George's "perpetual and blundering interferences" with wartime military plans (plainly Lloyd George did not get on with army commanders like Kitchener,

Haig, William Robertson or Frederick Maurice). By contrast, although Asquith's contribution to the British conduct of the War was not his finest achievement, Robertson could have pointed out that it was on Asquith's watch as Prime Minister that British-invented tanks went into action for the first time in the World War in mid September 1916.

Certainly Robertson attacked Lloyd George's performance at the 1919 Versailles Peace Conference as "the most ill-informed member of the Conference in European politics". While this may seem an unfair exaggeration, Clemenceau, the French Prime Minister, believed Lloyd George "knew nothing about the world beyond Great Britain"; and at about this time the economist Maynard Keynes felt that of the three leading participants at Versailles (from France, Britain and the U.S.A.) Lloyd George "carried the greatest burden of guilt for imposing a 'Carthaginian peace' on the defeated Germans": this was a view that seemed broadly consistent with that expressed by the politician turned historian Roy Hattersley in 2010. Robertson thought that one result of the Conference was "a Germany on the verge of absolute collapse". One indication of such a collapse was the maintenance of the Allied naval blockade which produced an alarmingly high German death rate related to quite widespread starvation by early 1919 (see Hattersley's *Lloyd George*, 2012 paperback ed., pp. 489-94). J.M.R. did not focus on whether Lloyd George, on becoming P.M., should have strenuously attempted to shorten the War through a negotiated peace with Imperial Germany which could have included German's ally Austria in 1917 or early 1918, and thereby saved much loss of life and destruction in Europe. Moreover, Robertson condemned Lloyd George's policy in Ireland, where under his premiership every Liberal ideal had been "trampled underfoot" with a war of "reciprocal brigandage". Robertson's 1923 book was noticed by historians Michael Bentley (1977) and S. Maccoby (1961) in their work on modern British Liberalism.

Robertson's concern for the freedom of oppressed peoples found expression when – weeks before Lloyd George and the American President Woodrow Wilson publicly called for an independent Poland in January 1918 – he paid eloquent tribute, at a London meeting, to Kosciuszko's inspiration in the struggle for Polish freedom. Lloyd George appeared to favour early recognition of Soviet Russia, which was soon at war with Poland (see Hattersley, p. 553; Antony Sutton, 1974, pp. 197, 200; Paul Johnson, 1983 ed., p. 74).

At a 1930s international disarmament conference there was a move for Britain to join in a ban on bombardment of towns from the air; but, as Lloyd George put it, "we insisted on reserving the right to bomb niggers!" (V.G. Kiernan, *Colonial Empires and Armies 1815-1960*, 1998 ed., pp. 200, 251, quoting Frances Stevenson's diary). In *Mein Kampf*, published in German in 1925-6, Hitler expressed deeply offensive and insulting racist views about African Negroes; and Lloyd George may have become aware of these before he showered praise on Hitler in the context of meeting him in 1936. Moreover, as a British wartime leader who talked rhetorically, even glibly, about a land fit for heroes, Lloyd George had an opportunity, which it clearly seems he did not take, as Britain's Prime Minister during and after the World War (1916-22) to insist on respectful and adequate commemoration and memorialisation (by name wherever possible) of over one hundred thousand loyal black and Asian soldiers from the British Empire who sacrificed their lives in the Great War (see *The Times* and other leading national newspapers in Britain for 22.4.2021 and 23.4.2021).

Mr. Shaw and 'The Maid' (n.d.: 1925)

This work represents Robertson's polemical attack in book form on George Bernard Shaw's treatment of the story of Joan of Arc (c. 1412-31), known as the Maid of Orleans, in his play *St. Joan*. On publication of his book Robertson promptly sent a copy to Shaw, whom he had first met in London of the 1880s, when they became friendly, and they had intermittently kept in touch or followed each other's career thereafter. Almost equally promptly Shaw returned the book, heavily annotated by him – on almost every page – in his minute, spidery handwriting, which is not always easy to read. Robertson then added his counter-comments, in green ink in his distinctive handwriting, in the book to Shaw's annotations. It does not appear that the book was sent back to Shaw for any further comments, and it seems that a line was drawn under the verbal sparring at that point.

Robertson was evidently keen to take issue with Shaw's quite often misleading presentation, and even understanding, of historical facts. J.M.R. was highly critical of Shaw's presentation in the play of a trial by the Inquisition, with Shaw's associated suggestion that such trials were conducted by the Inquisition in a humane way (see, for instance, pp. 73-4). For Shaw, said J.M.R., "Jeanne must be a she-Napoleon, a Marie Bashkirtseff, born out of due time, with an inoculation of George Eliot" (p. 45 – see also pp. 92, 103: Bashkirtseff was an artist whose published diary was admired by Shaw). Robertson's subsequent 1932 edition of *Courses of Study* gives quite an impressive and useful list of competent or commended works – at least half of them by writers in French – up to 1931 on the historical Jeanne d'Arc, her trial and life.

G.B.S. would probably have been better off if he had given greater emphasis to the line that he was a dramatist, free to adapt or ignore known facts, and not a historian (though he indicated that he had done historical research, and Robertson argued – on p. 30 – that G.B.S. was wrong "to pose as a historian entitled to flout a more responsible investigator who is really seeking objective truth"). But Shaw's handwritten comments are rather surprisingly tetchy and petulant, even occasionally abusive, when they are not defensive or even irrelevant. Robertson felt that Shaw unnecessarily presented King Charles VII of France as "a Dickens caricature, while Jeanne lectures to him out of George Eliot" (p. 54). J.M.R. added that Shaw had nevertheless provided a good dramatic touch giving "a real breath of mediaeval atmosphere" (p. 91) at one juncture.

The rationalist Joseph McCabe has a useful entry on Joan of Arc in his 1948 encyclopaedia (pp. 336-7), in the course of which he maintained that in *Mr. Shaw and 'The Maid'* Robertson "makes no serious inquiry into the question whether Joan was a witch", which McCabe implied she was. Admittedly in that context it may well have been advisable for J.M.R. to have consulted Margaret Murray's *The Witch-Cult in Western Europe* (1921) – McCabe gave the title incorrectly – but equally McCabe may have overlooked the point that on p. 74 (para. 1) of his 1925 book Robertson seemed to imply that he (J.M.R.) was open to the view that Joan was regarded as a witch. J.M.R.'s book was respectfully reviewed in the *New Criterion* by T.S. Eliot, who led a backlash against Shaw's play according to Damon Franke's academic *Modernist Heresies* (2008, p. 126), where Robertson's book is quoted and then listed in the bibliography.

Mr. Shaw and 'The Maid' was regarded as "excellent" by the literary freethinker William Kent (*John Burns*, 1950, p. 288), but clearly seemed to be viewed less favourably, also in 1950, by the Anglo-American theatre critic Eric Bentley, who declared, in an illogical line of argument: "Oddly enough the Rationalists agreed with the Catholics as to the villainy of Joan's judges; to doubt it would have been to doubt the whole basis of their anti-clericalism. And so it was possible for the Anglo-Catholic T.S. Eliot and the Rationalist J.M. Robertson to join hands ..." (*Bernard Shaw*, pp. 189-90). The implication appeared to be that Eliot was anti-clerical; certainly it would have been highly unusual for an Anglo-Catholic to have been suchlike. In any event, in the same work Eric Bentley showed himself to be unreliable or careless in referring (p. 11) to Robertson and Joseph McCabe as "Huxleyan agnostics" when it was well known that both men were atheists, with Robertson, for one, being consistently critical of Huxley. Moreover, according to the *Cambridge Biographical Encyclopedia* (1998 ed.) and the *Macmillan Encyclopedia* (1995 ed.) T.S. Eliot became an Anglo-Catholic in 1927, some three years after Shaw's *St. Joan* appeared.

The Natural History of Religion (Hume, with introduction by J.M.R., 1889)

As Robertson would indicate in *The Dynamics of Religion* (second edition, 1926, p. 171 etc.), he was influenced in his evidence-based thinking and avowed scientific approach, notably in his work on religion, by two eighteenth century British thinkers and writers he much esteemed and rated highly: David Hume and Edward Gibbon. He would produce a monograph on Gibbon, published in 1925, and an introduction dated 29 December 1929 to a selection from Gibbon's *The Decline and Fall of the Roman Empire (Gibbon on Christianity)*. Following in the footsteps of his friend Joseph Mazzini Wheeler, who turned out an edition (issued by the Freethought Publishing Company) of Hume's essay on Miracles, Robertson, through the same publisher, reprinted, with a fresh introduction, Hume's *The Natural History of Religion* in a complete and unexpurgated version designed to supersede the "extensively mutilated" and "piously fraudulent", if cheap, edition on sale in Britain in 1889. Robertson's later books like *A History of Freethought Ancient and Modern, Christianity and Mythology*, *Letters on Reasoning* and *Pagan Christs* reveal traces of the stimulation provided by Hume's work, not least *The Natural History of Religion*. This last-named work – in Robertson's words – "most explicitly asserts his Deism; but on account of its rationalistic treatment of concrete religion in general, which only nominally spared Christianity, it was that which first brought upon him much theological odium in England" (Introduction, p. vi). Robertson added that Hume "was certainly not one of the heroes of truth, or of the martyrs of progress. … This said, it remains to do justice to the incomparable insight and lucidity of his philosophical performance" (pp. xxi-xxii). Having then hailed Buckle as "a great sociologist" (p. xxii), J.M.R. would go on, in *Bolingbroke and Walpole* (1919), to place David Hume among "the variously serviceable beginners" in Britain of sociological study (p. 254). Robertson's *A Short History of Morals* (1920) would include quite a few references to Hume – but that was scarcely surprising.

New Essays towards a Critical Method (1897)

This collection of essays on literary subjects or themes – all written by Robertson from about 1884 onwards – may be regarded as a latter-day companion volume to his *Essays towards a Critical Method* (1889). The 1897 book comprises nine essays (if the Appendix is counted as in effect a separate essay). Of these, those on "The Art of Keats" and "Shelley and Poetry" may have been studied in about 1963 by Thabo Mbeki (a future President of South Africa) when at the University of Sussex he "wrote a thesis on the poetry of Percy Bysshe Shelley and John Keats" (Hadland and Rantao biography of Mbeki, 1999, p. 31). In the first essay, on "The Theory and Practice of Criticism" (some 53 pages long), Robertson analysed E.S. Dallas's *The Gay Science* (1866), which he hailed as "the most considerable English treatise yet penned on the philosophy of criticism". He then pointed out that the French critic Hippolyte Taine had posited "every work as a product of three causal forces, the race, the social and physical environment, the 'moment' or special influence of the time", but – J.M.R. added – "[Émile] Hennequin had previously shown the arbitrariness of Taine's implications as to race and environment" (pp. 18, 33). Taine's emphasis on the "moment" might partly explain Robertson's later allusion to the influence of "situation" as a causal factor in history (see *HF*, 1936, p. xxix).

In 1885 Robertson had established himself as one of the earliest British literary critics to understand the extent of Rufus Griswold's falsification in his scurrilous memoir of Edgar Allan Poe. (Rather ironically, Poe in his lifetime was accused of plagiarism regarding a popular book, published in 1839, on mollusc shells which he had edited and of which he was initially presented as the author, though he had apparently acted with the latter's approval: see *Daily Mail*, 9.7.2021, p. 62.) In his youth J.M.R. had learnt Poe's poem *The Raven* by heart, and in his 1885 essay on Poe he praised the American's poetic gifts but also declared that his best stories reflected "the same extraordinary creative energy and intellectual mastery as distinguish his verse". More than a quarter of a century later, Professor Killis Campbell at the University of Texas, in his edition of Poe's poems, would quote quite extensively from Robertson's essay; and four years after Killis Campbell, his colleague C. Alphonso Smith from the University of Virginia would hail Robertson's contribution as "on the whole the ablest brief treatment of Poe yet published in any language".

In his essay on Coleridge, Robertson identified three masterpieces from "a poet with some magical moments, never quite regained", with the stimulus of opium (pp. 137, 140). J.M.R.'s essay on Arthur Clough marked a pioneering break with a largely demeaning or dismissive attitude towards his poetry (see Frederic E. Faverty, ed., *The Victorian Poets*, 1968, and also Michael Thorpe, ed., *Arthur Hugh Clough*, 1972, who praised J.M.R.'s essay). Robertson seemed reasonably satisfied with his final piece – on "Accent, Quantity, and Feet" – as he mentioned it without disapproval decades later in *Courses of Study*, 1932, p. 174. In his essays focused on individual writers he arguably could have devoted more attention than he did to literary or artistic movements.

New Essays towards a Critical Method (with particular reference to the essay on Clough) appeared in the Bibliography for *The Cambridge History of English Literature* (1916) covering the nineteenth century; and Robertson's approach to scientific criticism, as expressed in his book, was endorsed by the music critic M.D. Calvocoressi in *The Principles and Methods of Musical Criticism* (1923). A second expert student of music who may have perused *New Essays* was the rationalist British conductor and composer Sir Henry J. Wood (not to be confused with one of Robertson's

Christian critics of the Myth Theory, H.G. Wood). The prolix anonymous reviewer of Robertson's book for *The Reformer* (15.11.1897) did not subject J.M.R.'s first and last essays - on technical, theoretical or general aspects of literary criticism - to any sustained or detailed analysis, although such analysis could have explored how Robertson's concept of a scientific attitude in literary appreciation related to "the science of consistency" (p. 17).

In 1999, in his Introduction to his book on *Romantic Atheism*, Martin Priestman declared (p. 1): "The emergence of declared atheism into common discourse has been traced by such historians of ideas as J.M. Robertson ... Such histories of thought, however, have had no particular brief to look at poetry as a special kind of discourse and have hence overlooked it except when it transparently overlaps with philosophy or polemic." In the Bibliography for his book Priestman listed only two of J.M.R.'s works, namely his 1929 and 1936 histories of freethought, apparently oblivious of the existence of *New Essays towards a Critical Method*, in which Robertson surveyed the literary achievements and endeavours of Shelley, Keats and Coleridge, who all featured quite prominently in Priestman's book.

"Our Relation to India" (1904)

This essay by J.M.R. appeared in the April 1904 issue of *The Reformer*, edited by his friend Hypatia Bradlaugh Bonner, who published articles of her own in this monthly such as "The Wrongs of India" during the first half of 1899 and "Starving India" during March and April 1900. Robertson's essay gave pointers and references to various informative works on India and seemed fully consistent with his long-standing sympathy and support for the burgeoning Indian nationalist movement. The article attracted the attention of one critic who wrote in to *The Reformer* to claim that "taken as a whole, it gives a very misleading impression of affairs in India, especially as regards irrigation" (issue for August 1904, p. 529); although J.M.R. vigorously defended himself.

In 1883 Robertson attacked the British acquisition of India as a "great national theft" and contemplated "with tranquillity the ultimate surrender of India to native management, and the writing of 'Finis' to the story of British Oriental Empire". In 1886, in his first lecture at South Place Institute in London, he strongly criticised Victorian imperialism and "the practice of international burglary". In 1891 he declared: "That inveterate indifference of the English public and their representatives to the right government of a territory over which they claim rule and possession, will hasten the inevitable separation of India" (*Modern Humanists*, p. 89). Many years later J.M.R. probably influenced the notable Indian rationalist Dr. R.P. Paranjpye, who heard him speak on varied subjects dozens of times. In February 1892 J.M.R., as *NR* editor, carried an obituary of an Indian National Congress joint secretary whose death was "a great loss to the Congress cause" (*NR*, 7.2.1892, p. 95). In July 1892 the *NR* placed on record Congress's deep appreciation of Bradlaugh's services on its behalf. In the 1894 biography of Bradlaugh, Robertson wrote that "Bradlaugh was all his life … the friend of India … he acquired by his work an amount of popularity among natives such as had never before been earned by an Englishman outside India"; and when Bradlaugh addressed the Indian National Congress in Bombay in December 1889, some 5000 participants rose to greet and cheer him (Vol. 2, pp. 198, 409-10). In 1899 J.M.R. indicated that imperialists "have no thought of giving self-government to India; they have scoffed at every step in the movement of the Indian National Congress, and they hate the ends at which it aims. They are exasperated at the suggestion that the Indian Civil Service should be gradually filled with natives …" (*Patriotism and Empire*, pp. 195-6 etc.).

Robertson expressed similar sentiments in books in 1920 (*Charles Bradlaugh*, p. 110) and in 1922 (*Voltaire*, p. 106). In 1925, for example, he acknowledged "the variety of conflicting racial and religious elements in Indian life" (*The Meaning of Liberalism*), p. 115) – a factor that would constitute a key stumbling-block twenty years or so later, with partition. In 1932 he devoted quite a long section to India under British rule in his *Courses of Study* (in which he noted W. Scawen Blunt's *Ideas about India* (1885), which the academic Priyamvada Gopal discussed in her 2019 book). Despite one unindexed, extremely brief and incidental reference to Robertson in the Notes (p. 494, n. 180) of her *Insurgent Empire: Anticolonial Resistance and British Dissent* (2019), it seems lopsided that Gopal did not include consideration by her of the contribution of freethinkers like Robertson, Bradlaugh, Hypatia Bradlaugh Bonner and William Archer in her sections on India (or, indeed, in Robertson's case, on Egypt). The books in English that Evelyn Waugh found in the Hindu-run bookshop in Goa in 1952 largely featured works by "old rationalists" may well have included books by J.M.R.

As Robertson's comments about India made in 1883 and 1891 (as cited above) were reproduced in or before 1904, he may have felt that it was not necessary for him in his *Reformer* essay to reiterate advocacy of Indian self-rule, but that his 1904 essay would carry more weight and acceptability if he outlined a case for immediate reforms (leading to self-rule). He indicated that the British administration of India was marked by "a bureaucracy under no Parliamentary scrutiny" dealing with "an alien subject population, destitute of all political rights" (op. cit. 1904, p. 212). At least some of J.M.R.'s proposals for reform in India would be echoed, if not copied, by his Labour acquaintance Ramsay MacDonald in the latter's *Labour and the Empire* (1907, p. 105), including employing more and more Indians in public offices. Robertson's Liberal Government introduced reforms in India in 1909. In the 1894 biography of Bradlaugh Robertson recorded and, indeed, welcomed "the persistence of the Congress movement" in India (Vol. 2, p. 199: see also Mira Matikkala, *Empire and Imperial Amibition*, 2011, pp. 108, 237, referring to this passage in the biography). In a section on India in *Courses of Study* (1932 ed., p. 335) J.M.R. declared: "The movement inevitably continued"; and, after noting a number of fairly recent works on the subject, he added: "Thus the intensification after 1914 was long prepared for; and such books … expressed the new aspirations for self-government that had arisen in Europe." Less than two decades later India was free.

Pagan Christs (1903; second edition, 1911)

While Robertson's *Studies in Religious Fallacy* (1900) included two essays on "The Jesus Legend and the Myth of the Twelve Apostles" and "The Myth of Judas Iscariot" – dating from 1894 and 1893, respectively – *Christianity and Mythology* (1900; 1910) and *Pagan Christs* (1903; 1911) were the only two of his important books published between the outbreak of the Boer War in 1899 and the start of the World War in 1914 to focus exclusively on the origins and emergence of Christianity and other ancient religions. Whereas Albert Schweitzer, in the printed version of lectures he delivered in Birmingham, UK, in

February 1922, cursorily noticed *Christianity and Mythology* in a footnote, a random sample of scholars and writers who acknowledged both *Pagan Christs* and *Christianity and Mythology* included: based in Britain, Ernest Crawley (1905); J. Estlin Carpenter (1911); Herbert J. Rossington (1911); Edward Carpenter (1920); Leonard Patterson (1921); Hugh E.M. Stutfield (1921); Arthur Findlay (1939); Herbert Cutner (1950); John Ferguson (1980); George Wells (1986, 1987); Larry Wright (2000); Lynn Picknett and Clive Prince (2008); in the USA, Shirley Jackson Case (1928); Harry Elmer Barnes (1931); Alvin Boyd Kuhn (1944); John G. Jackson (1976); Robert Ackerman (1987); Walter P. Weaver (1999); Robert M. Price (2006); in Germany, Arthur Drews (1910 Eng. trans.); in France, Maurice Goguel (1950) and Georges Ory (1968); and in Switzerland, Georges Berguer (1923).

In 1925 Maurice Goguel, immediately after referencing both *Christianity and Mythology* and *Pagan Christs*, declared: "Some ideas of Robertson resemble the astral theories developed by Niemojewski ... 1910); and by C.P. Fuhrmann (*Der Astralmythus von Christus*, 1912)" (*The Historical Jesus*, ed. Craig A. Evans, 2004, p. 320, note 33). But as these two scholars, as cited by Goguel, published their relevant works some years after J.M.R. had published the first editions of *Christianity and Mythology* and *Pagan Christs* and, in at least one case, after J.M.R. had published a second edition, it may be more accurate to say that the astral theories of Niemojewski and Fuhrmann resemble some ideas already developed by Robertson.

Jesus is a Greek form of the Hebrew name Joshua; and in *Pagan Christs* and elsewhere Robertson suggested that the Gospel Jesus was essentially based on Joshua as an ancient Palestinian saviour sun-god to whom human victims had been sacrificed, with this cult being eventually superseded by a sacramental meal combined with a mimic crucifixion and resurrection embodied in a mystery-drama of which the Gospel story gave a bare transcript. It may be relevant that the Greek word for a stage actor "is used seventeen times in the New Testament – only in the Synoptic Gospels and always in a saying of Jesus" (thirteen of them in Matthew: see Richard Batey, "Jesus and the Theatre", *New Test. Stud.* Vol. 30, 1984, p. 563 et seq.: cf. *Pagan Christs*, 1911 ed., pp. 197-99, etc.). In the words of the Marxist scholar Karl Kautsky some years later than Robertson: "Jesus dies, and the task is now to prove by a series of stage effects that a god had died" (*The Origin of Christianity*, orig. 1908). In his 1920 study of the Gospels, the Mythicist Gilbert Sadler referred readers to a section on the Passion-story in *Pagan Christs* (1911 ed.).

Robertson's thesis of a pre-Christian Joshua cult appeared to be largely supported by contemporary scholars and investigators like Thomas Whittaker, Gordon Rylands, Chapman Cohen, F.J. Gould, Macleod Yearsley, the Dutch scholar Bolland (as Goguel pointed out), the Frenchman Édouard Dujardin, and the German academic Arthur Drews (who, it is believed, influenced Lenin). Moreover, years after Robertson first put forward his mystery-drama theory, it appeared to receive some circumstantial corroboration with the revelation, from excavated Assyrian tablets, that the death and resurrection of the Babylonian saviour sun-god Marduk had been enacted in an annually performed mystery-drama centuries before the Christian era (see E. Sidney Hartland's article "Recent Babylonian Discoveries and the Passion of Jesus Christ", *LG*, March 1922, pp. 43-4). The Passion story in the Gospels closely resembles this mystery-drama, and there are clear allusions to Marduk elsewhere in the Bible. Babylonian influences on Judaic thought were outlined by

Robertson in *Pagan Christs* (1903 ed., pp. vi, 70-5; 1911 ed., pp. vi, 74-8), for example. The notable sociologist Robert Michels, in his study of patriotism (1929, German text, p. 74), referred to the importance of "Frazer und Robertson" in underscoring the significance of meals in nation-formation.

Pagan Christs has sections on "The Rationale of Religion", "Secondary God-Making", "Mithraism", and "The Religions of Ancient America" – not to mention Appendices – all replete with sources and references. The section on Mithraism – which the scholar Hugh Schonfield would draw upon for *The Essene Odyssey* (1984, pp. 154, 180) – originated in a lecture at South Place during 1889. In that lecture, apparently the first in Britain on Mithraism by a British freethinker, Robertson maintained that it had been the most widespread religion of the Western world "in those early centuries which we commonly call Christian". Decades later, in 1954, the remains of a second century Mithraic temple would be unearthed in London only about half a mile from where he had been speaking!

His section on "The Religions of Ancient America" originated in an 1891 South Place lecture in which he drew attention to "the high probability – I do not call it more – that the American races did come from Asia not very many thousands of years ago by way of Behring's Straits in the extreme north, at a time when men had already learned the primary arts of civilization". The best part of a century later this thesis appeared to be supported by archaeological and anthropological findings, including evidence of ancient artefacts discovered on the Soviet Kamchatka peninsula.

In his 1891 lecture Robertson concentrated on the Aztecs and Incas, drawing parallels between aspects of their religious and social systems and those found in other parts of the world. He perceptively stressed the deadly significance of the flat-topped Aztec pyramids (*Pagan Christs*, 1911 ed., pp. 362, 366). He thought that the ancient remains at Palenque (in Mexico) - which he never visited - indicated "a civilisation higher, on the side of art and architecture, and at the same time much older, than that of the Aztecs" (p. 348). The Palenque remains would be identified with the early Maya, whose script is the only ancient Mesoamerican writing system that has been substantially deciphered. In 2011 the historian Frank Welsh wrote: "the sole fragments of Mayan books that survive are either almanacs, ritual texts, or very basic annals, which might serve as prompts for oral amplification" (*The History of the World*, 2013 paperback ed., p. 92). This quite strongly suggests that Robertson's mystery-drama thesis was at least plausible. In the 1920s Max Schmidt pointed out that human sacrifice routinely took place at a new Inca's accession. In 1932 (*Courses of Study*, p. 390) J.M.R. commended Schmidt's later book (1929) on Peruvian art and culture, which devoted some 50 pages to Nasca (Nazca), with Nasca geoglyphs later attracting intense anthropological interest; rather as *Pagan Christs* arguably paved the way for Lord Raglan's *The Origins of Religion* (1949, Watts & Co.).

In 2003 Bill Cooke (op. cit., p. 51), without giving any specific example, criticised "the imprecision and dogmatism of Robertson's writings" in *Christianity and Mythology* and *Pagan Christs*. Cooke's claim seems, at the very least, an unfair and exaggerated characterization of each or either of these two books as a whole. It sits incongruously with J.M.R.'s statement in *Christianity and Mythology* that "I am not so presumptuous as to suppose that in the handling of this far-reaching controversy I have escaped fallacy or reached finality"; and he modestly added in his Epilogue: "If our analysis of the gospels as a congeries of myths be broadly accurate ... "(1910 ed., pp. xiii, 434). Moreover, in *Pagan Christs* he openly avowed his debt, for example, to Franz Cumont's work on Mithraism: "To M. Cumont I owe much fresh knowledge, and the correction of some errors ... and if I have ventured here and there to dissent from him, ... I do so only after due hesitation" (1911 ed., p. xxii). Cooke indicated that Robertson's two books "brought together an impressive quantity of mythical parallels to the Jesus story which churchmen of the time shrank from doing" (ibid.); but Cooke did not acknowledge that these parallels may have reflected a desire by Robertson to bring a greater sense of rigour and precision to the discussion. In 1936 the British Historicist A.D. Howell Smith described these two works by J.M.R. as "carefully documented" (see *BRUG*, pp. 99-100); and in 1980 the classical scholar John Ferguson did not refer to any supposed dogmatism or imprecision on Robertson's part in the latter's two hierological books (see Ferguson's *Jesus in the Tide of Time*, p. 158). *Pagan Christs* featured in the Bibliography to *Antecedents of Christianity* (1925) by the unconventional Anglican churchman C.P.G. Rose (see his book and also Peter Godwin's *When a Crocodile Eats the Sun*, 2007 ed., p. 145). During the Asquithian Liberal era the Christian controversialist H.G. Wood criticised *Christianity and Mythology* and, more particularly, *Pagan Christs* (for the Wood-Robertson debate before the Cambridge University Heretics Society in 1911 see Damon Franke, *Modernist Heresies*, 2008; for Wood's 1919 attacks on J.M.R. see Wood's *Rationalism and Historical Criticism*; and for his 1938 critique see G.A. Wells, op. cit. 1987).

In 1963 S.H. Hooke, Professor of Old Testament Studies at the University of London, asserted: "The Christ-myth of Drews and Robertson is now little more than a curiosity of literature, but ... it is very doubtful whether the attempt to purge Christianity of its mythical element can ever be successful." The novelist and poet D.H. Lawrence, who had experienced a crisis of faith when about twenty-one, admitted that his reading of Robertson, Robert Blatchford and such writers had "seriously modified" his religious beliefs. Decades later Professor G.A. Wells seemed to find the initial section of *Pagan Christs* on "The Rationale of Religion" particularly helpful (see *J.M. Robertson*, ed. Wells, 1987, p. 191).

J.M.R.'s Mythicist views were perhaps particularly influential on the Left. In Britain the socialist Robert Blatchford was one of those who popularized them. Later, Robertson's works helped to popularize the Myth Theory in the Soviet Union, much as he attacked the Bolshevik regime. In 1936 the Anglo-Australian Marxist writer Jack Lindsay declared: "it was Robertson's books that converted me to the Myth Theory, and I owe him a great debt." The British Marxist scientist J.B.S. Haldane acknowledged the importance of *Pagan Christs* (which was a reference point in America for Henry Frank's *Jesus: A Modern Study* in 1930 and for Tom Harpur's *The Pagan Christ* in 2004). Like J.M.R. in *Pagan Christs* and elsewhere, Freud's erstwhile collaborator Carl Jung highlighted the fish image in Christian iconography and a debt to Franz Cumont on Mithraism. Moreover, Freud and J.M.R. both read Hume, Spencer, E.B. Tylor, Feuerbach, Lecky, Ludwig Büchner and Sir James Frazer, not to mention Darwin (for Jung/Cumont and Freud/Frazer see John Kerr, *A Dangerous Method*, 2012 ed., p. 589).

Papers for the People (n.d.: 1896-7)

These twelve papers or pamphlets on matters of public

concern were produced by Robertson, and published by fellow freethinkers based in major English cities, over a twelve month period from about July 1896 onwards. The public issues addressed in these papers were, seriatim: "The Priest and the Child"; "The People and Their Leaders"; "Godism"; "The Blood Tax"; "Saving and Waste"; "Home Rule and Rule of Thumb"; "The Vote for Women"; "The Truth about Vaccination"; "What Has Christianity Done?"; "The Population Question"; "Railway Nationalisation"; and "Why Preserve the Monarchy?". As many of the Radical reforms, based on secularism, proposed by Robertson in this series involved pushing against religious interests, connections or presuppositions, freethinkers no doubt found it easier than at least some others to address the issues raised fully and honestly. The publishers declared: "This series of Pamphlets has already been boycotted by a large number of News-agents" (No. 6, unnumbered p. 1). As the substance of some of Robertson's papers – e.g. No. 8 – has been considered or touched upon at an earlier stage in the present book, the emphasis here is on other aspects or other papers in his series.

In the first paper he made the sociologically interesting observation that "It is doubtful whether more than one in three of the clergy now believe in the doctrines of hell and heaven, of salvation by blood, of miracles, of the answering of prayer, or of eternal life. Yet they are all prepared to go on teaching all these things" (p. 7). Having referred there to the "powerful bias of corporate interest" (p. 4), Robertson, using language that would also have resonated at least five decades later, drew attention in the next paper to "professional politicians" (p. 3) and "class interests" (p. 4). He went on in No. 2 (pp. 8-9) to advocate "Short Fixed Parliaments"; and in 1898 he would highlight "the harm of the old state of things, in which one magnetic leader periodically gave this or that signal to an army that had never been prepared for his choice" – for which an improvement would be that "the *group* of more prominent politicians shall show themselves in practical touch with their organised following, *taking* and giving counsel" (*The Reformer*, 15.2.1898, p. 340: emphasis added by J.M.R. for "group" and by the present writer for "taking"). Thus, some ten years before Robert Michels, Robertson seemed at least partially aware of the political problem of oligarchy. Moreover, his capacity for a human touch at a less abstract level was indicated when he declared in his second paper: "It is not that rich and poor people are born enemies, but their riches and their poverty make them so" (p. 6).

His third paper – on "Godism" – was selected, more than eighty years after its first appearance, for inclusion in *An Anthology of Atheism and Rationalism* (1980) by the American freethinker Gordon Stein, who maintained that Robertson's essay "gives an idea of his style and thought. It is probably one of his best short pieces and has been out of print since the 1890s" (p. 68). (In the same work Stein very briefly noticed J.M.R.'s *Christianity and Mythology, Pagan Christs, The Historical Jesus, The Jesus Problem*, and *Jesus and Judas*.)

In papers Nos. 4 and 7 he expressed a sense of solidarity or support regarding the aspirations of the international socialist movement and the rights and aspirations of women in Britain, respectively. In "The Blood Tax" (No. 4) he declared – and it seemed a reasonable or understandable declaration at the time – that the international socialist movement "is really destroying the spirit of national enmity, as between the workers of the different nations"; and "The Vote for Women" (No. 7) was devised in the same vein as his forceful statement in Parliament in March 1909 that "I am a supporter and have always been a supporter of women's suffrage".

Referring to Robertson's fifth paper – on "Saving and Waste" – the libertarian activist Chris Tame appeared to make a good point when he declared in 1987: "In 1896 Robertson argued that the entrepreneur fulfilled no productive role", adding "whereas in 1912 he said that the entrepreneur was 'as necessary a factor in industry as the "hands"' (*J.M. Robertson*, ed. G.A. Wells, p. 118), although there might be a semantic discussion as to what exactly J.M.R. meant by "productive".

In April 1897 Hypatia Bradlaugh Bonner, editor of *The Reformer*, recommended J.M.R.'s "very effective" "What Has Christianity Done?" (No.9) to one of her readers. On 18 July 1897 a reviewer in the "Book Chat" column of the *Freethinker* stated that Nos. 10 and 11 of *Papers for the People* "are written with force and ability, though the tone is perhaps more urgent than persuasive. Mr. Robertson is rather too impatient with illogical people, who…constitute the great majority of the population. On the other hand, it must be admitted that he generally advances strong arguments based upon adequate information" (p. 460). According to Jim Herrick, "a large proportion of the *Freethinker* was written by [G.W.] Foote in its first thirty years" (*Vision and Realism*, 1982, p. 34); and it may be presumed that the "Book Chat" column often reflected his general outlook. But tensions and conflicts over the allocation of secularist assets came to a head following Bradlaugh's death in 1891: "Robertson accused Foote of arbitrariness and irregularity in these proceedings and there was much animosity till the Memorial Hall Co. was finally wound up in 1897" (David Tribe, *100 Years of Freethought*, 1967, p. 42). That fraught background could help to explain the "Book Chat" columnist's claim that Robertson was "rather too impatient with illogical people". Certainly J.M.R. appeared to have a more harmonious relationship with Foote's successor, Chapman Cohen, who in 1938 wrote a series of *Pamphlets for the People*, which, rather unlike J.M.R.'s *Papers for the People*, tended to concentrate on religious and philosophical questions. Whereas Robertson's companion piece *The Future of Liberalism* (n.d.: 1897?) was noticed more than half a century later in A.M. McBriar's *Fabian Socialism and English Politics 1884-1918*, *Papers for the People* probably seemed to be more obviously a rallying call for citizens, individually or collectively, to take action, although both of Robertson's works attempted not only to give information, but also to influence or change attitudes.

Despite his reasonably friendly relationship with some individual Fabians, J.M.R. tended to be more radical than the Fabian Society, certainly during the half-decade 1895-1900, regarding which Bernard Porter maintained: "Before 1900 the Fabian Society had seldom shown any concern over, or even knowledge of, the wider world outside the bounds of the municipal corporations and the parish councils" (*Critics of Empire*, 1968, p. 109). This was reflected to some extent in *Papers for the People*, where in paper No. 12, for instance, Robertson championed the abolition of the monarchy, whereas the Webbs were berated by *Reynolds's Newspaper* in 1897 for proposing an oath of loyalty to the throne (see Antony Taylor, 1999, p. 135). Also J.M.R. produced the anti-imperialist *Patriotism and Empire* in 1899 whereas the Fabian Society issued its imperialist manifesto *Fabianism and the Empire* in 1900. *Papers for the People* formed part of a continuum of J.M.R.'s radical writings in the 1880s and 1890s.

Patriotism and Empire (1899)

In 2002 Peter J. Cain, a noted analyst of economic aspects of late British imperialism, declared: "Robertson is a neglected figure whose economic and sociological ideas deserve greater attention" (*Hobson and Imperialism*, p. 34n.). In 1998 Cain had issued an edition of Robertson's *Patriotism and Empire*, which was originally dedicated to the American internationalist Moncure Conway associated with London's South Place Ethical Society, and which was published in October 1899, more or less just as the Boer War was starting. Robertson's book called imperialism "the outstanding political problem" and "the prevailing fashion of political thought" (pp. 138, 142). In 1901 John G. Godard, author of *Patriotism and Ethics* – also published by Grant Richards – concluded that J.M.R.'s book "embodies a keen and masterly analysis of Imperialism" (p. 194n.).

Godard had quoted (p. 59) with approval J.M.R.'s aphorism: "Patriotism, conventionally defined as love of country, now turns out rather obviously to stand for love of more country" (p. 138) – a quotation that would be reproduced by two Finnish scholars, Edvard Westermarck (1917) and Timo Särkkä (2009), for example. Robertson's book also attracted the attention in 2011 of the Finnish academic Mira Matikkala, who pointed out that in this work J.M.R. linked imperialism not only with a crude and strident form of patriotism, but also with militarism. These three currents of thought flowed through Victorian music halls – Robertson sardonically half expected "a Moses of the Music-Hall" (p. 55) – and impinged on the work of W.E. Henley and Rudyard Kipling (see the extensive discussion in J.H. Grainger's *Patriotisms* (1986) of J.M.R.'s book, which also featured in the Bibliography of

Janet Henderson Robb's *The Primrose League 1883-1906*, published in New York in 1942). Robertson attacked the arguments for imperial expansion based on a perceived or alleged need for emigration, fresh markets, and trade to follow the (British) flag. He did not apparently have time to comment in *Patriotism and Empire* on Lord Rosebery's reference in May 1899 to "the larger patriotism that I have called imperialism" (quoted by Bernard Porter, op. cit. 1968, p. 60 & n. 3). J.M.R. did criticise Rudyard Kipling and W.E. Henley as prominent representatives of "the type of the Barbarian Sentimentalist" (p. 52), but he did not explicitly place Cecil Rhodes (who had quite recently been forced to resign as Prime Minister of Cape Colony after some five years in the post) in the same category. Indeed, the sole indexed entry for Rhodes merely offers two passing references to him in a quotation reproduced from Henley. As *Patriotism and Empire* was published over two years before Rhodes' death the former Prime Minister may have seen it or at least heard about it, particularly perhaps as Robertson made a much publicised political visit to South Africa in 1900.

Robertson's use of language seemed to find an echo in J.A. Hobson's opening sections of *The Psychology of Jingoism* (1901). Following in Bernard Porter's tentative footsteps in *Critics of Empire* (1968, p. 199), Peter Cain stated quite firmly in 1998: "Robertson actually anticipated Hobson's own elaboration and extension of his theory of financial imperialism in Part II of *Imperialism* and may even have prompted him to undertake it" (Introduction to his 1998 edition/ reprint, p. vii: Robertson and Hobson developed a friendly relationship during the 1890s). Although J.M.R. referred to "the general trading interests, which spontaneously leant to 'expansion' as a way of widening the market" (pp. 140-1), he did not specifically focus in detail on links between foreign investment and imperialism. (Such links, suggesting a cause and effect relationship between these two factors from the 1860s to the 1890s, were misleadingly implied by Hobson in his *Imperialism* (1902): see *Imperialism and Colonialism*, ed. G. Nadel and P. Curtis, 1964, p. 78 etc., and B. Porter's *Critics of Empire*, 1968, pp. 216-7.)

Nor, rather surprisingly, did Robertson's book identify Churches and their missionaries among imperialism's beneficiaries, although he did refer in passing to the "Church and the landlords, as the steadiest backers of the imperialist party" (p. 189). Arguably one of the merits of his *Patriotism and Empire* was that he seemed aware of the damage inflicted by imperialism on race relations. Thus, having instanced "hideous misery among the lower strata of the imperial State" (p. 178), he went on to declare: "No race is really raised, no community is really bettered, while it is held in subjection" (pp. 194-5) and to refer to "the countless infamies of the colonial handling of Maories and Basutos" (p. 197). He added: "The Anglo-Indian who strives and aims to bring the natives under him a little nearer self-rule is indeed doing as high a work as any done on the planet; but not one Anglo-Indian in ten seems to have any such thought" (p. 199).

Robertson did foresee that the U.S.A. would become an imperial power (p. 52), and that China would industrialize, with British capital relocating there (pp. 180-1, etc.). Robertson also indicated there was a risk, even a likelihood, of a deadly struggle between England and Germany (pp. 176-7). He certainly felt in 1899 that "the end in sight is an Armageddon of international piracy" (p. 191). He later revealed (*R.P.A. Annual*, 1915, p. 60n.) that a peace-loving German friend had translated *Patriotism and Empire*, of which the three parts are: "The Springs of Patriotism and Militarism"; "The Militarist

Regimen"; and "The Theory and Practice of Imperialism".

Norman Angell (Ralph Lane) relied upon *Patriotism and Empire* for his own *Patriotism under Three Flags* (1903). Although no reference to Robertson has been found in J.A. Hobson's *Imperialism, A Study* (1902), it seems almost certain that the latter took account of points in Robertson's 1899 book. Hobson's book influenced Lenin; and while no evidence has come to hand that Lenin consulted Robertson's work in preparing his own on imperialism, it seems perfectly possible that he did at some stage. Independently using concepts that Marxists could understand if not share, J.M.R. in *Patriotism and Empire* analysed, in largely economic terms, common roots of "patriotism", imperialism and militarism as reflecting and promoting the interests of the ruling classes. As he declared: "The only interests really furthered by fresh expansion [under imperialism] are those of the speculative trading class, the speculative capitalist class, the military and naval services, the industrial class which supplies war material, and generally those who look to an imperial civil service as a means of employment for themselves and their kin" (p. 187). Arguably Robertson should have provided more detail on whether he believed that industry and the business class as a whole profited from imperialism, although it seems reasonably clear that he mainly had in mind sections thereof as beneficiaries (see p. 178, for example). Moreover, his book was not disfigured by the anti-Semitism that marked Hobson's *Imperialism, The War in South Africa* (1900) and the latter's letter of 2 September 1899 to C.P. Scott (see Bernard Porter, *Critics of Empire*; Paul Kennedy and Anthony Nicholls (eds.), *Nationalist and Racialist Movements in Britain and Germany before 1914* (essay by Gisela Lebzelter on British anti-Semitism); and Lewis Feuer, *Imperialism and the Anti-Imperialist Mind*, for details).

He struck a distinctive note in supporting birth control in his discussion on emigration, where, after noting the scale of Italian emigration to the Americas, in a reference to the Italians being defeated in the battle of Adowa (1896) he stated that "their misgoverned motherland spends blood and treasure in a senseless clutch at waste places about Abyssinia" (p. 177). While he gave no detailed consideration to the British monarchy's role *vis-à-vis* imperialism, his book was justifiably praised by William Langer of Harvard (1951) as: "One of the earliest and one of the ablest indictments of imperialism as part of the capitalist ideology. Many later works draw on the arguments here presented" (*The Diplomacy of Imperialism, 1890-1902*, second edition, p. 96).

The case of Japan illustrated Robertson's capacity to develop his own argument. Towards the end of his final part (III, on imperialism) of *Patriotism and Empire* he declared: "the very policy of expansion itself may destroy the home industry it is professedly undertaken to further. Already the cheap labour of India and Japan is made the basis for a new competition with British manufactures" (p. 180). He then voiced implicit concern about turning Japan "into a duplicate of Lancashire" (p. 193). A few years later he shifted this late attention to Japan from the economic to the military aspects. In a rather remarkable article penned in 1904 during the Russo-Japanese War he warned that "the possible Imperialisation of Japan is another danger of the most serious kind", and he foresaw that a triumphant Japan could adopt an attitude of "general hostility towards British rule in the East". Thus he could see far beyond the more immediate concerns and calculations of the then British Prime Minister, Lord Salisbury, which were to discourage, through an Anglo-Japanese alliance and treaty (concluded in 1902), expansionism by Imperial Russia. In his article Robertson also indicated that the Russian disasters in the war with Japan were a "momentous warning" for a vulnerable British Empire and compared them to some extent with British reverses during the Boer War. Britain's alliance with Japan in effect came to an end years before Japan invaded and occupied Singapore in 1942.

The Philosophical Works of Francis Bacon (ed. with introduction by J.M.R., 1905)

Patriotism and Empire was reprinted in 1998. Similarly durable – and reprinted in 1970 – was Robertson's one-volume edition (1905) of *The Philosophical Works of Francis Bacon*, which the British philosopher Anthony Quinton would describe as entirely sufficient "for all but the most refined purposes" and use in his 1980 study of Bacon. As on other occasions, Robertson was assisted in his book-production by his dear friend Ernest Newman, who read the proofs; and the published book was heavily drawn upon by S.A.E. Hickson in *The Prince of Poets* (1926) on the Shakespeare question. J.M.R. would modestly refer to his own edition of Bacon, but without attaching his editorial name to it, in *Courses of Study* (1932, p. 110). His *Pioneer Humanists* (1907) would include an essay on Bacon, who has been hailed as one of the leading Western European thinkers of the seventeenth century, regarded as the first fully post-medieval century in the history of ideas (see Tom Rubens in *Ethical Record*, July 2014, p. 9).

For a number of enthusiastic, well-educated Marxists the ultimate accolade for Robertson and his work could well have related to the fact that his *Philosophical Works of Francis Bacon* (1905) was cited as a reliable source by the prominent

Russian Communist intellectual Nikolai Bukharin in his paper on dialectical materialism which, as the leader of the Soviet delegation, he presented to the International Congress on the History of Science and Technology held in London between 29 June and 3 July 1931, within about a mile or so of J.M.R.'s home – and with Special Branch taking a close interest in Bukharin's visit and obtaining copies of his papers (see John Costello (op. cit. 1988, pp. 163-4).

Pioneer Humanists (1907)

In 1936 the economist J.A. Hobson recorded of Robertson: "As I came to know him outside the arena of public controversy, I found him no less devoted to matters of artistic taste and imaginative literature, exhibiting a delicacy of expression which permeated all his writing, but which was best seen in his *Modern Humanists*" (*HF*, p. xxvii). Then, in 1949, Professor Harold Laski wrote of J.M.R.: "He was a literary critic of distinction, and his *Modern Humanists* (1891) contains some of the best work done in Great Britain since Matthew Arnold" (*Dictionary of National Biography 1931-1940*, p. 736). While this praise was no doubt sincerely bestowed, a similar candidate for it could be Robertson's *Pioneer Humanists*, which was arguably more readable and provided him with the advantage of a longer historical perspective (most of his designated modern humanists had died not long before 1891, and two of them – Ruskin and Spencer - were still alive then).

His 1907 book comprised absorbing essays on Machiavelli, Francis Bacon, Hobbes, Spinoza, Shaftesbury, Mandeville, Gibbon, and Mary Wollstonecraft. These eight studies presented vivid and sometimes eloquent pen-portraits of the thinkers as personalities, and introductions to their work, from a viewpoint combining aspects of literary criticism, sociology, historiography and philosophy, rather than any sustained philosophical analysis per se of their writings.

Hailing Machiavelli as the first great modern political thinker, Robertson maintained that maxims of his statecraft were "almost respectable beside the normal practice of his world, nay, beside the frequent practice of statecraft in our own day". (Robertson had already explored aspects of Machiavelli in "Machiavelli and Calvin" in Vol. 1 of his 1904 *Essays in Sociology*.) Students of Bacon, while detailing his errors, were "electrified by the penetrating truths, which are worded with the essential force of great oracles". J.M.R. drew thought-provoking comparisons between Hobbes and Spinoza; and he suggested that Spinoza influenced Shaftesbury, who was "one of the very first of our sociologists", just as Mandeville was "one of the real founders of utilitarianism". (In 1932, in *Courses of Study*, Robertson explained that he had discussed Bernard Mandeville's critics in the essay on him in *Pioneer Humanists*.) Robertson saluted Mary Wollstonecraft's service for women's rights. In 1948 Joseph McCabe endorsed his chapters on her and on Gibbon. (J.M.R. had written on Gibbon the historian in *NR* for 21.8.1892 and would devote a monograph to him in October 1925 as well as contribute a lengthy introduction to *Gibbon on Christianity* published in February 1930, with the last two works, like *Pioneer Humanists*, appearing under the imprint of Watts & Co.) Karl Popper's view of science in relation to Francis Bacon was largely presaged by Robertson (see Chris Tame in *J.M. Robertson*, 1987, ed. G.A. Wells, pp. 112-3, 118; also Ralph Blumenau, *Philosophy and Living*, 2002, p. 212, and 557).

Nicolas Walter of the R.P.A. performed a service to freethought in 1998 by informing, or reminding, his readers of the existence of *Pioneer Humanists* (*Humanism*, p. 64).

Poems, Essays and Fragments (James Thomson, ed. with preface by J.M.R., 1892)

Towards the end of 1984 a writer on Robertson declared: "Robertson's edition (1892) of *Poems, Essays and Fragments* by James Thomson was the first to give a broad selection, previously unpublished in book form, from both his prose and poetry, excluding *The City of Dreadful Night*. That remarkable work by a leading Victorian poet of pessimism projected the City as a symbol of loss of faith or purpose traceable, in twentieth century verse, to *The Waste Land* and T.S. Eliot, with whom Robertson would establish a friendly relationship" (*BRUG*, p. 57). It was no doubt a coincidence that only a few months later Robert Crawford would publish an article entitled "James Thomson and T.S. Eliot" in which he wrote: "the relation between Thomson's poetry and that of Eliot has never been examined closely. This essay carries out such an examination" (*Victorian Poetry*, Vol. 23, No. 1, Spring 1985, p. 23). What was less understandable – in view of the quotation above – was the absence of any reference to J.M.R. in that essay. There appeared to be a similar phenomenon when in 1932 a selection of Thomson's poetry carried an introduction by the poet Edmund Blunden which referred the reader to the biography (1894) of Charles Bradlaugh jointly written by Hypatia Bradlaugh Bonner and J.M.R., but without any mention whatsoever of the latter's involvement and contribution regarding both Bradlaugh and Thomson. In his 1892 Preface to his edition Robertson said of Thomson ('B.V.'): "In his prose, to a critical eye, he is almost always a quite secure and accomplished craftsman; in his verse, even the greatest, he was always capable of lapsing from perfection, of eking out his gold with putty" (p. vi). Robertson's friend, the bookseller Bertram Dobell, was stung by his forthright criticism of Thomson's poetry, but their relationship survived. Publication of Robertson's collection was quite quickly followed by his "Critical Chat" on 'B.V.' in which he declared that "Thomson's true vehicle was prose" (*NR*, 15.1.1893, p. 42). J.M.R.'s edition included five essays previously unpublished in one volume, and none of the essays he selected overlapped with any material in G.W. Foote's fine collection (1884) of articles by 'B.V.' In 1964 Charles Vachot, writing in French, was quite complimentary, in his study of James Thomson, about Robertson's edition.

The Political Economy of Free Trade (1928)

Apparently believing that freethought and Free Trade were complementary, Robertson presented much valuable information – in *Trade and Tariffs* (1908), *Free Trade* (1919), *The Political Economy of Free Trade* (1928), and elsewhere – on the history of Free Trade and Protectionism. Not least among the three works itemised, the last-named is easy to read and understand. It offers an authoritative account of "the struggle for Free Trade" and "discoveries of Free Trade" (pp. 98, 100), principally in Britain, interspersed with criticism of politicians like Joseph Chamberlain, Stanley Baldwin, Bonar Law and Leo Amery (the last-named while he was Colonial Secretary), and with some personal anecdotes and reminiscences (for example, on his wintering in Germany in 1887, when he stayed for six weeks with the kindly atheist and man of science Ludwig Büchner, whose literary links with his older brother Georg Robertson was one of the first in Britain to appreciate).

In *The Political Economy of Free Trade*, written in the autumn of 1926, J.M.R. pointed out that trade played a leading part in the Renaissance, and that in the early years of the twentieth century Britain had the lowest working hours, in relation to prosperity, in the whole industrial world, while Free Trade tended to increase prosperity all round, with Walpole as "the first English premier with free-trade leanings" (pp. 101, 118, 76, 61, seriatim). Robertson tended to see the defence of Free Trade against the rising forces of "tariffism" in class terms. He mounted a strong attack on Joseph "Chamberlain, than whom no politician was ever more skilled in playing on prejudice, whether of class, nation, or race … He told his countrymen that the [Free Trade] Cobden Club was largely supported by foreign subscribers; and when this was officially declared to be utterly false, with an offer to exhibit the Club's books, he made neither apology nor retractation. He falsified quotations from Cobden and Mongredien by way of confuting Harcourt and other free-traders; and when the true quotations were given he still made neither retractation nor correction" (p. 134). Possibly through his relationship with Beatrice Potter (later Webb), Chamberlain may have learned of Karl Marx's falsification, in his 1870s French edition of *Das Kapital*, of material and quotations from the British (Parliamentary) Blue Books and, in effect, decided that what was sauce for the goose was sauce for the gander so far as misrepresentation and falsification were concerned. J.M.R. touched on the thorny issue of post-war reparations by Germany (the imposition of which he had publicly criticised by 1918, before Keynes in 1919).

He maintained that the Russian Communists "have set up the

highest tariff walls in Europe" (p.181): an important issue that British historians and commentators on Stalin's Russia have tended to shy away from. Robertson's comment followed Stalin's support in May 1922 for a proposal by Nikolai Bukharin to rescind the state monopoly on foreign trade – a change firmly opposed by Lenin (Dmitri Volkogonov, *Stalin*, 1991 Eng. trans., p. 71: in 1931 Bukharin – a perpetrator and victim of Stalinism – would come within about half a mile of Robertson's Kensington home in the course of attending the International Congress, in London, on the History of Science and Technology). In 1929 A.S. Comyns Carr and D. Rowland Evans stated: "Tariffs are a menace to world peace" (*The Lure of Safeguarding*, p. 126); and in 1940 Henry B. Parkes declared: "what causes war is not capitalism but trade barriers" (*Marxism*, p. 142; also 141). Parkes added: "any form of planned economy (Communist as well as Fascist) must reduce its reliance on foreign trade to a minimum – partly for military reasons" (p. 142: on the basis of Parkes's stark terms J.M.R. may be seen as supporting a mixed economy). Robertson believed in 1928 that if a Second World War occurred, "civilization itself would be in process of dissolution" (J.M.R. op. cit., p. 165).

His book would be acknowledged by Ludwell Denny in *America Conquers Britain* (1930) and by S. Maccoby in *English Radicalism: The End?* (1961). As Gottfried von Haberler would point out in 1933 – the year of Robertson's death – there was an affinity between Free Trade and internationalism (*The Theory of International Trade*, 1936 Eng. trans., p. 225). A copy of *The Political Economy of Free Trade* was to be found in the Parliament of Zimbabwe Library quite soon after independence in 1980.

The Problem of 'Hamlet' (1919)

In *The Problem of 'Hamlet'* Robertson elaborated on the analysis he had presented five years earlier in his *Elizabethan Literature*, where he had written: "In *Hamlet*, the most famous of his plays, he was certainly hampered by the previous tragedy of Kyd, which he recast. In that, the assumed madness of the hero, remotely derived from an old saga, was matter for mirth, as madness always was to the rude and crude Elizabethan audience; and the added madness of Ophelia would serve the same purpose. The first he turns to truly tragic ends, and the second he makes matter of pity and tears ... In point of delicacy and vividness of character delineation ... *Hamlet* transcends all previous tragedy: the portraiture is as freshly powerful as the versification. Still there remain incongruities involved in the structure of the original. Hamlet's brutal words over the slain Polonius, and his savage motive for sparing the praying King, remain on the old barbaric plane; and the placing of the 'To be' soliloquy, with its reverie on the 'undiscovered country', *after* the scenes in which Hamlet has actually met the 'returned traveller', tells of readjustment which missed coherence. The barbaric plot discords with the brooding psychology which now pervades it" (pp. 185-6). As J.M.R. put it in 1919: the plot "retained a strictly barbaric action while the hero was transformed into a supersubtle Elizabethan" (p. 74). In 1951 the American critic Harold C. Goddard angrily disagreed with Robertson's view that *Hamlet* was blemished by the incongruity or tension between the retention of a "barbaric" plot and an attempt to transform the hero into "a supersubtle Elizabethan" (*The Meaning of Shakespeare*, p. 335, where J.M.R.'s 1919 work is quoted without any identifying specifics). Robertson's theory of *Hamlet* convinced T.S. Eliot, who soon after its appearance in 1919 declared: "the play is most certainly an artistic failure"; and, despite orthodoxy's counterblasts, Eliot had not emphatically repudiated Robertson's theory seventeen years later. In 1926, referring to Robertson's 1919 book, the unorthodox critic Herbert Read, who appeared to respect and esteem J.M.R., maintained that J.M.R. highlighted "incoherent" and "incongruous" elements of the tragedy *Hamlet* "with so much force" (*Reason and Romanticism*, p. 100: see also *BRUG*, pp. 69-70).

It is not very well known that Robertson had written in a similar fashion some three decades earlier, in 1885 in *The Upshot of 'Hamlet'*, where he gave voice to his belief that Shakespeare had set about re-writing old plays so as to furnish his theatre company "with a more vigorously written set of parts than was supplied by the plays before him", and that *Hamlet* was "demonstrably produced in this spirit". Following the outline of an older play or narrative which formed the basis for *Hamlet* as we know it – Robertson suggested – Shakespeare largely transformed the drama, changing the "barbaric" or "half-sophisticated Hamlet of the old play – into the many-sided, subtle-minded creation which we have all brooded over". But, Robertson presumed, because Shakespeare was "composing or adapting with extreme rapidity", he could not remove all blemishes or incongruities from the drama such as those listed by Robertson, resulting in "this wonderful play" becoming a "heterogeneous product". Ten years later, J.M.R. followed up *The Upshot of 'Hamlet'* with a paper entitled "Is 'Hamlet' a Consistent Creation?" in the *Free Review* for July 1895, which he edited at that time.

After about 1920 John Dover Wilson became more or less convinced that a tragedy by Thomas Kyd on the Hamlet theme had influenced the making of Shakespeare's *Hamlet* as we know it (see introduction to his second, 1936, ed. of *Hamlet*, pp. xix, xxi, xxiii). However, there may have been a degree of political risk attached to Shakespeare's presumed recasting or transformation of Kyd's play (now lost) during Queen Elizabeth's reign as Kyd had been arrested and detained by order of the Privy Council, and quite probably tortured, in May 1593 on account of mutinous anti-State work attributed to him. Although eventually released – his freethinking friend Christopher Marlowe having been slain in the meantime – Kyd still felt he was under suspicion of atheism, fell on hard times and (on the basis of J.D. Wilson's conclusions) in effect agreed to sell his play on Hamlet to Shakespeare's drama company to make ends meet. If so, Shakespeare may well have been at least partly motivated to help Kyd out. The esteemed female Shakespearean scholar Anne Barton seemed inclined to accept that Shakespeare's *Hamlet* was at least partly based on a now lost play by Kyd (see her introduction to the 1980 Penguin ed. of *Hamlet*, pp. 15-16). Moreover, the First Folio (F1) reference to an apparently non-Christian "enurn'd" (Act I, Scene 4, line 49) might suggest a lingering trace of Kyd's influence.

In 1940 – when Britain was already at war with Nazi Germany – *The Problem of 'Hamlet'* and its sequel *'Hamlet' Once More* (1923) were noticed, in a reasonably urbane way, by Hans Glunz in *Der 'Hamlet' Shakespeares* in Frankfurt am Main. Robertson's *The Problem of 'Hamlet'* was discussed by the Freudian (and R.P.A. Honorary Associate) Ernest Jones in his *Hamlet and Oedipus* (1949); and in 1986 William Empson's *Essays on Shakespeare* noted J.M.R.'s 1919 book and his *Literary Detection: A Symposium on 'Macbeth'* (1931). The *Problem of 'Hamlet'* was taken into account in 1961 in a work on Shakespeare's Quartos by the American literary critic Hardin Craig, who had drawn attention to it in 1950, in *The*

Enchanted Glass, where he also relied on Emil J. Trechmann's English translation (1927) of Montaigne's *Essays*, which carried an introduction by Robertson. J.M.R.'s *The Problem of 'Hamlet'* was quite thoroughly, if critically, studied by George Ian Duthie in *The 'Bad' Quarto of 'Hamlet'* (1941) and by Roy Walker in *The Time Is Out of Joint* (1948). However, Duthie admitted (p. 196) concerning Robertson: "he has one very powerful argument for his position with regard to the part played in Q1 by the Queen. He and others point out that in those respects in which Q1 differs from Q2 and F1 it agrees with the prose story of Belleforest" (pp. 196-7: Belleforest is believed to have provided, directly or indirectly, a source for the play *Hamlet* attributed to Shakespeare). J.M.R.'s 1919 book was treated reasonably sympathetically in W.J. Lawrence's *Shakespeare's Workshop* (1928) and arguably less so in Kenneth Muir's *Shakespeare's Tragic Sequence* (1972: no evidence has emerged that Muir's Communism accounted for his critique).

In more recent Shakespearean criticism *The Problem of 'Hamlet'* has been treated in a generally more respectful and favourable way by Zachery Lesser of the University of Pennsylvania in his *'Hamlet' After Q1* (2015). Professor Lesser in effect followed in the footsteps of the British scholar Ian MacKillop, who credited Robertson with fruitfully viewing *'Hamlet'* as a layered text resulting from Shakespeare altering or incorporating the work of other Elizabethan dramatists (see MacKillop in *J.M. Robertson*, ed. G.A. Wells, 1987, p. 61; Lesser, 2015, p. 173). Describing J.M.R. as "the most important" of the disintegrationists, Lesser declared that the disintegrationist literary critics "laid the foundations for much of the important Shakespeare scholarship of the twentieth century" (p. 174; see also p. 182). Admittedly Lesser went on to refer to "the extreme positions that Robertson ultimately advocated" (p. 184) and to J.M.R. becoming "discredited by the extremes of his authorship attributions" (p. 255, n. 134); but on neither page did Lesser present or refer to any examples or evidence of J.M.R.'s alleged extremism as a Shakespearean critic. Moreover, even if Lesser's claim regarding this is accepted, it would not follow that Robertson's other observations in this field were all devoid of merit, value or relevance (for which see entries by the present writer relating to J.M.R.'s works on Shakespeare, of which Lesser made quite extensive use, at least in the case of the 1919 and 1923 books on *'Hamlet')*. Lesser pointed out that Robertson focused on the problem of delay in *'Hamlet'*.

The Problem of 'The Merry Wives of Windsor' (1918)

In November 1917 Robertson read a paper on "The Problem of 'The Merry Wives of Windsor'" to the Shakespeare Association. This was published (amounting to some 32 pages) soon afterwards to reach a wider audience. In his piece J.M.R. sought to explain his belief that Shakespeare was working upon older material (a theme on which he would elaborate in *The Problem of 'Hamlet')*, and that the Bard's contemporary George Chapman had a share in the text of the play, a comedy, which subsequently appeared in the First Folio. He suggested that the young Shakespeare probably had little option but to retain comic parts loved by the "groundlings", and that the caricatured figure of Dr. Caius owed much to Chapman (see also J.M.R.'s *Shakespeare and Chapman*, 1917, p. 291, for example). As the critic Bill Bryson pointed out in 2016: "to Elizabethan playwrights plots and characters were common property. ... What Shakespeare did, of course, was take pedestrian pieces of work and endow them with distinction and, very often, greatness" (*Shakespeare*, updated 2016 ed., pp. 98, 99). In his 1918 publication on *The Merry Wives of Windsor*, but not in his *Shakespeare and Chapman* (1917), J.M.R. attributed to Chapman "a much larger share than Shakespeare's in the *Merry Wives*" (*'Hamlet' Once More*, 1923, p. 144). In neither publication did Robertson propose or endorse the idea of what Odin Dekkers would call "Chapman's supposed authorship of *The Merry Wives of Windsor*", a view which Dekkers would imply was held by Robertson (see *J.M.Robertson*, 1998, p. 186).

Pierre Porohovshikov, who thought, without presenting any evidence, that the Earl of Oxford – on this occasion not the Earl of Rutland – may have written or contributed to *The Merry Wives of Windsor*, admitted, with an eye on Shakespeare, that this play was "characteristically different from the master's usual matter and style" (*Shakespeare Unmasked*, 1955, p. 304). Robertson's musical friend Ernest Newman, referring to J.M.R.'s work, felt that Shakespeare was responsible for "some strokes of humour and certain felicities of style" in the play, where "incongruities abound" (*Opera Nights*, 1943, p. 392). J.M.R.'s findings in his work were also praised by his medically trained friend Macleod Yearsley in *The Lancet* (24 November 1928). For S.C. Sen Gupta in 1950, Robertson's "important" research on the play indicated that "the character of Falstaff developed on two independent lines" which appeared to converge "at some late stage", with the present text being based on an original play "produced not long after 1592" (*Shakespearian Comedy*, p. 267 etc.). Robertson's 1917-18 contribution was briefly noticed in 1932, albeit in moderate and seemingly respectful language, by his rather irascible critic Georges Connes, Professor at the Dijon Faculty of Letters in France.

The Problems of the Shakespeare Sonnets (1926)

Soon after Robertson's death in early January 1933, the Anglo-American literary critic Logan Pearsall Smith indicated that along with J.M. Robertson he felt that Shakespeare, although a great dramatist, was pre-eminently a poet (*On Reading Shakespeare*, 1933, pp. 153-4 n.). Rather as Robertson believed that not all 37 plays attributed to Shakespeare were written by him and him alone, so he thought that not all the 154 Sonnets associated with him were by him. In *The Problems of the Shakespeare Sonnets* – a book which arguably has received insufficient attention – Robertson rejected about fifty Sonnets as probably non-Shakespearean in the course of his detailed study of the Sonnets and of diverse, indeed bewildering, theories about them which more or less inevitably left many highlighted questions, complexities and conjectures on the subject unanswered. In the Master of the Revels' accounts for 1604-05 Shakespeare is identified as the author of the Sonnets (Bill Bryson, *Shakespeare*, 2016 updated edition, p. 181). But that is far from proving that he wrote all of the Sonnets (or plays) attributed to him.

Robertson's inference that Thomas Thorpe's publication of the Sonnets in 1609 was undertaken "without Shakespeare's knowledge or permission" and that Thorpe's edition "was suppressed before it had much sale" (see pp. 118, 120 and 257 of his 1926 book) could be consistent with embarrassment concerning sexuality or relationships as delineated in the Sonnets, or with issues relating to more than one person having written the Sonnets. The suppression theory advanced by Robertson (as indicated above) – and supported by John Dover Wilson – was regarded, in the 1940s, as plausible by Hyder E. Rollins, a highly respected American editor (1944) of Shakespeare's Sonnets.

It has been claimed that the person addressed in Sonnet 18 ("Shall I compare thee to a summer's day?") is, unusually, a male. But J.M.R. wrote that this was "not certainly so: it is only the effect of contiguity that gives the presumption. But No. 20 expressly and extravagantly celebrates the beauty of a male" (p. 143) – a view of Sonnet 20 largely shared years later by Stanley Wells, for example. Robertson was inclined to believe that Shakespeare did not write Sonnet 20 (see p. 184). He noted that a couple of lines in Sonnet 54 had allegedly been preceded by a couple of lines in *Hamlet*, Act I, Scene 3, lines 39-40, among "the few parallels between the Sonnets and the 'late' Plays" (p. 160).

His suggestion (p. 142) that Sonnet 55 was intended for inclusion in a volume of love poetry was followed up sympathetically by Mona Wilson in her 1931 work on Sir Philip Sidney and by John Dover Wilson in his 1966 commentary on the Shakespeare Sonnets. Robertson declared that Sonnet 66 was "surely Shakespearean" (p. 202): in this Sonnet "art made tongue-tied by authority", and even "purest faith unhappily forsworn", indicated a desire for greater freedom of speech and of thought; and in a later Sonnet (107), J.M.R. felt, there was an oblique reference to Queen Elizabeth's death (p. 35). Sonnet 94, Robertson pointed out, included a line ("Lilies that fester smell far worse than weeds") that also occurred – Scene 3, line 451 – in the anonymous play *Edward III* (published 1596), which he believed (pp. 156-7, 165n., 60) had been largely written by Marlowe, though partly rewritten by Greene, to the latter of whom Robertson attributed the "Lilies that fester" line in the play (see also J.M.R.'s *Elizabethan Literature*, 1914, p. 105. For this view of the Marlowe-Greene contribution to the authorship of

Edward III, he referred the reader in 1926 to his *Introduction to the Study of the Shakespeare Canon*). Decades later John Kerrigan – who was aware of the body of Robertson's work on Shakespeare – also drew attention, in his edition of Shakespeare's Sonnets, to the fact that the "Lilies" line occurs in both *Edward III* and Sonnet 94. In 2007 David West, in his edition of Shakespeare's *Sonnets*, quoted (though not with complete fidelity, on p. 307) from J.M.R.'s 1926 book (p. 85), where strong criticism was expressed regarding the poor quality of Sonnet 99.

Janet G. Scott (1929) in France and Barbara Mackenzie (1946) in South Africa both independently acknowledged J.M.R.'s contribution, but worked on the basis that all the Sonnets attributed to Shakespeare were by him. Mackenzie, however, admitted: "Many arguments have been set forth against the assumption of a single authorship of the sonnets, but they are all based on internal evidence." Moreover, the poet and critic T.S. Eliot described *The Problems of the Shakespeare Sonnets* (1926) as "indispensable: certainly it is the best discussion of the subject that I have ever read". Indeed, 1926 was rather a good year for J.M.R.: it saw the publication of a revised edition of *The Dynamics of Religion*, in addition to his book on the Shakespeare Sonnets; he was rather unexpectedly praised by the literary critic J. Middleton Murry for his stimulating contributions to Shakespearean criticism; and he celebrated his seventieth birthday in the company of friends and admirers. Decades later James Schiffer, as editor at the end of the century of Shakespeare's Sonnets, made some direct use of Robertson's 1926 work; and Macdonald P. Jackson (2014) took account of J.M.R.'s book (and of his *Shakespeare and Chapman*).

Rationalism (1912)

In 1941 – a critical year in the Second World War – the literary critic George Sampson, considering Robertson's contribution as a Shakespeare scholar, referred to J.M.R. in passing as "an unusually honest politician" and as "an intrepid advocate of rationalism" (*The Concise Cambridge History of English Literature*, p. 1031). In the latter capacity he was seen to advantage in his slim and accessible book entitled *Rationalism*, which seemed to be intended more for the man (or woman) in the street than for a philosopher in a study. Robertson virtually concluded his concise exposition of his subject on an eloquent note thus: "it is flatly inconceivable that the spirit which challenges all authority and anomaly in doctrine can tend to conserve either tyranny or social and political inequality. … rationalism, on the side of thought, must forever mean liberty, equality, fraternity, 'the giving and receiving of reasons', the complete reciprocity of judgment. To all races, all castes, it makes the same appeal, being as universalist as science, naming no master, proffering no ritual, holding out no threat" (1912, pp. 80, 81). More than a century later perhaps the most striking feature of the passages quoted is the writer's emphasis on the egalitarian, and specifically the non-racial, aspects of rationalism. In 2003 a commentator on the British rationalist movement maintained that in a passage in his book (p. 8) Robertson confused being independent of authority with being antagonistic to it (Bill Cooke, *The Blasphemy Depot*, pp. 212, 347). But this distinction could appear blurred or academic when, in the passage (on p. 8) complained about, Robertson indicated that rationalists had been confronted by forms of authority "which demand allegiance".

The Rationalist Press Association may well have had

publications like Robertson's *Rationalism* in mind when in its Report for 1912 the R.P.A. declared: "theological reactionaries have made desperate endeavours to ensure the boycotting of all books challenging the credentials of the orthodox religions" (quoted by Adam Gowans Whyte, *The Story of the R.P.A.*, 1949, p. 72: J.M.R.'s book was published by Constable and Co.). In 1937, in Sydney, Australia, the Christian David Simpson would grudgingly admit: "the Rationalist Press Association may seem a formidable battalion in the army of the godless, and probably is so" (*The March of the Godless*, p. 119). Somewhat similarly, in 1919 H.G. Wood grudgingly admitted "That Mr. Robertson is guided in part by scientific considerations need not be denied" (*Rationalism and Historical Criticism*, p. 54). Wood added (p. 58): "He is a kind of intellectual Ishmaelite." This latter comment may have been seen by Robertson's one-time journalist colleague Hector Carswell Macpherson shortly before Macpherson, in a letter to *The British Weekly* (11.11.1920, p. 110), said that J.M.R. had been "a kind of journalistic Ishmaelite". Be that as it may, Wood, after a late reference to Robertson's *Rationalism* (1912), concluded his own work with the curious claim that Rationalism "is plainly ceasing to be the servant of reason" (p. 63).

In his book, as elsewhere, Robertson attacked the views on religion of the top Tory Arthur Balfour, with whom he clashed in the House of Commons, but who apparently listened attentively when J.M.R. spoke in the House. (In the 1894 Bradlaugh biography, Vol. 2, pp. 386-7, J.M.R. had seemed to give Balfour some limited credit for denying, to Bradlaugh's face in 1888, during a Commons discussion of over-population and emigration, that he had ever used "wicked" language against Bradlaugh.) Possibly counter-intuitively, Robertson influenced at least two music critics, with Neville

Cardus writing of himself and Ernest Newman: "we are both rationalists; and both of us began as students of [Émile] Hennequin and J.M. Robertson and the 'scientific method' of criticism" (*Autobiography*, 1947, pp. 215-6). Arguably Robertson's short introduction to his subject (1912, a total of just over 80 pages) was less philosophically impressive than Morris Cohen's *Reason and Nature: An Essay on the Meaning of Scientific Method* (1931), which was none the less more than double the length of *Rationalism*, and which J.M.R. noticed in glowing terms in his *Courses of Study* (1932 ed., p. 130).

In *Rationalism* and his earlier *Letters on Reasoning* he devoted little explicit space to the role of imagination in human life; and it would have been interesting if in *Rationalism* he had explored issues such as the extent to which a person showing signs of illogical thinking could still behave rationally. As Ernest Newman wrote of Robertson: "he never deluded himself that reason had only to show itself in the public places for an enraptured humanity to forsake everything else to run after it. All he held was that, imperfect as the light of reason may sometimes show itself to be, it is still the best, if not the only, light we have to rely on as we stumble through the darkness of our lives …" (*HF*, 1936, Vol. I, p. xxv).

Rudyard Kipling: A Criticism (n.d.: 1905)

In 1936 Ernest Newman wrote of Robertson: "No one who worked with him, talked with him, or even read him with the sincere desire to learn from him, can either forget or over-estimate the intellectual debt they owe him" (*HF*, p. xxvi). It was quite probably thanks to J.M.R.'s encouragement or influence that Newman – using the pseudonym Hugh Mortimer Cecil – excoriated Arthur Balfour (a future Prime Minister) in his *Pseudo-Philosophy*, published in 1897 by "The University Press", which in that same year also published three of Robertson's books (see H. George Farmer on "Ernest Newman" in the *Freethinker*, 16.6.1961, p. 191: both Newman and Robertson wrote for the *National Reformer*, each having made contact with the other by 1889).

In *The Meaning of Liberalism*, published in their lifetime, J.M.R. criticised both Balfour and Rudyard Kipling, who for him were on the other side of the political fence from himself. But in *Patriotism and Empire* he focused his attention on Kipling of the two, calling him one of the most distinguished members of the "Barbarian Sentimentalist" school (p. 52). Kipling appeared to be more strident than Balfour in his identification with imperialism, although Balfour, more noted for his elegant obscurantism and seeming dialectical subtlety, bluntly exposed his own racism when on 31 July 1906 he declared in the Commons: "We have to face facts; men are not born equal, the white and black races are not born with equal capacities: they are born with different capacities which education cannot and will not change" (see Bernard Porter, *Critics of Empire*, 1968, p. 306; see also 294n. Balfour expressed racist views in Parliament in distinctly similar terms in 1910: see W. David McIntyre, *Colonies into Commonwealth*, 1974 ed., p. 115). Robertson believed that, given the fact of Empire, Britain should guide its subject peoples towards self-rule.

In his *Rudyard Kipling* (1905) – noted by *The Cambridge Bibliography of English Literature* (Vol. 3, 1940) – Robertson convicted Kipling of vulgar hatred for other races, adding that "it will be found to be a rule for all his work that men of all races figure in it as foul or fair in respect of their hostility or devotion to the British Empire" (p. 26). Robertson conceded that "with his artistic sensibilities, he has flashes of higher inspiration and aspiration. On the strength of one such flash, he wrote the 'Recessional'." Kipling had "gifts for imagination and utterance", but was "beyond the pale of great art … because of his intellectual limitations, which keep him school-boyish, parochial, morally vulgar" (see pp. 27-9). J.M.R. had already compared Kipling unfavourably with the French writer Guy de Maupassant (*NR*, 16.7.1893, p. 42), and with the little known Ukrainian novelist Ignaty Potapenko (see J.M.R.'s *Criticisms*, Vol. 2, 1903) decades before Ukraine became independent of the remnants of the Soviet Union.

J.M.R.'s booklet was published in Madras, where the British authorities conceivably kept an eye on its distribution and on *The Indian Review* from which it was reprinted – in the interests of the British Prime Minister: Balfour (whose awareness of the political situation in Asia at this time was illustrated by Britain's signing a treaty of alliance with Japan).

The Saxon and the Celt (1897)

A few years after Robertson's death the American scholar Jacques Barzun wrote: "from 1870 to 1914 English public opinion was saturated with the notion of a superior Anglo-Saxon race, of which England produced the fine flower. The decadence of France, Italy, and Spain was contrasted with the political and economic success of the Teutonic sister-nations, England and Germany, and this self-righteous pride was heightened by racial contempt for the Irish." As Barzun went on in the next sentence (*Race: A Study in Modern Superstition*,

1938 UK ed., p. 105) to mention Robertson's *The Germans* alone of his works, the reader may not have suspected that J.M.R. had addressed such questions some twenty years earlier in *The Saxon and the Celt* (1897). Largely devoted to the Irish problem – it included a statesman-like programme for state-aided social and economic development and a federal constitution in Ireland, with provision for Ulster – *The Saxon and the Celt* remained a perceptive pioneering exposé of the bogus use of race to explain social and political history. (In 1868 W.R. Greg had referred to Ireland as "a land originally peopled by a thousand Saxons and a thousand Celts": quoted by Patrick Brantlinger, *Taming Cannibals*, 2011, p. 139.)

As L.P. Curtis, Jr., pointed out in 1968, Robertson's "remarkably cogent book" included an introductory section in which he marshalled historical and ethnological evidence "to dispose of the idea that the Celts of Ireland were a distinct race" (*Anglo-Saxons and Celts*, p. 104). J.M.R. followed this up by refuting Theodor Mommsen's lengthy denigration of the ancient Celts and modern Irish, of whom the German historian concluded: "It is, and remains, at all times and all places, the same indolent and … thoroughly useless nation" (quoted by J.M.R., 1897, p. 191). Mommsen's sentiments bear a distinct similarity to those expressed by Friedrich Engels – not recorded by Robertson – in *The Condition of the Working Class in England* (authorised Eng. ed. 1892, passage beginning "The southern facile character of the Irishman": this passage is cited by Leslie Page, *Karl Marx and the Critical Examination of His Works*, 1987, p. 105, and in a rather misleadingly truncated form by Tristram Hunt, *The Frock-Coated Communist*, 2010 ed., p. 107). In his book Robertson was much more critical of the barbaric Germani than Engels had appeared to be in *The Origin of the Family*, which went through several editions and translations between 1884 and 1891. J.M.R. went on to expose the distortions of British commentators like J.R. Green, the Duke of Argyll, Goldwin Smith, J.A. Froude, and Arthur Balfour. (In 2002 Ronald Hyam seemed to follow in Robertson's footsteps by critically surveying the anti-Irish attitudes of J.R. Green, Froude and Balfour – see his *Britain's Imperial Century, 1815-1914*, third ed., p. 169.) If, as Hugh A. MacDougall (1982) maintained, many of the racial shibboleths J.M.R. attacked had been discarded by scholars a generation later, Robertson's work had not been in vain. MacDougall referred to both *The Saxon and the Celt* (1897) and *The Germans* (1916) by J.M.R. In 1921 MacDougall's namesake William McDougall, Professor of Psychology at Harvard, placed J.M.R. as one of three "critics of the race-dogmatists" (*National Welfare and National Decay*, pp. 51, 55). William McDougall had already influenced Cyril Burt.

In 1982 Nancy Stepan at Yale University declared: "The use of race to explain political and social history, for example, had been criticised by the sociologist Robertson as early as 1897, in *The Saxon and the Celt*. … Altogether, Robertson gave a penetrating analysis of the pitfalls of race science" (*The Idea of Race in Science*, pp. 144-5, 216). Somewhat similarly, if also somewhat quirkily, Thomas Gossett in 1963, and again in 1997, described *The Saxon and the Celt* as "one of the wittiest and most devastating books of the [nineteenth] century on the subject of race" (*Race*, 1997 ed., p. 412). This followed the view of the British philosopher C.E.M. Joad in 1934 that in his 1897 book Robertson's chief concern was "to combat the fashionable contemporary interpretation of the events of national history and the traits of national character in terms of innate racial differences" (*Encyclopaedia of the Social Sciences*, Vol. XIII, p. 411: U.S.A.). A similar favourable view of Robertson's book had been expressed in 1898 by Charles Seignobos of the Sorbonne.

That J.M.R. sometimes lapsed in his task is illustrated by the fact that in *The Saxon and the Celt* he described the Jews as a "race"; although a century later the Jewish Communist historian Eric Hobsbawm appeared to slip in a similar way, in his autobiography *Interesting Times*, (2002, p. 24). In his book Robertson critically examined issues associated with J.R. Green's notion of "the German race" (for which see Sheridan Gilley's essay in *Immigrants and Minorities in British Society*, ed. Colin Holmes, 1978). Robertson criticised "the extraordinary abasement of public opinion before the personality of the emperor" in Germany (p. 27): Kaiser Wilhelm II would go on to commit racial genocide in Africa and to become rabidly anti-Semitic. In *The Germans* J.M.R. alluded a number of times to *The Saxon and the Celt*, and he likewise cited Friedrich Hertz's *Modern Race Theories* (1904). In his own sociological work on race Hertz indicated his appreciation of the contribution of others like J.M.R., who returned the compliment in 1932 with favourable references to Hertz in *Courses of Study*. Quite soon afterwards Hertz was attacked by the Nazis as a Jew, and in 1938 he left Austria to settle in London, where he would probably have met Robertson had the latter lived long enough. The ground covered by Robertson was not re-examined in Simon Jenkins's *The Celts* (2022).

Shakespeare and Chapman (1917)

Within months of its publication in 1897 J.M.R.'s *The Saxon and the Celt* was hailed by Charles Seignobos of the Sorbonne in Paris as "a very good criticism" of the notion of race (*Introduction to the Study of History*, 1966 reprint of 1898 Eng. trans., p. 241n.: in the same book Charles

Langlois commended *Buckle and His Critics*). By contrast his compatriot Jean Jacquot, associated with the University of Lyon(s), was highly critical in 1951 of Robertson's *Shakespeare and Chapman* (1917), accusing J.M.R. of "constructing a vast edifice above shaky or arbitrary foundations" (*George Chapman*, pp. 298-9) in his claims regarding Chapman's hand in plays attributed to Shakespeare.

In 1934 Havelock Ellis declared that "J.M. Robertson, who suffered from a sort of Chapman-complex, saw Chapman nearly everywhere in Shakespeare, from *Love's Labour's Lost* to *The Tempest*, not to mention some of the sonnets" (*Chapman*, p. 38). But Havelock Ellis (who had been praised by J.M.R. in *NR*, 16.12.1888, p. 390) was exaggerating: in *Shakespeare and Chapman* Robertson focused on four plays (*Timon of Athens*, *Love's Labour's Lost*, *Pericles*, and *Troilus and Cressida*) which he felt contained indications that Chapman had had a share in their composition; and even if the count is extended to include all of twelve other plays in the Shakespeare Canon, studied by Robertson, suggesting possible interventions by Chapman, the total of supposedly Chapmanesque plays would still be distinctly less than half of the 37 plays conventionally claimed for Shakespeare.

In 1942 George Bernard Shaw told Hesketh Pearson that "Robertson, who was a Chapmaniac," attributed *All's Well That Ends Well* and *Measure for Measure* to Chapman (Pearson, *G.B.S. – a postscript*, 1951, p. 137). But Shaw – unchecked, it seems, by Hesketh Pearson – did less than justice to J.M.R.'s generally measured and tentative approach in his ascriptions to Chapman. This appeared to be illustrated, at least to some extent, in the case of the American Professor Joseph Q. Adams, who declared that in *Shakespeare and Chapman* Robertson, "assuming it as proved that the Rival

Poet was George Chapman", had assigned the poem *A Lover's Complaint* to Chapman, with Adams adding: "Both hypotheses seem fanciful and unlikely" (*A Life of William Shakespeare*, 1923, p. 183). Yet quite apart from the fact that a well respected Victorian scholar like Professor William Minto had already identified Chapman as the Rival Poet, there was at least a whiff of Robertson being relatively guarded when he wrote in *Shakespeare and Chapman*: "If not the rival poet, certainly the author of *A Lover's Complaint*, can now, I think, be proved to be Chapman" (p. 10). A decade or so later, Robertson maintained: "I am content to leave the thesis of Chapman's being the rival poet to take its chances ..." (*The Problems of the Shakespeare Sonnets*, p. 240). Half a century later two critics, commenting on lines in Shakespeare's Sonnet 86, declared: "If, however, a convincing case were made out for Chapman being the rival poet, these difficult lines could be coherently interpreted" (W.G. Ingram and T. Redpath, *Shakespeare's Sonnets*, 1978, as quoted in David West, same title, 2007, p. 268).

None the less, the onslaught against Robertson and his *Shakespeare and Chapman* was continued in 1966 by S. Schoenbaum, albeit at quite some length, without any of Shaw's wit and with a generous dose of vitriol and vituperation. On the other hand, J.M.R.'s reasons for discerning Chapman's presence in a play like *Timon of Athens* received support from Professor T.M. Parrott, American editor of Chapman's works. Moreover, Terence Spencer referred to Robertson's skilful re-examination of data "in his *Shakespeare and Chapman* (1917) (see especially pp. 133-4), where several valuable observations are unfortunately likely to be neglected" because of J.M.R.'s authorship theories (*Shakespeare Survey*, 1953, p. 78). In 1923 Robertson had maintained that in his 1917 book he had "advanced evidence for the ascription to Chapman of a large share in *All's Well That Ends Well*, and of the actual authorship of the masque in *The Tempest*" (*'Hamlet' Once More*, p. 144). Robertson's contention that George Chapman had quite a strong hand, so to speak, in the *Troilus and Cressida* attributed to Shakespeare appeared to receive a de facto general endorsement in 1980 from Daniel Massa, a Lecturer in English at the University of Malta, in his Notes (pp. 10-11) for an edition, aimed at students, of the play; and in 1993 Barbara E. Bowen, in her study of the play, wrote of Homer's English translator: "The precursor with which Shakespeare's play has most at stake may turn out to be Chapman (whose *Iliad* began appearing in 1598)" (*Gender in the Theater of War*, p. 128: New York & London).

The literary critic George Sampson (1941) seems to have thought quite highly of *Shakespeare and Chapman*; yet Kenneth Muir (in *Shakespeare the Professional*, 1973, pp. 204-209) criticised J.M.R.'s analysis of word-use so as to weaken, though failing to destroy, the latter's thesis of Chapman's authorship of *A Lover's Complaint*. The consensus of scholarly opinion appears to endorse Robertson's conclusion over a century ago that *Alphonsus Emperor of Germany* was "heedlessly ascribed to Chapman" (*Elizabethan Literature*, 1914, p. 245).

In his massive *The Masks of Macbeth* (1978) the American critic Marvin Rosenberg noticed only *Shakespeare and Chapman* among J.M.R.'s works in the Main Bibliography, and, rather curiously, seems to have overlooked Robertson's *Literary Detection* (1931), which was wholly devoted to *Macbeth*.

The Shakespeare Canon (1922-32)

In 1902-3 Robertson published, in two volumes, a diverse collection of essays on literary subjects under the generic title *Criticisms*. These included pieces on Andrew Marvell (widely regarded as an icon of liberalism by Victorians), Jane Austen, Hawthorne, Henley, Edward Carpenter, "The Murder Novel", Zola, Thackeray (much admired as a novelist by Robertson), Schopenhauer, Heine, Heinrich von Kleist, and Edmond Scherer. Although they also featured essays on "Elizabethan Lyrics" and even Robert Herrick, not one was exclusively devoted to Shakespeare. Two decades later, however, J.M.R. began to publish a series, spanning five volumes, bearing the brief overarching title *The Shakespeare Canon* (1922-32). These examined issues relating to the origination and authorship of: *Henry V, Julius Caesar*, and *Richard III* (1922); *The Two Gentlemen of Verona, Richard II, The Comedy of Errors*, and *Measure for Measure* (1923); *All's Well That Ends Well*, and *Romeo and Juliet* (1925); *Henry VI* (1930); and *Henry VI*, continued (1932).

Although they have received comparatively little attention from the literary Establishment since the end of the Second World War, with the tremendous growth of the Shakespeare industry, and although J.M.R. himself is not understood to have mentioned any of these five volumes in his *Courses of Study* (1932), among British literary critics George Sampson believed in 1941 that "Robertson's greatest contribution to his subject is contained in *The Shakespeare Canon* (Part I, 1922; Part II, 1923) and *An Introduction to the Study of the Shakespeare Canon* (1924)" (*The Concise Cambridge History of English Literature*, p. 1032). There were at least half a dozen references in J.M.R.'s *The Problems of the*

Shakespeare Sonnets (1926) to Parts 1 to 3 of his *The Shakespeare Canon*; and in 2014 John Jowett specified those same Parts in the References section (p. 186) of his article "Disintegration, 1924" in the journal *Shakespeare* (Vol. 10, Issue no. 2), where his main text touched very briefly, even peremptorily, a couple of times upon Robertson's disintegrationist work.

As F.S. Boas observed in 1940, in *The Shakespeare Canon* – complemented in some respects by other Robertsonian works such as *Shakespeare and Chapman* (1917), *The Problem of 'Hamlet'* (1919), *The Problems of the Shakespeare Sonnets* (1926), and *Marlowe* (1931) – J.M.R. detected the hand of Shakespeare's contemporaries like Chapman, Marlowe, Kyd and Peele in an extensive range of plays attributed to Shakespeare. In *Shakespeare and Chapman* Robertson had already assigned Clarence's dream in *Richard III* to Marlowe (p. 274n.). Having read J.M.R.'s comments on *Richard III* in *The Shakespeare Canon*, T.S. Eliot became "not so confident" that all the lines in Clarence's account of his dream (Act I, Scene 4) were written by Shakespeare (Eliot in 1927: *Selected Essays*, 1972 ed., pp. 89-90). In 1923 William Wells corroborated Robertson's contention – expounded only the year before – that Marlowe had a hand in *Julius Caesar* (notably in Antony's oration). Robertson felt that *The Comedy of Errors* was largely Marlowe's work, and that Kit Marlowe's influence was also discernible in the presentation of the characters Romeo and Juliet.

In the 1929-33 period at least, John Dover Wilson appeared to agree with J.M.R.'s conclusions regarding *Measure for Measure* and *All's Well That Ends Well* to the extent that he, Dover Wilson, accepted that those two plays "are almost certainly the result of collaboration between Shakespeare and some second-rate dramatist to whom was entrusted the final shaping of the material" (*Aspects of Shakespeare*, 1933, p. 203). Of the plays conventionally attributed to Shakespeare, Boas admitted that "in some instances" they may have been "the result of successive revisions by Shakspere of his own earlier work or, as often as not, plays from some inferior hand" (*Shakspere and His Predecessors*, 1940, pp. xxi-xxii). Moreover, Kenneth Muir was not very convincing, it may be felt, in seeking to discount Robertson's searchlight on words that occur both in the poem *A Lover's Complaint* and in Chapman's works, but not elsewhere in Shakespeare.

Robertson's volumes on *The Shakespeare Canon* were much esteemed by scholarly and intellectual men like Sir John Squire, Gilbert Murray and Chapman Cohen; and his literary criticism of the Canon to a greater or lesser extent influenced such diverse students of Shakespeare as Professor Dover Wilson, Dugdale Sykes, Augustus Ralli and the German translator Hans Rothe. However, to the surprise of many he appeared to settle on embracing a boldly imprudent belief that *A Midsummer Night's Dream* was the only play that was wholly Shakespeare's in origin and execution (see Odin Dekkers, 1998, p. 176). J.M.R. later cited the *Dream* as an example to rebut the accusation that he was always looking for a Shakespeare at the top of his achievement.

In 1969 the literary critic John Gross pronounced Robertson's *Criticisms* "the work of a singularly honest man", but went on to distance himself from "the abandon with which he assigned great stretches of the plays to Marlowe, Chapman and others. His arguments, as always, were forcefully expressed, but too arbitrary, too wilful, too acrimonious" (*The Rise and Fall of the Man of Letters*, p. 125). Certainly Robertson could have offered a more extended discussion or explanation as to how his conclusions cohered, how work by Marlowe and Chapman (two quite different men) came to be found, according to J.M.R., in plays attributed to Shakespeare. But J.M.R. generally openly acknowledged instances when he was engaging in supposition; he often gave reasons or evidence, even if circumstantial, for his views; and he was quite often responding to attacks on him by critics like E.K. Chambers and J. Dover Wilson. Indeed, Robertson's critics were not guiltless of comments on him which were "too arbitrary, too wilful", for example when in 1941 George Ian Duthie perpetrated a glaring *non sequitur* in dismissing an instance where J.M.R. in *The Shakespeare Canon* identified Marlowe's authorship (*The 'Bad' Quarto of 'Hamlet'*, p. 44, n. 1).

If Robertson was guilty of "ironclad rationalism", as Gross indicated (on p.126) he was, J.M.R., in adopting a scientific, evidence-based approach buttressed by logical argument and respect for known facts, would have been unlikely to fit easily into Gross's category of "too arbitrary, too wilful, too acrimonious". Moreover, John Gross taught English literature at Cambridge University at a time (the 1960s) when F.R. Leavis, a renowned don of very decided opinions, was a senior colleague of his in the English faculty there; and it is an intriguing fact that Leavis also disparaged Robertson as an "iron-clad rationalist", as he did to at least one of his undergraduate students, Ian MacKillop (see *J.M. Robertson*, ed. G.A. Wells, 1987, p. 59). This was rather ironic as in his 1969 book Gross criticised Leavis for condoning, if not encouraging, the cultivation by at least some of his adherents of "many of the characteristics normally associated with a religious or ideological sect", including "the ritualistic use of approved or disapproved names" (pp. 281-2) – which, it may be thought, could include "J.M. Robertson" or "iron-clad rationalist".

Volumes of *The Shakespeare Canon* appeared in the bibliography of Zachery Lesser's book *'Hamlet' After Q1* (2015) and were listed (together with *The Problems of the Shakespeare Sonnets* and *The Baconian Heresy*) in that of Pierre Porohovshikov's *Shakespeare Unmasked* (1955).

A Short History of Christianity (1902; second ed., 1913; third, 1931)

This is a notably stimulating scholarly introduction to its subject. It has few and brief footnotes and no appendices replying to critics. It is also the only one of this great freethinker's books which is devoted not only to exploring the primitive origins and early development of Christianity, but also to tracing its subsequent history to take account of the rise of Islam, the medieval period, and generously defined modern times (only cursorily and fitfully regarding the early twentieth century). In surveying the evolution of Christianity from the second century AD to the rise of Islam, Robertson pointed out that his accounts could be checked against those provided by historians like Neander, Mosheim and Milman (p. 412, 1902 ed.; p. 334, 1913 ed.); or as Professor G.A. Wells put it in that context: "A strong point in favour of Robertson's construction is that it is very largely based on what Christian ecclesiastical historians had themselves conceded" (*J.M. Robertson*, ed. G.A. Wells, 1987, p. 179). In 1902 J.M.R. was able to refer to the Moslem conquest of Crete early in the ninth century and to the Byzantine recovery of Crete in the tenth (pp. 306-7), but not to the much more recent discovery of the recourse to human sacrifice in or until 1560 BC to appease the forces of nature by the ancient Minoans (for whom the bull was a key symbolic creature: see *Daily Mail*, 10.4.2020, p. 17).

In 1932 Robertson explained that in his *Short History* he had attempted "to trace from the first the economic determination of the historic process, usually ignored in academic histories. … when academic writers discuss, say, the failure of Mithraism to survive, they invariably assume that its defect of popular 'appeal' is the sole explanation, never positing the fact that the Christian Church, *copying Jewish example*, established a popular economic organisation (which Mithraism did not), and thereby survived. We get, on the contrary, the untrue generalisation that it is the persecuted creeds that survive. This is obviously false as to Manichaeism, and the Christian Church in the lands in which Islam conquered" (*Courses of Study*, p. 92: J.M.R.'s emphasis).

Just as the third part (on "The Gospel Myths") of *Christianity and Mythology* was published in a German translation in Jena in 1910; so an authorized German translation of his *Short History of Christianity* was published in Frankfurt am Main that same year with an introduction by the German Mythicist Arthur Drews. Both German translations were noted in Italy in 1912 by Mario Puglisi in his work entitled (if translated into English) *Jesus and the Christ Myth*, where he also took account of the first edition of *Pagan Christs*.

In the first part of his *Short History* J.M.R. presented material that also appeared in *Pagan Christs* (or *Christianity and Mythology*) on similarities or parallels between primitive Christianity and aspects of various ancient religions, including references to the bull-symbol and the Goat-God; and it may be of some significance to the Myth Theory that in the Old Testament Psalm 50, for example, presents God proclaiming to the people of Israel that he does not need sacrificial offerings of bulls or he-goats for nourishment.

In his section on the Essenes Robertson gave a remarkably accurate account in 1902: "How far Essenism reacted on early Jesuism cannot be ascertained. ... it is clear that there was no such close resemblance between the movements as has been supposed by the writers who seek to identify them; but they tell of a similar mental climate. The non-mention of Essenism in the gospels is to be explained by the fact that the two systems were not rivals" (p. 62; 1913, p. 51). This seems confirmed by the discovery (1947) of the Dead Sea Scrolls (see *New Humanist*, Summer 1985, p. 20; cf. Archibald Robertson, J.M.R.'s namesake, *The Origins of Christianity*, revised ed., p. 215 – "there is nothing in the Dead Sea Scrolls about the incarnation of the Son of God, or about the Atonement, or about the resurrection ... about the virgin birth, the immaculate conception, transubstantiation ..."). In J.M.R.'s book the section on "Myth of the Twelve Apostles" had been preceded by similar material in his *Studies in Religious Fallacy* and also in *Christianity and Mythology* (1900), with the latter being noted in the Soviet Union by I. Kryvelev in *Christ: Myth or Reality?* (1987). Presenting religion as a barrier to human progress, Robertson's *Short History* was quoted or referenced by Paul Tobin (2009), Robert Van Voorst (2000), Maurice Goguel (1950 and 1925), Archibald Robertson (1946), A.D. Howell Smith (1942: *Why I Am A Rationalist*), "A Hindu" (*The Bible Examined*, India, 1938), "A London Journalist" (*Britain Without God*, 1935), Charles Guignebert (1935), Thomas Whittaker (1933, fourth ed.), Shirley Jackson Case (1928), and Ernest Crawley (1905).

In the 1970s a professional rationalist like Hector Hawton (in *Controversy*) in Britain, or John G. Jackson (in *Pagan Origins of the Christ Myth*) in the U.S.A., relied upon J.M.R.'s *Short History of Christianity* as a source, with both these writers also taking account of his *Christianity and Mythology*; and while the Anglo-Australian Marxist literary critic and historian Jack Lindsay and the British Independent Labour Party member John L. Robinson may have paid due attention to J.M.R.'s *Short History*, they certainly acknowledged a significant debt they owed him for his work relating to the Myth Theory.

A Short History of Morals (1920)

Robertson's book does not concentrate on a succession of legal cases or incidents directly involving censorship, pornography, sexual attitudes and behaviour, or alleged corruption of morals. This work provides a fitfully illuminating account of the evolution of moral ideas and ethical systems from primitive man, through the eras of ancient Greek, Roman, Chinese, Buddhist, Christian and rationalist doctrines, to Schopenhauer and "subsisting ethical issues". His survey of Greek ethical doctrines seems unnecessarily short and incomplete, and for some reason he in effect excluded Islamic and Hindu thought. In tracing the history of moral philosophy since the eighteenth century he concentrated largely on Britain and Germany, with some surprising omissions of individual German, French and other philosophers.

By contrast, his treatment of British ethical thinkers from Hobbes to John Stuart Mill was extensive and thorough. As Joseph McCabe commented regarding utilitarianism: "Details of the long struggle, from Hobbes and Locke to the end of the nineteenth century, must be read in J.M. Robertson's *Short History of Morals* (1920)" (*A Rationalist Encyclopaedia*, 1948,

p. 194: however, McCabe was more critical of *A Short History of Christianity*, where he felt Robertson had grossly over-recorded the number of Christian martyrs in the Diocletian Persecution in the Roman Empire). McCabe also commended, in his 1948 work (p. 156), J.M.R.'s "good account" in his 1920 book of aspects of the determinism v. free will controversy. Arguably Robertson broke fresh ground with his tribute to the Rev. John Gay, who in the eighteenth century was the author of "one of the most important contributions ever made to the solution of the problem of the origins of morality" (1920, p. 283: see also 279-80). J.M.R.'s book on moral philosophy also offered scattered or short comments by him on F.H. Bradley, T.H. Green, and G.E. Moore. More than a decade after Robertson's death *A Short History of Morals* was listed – together with his *History of Freethought* (1936 edition, arguably his greatest work) – in the Secondary Sources of Walter M. Merrill's 1949 study of Bolingbroke's deism: *From Statesman To Philosopher*. J.M.R.'s 1920 book featured in the section "References to Mandeville's Work" of F.B. Kaye's edition of *The Fable of the Bees*, where Kaye drew attention to Robertson's "illuminating comment on and summary of Mandeville's position" (1957 reprint, Vol. 2, p. 451); and in early 1921 the *Literary Guide* reported that Sir Robert Stout – who would be remembered for his public service as Prime Minister and Chief Justice of New Zealand – had praised Robertson's book.

Robertson referred, albeit briefly, to "appalling potentialities of evil" in the light of the First World War, "those who are now beginning to ask what is the total reaction of a great war upon society", and the fact that "after a century fuller of ethical discussion than any previous age, we have had the World War". In his last couple of years or so he began to grapple intellectually with links in Europe between violence, chaos and uncertainty associated with the World War and the rise of totalitarianism. In September 1931 Stalin's murderous excesses enabled Robertson to declare: "the brutality of the latest Communism, working gross social failure, is ominous" (*A Short History of Christianity*, third ed., p. 246). In January 1932 J.M.R. wrote: "Democracy, so to speak, is the last chance … now we see in parts of Europe the fear of democratic chaos inspiring new forms of authoritarianism; the Soviet at one end and at the other that of the Italian Duce, who had been mentally evolved as a Socialist." It seems unlikely that he would have been surprised to learn of the virtually simultaneous support and admiration for Mussolini, Stalin and Hitler expressed by his one-time friend George Bernard Shaw, who professed himself a socialist (Shaw had also advocated the physical extermination of people seen as resisting or impeding the development of a socialist society: see Giles Udy, *Labour and the Gulag*, 2017, Chapter 37, for shocking confirmation and details). Although no evidence has come to hand that he ever did so, Robertson could have pointed out that the German National Socialists claimed (however perversely and opportunistically) a degree of affinity with socialism (see Louis Lochner, *What About Germany?* 1943, p. 25, and K.D. Bracher, *The German Dictatorship*, 1973 Eng. trans., pp. 186, 230-1: Bracher does not mention Lochner).

He devoted part of his concluding chapter on "subsisting ethical issues" to what may have seemed to be relatively minor issues in themselves like drunkenness and pensions for mothers when weightier post-war questions could have been considered. On the other hand, drunkenness and alcoholism had long been a stain on the fabric of British society; and pensions for mothers could have opened the door to a timely conversation about child-care provision and facilities. In his book birth control did not receive the degree of prominence later devoted to it in Max Hodann's *History of Modern Morals* (1937), which was translated from the German, and possibly partly researched, by the socialist feminist F.W. Stella Browne, who had reviewed Robertson's *War and Civilization* and would have been aware of J.M.R.'s secularist contribution, including his advocacy of birth control and not excluding his support of the 1888 match girls' strike.

Socialism and Malthusianism (1885)

In Robertson's concern for the creation of a more just and egalitarian society, the question of birth control (or neo-Malthusianism) was of critical importance. As an advocate of birth control he believed he was responding in a scientific spirit to one of the great social questions of the day. In an article in Bradlaugh's *National Reformer* in February 1885 he maintained that "the Malthusian is an influence for good of the most important kind – so far as he does not teach that his is the only reform necessary". Robertson's use, in this article, of the term "neo-Malthusian" would be considered almost half a century later by Professor Norman Himes, a noted American historian of birth control, to be possibly the first such use in the English language (though in fact it had appeared at least several years earlier).

However, Robertson's *National Reformer* article on "Socialism and Malthusianism" – reprinted as a pamphlet by Bradlaugh's Freethought Publishing Company later in 1885 – established J.M.R. as probably the first British Radical after Marx's death to criticise at some length socialists who in their quest for utopia ignored or discounted the population problem, to which the Marxist conception of history had paid scant attention. He pointed out that the economic thinker cheaply derided as "Parson Malthus" had never taught that poverty was bound to disappear if only population growth were restrained by birth control. Equally, J.M.R. indicated, there was nothing to justify a belief that once poverty is abolished, the rate of population growth would automatically decline satisfactorily. In this context the Soviet *A Dictionary of Philosophy* (1967, published in Moscow and edited by M. Rosenthal and P. Yudin) maintained that "Malthus' theory is completely untenable and reactionary" and categorically declared: "Marx and Engels said that overpopulation and the attendant poverty of the masses are caused by the capitalist system" (see pp. 264-5), with the questionable implication that overpopulation would or could not occur under Communism.

Engels' comrade Marx did not explain how over-population would be prevented in the reconstructed society. But, in writing to Karl Kautsky in 1881, Engels acknowledged that a communist society might need to recognise a need for population restraint (see Lewis Feuer, *Marx and Engels*, 1959, 1969 ed., p. 32; to which it may be added that no indexed reference to such terms as birth control, contraception, population question or neo-Malthusianism has been found in such books as Marxian histories of the British Labour Party and movement by Tony Cliff and Andrew J. Davies respectively, Daniel Weinbren's *Generating Socialism*, or Tristram Hunt's biography of Engels). Yet in 1988 the esteemed social historian William J. Fishman regurgitated a report that in the East End in 1888 "knowledge of contraception among the poor was practically nil".

As editor (1891-3) of the *National Reformer* Robertson regularly carried birth control advertisements; and the British socialist

Robert Blatchford, who was much influenced by Robertson's thinking, disseminated a pro-birth control message in his journal *Clarion*. In 1918 Robertson drew attention to the fact that in 1913 Rosa Luxemburg and Clara Zetkin at mass meetings of the German Social Democratic Party had urged hostile German workers to increase the size of their families (*The Economics of Progress*, pp. 277-8). He refrained from adding that this was ironic as from 1914 onwards a huge number of Germans, mostly men (later estimated to be over a million), were killed in the World War which notably included the battles of Verdun and the Somme. His 1885 piece was welcomed by *The Malthusian*, yet in 1903 he would be cross-examined in court on his essay in the context of a lawsuit that he brought for libel, but lost, with his morale subsequently being boosted by the loyalty and generosity of many friends, including Ernest Newman, who raised funds to meet his costs (and prevent J.M.R. putting some of his books up for sale from his library).

Spoken Essays (1925)

The Prefatory Note to this published collection of eight essays states that all of them, except for the one on *Hamlet*, were originally read to the South Place Ethical Society in London "during 1923". Unfortunately, this is not absolutely correct, as a scan of South Place's *Monthly Record* for 1921-25 inclusive indicates that "The Theism of Earl Balfour" and "Rationalism and Religion" originated as lectures on 6 January 1924 and 21 December 1924, respectively. The text of these most recent lectures appeared towards the end of his book, where he took account of "many English statements of a 'religion of the future'", as he later recorded in *Courses of Study*

(1932 ed., p. 64). It may be added that it has been claimed that J.M.R. "always commanded … the respectful attention of Mr. Balfour" in the Commons (Harry Jones, *Liberalism and the House of Lords*, 1912, p. 181) – although Balfour's emotionally charged responses in the House were not always very respectful. In advocating using and following reason, J.M.R. in *Spoken Essays* (p. 187) set store by "our checked and tested thought", but seemed imprecise as to how, and how far, an ordinary citizen, with limited resources (including time), could be expected to conduct such checks and tests even in a democracy.

"Utopia" – the first lecture delivered (on 10 June 1923) and printed in the collection – "offered a biting critique of H.G. Wells' authoritarian Fabian socialism as well as of romantic utopias in general", in the well chosen words of the libertarian Chris Tame (*J.M. Robertson*, ed. G.A. Wells, 1987, p. 106). The second lecture – delivered on 2 September 1923 – was on the religiously fanatical and imperialistic Oliver Cromwell, whose reputation (not least with Victorian historians) Robertson had strongly attacked in an essay on the tercentenary of his birth. The next lecture was on "The Theology of Earthquakes" – while another one was on the related topic of "The Theory of Cosmic Purpose". The fourth lecture as printed was devoted to "The Meaning of Utilitarianism", which for him provided a rational basis for ethics without recourse to a religious dimension. As Robertson put it: "The Rationalist knows that he does *not* need a church, a priest, a sacrament, a ceremonial, to live a sane and cheerful intellectual life" (p. 212: J.M.R.'s emphasis). This tied in with the assessment by J.P. Gilmour, who had been J.M.R.'s friend for fifty years, that "Robertson was constitutionally good-tempered and blithe, of a robust will, and a valiant spirit" (*HF*, 1936, p. xix: see also p. xii for J.M.R. on "tested truth").

J.M.R criticised the Positivism of Auguste Comte (not to be confused with Charles Comte, whom Robertson admired and in 1895 credited with having offered – along with Buckle – a perspective that could make scholars "less dithyrambic over the service done to sociology by Marx"). With regard to Robertson's *The Problem of 'Hamlet'* (1919) and, more particularly, to his lecture and essay "The Naturalistic Theory of 'Hamlet'" (the latter reproduced in *Spoken Essays*), the literary critic Ian MacKillop felt that Robertson's theory of *Hamlet* fruitfully "allows him to see layers of varying styles in the play, to admit that the text is a mosaic" (*J.M. Robertson*, 1987, p. 61). He added that Robertson believed that Shakespeare's extraordinary mind was influenced by his appreciation of Montaigne.

Studies in Religious Fallacy (1900)

It is disappointing that, in a notable and valuable study (1964), spanning some 650 pages, of Robertson the freethinker and Radical, the devout American Christian Conrad Kaczkowski listed (p. 199) *Studies in Religious Fallacy* among six "major works on the religion question" produced by Robertson between 1897 and 1903 – but otherwise ignored it. Robertson's book comprised eleven polemical essays or reviews that had essentially been published separately during the 1890s (though the first one in the collection dated from 1884).

Perhaps inevitably – not least in view of its title – there is a *fin de siècle* feel to Robertson's book, with the author looking back at events in the nineteenth century rather than looking forward to developments in the twentieth. Thus in an essay produced in Gladstone's lifetime J.M.R. gave a brilliant summary of the elder statesman's U-turns, backpedalling and political lurches in the course of his long career, while Mrs. Besant's permutations, though serious, "were never the index of her self-interest" ("Mr. Gladstone on the Atonement", orig. 1894, pp. 100-101). Robertson also placed on record that freethought meetings were still occasionally "broken up by the violence of Christians" ("The Feeling for Religion", p. 217). A secularist reviewer wrote that J.M.R. "surveys the world of lore with a telescope and examines it with a microscope" (*The Reformer*, February 1900, p. 115): Harold Laski used similar language in 1936 about Robertson.

While it seems impossible to summarise all eleven essays within the space available here, it may be noted that at least two of them, "The Jesus Legend and the Myth of the Twelve Apostles" and "The Myth of Judas Iscariot", were subsumed in larger works like *Christianity and Mythology* and *Pagan Christs*, where he took account of works by Andrew Lang, a contemporary anthropologist and classical scholar to whom Robertson also devoted two essays in his collection: "Mr. Lang on the Origin of Religion" and "Mr. Lang on Miracles", where Robertson the logician seemed merciless with his dissecting scalpel.

J.M.R.'s first essay in his *Studies* is on Henry Drummond and his *Natural Law in the Spiritual World* – a subject already touched upon elsewhere in the present work. In "The Tory Religion", dating from 1897, J.M.R. criticised Arthur Balfour, as he would periodically over some three decades or more in all. In "Freeman on Christianity", dating from 1895, Robertson declared that the late, learned historian Edward Freeman was "partly incapacitated by prejudice and … learned ignorance" (p. 176) – a judgement that would later appear to be fully justified by virtue of Freeman's racist, insulting and demeaning comments about Jews (to some extent touched upon by J.M.R. on pp. 180-2), black Americans and Irishmen. Robertson was similarly scathing about Tolstoy's ignorance ("Tolstoy and the Ethics of Jesus": pp. 197, 192 etc.). In "The Feeling for Religion" J.M.R. struck a characteristically Robertsonian note when he asked: "If religion be wholly of the heart, why these reams of Christian Evidences, these philosophic batteries against the Atheist?" (p. 212).

Published by the newly founded Rationalist Press Association despite its slender resources, *Studies in Religious Fallacy* is easy to read as an introduction to works like *Christianity and Mythology* and *Pagan Christs*. In the Association's Report for 1900 the R.P.A. Directors affirmed that they were "confident that the utterances of independent investigators such as Professor Haeckel and Mr. Robertson deserve far more attention from the thoughtful public than is commonly bestowed on them" (quoted by Adam Gowans Whyte, *The Story of the R.P.A.*, 1949, p. 50).

Thomas Paine: An Investigation (1888)

In 1888 Charles Bradlaugh and Annie Besant, through their Freethought Publishing Company, issued Robertson's *Thomas Paine: An Investigation*, which had been serialised in the *National Reformer* earlier that year. This was a devastating yet fair-minded refutation of Leslie Stephen's calumnies against Paine as a man and as a teacher and thinker (principally in Paine's *The Age of Reason*) as outlined in Stephen's *English Thought in the Eighteenth Century*. In his 1888 pamphlet Robertson took Leslie Stephen to task for his misleading and caricatured description of Paine's recourse to alcohol, and for disparaging Paine as a writer. J.M.R. criticised Stephen for lauding Edmund Burke as a superior political thinker to Paine, resulting in Robertson declaring: "Even Mr. Gladstone has admitted that it was mainly Burke's propaganda that forced on the Reign of Terror, by setting half Europe against the French people" (*NR*, 27.8.1893, numbered problematically as p. 130: in *Studies in Religious Fallacy* Robertson discussed Gladstone's religious views in two essays relating to the Atonement and Bishop Butler, respectively).

In due course Stephen gave a frank public apology for his comments about Paine's drinking; but in August and September 1893 J.M.R. pointed out in the *National Reformer* that Stephen had still not recanted his disparagement of Paine's work. In correspondence with the journalist Hector Macpherson, who seems to have been in friendly contact with Robertson, Leslie Stephen revealed that he keenly felt J.M.R.'s attack. A clear indication of Stephen's feelings also emerged when he informed another correspondent that Robertson "boasts of being a thorough-going atheist and materialist. He dislikes me as a thorough radical dislikes a Whig and thinks me both cowardly and illogical as well as insincere. He had a special grudge against me because in that eighteenth-century book I rashly accepted certain statements about Paine's drunkenness, & c. I confessed my mistake in an article in the Fortnightly [*sic*], but he thought my confession inadequate" (see *T.P.'s Weekly* for 21 May 1909 and F.W. Maitland's 1906 biography of Stephen). Robertson would deny that he had ever called Stephen cowardly or insincere and would present quite a rounded, even rather compassionate, appreciation of him in his 1929 history of freethought.

Robertson's analysis in 1888 did much to vindicate Paine and to pave the way for Moncure Conway's classic *Life of Thomas Paine* (1892), in which Conway recorded a debt to his friend Robertson and referred to Stephen's unquestioning acceptance in his *English Thought* of false accusations (which Stephen later repudiated) about Paine.

In his 1891 introduction to an edition of Paine's *Rights of Man*, J.M. Wheeler quoted from Robertson's work on the pioneer democrat; and half a century after its original publication, Robertson's *Thomas Paine* would be serialised in the *Freethinker* and then reissued as a pamphlet, thanks to G.W. Foote's successor, Chapman Cohen, of whom Cohen's debating opponent, the philosopher Cyril Joad, declared in 1928: "All that Mr. Chapman Cohen has owed to Mr. Robertson I, too, have owed; Mr. Robertson has had an incalculable influence in moulding the thought of my generation, perhaps even more than that of Mr. Chapman Cohen's generation." Although Cohen's 1937 introduction to an edition of *The Age of Reason* referred extremely briefly to Stephen's disregard for Paine, and although Noel Annan's 1984 study of Leslie Stephen showed awareness of Robertson's works, neither mentioned J.M.R.'s 1888 pamphlet, which was much admired by Cohen's scholarly colleague Herbert Cutner and years later, in 1971, by Robert Morrell, Secretary of the British Thomas Paine Society.

In October 1895 – just after J.M.R. had ceased to be its editor – *The Free Review* reported an instance where a leader-writer on the *Standard* had recently vilified Paine (see *The Free Review* for the date specified, pp. 111-12). Then in the U.S.A. in 1901 – the year in which he became the American President – and more categorically in 1918 Theodore Roosevelt retracted his original description of Paine as a "filthy little atheist", in a kind of echo of Leslie Stephen's recantation in England (see the American *Progressive World*, June 1968, pp. 34-5, for the Roosevelt case).

Later, in England of the 1940s, Robertson's introduction as reproduced in the 1938 Thinker's Library edition of Thomas Paine's *The Age of Reason* may well have been read by the then teenage Eric Gordon, who later became a journalistic legend in North London and further afield, as reading *The Age of Reason* and probably other works by Paine was apparently instrumental in his abandoned training to become a rabbi. The R.P.A.'s Thinker's Library volumes were cheap enough for at least some working-class people to buy (or borrow from a library); and a number of Communist writers, intellectuals and fellow-travellers had already joined the R.P.A. or had work published in the Thinker's Library series. Eric Gordon soon became an ardent Communist, but subsequently fell foul of the Chinese Communist regime, which regarded him as too much of a freethinker and placed him under a form of house arrest for some two years. But even before Eric Gordon had begun to read *The Age of Reason*, Robertson's biographical introduction to it had been noticed, and quoted from, by the Australian Christian David Simpson in his *The March of the Godless* (1937, Sydney, pp. 14-5) in a way that could be regarded as a kind of compliment.

Trade and Tariffs (1908)

In October 1908 a press review indicated that Robertson's book *Trade and Tariffs* constituted a Nasmyth steam hammer to crack a nut relating to the Free Trade issue. The reviewer was Leo Chiozza Money, who appeared to be a rising political star in the Liberal firmament, with a special interest in economic matters. But as Britain would cease to be a Free Trade country within twenty-five years, Robertson was justified in feeling concerned about attacks on Free Trade (such as those quite recently spearheaded by Joseph Chamberlain). Whether or not the reviewer was possibly motivated in his comments by a touch of jealousy, a younger man, Walter Citrine, took a more positive view of *Trade and Tariffs*, which he found helpful in promoting his career as a workers' leader who became General Secretary of the Trades Union Congress in Britain. As Citrine explained: "The time arrived [in about 1909] when I was asked whether I would give an address on some subject of my own choice to the members of the I.L.P. [Independent Labour Party] in Wallasey. I swotted up a subject which was of intense current interest. I borrowed a book by J.M. Robertson from the public library in Wallasey. It was on free trade and tariffs. The author was a highly competent writer and a strong free-trader. I memorized whole passages from this book, and, having carefully summarized Robertson's arguments, I went along to the meeting armed with copious notes to deliver my address. I created a favourable impression. As time went on I took the chair at other meetings … gaining experience all the time" (*Men and Work*, Vol. 1, 1964, p. 62).

Trade and Tariffs took account of information such as that provided by the lengthy debate between Robertson and Samuel Storey in Newcastle-upon-Tyne in 1905 on the issue of Free Trade. Violet Bonham Carter, in her day a prominent Liberal politician, would recall "the patience and apparent pleasure with which vast audiences would follow close-knit argument buttressed by hard, dry facts – import and export statistics and Board of Trade returns", adding: "I remember hearing that the Newcastle Hippodrome, holding some three thousand people, was sold out for several nights in succession while the Free Trade v. Protection case was debated by a distinguished but rather dry and academic Liberal, J.M. Robertson, and a Conservative protagonist of Tariffs" (*Winston Churchill As I Knew Him*, 1965, p. 118). That Asquith's daughter's recollection, sixty years after the event, may not have been entirely fair or trustworthy is suggested by the fact that she omitted to mention that the debate in question took place in the context of the 1905 general election, and that J.M.R.'s friend Dr. Alfred Cox had recorded that Storey was a Liberal.

In 1921 the University of London economist T.E. Gregory noted the "vigorous polemic" in *Trade and Tariffs*, which represented J.M.R.'s major economic work in the Edwardian period. The 1908 book gave much valuable information, including statistical data, on the history of Free Trade and Protectionism. Robertson himself highlighted his treatment of Holland, declaring in 1932: "A sociological sketch of the entire development of Holland has been attempted by the editor [J.M.R.] in his *Evolution of States*; and her later commercial history is noted in *Trade and Tariffs*" (*Courses of Study*, p. 284). Moreover, he referred, albeit in passing (p. 196), in *The Economics of Progress* (1918) to his coverage in his 1908 work (p. 100) of the antagonistic economic relationship between Britain and the U.S.A. in the nineteenth century. An anonymous reviewer in *The Nation* for 31 October 1908 – possibly J.A. Hobson – presented J.M.R. as arguably "the best equipped defender of Free Trade in the country. He is a trained economist with immense historical erudition, an acute logician, and a mighty hunter of myths and fallacies." (Robertson had taught economics at the Hall of Science Schools during 1885-86.)

The three reports (1916) by the Board of Trade Committee

on (food) Prices, chaired by Robertson, attracted the attention of another prophet of the Welfare State and a fellow Liberal, William Beveridge (*British Food Control*, 1928; see also *BRUG*, pp. 17-21). In 1917 the Labour Minister Arthur Henderson wanted J.M.R. to represent the case for Free Trade on a Government committee. J.M.R.'s criticism (1931) of comments by G.D.H. Cole on Free Trade as uninformed was in effect supported by Robert Conquest (*Tyrants and Typewriters*, 1989, pp. 175-6).

Robertson died in 1933; but Free Trade enjoyed something of a renaissance after the Second World War. As an authoritative work of reference explained in 1995: "the collapse of the world economy in the 1930s produced a wholesale retreat into protections with tariffs, quotas and exchange rate restrictions multiplying rapidly. This was self-defeating and simply exacerbated the Depression. In 1944 Bretton Woods produced the institutional framework within which post-war international economic policy was to develop. The IMF, World Bank and specifically GATT came into being with the objective of restoring a liberal trading order. Successive rounds of multi-lateral tariff reductions over the next 30-40 years helped world trade to grow … fuelling the post-war boom" (*The History Today Companion to British History*, ed. J. Gardiner & N. Wenborn, p. 321: "Free Trade").

The Truth about the War (1902)

During the second Boer War (1899-1902) Robertson visited South Africa as a special correspondent; and his national newspaper reports and articles were later thought to have done much to help change and mobilize sections of British public opinion concerning the war. Even so, on the eve of the Boer War Lord Selborne, Under-Secretary of State at the Colonial Office – for one – seemed distinctly concerned as to whether British voters (particularly middle class voters) would support the Government in the event of hostilities with the Boers, writing to Lord Milner in South Africa on 7 October 1899: "You cannot realise the enormous difficulty we have had with public opinion at home" (quoted by Bernard Porter, *The Absent-Minded Imperialists*, 2004, 2006 paperback ed., pp. 234, 407).

Robertson's visit to South Africa confirmed his opposition to the British Government's policy there. While the British public was not shown pioneering film footage, taken on behalf of the British Government, of distressing scenes of emaciated Boers detained in South Africa, J.M.R. on his return addressed crowded meetings all over Britain to condemn the war (which spawned concentration camps and a scorched earth policy), with his lantern slides of its horrors matching the eloquence of his words, defying jingoistic hysteria and physical violence from Government supporters. (For the specific 'official' Boer War film footage referred to, see the film "Britain in Colour", Episode 2, screened by the TV Channel "Smithsonian" in Britain on Boxing Day evening 2021, and, more generally, Bernard Porter, op. cit. 2006 ed., pp. 177-8. Moreover, in March 1900 Lloyd George was struck on the head with a heavy stick almost immediately after speaking at a pro-Boer rally in Bangor; and Robertson's wife is believed to have carried a walking-stick with a bulbous grip – almost a kind of South African knobkerrie! – as a precaution when, on at least one occasion, she accompanied her husband to attend an anti-imperialist meeting in London during the Boer War.) Robertson was also vilified in the London press as a traitor to his country's interests (see Timo Särkkä, *Hobson's*

Imperialism, 2009, p. 72, and *Wrecking the Empire*, J.M.R.'s introductory remarks). Quite a few of Robertson's published dispatches from South Africa were written in Natal; and more than a century later British military policy there in the early stages of the war would be severely criticised in Hugh Rethman's *The Natal Campaign* (2017).

J.M.R.'s pro-Boer writings included a trenchant, hard-hitting reply to the then chauvinistic Arthur Conan Doyle in the form of an Open Letter to him entitled *The Truth about the War* (covering some 48 pages) under the auspices of the radical *New Age* periodical and New Age Press. ("Macrobius" – a pseudonym definitely familiar to J.M.R. – had already attacked Dr. Doyle's Deism in an article under that title in Hypatia Bradlaugh Bonner's *The Reformer* for May 1897, with the article bearing at least some of the hallmarks of J.M.R.'s style.) In his Open Letter Robertson declared: "any careful reader of your History [regarding the war] could see how little trouble you commonly took either to find facts or to weigh them. But in a country which is in large part content to take its sociology from Mr. Kipling, its morals from Mr. Chamberlain, and its code of statesmanship from Lord Milner, you may, I grant, fairly assume that the study of military causation is in the scope of the creator of Brigadier Gerard" (in 1899 a secularist based in Cape Town blamed both Joseph Chamberlain and Lord Milner for the outbreak of the second Boer War: see Edward Royle, op. cit. 1980, pp. 211, 217).

With an aggressive British imperialism serving the interests of British capitalism, British troops invaded the two Boer republics of the Transvaal and the Orange Free State (both formally annexed by Britain in 1902); and faced with stubborn resistance in the form of guerrilla warfare by the Boers, the British authorities opened concentration camps with "thousands of women and children herded within barbed wire folds, forbidden to go out on their own: kept in a state of semi-starvation and filth and raggedness; and dying like flies", as a disgusted correspondent – apparently a first-hand observer – graphically explained in a letter of 12 May 1901 to J.M.R. Composed before the war ended, Robertson's Open Letter took account of the causes and course of the war; and it concluded with strongly felt, severe criticism of Conan Doyle, addressed by Robertson "in the name of national honour, which you and yours have trodden in the mire, … of the ideals of justice and humanity which you have shamed … you and your party are not the nation". Robertson's testimony constituted one of the few sources of reliable or considered information available to the British public on adverse or negative aspects of the war.

A fortnight before a peace agreement was signed, Robertson computed, with considerable accuracy in the circumstances, the devastating human and material losses associated with the Boer War. He concluded that the war meant "above all the creation in South Africa of such an intensity of Dutch hatred for British rule as must make government there a desperate hazard for generations to come": a residual trace of such Afrikaner bitterness could be discerned in P.W. Botha's statement on the March 1984 Nkomati Accord. Robertson's pamphlet – which went through four editions in 1902 – would be noticed by R.G. Hackett (1994) in Britain and Paula Krebs (1999) from the United States in their respective books on the Boer War.

The Truth about the War is not to be confused with *Truth and the War* (1916), which is about the First World War and in which J.M.R. is mentioned in passing, by Edmund Dene Morel, a veteran campaigner critical of aspects of imperialism. In

1932 Robertson, in *Courses of Study*, noticed Morel's work, published in 1912, on Morocco, which was a topic to which Morel devoted a whole chapter in his *Truth and the War*.

War and Civilization (January 1916; second edition, September 1917)

This polemical work represents Robertson's reply in the form of an Open Letter to a Swedish academic, Dr. Gustaf Steffen (Professor of Economics and Sociology, Stockholm), who supported the German side in the First World War. Just as J.M.R. was one of the more distinguished of the few in Britain between about 1899 and 1919 who combined scholarly political commentary and polemic from a pro-Free Trade and radical perspective with energetically holding public office at a national level; so he was one of the comparatively few British M.P.s, who also were or had been Ministers, to engage in open and sustained ideological conflict with supporters of German militarism and aggression during the First World War.

In 1935 the Nazi propagandist Hermann Wanderscheck noted J.M.R.'s book *The Germans* (as would Ashley Montagu in his 1974 book on race, *Man's Most Dangerous Myth*). But Wanderscheck also noticed what was in effect Robertson's companion volume, *War and Civilization*, in which Robertson developed his contention that the German people as a whole had been brutalized by the pervasive psychology of militarism and the spirit of imperial expansionism. Although neither of his two 1916 books focused on Germany's colonial record in Africa, there was plausibly an oblique or veiled reference to Imperial Germany's extermination of many hundreds, if not thousands, of Nama ('Hottentots') when J.M.R. wrote to Professor Steffen: "If a white man (say, a Professor) who had gratuitously killed a Hottentot were to tell me that his superior culture justified him, I should pronounce him twice a scoundrel for offering such a defence" (*War and Civilization*, p. 15: see also David Olusoga and Casper Erichsen, *The Kaiser's Holocaust*, 2010).   As Britain and Germany were competing imperial powers, Robertson did less than justice to the penetrating analysis he had already made of imperialism (he may have decided to concentrate on the continent where the fighting seemed bloodiest: Europe).

He criticised the idea of an innate racial or national psychology; although he suggested that national states of mind were influenced by institutions, propaganda, literature, art, and recent experience.   Although he condemned Germany's invasion of Belgium, he also referred with apparent disapproval to "Belgian cruelties in Congoland" (op. cit., 1917, p. 48). He did not hold Imperial Germany solely responsible for the World War; but he felt that Germany had precipitated it (see *War and Civilization*, 1917 ed., p. 54; *The Germans*, pp. 102-3).   He pointed out that Steffen did not attempt to defend the German invasion of Belgium (op. cit., 1917, p. 124), and that the Armenian massacres by Germany's ally Turkey had been endorsed in Germany (pp. 126, 135).   He noted "the brutality of the drill-sergeant" and "the selfish arrogance" (p. 138) of many German army officers that were commonly talked about in Germany in the 1880s (when he lived there for a short while in 1887, at almost exactly the same time as Austen Chamberlain noticed and recorded a similar disturbing phenomenon in Berlin: for Chamberlain see Peter Winzen in *Nationalist and Racialist Movements in Britain and Germany before 1914*, 1981, pp. 161, 169).   J.M.R. also touched, albeit very briefly, on German anti-Semitism (1917, pp. 104-5).

The Italian historian Benedetto Croce commented on the bellicose atmosphere in Germany between 1912 and 1914 (*History of Europe in the Nineteenth Century*, Eng. trans. 1933, p. 337). Robertson indicated that Germany's omission to make any pre-war provision to safeguard its food supply as good as proved that Germany was not fearing an attack (1917 ed., 149). Indeed, Germany intended to attack Britain and particularly its maritime power at a later stage in the war (pp. 23, 45). From September 1910 until shortly before his death in August 1913 the German socialist leader August Bebel secretly supplied the British Government with numerous politico-military reports suggesting, inter alia, that the German Government intended to mount a surprise naval attack on Britain. From July 1914 the newly widened Kiel Canal enabled German warships to sail quickly from the Baltic to the North Sea. Britain's transfer of Heligoland (which was used as a German naval base in both world wars) to Germany in 1890 had seemed to indicate that Britain did not expect to become embroiled in an armed conflict in Europe. Moreover, Robertson maintained that, according to the veteran Italian statesman Giovanni Giolitti, Germany's ally "Austria had planned and proposed to attack Serbia in 1913" (op. cit., 1917, p. 42). Giolitti's claim, as reported by J.M.R., was not automatically invalidated by the accusations of bribery, corruption and incompetence levelled against this veteran Prime Minister by other Italians (for which see Caroline Moorehead, *A Bold and Dangerous Family*, 2017, p. 34).

In 1940 in Nazi Germany Dr. Edgar Mertner noticed his criticism (1905) of Rudyard Kipling, and the Gestapo placed Robertson (dead for seven years) on their search list of British writers. But, as J.M.R. acknowledged more than once, he owed much to aspects of German culture; and he also benefited from contact with Austrian intellectual life. In *Buckle and His Critics* (1895) he discussed Ludwig Gumplowicz's *The Race Struggle (Der Rassenkampf)*, which Karl Kautsky critiqued some three decades later in his massive *The Materialist Conception of History* (abridged Eng. trans., 1988 ed., pp. 123-4), although Kautsky had reviewed Gumplowicz's book in the year of its publication (1883). In a survey of the history of sociology (in *Courses of Study* for 1932) Robertson appeared to rank Ratzenhofer above his fellow Austrian Gumplowicz, who had the highest regard for his compatriot as a sociologist. In the same volume J.M.R. also acknowledged Freud's contribution.

In *War and Civilization* four chapter headings focused specifically on facets of German involvement in the War, and none on Austria or the Austro-Hungarian Empire, which was widely seen, in Britain at least, as Kaiser Wilhelm II's junior partner. In fact, the main lines of Robertson's indictment of Imperial Germany would appear to be vindicated a few years later as a result of Kautsky being officially allowed access, following Germany's defeat in 1918, to highly sensitive, senior level German Government documents relating to the War. Privileged study of these papers enabled Kautsky to maintain that "the political, diplomatic, and military elites of imperial Germany conspired with the Austrian leadership to dupe both peoples into a senseless war" (Gary P. Steenson, op. cit. 1991, p. 225). Later Kautsky himself – an Austrian who, like Freud, would escape from the Nazis in 1938 – referred to "the World War ignited by Kaiser Wilhelm's policies" (*The Materialist Conception of History*, 1988 ed., p. 483).

Robertson's wartime book contained a less than flattering passing reference (1917 ed., p. 152) to Professor Eduard Meyer of Berlin, who, in J.M.R.'s words, "professes to be convinced that immeasurable war had to be forced on Europe because Austria 'must not be humiliated'". In the same year, under the title *Britain versus Germany*, Robertson published an Open Letter to Meyer in which he took the Professor to task for his virtual glorification of the State. Meyer seems to have responded, in his massive, three-volume *Origin and Beginnings of Christianity (Ursprung und Anfänge des Christentums*, published in German between 1921 and 1923), by ignoring Robertson's contribution, spanning some half a dozen scholarly and substantial works, in the same field, from 1900 onwards.

J.M.R. pointed out in *War and Civilization* that Steffen trusted that a German victory in the World War "will mean the *triumph of Socialism in Germany, and therefore in the countries which Germany may subdue*" (p. 119: Robertson's emphasis). It was already known that in 1887 Engels had declared: "no war is any longer possible for Prussia-Germany except a world war ... of an extension and violence hitherto undreamt of. ... to open the last great war dance – that will suit us all right." But in the wake of the Second World War it would become more and more widely known that in the context of the Franco-Prussian War Marx had written to Engels in July 1870: "The French need a thrashing. If the Prussians win, centralisation of the state power will be useful for the centralisation of the German working class"; and he added regarding the Germans: "Their predominance over the French on the world stage would also mean the predominance of our theory over Proudhon's, etc." (see Leslie R. Page, op. cit. 1987, pp. 113 (Engels), 112 (Marx): part of the Marx passage appears, also in translation, in the Appendix to the present work).

Another arena or opening for left-wing ideas would be provided by Tyneside in the years immediately preceding the First World War. As the local historian Jo Bath would explain regarding this period: "Tyneside was also a crucible of ideas, with a strong tradition of engagement with religion, politics, intellectual pursuits, trade unionism and the suffrage movement" (George Orwell's literary and socialist friend Jack Common grew up in the Newcastle area before and during the World War, when the Bolshevik theoretician Nikolai Bukharin was arrested in Newcastle in 1915). But as an industrial and population centre Tyneside – which contained Robertson's constituency – also made an important contribution to England's war effort between 1914 and 1918 (see entry for *Fiscal Fraud and Folly*, and see Jo Bath, *Tyneside: Remembering 1914-18*, 2015, pp. 10, 125, and generally).

On 3 December 1917 Robertson, in a Parliamentary speech, mounted an attack (described as "admirable" by the historian and educationalist H.A.L. Fisher) on a Bill – which J.M.R. clearly felt was unworthy of the House of Commons - designed to damage a prominent German-oriented company in the metal trade (see Fisher's *Coalition Diaries and Letters*, 2006 ed., Vol. 1, p. 169, and Simon Ball, *The Guardsmen*, 2004, pp. 137-40); and J.M.R. consistently warned against punitive German reparations. Then in late 1932 Robertson warned prophetically: "Inasmuch as the danger to the world's peace emerges in terms of the 'nationalism' of German and other sufferers by the territorial revisions of 1919..." (*Courses of Study*, p. 402). In *War and Civilization* he had referred to German "financiers who had hoped to wring vast 'indemnities' from France and Russia" (p. 148). But equally if not more striking was Robertson's conclusion that Germany had been using science as a terror weapon in war (pp. 144-5), foreshadowing his Parliamentary warning in August 1918 that in a post-war Europe armed to the teeth: "Every device of science for the destruction of life on the largest possible scale will be the order of the day. There will be no question, then, about Hague Conventions ..." (see *BRUG*, 1984, pp. 34-5).

Robertson's Parliamentary warning on 8 August 1918 about the grave danger of an even more terrible war in the foreseeable future enhanced a speech that included an eloquent tribute to Karl Liebknecht, the rebellious German socialist leader whose "heroic protests" against the aggression of the German war machine J.M.R. had already noted in 1915 (*LG*, 1.2.1915, p. 17), when, at nearly sixty, J.M.R. also offered "if need be" to "lay down my own life" to resist "the military dominion of Germany" (*The R.P.A. Annual 1915*, p. 60). Then, in 1917, Robertson concluded his Postscript to the second edition of *War and Civilization* by referring to Liebknecht as one "whose voice is no longer allowed to be heard" (p. 156). Less than eighteen months later, after becoming a co-founder of the German Communist Party, Liebknecht was murdered – together with Rosa Luxemburg – by authorities acting on behalf of the Weimar Republic's Defence Minister Gustav Noske, a Social Democrat, whose repressive steps, in 1919 in Berlin and in Bavaria, arguably indirectly helped the Nazis in their rise to power. (Another left-wing political outsider praised or defended in *War and Civilization* was, in addition to Liebknecht, the Russian anarchist Kropotkin.)

While Robertson's strictures in his book on German militarism and aggression might possibly seem unduly harsh today, none of them was contradicted by Nazi atrocities and massacres in the Soviet Union and in Eastern Europe generally, including the Nazi death camps, less than three decades after *War and Civilization* appeared. J.M.R. later highlighted "a grave indictment against the administration of Samoa by New Zealand since the War" (*Courses of Study*, 1932 ed., p. 397), following the end of Imperial Germany's rule in Samoa.

Wrecking the Empire (1901)

In 1900 Robertson visited South Africa as an investigative journalist to report on the working of martial law and the course of the Boer War there, having been commissioned to do so by the *Morning Leader*, which was one of the few London newspapers opposed to the war. (*The Morning Leader* took part in the campaign in England on behalf of the persecuted Spanish libertarian Francisco Ferrer some years later, when, according to Ferrer's daughter Sol, it was regarded as a Conservative paper.) Scores of J.M.R.'s letters, written in Cape Colony and Natal during a period from June to October 1900, duly appeared in that newspaper over the signature "Scrutator". They are thought to have provided the Liberal Opposition leader Campbell-Bannerman with useful ammunition for the October 1900 general election (see Conrad Kaczkowski, op. cit. 1964, pp. 58, 412). Robertson then revisited his letters, and sixty-nine of them, together with a lengthy preface and an appendix, were published in book form under his own name as *Wrecking the Empire*, for which the demand was apparently so great that the first edition was sold out before it appeared (see *The Reformer*, 15.5.1901, pp. 257, 318). The book was soon boycotted by jingoistic booksellers. The publisher was Grant Richards, who years later would publish *The Ragged Trousered Philanthropists* by the socialist "Robert Tressell" – Robert Noonan – who lived in South Africa, apparently with pro-Boer sympathies, throughout the time J.M.R. was there.

During his stay in South Africa Robertson came across the political activist F.W. Pethick-Lawrence, who later recorded: "I spent many an evening with Olive Schreiner and her husband Cronwright; and we were often joined by Cartwright of the

South African News and J.M. Robertson who, like myself, was on a visit to the Cape. Many were the discussions we had on religious and social questions. The lighter side was also not forgotten, and I remember in particular a famous 35-mile drive we all had round Table Mountain in a wagonette drawn by three horses driven by a Malay coachman wearing an enormous straw hat" (*Fate Has Been Kind*, n.d., 1943? p. 53).

To the anger of British imperialists Robertson's book offered "carefully-sifted evidence of the devastation of the Boer territories, of farm-burning, looting, sufferings of women and children, of wholesale arrests, false charges, iniquitous sentences, of gross injustice in the application of martial law ..." (*The Reformer* review, 15.5.1901, pp. 318-9). Such behaviour, J.M.R. believed, was "preparing the dismemberment of the British Empire", which should be phased out in a measured, peaceful way. In his forceful maiden speech in Parliament (1906), devoted to the treatment of South African blacks, he urged the British Government to develop their education and agricultural potential. On 6 April 1908 he addressed the Aborigines' Protection Society on the treatment of natives in Natal. He later declared: "in Protestant Natal today there is a general determination among the white population to keep the natives uneducated, lest knowledge should give them power" (*Pagan Christs*, 1911 ed., p. 382).

He also raised questions in Parliament about the position of Indians imprisoned in South Africa (October 1907); and Mohandas Gandhi may have remembered that the M.P. raising these questions was the activist taking over the editorship of the *National Reformer* from Bradlaugh, whose funeral both he and Robertson had attended, the latter as a pall-bearer. (Gandhi's biographer Ramachandra Guha -

2013, p. 51 - mixed up the date of Bradlaugh's death with that of his funeral.) As reported in 1911, J.M.R. had concluded that "none of the *a priori* arguments against autonomy for any race have any scientific validity" (quoted in *Imperial Sceptics*, 2010, p. 12, by Gregory Claeys). J.M.R. foresaw the "probability of enormous evil" regarding race relations in Africa. Moreover, in 1903 J.M.R. indicated that, with changing socio-economic conditions, white settlers would begin to withdraw from (then) Rhodesia and South Africa within "a few more generations" – a remarkably prescient forecast in the circumstances, at a time when to many in or from Britain the British Empire held no foreseeable prospect, or only an extremely remote prospect, of black (or brown) majority rule. (See Robertson's article he referenced in *Courses of Study*, 1932 ed., p. 395, "Black and White in Africa", where, despite the trauma associated with the Boer War, he suggested, with a high degree of accuracy, that "in the near future the common self-interest of Dutch and British will restore the former repressive attitude of whites towards blacks" in South Africa.) It would take generations for racial discrimination, as entrenched in law, to be dismantled in Rhodesia (Zimbabwe) and South Africa. Even so, the life-span of the British Empire was distinctly shorter than that of the Assyrian Empire (an ancient empire J.M.R. surveyed in *Courses of Study*, 1932 ed., pp. 221-22).

In 1994 R.G. Hackett stated that *Wrecking the Empire* presented a "comprehensive account of alleged misdeeds of the British" during the Boer War (*South African War Books*, p. 180); and there are unindexed references to J.M.R.'s book in Bernard Porter's two books on aspects of British imperialism published in 1968 (p. 163n., cf. p. 345) and 2004 (2006 ed., p. 409, cf. p. 441), respectively, with both works also noticing *Patriotism and Empire*. Robertson cast his bread upon the waters, and his 1901 book was picked up by H.R.D. Anders in Berlin for a work on Shakespeare, and by Bentley Gilbert in London for a work on the evolution of national insurance in Britain (in 1904 and 1966, respectively).

Field Marshal Lord Carver's book (1999) on the Boer War, which focused on its military aspects from a British army perspective, indicated that by 1900 200,000 British troops were fighting some 30,000 Boers at most. It also recorded, quoting Lord Roberts's own words, that his policy of burning Boer farms dated from 14 June 1900 (p. 168). That policy was condemned by a steadfast British opponent of the war like J.M. Robertson (who visited war-torn South Africa). Yet Carver's book did not notice him or his *Wrecking the Empire* (1901), with both being critical of Lord Roberts, as was J.M.R.'s contribution to *Essays towards Peace* (1913). Lord Carver thought Roberts an "excessively self-satisfied" general who had hardly distinguished himself during the Boer War (p. 257). Carver did not follow some Victorian secularists in blaming prominent British imperialists explicitly by name for the outbreak of the war, although he acknowledged "Milner's aggressive stance" shortly before it started (p. 11). An army chief Sir Charles Warren was described as "bad tempered, wanting-in-tact" by Lord Roberts, who longed to get rid of him in the high command in South Africa and force him out of the territory early in 1900 (Carver, pp. 91-2, 254). This was somewhat ironic as Warren, when a reactionary Commissioner of Police for London, had banned all public meetings in Trafalgar Square in November 1887, thereby sparking "Bloody Sunday" (a "deplorable" episode - J.M.R.'s word - in which three people died through police brutality).

APPENDIX: Robertson, Marx, Engels and Communism

The Marxist Rosa Luxemburg once declared: "Marxism lays claim only to temporary truth; dialectic through and through, it contains within itself the seeds of its own destruction." Karl Marx was a revolutionary thinker and prophet who dedicated his life to what he considered to be the liberation of humanity. Yet terrible crimes have been committed in his name; and many of his ideas have had to be substantially modified in the light of historical events shaped largely by his influence. His theory of value was the corner-stone of his economic analysis of capitalism. Yet according to the eminent rationalist radical J.M. Robertson (1856-1933): "Marx constructed an *a priori* concept of Value which answers to nothing in Nature" (*The Decadence*, 1929, p. 55); and it has often been said that Marx himself, in volume three of *Das Kapital*, all but abandoned his theory as expounded in the first volume (where he identified the division of labour, a major factor in alienation, as reducing man to "an appendage of a machine"). Robertson was more positive: "Our first traces of 'civilisation', strictly speaking, are in towns – *civitates*; and their civilisation consists largely in the development of the useful arts by division of labour" (*Pagan Christs*, second edition, 1911, p. 37).

For Engels, writing in *Anti-Dühring*: "It was slavery that first made possible the division of labour between agriculture and industry on a considerable scale, and along with this, the flower of the ancient world, Hellenism. Without slavery, no

Greek state, no Greek art and science. ... The introduction of slavery under the conditions of that time was a great step forward." This view was keenly contested by Robertson in *The Evolution of States* (pp. 62-3): "All the ancient States, before Greece, stood on slavery: then it was not slavery that yielded her special culture. What she gained from older civilisations was the knowledge and the arts developed by *specialisation* of pursuits; and such specialisation was not necessarily dependent on slavery, which could abound without it. It was in the special employment, finally, of the exceptionally large free population of Athens that the greatest artistic output was reached" (Robertson's emphasis).

Marx and Engels had propounded the doctrine of inevitable economic crises, increasing in frequency and magnitude to culminate in the apocalyptic overthrow of capitalism. Yet, this doctrine was stultified by Engels himself when, at the end of his life, he recognised that "the old breeding grounds of crises and opportunities for the growth of crises have been eliminated or strongly reduced". Indeed, one Marxist prophecy after another has come to naught, e.g. the numerical eclipse of the middle class and the ever-swelling ranks of an increasingly impoverished and discontented proletariat. Marx apparently believed that capitalism could not adapt to survive; yet the Great Depression (1929-1933) failed to produce a Marxist revolution. Marx's materialist concept was, said Engels, "destined to do for history what Darwin's theory has done for biology"; yet Darwinian evolutionism was a far cry from the Hegelian dialectic absorbed by Marxism.

Marx's reformist approach as regards Britain, the United States, Holland, even France and Germany, was consistent with that of Robertson, who declared: "any other way of getting rid of capitalism than by gradual evolution is absolutely chimerical, unless the zealots are to content themselves with a universal industrial smash in which wealth and leisure and culture will alike disappear, and the survivors will resume the primal task of getting a bare living from the soil. ... If it be insisted that revolution is a mode of evolution, it cannot at the same time be denied that evolution is a protracted revolution" (*The Economics of Progress*, pp. 176, 286). In 1927 the British socialist William Stephen Sanders provided some confirmatory material on Engels' belief in a form of evolution, certainly during his closing years (see *Early Socialist Days*, p. 81).

Engels wrote to Marx in 1858: "The English proletariat is actually becoming more and more bourgeois" (quoted by Tristram Hunt, *The Frock-Coated Communist*, 2010 ed., p. 190, and by Francis Wheen, *Karl Marx*, 2000 ed., p. 206); and this process has gained momentum. Despite the perpetuation of immense differences in personal wealth, revolutionary class-consciousness on the part of the so-called proletariat has largely faded, if not evaporated, in Britain, as in other highly developed industrial states, mainly as a result of increased and more widespread affluence. The 1848 revolutions, and even the Paris Commune of 1871, did not arise and develop in accordance with the postulates of Marxism. The "socialist" revolutions of Lenin, Mao Tse-tung and Fidel Castro, which emerged from the womb of predominantly *agrarian* societies, were more in line with Bakunin's political primitivism than with Marx's view that the revolution would be set in motion by the workers of the most advanced capitalist countries. For many Marxists, the Russian peasantry could skip the bourgeois stage of their development only if sustained by a successful socialist revolution in Western Europe; and twenty years before the Spartacist uprising, Robertson wrote of Germany's "apparent progress towards the political condition of Russia, the extraordinary abasement of public opinion before the personality of the emperor, the rapid gravitation of all the forces of freedom and progress to the side of Socialism, with the prospect of a death-struggle between that ideal and its opposite" (*The Saxon and the Celt*, p. 27). Rosa Luxemburg expressed somewhat similar sentiments in 1910: "If once the revolutionary period is fully unfolded, if the clouds of battle are already rising high, then no brake-pulling by the [S.P.D. German Socialist] party leaders will be able to accomplish much, for the masses will simply shove aside their leaders who set themselves against the storm of the movement" (quoted by Harry Harmer, *Rosa Luxemburg*, 2008, p. 80; see also p. 71). Yet the urban revolt of the German Spartacists was a tragic failure. In January 1919 the Spartacist leaders Luxemburg and Karl Liebknecht were brutally murdered in Berlin by the Freikorps, whose founder and commanding general was a convinced monarchist who knew that many of his men had fought with fanatical devotion in the Kaiser's wartime army. Hitler, by contrast, charged with high treason in 1923, served a short prison sentence and became German Chancellor within a decade! J.M.R.'s 1932 *Courses of Study* commended Vladimir Simkhovitch's classic *Marxism versus Socialism*; and Robertson's criticism (1925, etc.) of Marx's attachment to "inevitable" developments preceded Leopold Schwarzschild's strident criticism by over two decades.

As Engels said: "history is the cruellest of all goddesses"'; and in 1895 he described as illusions early views held by Marx and himself, and he admitted that history had altered the conditions under which the proletariat were to struggle. It may be considered that Marx failed to foresee the phenomenal growth of the trade union movement in Britain. Robertson, who lived through the only general strike (so far) in British history, might have pointed out that trade unions have evolved to accept social "responsibility" as an integral part of capitalism rather than as a force for labour's emancipation *from* capitalism, and have arguably become willing bureaucratic agencies of control for ruling élites in wartime. In an age characterised by the emergence of a "managerial revolution", Robertson correctly observed that Marxists often confused the wage-earning manager with the "idle" capitalist to whom he paid interest. In 1892 (*NR*, 4.12.92) Robertson criticised Engels' demonisation of "the bourgeoisie".

During the 1980s the present writer, more or less by chance, made the acquaintance of Eric and Marie Gordon, who had been released from Mao's Communist China in October 1969 after being arbitrarily imprisoned, and closely guarded, together with their young son in one small room in Peking (Beijing) for some two years for an alleged anti-Maoist stance during the Cultural Revolution. Eric Gordon, a pro-Communist British journalist, was also subjected to solitary confinement during his ordeal, which was apparently linked to his pointing out that Mao had not been the early military leader of the Chinese Communist army, which in a military sense was really led at this stage by Chu Teh, from a poor peasant family (see Eric Gordon's article "Mao's legacy" in *Islington Tribune* of 8 February 2019). Chu Teh – also known as Zhu De or Chu-The in English texts – was much admired by the highly influential American Communist agent and journalist Agnes Smedley, who after years in China died in England in 1950 and left her estate to him with a request that her ashes "be laid to rest at any place designated by General Chu-The or his heirs" (Norman Polmar and Thomas B. Allen, *Spy Book*, 1997, p. 518).

Marx the revolutionary journalist who opposed the censor did not foresee the rise of the mass media, with the consequent power of ruling élites, through their control and manipulation of the media, to indoctrinate and sway public opinion, and thus fortify their own position. Modern totalitarianism can process the masses so successfully that the mass-society becomes the architect of its own enslavement. In the so-called free world what Marx called the "fetishism of commodities" seems to have been enhanced by the fetishism of sex. Moreover in 1848 Marx and Engels declared: "National differences and antagonisms between peoples are daily more and more vanishing." Yet under the impact of capitalist technology, expanding populations and the growth of nationalism and racialism, alienation has conceivably increased, and bourgeois capitalism may have tended to develop into bureaucratic collectivism rather than socialism.

Of the ten commandments for a socialist programme outlined in the *Communist Manifesto* (which, according to Tcherkesoff, was taken largely from Victor Considérant), no fewer than nine called for the enlargement of the State; and in 1880 Engels declared that once the State had undertaken "possession of the means of production in the name of society", it would begin to wither away. In 1884 he apparently believed that the dissolution of the State was at hand and that the whole machinery of the State would soon be relegated to "the museum of antiquities, by the side of the spinning wheel and the bronze axe". Engels' optimism was not shared by Robertson the practical politician, who, on the eve of a world war between the imperialist nations, remarked that an appetite for extended dominion was an inherent characteristic of States. The ideological basis of Soviet society was supposedly laid by Marx and Engels; yet decades after the Bolshevik Revolution, the State was probably nowhere stronger than in Russia, where it showed no sign of withering away – despite Lenin's reaffirmation of

Engels' prediction. Marx and Engels themselves suggested that the State was a manifestation of human alienation; yet the State has emerged as a cohesive force, sustained by loyalties that cut across class differences, and its power has increased immeasurably since Marx's day.

While Marx saw love of freedom and love of domination as the two motive-forces of social life, he did not really explain how everyone is at once oppressor and oppressed, in varying degrees according to one's position in the social hierarchy. He devoted little attention to the struggles *within* classes; and his emphasis on the ownership of property as the main determinant of class – valuable though it was – was an over-simplification. Indeed, he never fully defined a social class. He was inclined to forget that even in a class society there could be a relative absence of economic antagonism between classes. His materialist concept of history tended to minimise the record of class co-operation, the impact of personality and the driving force of human irrationality. In a private letter (hitherto unpublished) Robertson declared: "All social reconstruction is a praxis, calling for a practical skill that is quite distinct from power of abstract theorising; and very few Socialists have that form of wisdom, Marx certainly had not. … Broadly speaking, all thinking in terms of 'class consciousness' is for me suspect." J.M.R. suggested that the character of religious sects or conflicts was not necessarily or wholly determined by class consciousness or class conflict.

Robertson defined religion as "the sum (a) of men's ideas of their relation to the imagined forces of the cosmos; (b) of their relation to each other as determined by their views of that, or by teachers who authoritatively recast those views; and (c) of the practices set up by those ideas" (*Pagan Christs*, second edition, p. 58). Religion, said Engels, "stands furthest away from material life and seems to be most alien to it. Religion arose in very primitive times from erroneous, primitive conceptions of men about their own nature and external nature surrounding them" (from *Ludwig Feuerbach and the End of Classical German Philosophy*, 1888 ed.: see Lewis S. Feuer (ed.), *Marx and Engels*, 1969 ed., p. 278). J.M.R. stressed the role of fear and adoration, "a social habit of conformity" and economic forces in the origination, perpetuation and survival of religions.

When Marx's wife attended Bradlaugh's Sunday meetings, their daughter Eleanor recorded her father's reaction: "He told mother that if she wanted edification or satisfaction of her metaphysical needs she would find them in the Jewish prophets rather than in Mr. Bradlaugh's shallow reasonings" (see Lewis Feuer, *Marx and Engels: Basic Writings on Politics and Philosophy*, 1969 paperback ed., p. 35). Bradlaugh's disciple Robertson would have been greatly struck by this remark, with the apparent recognition of "metaphysical needs" by the foremost exponent of the materialist theory of history. Just as Christianity appealed to slaves in the ancient world, so Marxism championed the wage-slaves of the modern era. Marx, the Hebraic prophet of socialism, secularised the doctrine of the Redemption: Marx conceived of the future classless society as achieving the "re-integration or return of man to himself", as a partial reflection, at a higher evolutionary stage, of man's primitive communism, which was vitiated by the development of private property. In *Das Kapital* he referred to "human nature in general, and human nature as modified in each historical epoch". (See G.A. Cohen, *Karl Marx's Theory of History*, 1978, 1979 reprint, p. 151, for example.) Yet Marx arguably did not present as detailed an analysis of this distinction as was possible or desirable; and if human nature has been so thoroughly deformed by centuries of exploitation, can man "return to himself"? If, as Marx suggested, modern man and his consciousness are determined by a social environment where justice is an illusion, can man create a truly just society?

Robertson drew attention to the paradox that Marxists proclaimed the historical inevitability of the victory of communism, and yet appealed to human volition by seeking to arouse in the proletarians revolutionary consciousness of their historic mission. It was, he said, one of life's ironies that the classless society was to be created through class hatred, that a fraternal society was to be built up by the forces of malevolence. The Marxian gospel, he said, promised the faithful a political Day of Judgement: "At that day, by military force, a society reduced to misery by systematic capitalism would be turned upside down, swiftly reconstructed by martial law, and then set agoing on ideal principles, to be happy ever after" (*The Decadence*, 1929, p. 54). For Marx the Paris Commune was "forever … the glorious harbinger of a new society", and Engels called the Commune "the dictatorship of the proletariat" (see Feuer, op. cit. 1969, pp. 429, 402); yet no social revolution followed the French Commune, which was brutally suppressed. How, then, were the proletariat to know when the hour had struck for the decisive overthrow of capitalism, for the successful socialist revolution? Moreover, Marx never really faced up to the destructive effects of violence on its practitioners.

Declared Robertson: "Marx puts a catastrophic and finally static theory of social destiny under a pseudo-evolutionary form. Imposed by his personality and that of Lassalle on generations of German workmen, whom it [Marx's philosophy] hypnotised with a quasi-religious hope, analogous to that of the 'Second Advent', it is thus in itself an extremely interesting sociological phenomenon." A system of ideas like Marxism, which essentially reflects a class struggle, could play no vital part in the evolution of a classless society. Even so, on the structure and administration of the triumphant communist economy Marx offered about as little guidance as he did on the tactics and organisation to be adopted by the proletariat to carry through the revolution.

Marx and Engels spoke of "the idiocy of rural life", and Marx said: "the country that is more developed industrially only shows to the less developed the image of its own future"; yet Marx's "huntin' and fishin'" concept of communism was distinctly rustic. Marx and Engels expected the division of labour to wither away in the future communist society. Ironically, predominantly industrial states today are characterised not only by increased leisure and automation, but also by the growing complexity and specialisation of social life. Under communism, alienation, the play of dialectic and centuries-old class struggle would apparently be resolved; yet to live in a continual state of tension, dissatisfaction and uncertainty seems to be an ineradicable feature of man's estate, and Marx failed to appreciate that strife could continue in a classless society. In some respects, therefore, Marx was at least as utopian as the Utopian Socialists of whom he and Engels were so critical.

In a twentieth century of unparalleled destruction, when the self-annihilation of the human race was at least a technological possibility, the concept of a future earthly paradise seemed even more a projection of wish-fulfilment than in Marx's day. Marx's assertion that "mankind always sets itself only such tasks as it can solve" (G.A. Cohen translation, p. viii) is far less confidently held today, and may be regarded as a legacy of the eighteenth century belief in progress and reason.

Robertson wondered what would be the fate of artists and clergymen – indeed, of freedom of expression itself – under a Socialist regime dedicated to "productive" work and possessing a State monopoly of printing and publication. That he was justified in raising such issues in January 1908 in a debate on the practicability of socialism was borne out a decade and more later when in Russia, following the October 1917 Revolution, the Russian Orthodox Church was vigorously repressed, with its priests vulnerable to viciously vindictive assault, and in 1920 Yevgeny Zamyatin (who only three years earlier had worked in Tyneside, which Robertson had represented politically) declared: "True literature only exists when it is created by madmen, hermits, heretics, dreamers, rebels and sceptics, and not by reliable clerks … we won't have any genuine literature until we have been cured of this new kind of Catholicism which is just as afraid of heresy as the old one was" (quoted by Dmitri Volkogonov, *Stalin*, 1991 ed., p. 129). The concern expressed by J.M.R. in January 1908 and by Zamyatin in 1920 was vindicated from 1934 onwards as a result of the uniform imposition in Stalin's Russia of the dogma of "Socialist Realism", reinforced by an "ideological strait-jacket" (Chris Ward, 1995 ed.) and a "rigid censorship of the arts" (Nicholas Comfort, 2005). Under this regime so-called art "had to be imbued with optimism and to present an idealized view of workers and peasants" (Archie Brown, *The Rise and Fall of Communism*, 2009, p. 263); and this Soviet orthodoxy may well have been partly intended to mask, or divert attention from, the Communist state's brutal and murderous treatment of the more prosperous peasants known as kulaks, with this ruinously homicidal and suicidal agricultural policy reaching a crescendo by 1934. Moreover, if values are taken by Marxists to be historically relative, why do we enjoy art created hundreds of years ago and expressing a way of life alien to ours in many ways? Marx gave no satisfactory answer in Marxian terms.

Marx's confidence in the proletariat (who he thought would become increasingly socialistic) appears to have been excessive. If, as Marx believed, "the emancipation of the working classes must be won by the working classes themselves", it is ironic that quite a number of Marxist and Communist leaders have been non-proletarian, indeed bourgeois. Marx's concept of a revolutionary mass movement was undermined by Lenin's emphasis on an elitist party of professional revolutionaries. Marx's belief that international capitalism would be confronted and overthrown by an internationally unified proletariat has been dismally confounded. The First World War, Robertson declared, came about "unhindered by the Marxists" (*A History of Freethought in the Nineteenth Century*, 1929, p. 574). From one perspective, "unhindered" was an appropriate word for Robertson to use as the Second International failed not only to prevent the World War from starting, but also to muster and organise resistance to it once it had started (see *International Socialism* 143, Summer 2014, p. 107, for example). From another angle, even "unhindered" was a rather generous term to apply to the Marxists and socialists on the basis that it did not fully reflect the fact that the German and French social democratic parliamentarians, for instance, went out of their way to vote unanimously for their respective Governments' war credits.

Although Bakunin was alive to the prospect of total war, Marx and the military critic Engels, during the "Hundred Years Peace" before Sarajevo, concentrated mainly on the class struggle and failed to work out a sustained theory of the political significance of armed conflicts *between nations*. Yet, in the twentieth century, such conflicts over-shadowed the class struggle within nations. Arguably Marx and Engels did not appreciate the extent to which the struggles and armed conflicts between imperialist powers for colonies and overseas markets were themselves the outcome of capitalist development; yet before the publication of the classic treatises of Hobson and Lenin, Robertson said of imperialist expansion: "The only interests really furthered by fresh expansion are those of the speculative trading class, the speculative capitalist class, the military and naval services, the industrial class which supplies war material, and generally those who look to an imperial civil service as a means of employment for themselves and their kin" (*Patriotism and Empire*, third edition, 1900, p. 187; see also pp. 177-8).

Robertson (who was one of the most advanced radicals in Britain before the rise of the Labour Party) added that a secondary aim of imperial expansion was "to put off the day of reckoning as between capital and labour" (op. cit., p. 188). Rather ironically this latter aim of imperial expansion had been identified some four years earlier in London by the arch-imperialist Cecil Rhodes, who after attending a fraught public meeting of distressed unemployed in the East End had become even more convinced that imperialism could and should provide "a solution for the social problem" and specifically prevent "a bloody civil war" by offering new outlets and opportunities for unemployed British people emigrating to the colonies, seen as "new lands to settle the surplus population" (Rhodes quoted by the Russian Communist historian Apollon Davidson, *Cecil Rhodes and His Time*, 1988 ed., pp. 413-14). In *Patriotism and Empire* Robertson concluded: "While imperialism prospers, there will be no vital social reform" (p. 189).

Marx and Engels were contaminated by aspects of German

nationalism and racialism. Marx, who claimed to have discovered "the rational kernel within the mystical shell" of Hegelian dialectic and who sprang from the ranks of the Jewish bourgeoisie, was himself an anti-bourgeois with leaning towards anti-Semitism! Declared Marx: "What is the worldly cult of the Jew? Huckstering. What is his worldly God? Money." But as Robertson pointed out in *The Saxon and the Celt*: "while the self-styled Aryan prates of the predominance of his species, the lands in which his tongue is spoken are chronically convulsed by wild outcry against the domination of the Semite, who wields the all-compelling power of the purse; yet at the same time, as if to show at a glance the nullity of the theory which in turn makes him merely a manipulator of money, contributes to 'the general deed of man' the most opposing influences, producing at once Lassalle and Rothschild, Marx and Hirsch, Ricardo and Disraeli" (1897, p. 112).

Marx, the leading light of the First International, adopted a German nationalist attitude towards Schleswig-Holstein (which Bismarck took from Denmark) and towards Bohemia. He apparently believed in the relative inferiority of the Negroes no less than in the innate superiority of the Germans to the Slavs; and he referred approvingly to "the historical tendency and the physical and intellectual power of the German nation to subdue, absorb and assimilate its ancient eastern neighbours". In the Franco-Prussian War, Marx supported Bismarck, condemned the anti-Bismarckian attitude of the German Socialists Bebel and Wilhelm Liebknecht, and declared: "The French need a thrashing. … The German working class are in theory and organisation superior to the French. Their dominance over the French on the world stage would also mean the dominance of our theory over Proudhon's."

At a time when the racialist historians of the "Teutonic school" were coming to the fore in England and Germany, Engels produced his sociological romance *The Origin of the Family* (1884). In this work, Engels extolled the racial purity, chastity and respect for women which were supposedly characteristic of the barbaric Germani, with "their personal efficiency and bravery, their love of liberty, and their democratic instinct". Engels died before his thesis was in effect demolished by Robertson in *The Saxon and the Celt* (1897), where the Scot handled evidence in a scientific spirit that seemed beyond Marx's over-enthusiastic collaborator.

J.M. Robertson was perhaps the greatest literary scholar of plebeian origins ever born and bred in the British Isles. There is no evidence that he slavishly accepted Marxian interpretations (on the contrary!); yet there was often a striking similarity of view between him and outright Marxists which did not devalue his own contribution any more than Marx's contribution was stultified by his own considerable debt to his predecessors and contemporaries.

In the conclusion to his *Critique of Political Economy*, Marx had asked why ancient Greek art and epic "still constitute with us a source of aesthetic enjoyment and in certain respects prevail as the standard and model beyond attainment". His answer indicated a difficulty inherent in Marxian aesthetics: "Why should the social childhood of mankind, where it had reached its most beautiful development, not exert an eternal charm as an age that will never return?" In his classic *Short History of Christianity* (second edition, p. 163), Robertson eloquently elaborated this theme of a lost Greek "golden age":

> Pagan Greece lives for ever in men's thought as a dream of grace and beauty and enchanted speech; and though

behind the shining vision of art and song there lingers immovably a sombre memory of strife and servitude, the art and the song are a deathless gift to mankind. At every summit of its attainment our civilization looks back to them with an unquenchable envy, an impotent desire, as of a race disinherited.

"The rise of Christianity is to be explained in terms of social metabolism; it points to the emergence of the ideals of a slave class in place of those of a ruling and military class." With this description of a Nietzschean transvaluation of values Robertson may be said to have adumbrated the thesis that was to be developed a decade later by the Marxist scholar Karl Kautsky in his valuable *Origin of Christianity* (1908). Of Kautsky's book he said: "It has some strong grounds, and it is beset by very serious difficulties, which Kautsky, I think, has not met. When he [i.e. Kautsky] denies that there were Hellenistic experiments and propagandas which in a later period could have set some Christian enthusiasts upon inventing a communistic beginning for the Church, he seems to ignore his own argument from the Epistle of James, and evidence which he could have found in Kalthoff. But unless the communistic theory ... is pressed as giving the *whole* origin of Christianity, it remains a part rather of the sociological problem than of the hierological inquiry" (*The Historical Jesus*, pp. 190-1: J.M.R.'s emphasis). Robertson added: "there is a primary *religious* factor and problem ... There was a sacramental cult before there could be any communism" (J.M.R.'s emphasis). Here Robertson was more restrained than Erich Fromm would be decades later, in 1963, when, in *The Dogma of Christ* (p. 34n.), he berated Kautsky for writing off the role of pious fanaticism or fantasies in early Christianity. Fromm has been identified with an empirical trend in modern humanist philosophy; and his neo-Marxist associate Max Horkheimer may have drawn upon J.M.R.'s work on Montaigne.

Arguably Robertson approximated to a Marxian analysis when he wrote: "in not a single country could the Reformation have been accomplished without enlisting the powerful classes or corporations, or alternatively the *de facto* governments, by proffering the plunder of the Church. Only in a few Swiss cantons, and in Holland, does the confiscation seem to have been made to the common good." Marx believed: "Luther destroyed the enslavement that sprang from devotion, only to put in its place the enslavement that springs from conviction." (Cf. David McLellan, op. cit. 1976 ed., p. 92.) Declared Robertson: "Luther and Calvin alike did but set up an infallible book and a local tyranny against an infallible pope and a tyranny centring at Rome" (*HF*, 1936, Vol. 1, p. 483). Just as Gerrard Winstanley and the Diggers became Marxian heroes, so Robertson championed the Leveller John Lilburne while Victorian historians were busy extolling the authoritarian and religiously fanatical Cromwell, a founding father of the English (or British) Empire.

In the context of the R.P.A. President, Professor Graham Wallas, referring at an R.P.A. Dinner in June 1926 to the economic power of anti-rationalist institutions over the years, one of the after-dinner speakers, Dr. Peter Chalmers Mitchell, heaped praise on J.M.R.'s *The Dynamics of Religion*, where "the author's gift of exposition makes the work as fresh and as valuable today as when it was written" and complimented the R.P.A. on re-publishing (in a revised edition) this "book of such permanent value". Almost two years later Chalmers Mitchell, at a private dinner party attended by Robertson and the latter's friend Macleod Yearsley, revealed himself to be, in Yearsley's words, "an ardent Bolshevik" (for virtual confirmation of which see David Caute's *The Fellow-Travellers*, 1973).

Of the foremost British pioneer in co-operative socialism, J.M.R. rightly said: Owen "had in him much of the idealism which inspired the quasi-communistic religious movements of earlier times. He was credulous of the potency of goodwill to regenerate the earth. And his own early and signal success at New Lanark … gave to his benevolent bias the fixity of a conviction borne out by a great experience" (*The Meaning of Liberalism*, 1925 ed., pp. 137-8). Here, at least Robertson joined hands – so to speak – with Engels in his interpretation of this utopian socialist, whose disciples may be said to have included Karl Marx himself. Robertson emphasised "the great and ill-acknowledged doctrinal debt of Marx to the earlier English Socialists, in particular to William Thompson, some of whose main doctrines he adopted". J.M.R. also referred to "the early English Socialists and land nationalisers, William Ogilvie, Thomas Spence, Charles Hall, William Thompson, Thomas Hodgskin, and J.F. Bray, who, with Godwin and Robert Owen, are the true founders of modern Socialism and 'scientific Anarchism'" (see *Courses of Study*, 1932 ed., pp. 186, 185).

Robertson's preparatory background reading for *The Fallacy of Saving* may have benefited from a perusal of *Das Kapital*, which his 1892 book clearly indicated (p. 63n., etc.) he had studied. Certainly Robertson was well aware of the affinities between Marx's materialist theory of history and Buckle's analysis, which Marx partly complemented and which J.M.R. largely accepted. In his masterly *Buckle and His Critics* (1895), he declared (pp. 432-3):

> the teaching of Marx has not passed away. As a system of economic logic, indeed, it has been sufficiently

triturated; and its strange stress on the formula of "surplus value" is apt to make one do less than justice to its scientific value. But there is in *Das Kapital* a sociological teaching of permanent importance, and that is the principle which has been stated by his followers as "Economic determinism". That principle is not a new one for the students of Buckle; but it is newly applied by the school of Marx, in terms of the economic life not of the primary civilisations but of the most complex industrial civilisation of today. … Marx represents the results of a German theorist's stay in and study of industrial England, with … the stimulus of French schemes of organisation… The socialism of Marx is a complex of the sociological cultures of three environments; and it is some confirmation of our doctrine of the effects of cross-fertilisation of ideas that this result should be the most effective performance in its kind. … the doctrine that all social phases, early and late, are to be explained in terms of economic conditions, is indeed of profound importance, but … used as a sole interpretative principle it may lead to all manner of errors.

Marx believed that social developments were the result of "natural laws which work with iron necessity towards inevitable results" (highlighted in 1948 by Schwarzschild, quoted by Leslie R. Page, op. cit. 1987, p. 33); whereas for Robertson, and similarly for Buckle, the ability of the scientific historian to forecast the shape of things to come was distinctly circumscribed (see also p. 375 of the present work).

In the 1890s and, again, in the revolutionary year 1917, Robertson proposed a whole series of measures which in Marxist terminology would "necessitate further inroads upon the old social order, and are unavoidable as a means of entirely revolutionising the mode of production". These measures included: taxation of land-values and the ultimate nationalisation of land; a graduated income tax and a tax on capital; State banking; railway nationalisation and municipalisation of tramways; profit-sharing schemes for industrial workers and a programme of public works to tackle unemployment; and "the extension of the principle of Free Education to the higher schools and Universities". These proposals bore a striking, though no doubt unintended, resemblance to the ten-point programme outlined in the *Communist Manifesto*, which J.M.R. had read.

Marx described the modern industrial worker as "a mere machine for producing alien wealth, broken in body and brutalised in mind"; Robertson spoke of "that burden of joyless, mechanical, mindless toil at the machine". In proposing railway nationalisation, J.M.R. said: "it remains to urge upon the workers that it is only by such steps as the one here proposed that any vital progress can be made towards the betterment of their lot in general, towards the removal of idle wealth, towards equality of comfort, towards social justice. The matter lies in their own hands." This appeal to the workers was akin to the concept – enunciated by Flora Tristan in 1843, and by Marx (in his inaugural address for the International) in 1864 – that "the emancipation of the working classes must be won by the working classes themselves". Like Marx, Robertson believed that, in England at least, a transition to socialism could be accomplished entirely by peaceful means; and in 1885 Engels went so far as to assert, quite seriously: "since 1848 the English Parliament has undoubtedly been the most revolutionary body in the world" (significantly, the letter from which this remark is taken – letter of 15 June 1885, to J.P. Becker – was omitted from the editions up to 1962 of the Moscow miscellany *Marx-Engels on Britain*).

At about the time of the infamous Jameson Raid (in which, it seems, Joseph Chamberlain was complicit), Robertson wrote: "Whatever of glory and social distinction goes with the trade of war is reaped by the upper classes. It is the blood of the common people that flows like water to carry out the quarrels of the ruling classes." "Capitalism began the war," said J.M.R. of the Boer War, which seems to have been instigated by the English ruling class to secure undisturbed possession of the Transvaal gold mines; and in his opposition to this war Robertson joined forces with the Marxist H.M. Hyndman – though the noted German socialist Wilhelm Liebknecht attempted to explain, if not condone, the British Government's action as "political necessity".

On 3 August 1914, two days after declaring war on Russia, Imperial Germany declared war on France and began invading Belgium. The next day, all the hundred and eleven German Social Democratic deputies voted for the Kaiser's war credits. On 2 December, a solitary German deputy, the socialist Karl Liebknecht (son of Wilhelm), defied party discipline to vote against war credits – and three years later, J.M. Robertson wrote of pro-German socialists: "While the Socialist majority, who truckled to the Kaiser and exhorted the Belgian Socialists to submit, are scheming for a peace which shall leave the plunder of Belgium in German hands, Liebknecht, I read, is dying in prison. Which of you all, I wonder, is most to be envied? I think I would rather be Liebknecht!" (*War and Civilization*, 1917 ed., p. 156). In his masterly swan-song in the British Parliament (August, 1918), Robertson paid eloquent tribute to the courage of Karl Liebknecht, who was soon to be murdered with the approval of the Social Democratic Defence Minister. Robertson rightly pointed to *Political Parties* by Robert Michels as "a treatise of some weight"; but if only he had commented in depth on Michels' contention that even European socialist parties, ostensibly devoted to the negation of élite control, conformed to the "iron law of oligarchy".

In *The Decadence* (p. 24), Robertson, who recognised that every empire contained within itself the seeds of its own decay, said of European imperialism: "In 1929, Winston Churchill was writing that in 1918 England had reached the highest point in her history. He could not conceive, doubtless, that already the arc was on the downward turn, and that in 1948 this would be obvious to English as well as to alien eyes. Yet in the World War four empires had been smitten to fragments because their rulers had lacked vision." 1948 was the year after the Indian sub-continent gained political freedom from British imperial rule. But in 1938 Robertson's analysis was substantially reiterated by the English Communist historian A.L. Morton, who regarded the First World War as a global "turning point, marking the passing over of European Imperialism into decline". Certainly Churchill's funeral in 1965 symbolised the death of English imperialism.

In 1932 Robertson emphasized "the historic fact that the Soviets came into existence before the Bolshevists seized power, and that primarily Sovietism and Bolshevism were different things" (*Courses of Study*, p. 305). J.M.R.'s apposite comment was consistent with the fact that once the Bolsheviks gained a majority in the Moscow and Petrograd Soviets in September 1917, they in effect used the Soviets (or councils), which had owed much to the Mensheviks, to widen support for the Bolshevik cause by appearing to be aligned with the reputed democratic credentials of the Soviets, which Lenin's Bolsheviks actually despised (see Dmitri Volkogonov,

Lenin, 1995 Eng. ed., p. 161; Robert Service, *Lenin*, 2000, p. 176; Bertram Wolfe, *Three Who Made a Revolution*, 1966 ed., pp. 415-18; Ralph Miliband in *After the Fall* (ed. Robin Blackburn), 1991, pp. 12, 17). Robertson opposed the blatantly undemocratic Bolshevik régime with much of the vigour with which, presumably, Marx and Engels themselves would have opposed it (cf. Harry Harmer, *Rosa Luxemburg*, 2008, p. 115). In 1925 J.M.R. exclaimed: "The absolute denial of freedom of criticism to opponents of the Bolshevik system in Russia is a black infamy, discrediting to the last degree all Bolshevik profession to seek freedom at all" (*The Meaning of Liberalism*, p. 163). He thus joined hands – so to speak – with Rosa Luxemburg, the Marxist martyr who, in memorable words, had prophetically discerned the seeds of what would become Stalinism in the suppression of political freedom by Lenin and Trotsky:

> With the repression of political life in the land as a whole, life in the Soviets must also become more and more crippled. Without general elections, without unrestricted freedom of press and assembly, without a free struggle of opinion, life dies out in every public institution, becomes a mere semblance of life, in which only the bureaucracy remains the active element. (*The Russian Revolution*)

Maxim Gorky – who was singled out as a freethinker by J.M.R., and who may have been poisoned on Stalin's orders – called the Leninist Revolution "a cruel experiment, doomed to failure in advance". Robertson was in substantial agreement with this view, and in 1931 he declared: "the brutality of the latest Communism, working gross social failure, is ominous." Two years earlier, he had pointed out that "the Russian cataclysm took place in a field of the most widespread ignorance, long maintained by religious machinery. It is no augury for more civilized lands" (*A Short History of Christianity*, third ed., p. 246; *A History of Freethought in the Nineteenth Century*, 1929, pp. 616-7. Many decades later a despotic and incredibly aggressive new Tsar, Vladimir Putin, would be blessed by the Russian Orthodox Church).

Robertson's attitude to Soviet Russia may be contrasted with that of John Maynard Keynes (who likewise attended post-war Liberal Summer Schools in England, though not necessarily at the same time as J.M.R.). In 1925 Keynes was impressed, on a visit to Russia, by the "religious" quality of the Communist régime. During December 1917-February 1918 he had described himself, in letters to his mother, as "buoyantly Bolshevik", refusing to accept the delayed award of a decoration from the socialistic Kerensky's Russian Provisional Government (R.F. Harrod's *Life of Keynes*, 1951, pp. 365, 223-5). Indeed: "In *The Economic Consequences* [*of the Peace*] Keynes vigorously opposed the policy of intervention by the allies against the Bolshevik forces and criticised the economic blockade against Soviet Russia" (Zygmund Dobbs, *Keynes at Harvard*, 1962 ed., p. 47, referring to Keynes op. cit., p. 294). When in May 1924 the British Communist Ivor Montagu successfully invited members of a Soviet trade union delegation staying in London to visit Cambridge, "the visitors were especially keen to have the lodgings of John Maynard Keynes at King's pointed out to them", ostensibly, at least, because "they were impressed by his contributions as an economist to post-war debates on international relations" (Russell Campbell, *Codename Intelligentsia*, 2018, p. 32). However, Keynes' criticism of the Soviet Union in *A Short View of Russia* – even in its original serialised periodical form in October 1925 – seems to have followed J.M.R.'s forthright verdict (1925) on the Bolshevik régime that "No worse tyranny has ever subsisted in Europe". Apparently suspicious of

Stalin the new tsar, Robertson in 1932 dismissed his political report to the Sixteenth Congress of the Soviet Communist Party in 1930 as "not informative" (*Courses of Study*, pp. 188-9). Moreover, during 1931-2 J.M.R. thwarted what seems to have been a pro-Communist attempted take-over of the R.P.A. in the name of "scientific humanism" spearheaded by his Communist namesake Archibald Robertson and other activists (see *BRUG*, p. 90, for details).

Said J.M.R.: "The spirit of freedom and toleration in the modern world has been predominantly anti-religious; and the spirit of social reconstruction has been no less so. Paine and Owen, Lincoln, Bradlaugh, Garibaldi, Stepniak, Marx, were all Freethinkers." For Robertson, religion dehumanised man; for Marx, it was "the opium of the people", alienating men from truly human ends. Darwinian evolutionism dealt Christianity a well nigh fatal blow, as Robertson realised. Both he and Lenin acknowledged the remarkable popularity of *The Riddle of the Universe* by Darwin's German apostle Haeckel, whose book, Lenin said, became "a weapon in the class struggle"; just as Marxists saw *The Origin of Species* as providing a basis in natural science for the class struggle in society.

Stalin, who was a voracious reader and ruthless operator, lured the novelist Gorky back to the Soviet Union in 1931 from exile in Italy and, that same year, may well have ordered, or approved, the creation of the myth that Marx tried to dedicate part of *Das Kapital* to Darwin through the Marx-Engels Institute in Moscow pretending that Darwin's letter of 13 October 1880, relating to a dedication, was addressed to Marx when in fact it was addressed to his disciple Edward Aveling. J.M.R.'s *Buckle and His Critics* (1895) mentioned Darwin quite frequently and Marx a couple of times, but did not explore or point to purported links between Marx and Darwin. Decades later

Robertson declared in May 1929: "We have to remember that Marx came before Darwin, and that his converts, first and last, were men who had not learned to think in terms of the law of evolution" (*The Decadence*, p. 55). Robertson seems to have been correct in the sense that *The Communist Manifesto* (1848) had been published before Darwin's *Origin of Species* (1859), or, as J.M.R. put it in *A History of Freethought in the Nineteenth Century* (1929), Marx had been "framing his theory of economic causation before the doctrine of evolution had been inductively established" (cf. Engels in 1888: see *The Communist Manifesto*, Penguin Classics ed., 2002, p. 203). Following political repression in Europe, "between 1850 and 1870, the *Manifesto* was remembered by no more than a few hundred German-speaking veterans of the 1848 revolutions" (Gareth Stedman Jones, Penguin Classics ed., p. 16). J.M.R. may have met some of them in Germany in 1887. However, *Das Kapital* (1867) reflected a degree of interest in Darwin (see G.A. Cohen, *Karl Marx's Theory of History*, 1979 ed., pp. 99 n. 6, 291).

Significantly, neither Lenin nor Robertson was acquainted with Marx's explicitly humanist *Economic and Philosophical Manuscripts* of 1844, which were published in German in 1932, and did not reach a mass English-speaking audience before 1961. Meanwhile, Robertson had died in January 1933, before he could analyse these seminal writings of the young Marx, which "were suppressed in the Soviet Union" (Gill Hands, *Marx*, 2007 ed., p. 140). There can be little doubt, however, that J.M.R. would have applauded Marx's magnificent statement: "The criticism of religion ends with the teaching that *man is the highest being for man*, it ends with the categorical imperative to overthrow all conditions in which man is a debased, forsaken, contemptible being forced into servitude." Marx prophesied that out of the ruins of man's prehistory there would rise "a higher type of society, whose fundamental principle is the full and free development of every individual". Only a few years before his death, Robertson pointed to the Marxian socialist formula, *From each according to his abilities, to each according to his needs*, as the highest of social ideals; and he declared: "we cannot say that ultimate Socialism will be felt by anybody as a restraint on liberty. Is it at all unlikely that our posterity will regard our economic 'liberty' somewhat as we now regard that of savages!"

Although Robertson in 1894, like Marx at an earlier point, was apparently contemplating the possibility of settling in America, it seems certain that J.M.R. was never in any form of contact with Marx (to whom J.M.R.'s secularist colleague Robert Banner of Edinburgh had written as an ardent socialist in 1880: see Francis Wheen, *Karl Marx*, 2000 paperback ed., pp. 369-70, 419). In 1927 William Stephen Sanders, in *Early Socialist Days*, paid tribute to Robert Banner's services to socialism in the Woolwich area associated with Britain's capital city. Nor has any evidence emerged that Robertson was ever in direct personal contact with Friedrich Engels, who sent no known reply to J.M.R.'s highly critical review, as editor, in the *National Reformer* for 4 December 1892 of Engels' *Socialism: Utopian and Scientific*. When Robertson declared in *The Meaning of Liberalism*, after the German's death, that Engels "never learned any humility" (p. 136, 1925 ed.), he seemed to have in mind Engels' erroneous forecasts and misjudgements. But the comment could also suggest a degree of personal knowledge of Engels and his weaknesses, which Robertson could have picked up through his erstwhile friend G.B. Shaw, who knew Engels (see David Caute, *The Fellow-Travellers*, 1973, p. 90; cf. Tristram Hunt, 2010 ed., p. 321), or through those close to Marx's daughter Eleanor or to Edward Aveling. Stalin may have been suitably impressed when he met Shaw in 1931 that the latter had known Engels; but this did not save both Stalin and Shaw, on account of their denial of the reality of the Soviet famine, from becoming the two most hated men in Russia, as the *Manchester Guardian* readers were informed on 29 March 1933 (by the British diplomat Gareth Jones, who was murdered two years later, probably by Stalin's agents: see Martin Sixsmith, *Russia*, 2011, pp. 263-5, 555).

In 1849 Engels – and, by implication, also Marx – appeared to condone the prospect of the elimination of "entire reactionary peoples" (see Leslie Page, *Karl Marx and the Critical Examination of His Works*, 1987, p. 102). Later Stalin took quite a close interest in Engels' works (Dmitri Volkogonov, op. cit. p. 552; Tristram Hunt, op. cit., p. 364). Certainly Stalin's atrocious record of mass murder virtually extended to encompass genocide through enforced starvation and famine in Ukraine, where some five million perished in this way in 1932-33 (Helen Rappaport, *Joseph Stalin*, 1999, p. 52; *The Week*, 26.2.2022, p. 13), at a time when J.M.R. was unable to investigate, although Robertson did refer in 1925 to "the Bolshevik dragooning of Georgia" - a crime repeated by Putin's Russia between 2008 and 2024. Stalin took steps to ensure that the existence of the Ukraine terror-famine would be denied or discounted by G.B. Shaw and Sidney and Beatrice Webb, who were among distinguished visitors to Russia between 1931 and 1933, and who had known Robertson years earlier (see Christopher Andrew and Oleg Gordievsky, *KGB*, 1990, p. 97, etc.). The recourse to mass murder, if not genocide, would be repeated in Communist China and in Pol Pot's Communist Cambodia (Kampuchea); and the 1994 genocide of the Tutsi in Rwanda would be denied by *Living Marxism* in Britain (for which see Linda Melvern, *Intent to Deceive*, 2020).

Meanwhile, Aveling had been a co-translator of the first English edition of Volume 1 of *Das Kapital*. This edition was published in London in 1887 by Swan Sonnenschein, which from 1891 onwards also published a number of Robertson's books. (Volume 1 was the only volume of *Das Kapital* to appear in any language in Marx's lifetime, in fact originally in Berlin in 1867.) In Vol. 1, Part 4, Chapter 15, Section 7 was entitled "Repulsion and Attraction of Workpeople by the Factory System". In *The Evolution of States* (1912) – and, before that, in what was, in effect, its first edition (*An Introduction to English Politics*, 1900) – Robertson applied the attraction-repulsion principle to European political development over a wide field historically. Whether he did this completely independently of Marx's influence or not is not known. Yet in *Buckle and His Critics* (1895) he had paid a fine tribute to the "scientific value" and "sociological teaching of permanent importance" of *Das Kapital*, of which Volume 2, edited by Engels, appeared in 1885; while Volume 3, on which Engels worked between 1885 and 1894, was published only about a year or so before J.M.R.'s book on Buckle. In Vol. 3 Marx's attempted explanations of cyclical crises, including a perceived falling rate of profit under capitalism, were all open to objections presented by David Conway in *A Farewell to Marx* (1987, pp. 138-40); and in 2013 a commentator on Marx's *Capital* in the Wordsworth Editions series concluded that "the modern consensus is that the economic theories espoused in Volume 3 are 'seriously flawed'" (p. xxiv). Robertson declared in 1929: "It must have been the semblance of exact economic procedure that lured so many men of otherwise good intelligence into the conviction that they were reading a scientific theorem when they were but accepting a 'cooked' equation" (*The Decadence*, p. 55).

Moreover, there is a plausible indication not only that

Robertson had studied Marx's published Notes to Volume 1 of *Das Kapital*, but also that J.M.R. may have had that volume in mind when he was composing the script of his 1917 lectures later published as *The Economics of Progress* (1918): for in that work as published – very approximately four times shorter than Marx's Volume 1 – Robertson noticed economists, commentators and public figures like Frédéric Bastiat, Thomas De Quincey, John Ramsay McCulloch, James Mill, Dudley North, Ricardo (of whom J.M.R. was more appreciative than Marx was), Wilhelm Roscher, J.B. Say, Nassau Senior, Sismondi, Sir Edward West, and Andrew Yarranton, all of whom also featured in Marx's Vol. 1 Notes. Of these twelve men, few of them could even remotely be regarded as household names in Victorian or post-Victorian England, where at least a couple of those mentioned in both books (by Marx and Robertson respectively) were virtually unknown. As this list of twelve in common is not claimed to be exhaustive, the longer such a list, the less likely it seems that the appearance of the same names in both works could be entirely attributed to coincidence.

In a Note added to the third German edition (1883) of *Das Kapital* Vol. 1 (Part 5, Chapter 18) Engels unguardedly included a highly perceptive if little known quotation from Johann Karl Rodbertus' letters in which Marx's contemporary and fellow economist declared: "Altogether, Marx's book is not so much an investigation into capital, as a polemic against the present form of capital, a form which he confounds with the concept itself of capital" (see Karl Marx, *Capital*, Wordsworth Classics of World Literature Edition, 2013, p. 1092). (The social philosophy of Rodbertus – who had accused Marx of plagiarism – was noticed by Robertson in *Courses of Study*.) It has been quite widely believed that Marx tended to form his theory, conclusion or opinion first, and then look for evidence to support it. As the French sociologist Émile Durkheim wrote in relation to *Das Kapital*: "The researches … were undertaken to establish a doctrine … previously conceived, rather than the doctrine being a result of the research" (*Selected Writings*, 1981 ed., pp. 156-7, as quoted by Leslie Page, op. cit. 1987, pp. 122, 139). It is not known for certain – although it is likely – that Robertson was aware of this comment by Durkheim, who was hailed by J.M.R. as "one of the ablest of modern sociologists" (*Courses of Study*, 1932 ed., p. 216). Be that as it may, Robertson stated in 1929: "Marx made only a selection of misunderstood facts, to carry his point" (*The Decadence*, p. 50). This was five decades before the Marxist/Communist historian Eric Hobsbawm admitted: "Marx himself was committed to a specific goal of human history – communism – and a specific role for the proletariat before he developed the historical analysis which, as he believed, demonstrated its ineluctability" (*New Left Review*, Jan.-Feb. 1981, as quoted by Leslie Page, op. cit. 1987, p. 139, n. 15). What Professor Hobsbawm seems to have found more difficult to acknowledge was the conception or possibility that in his determination to present supporting evidence for his analysis Marx resorted to misrepresenting, manipulating or falsifying information (see Leslie Page, op. cit. 1987, pp. 46-8).

Although Robertson did not attempt to describe, analyse or interpret capitalism on a grand scale or with the detail, sometimes ill-digested and tedious, sometimes associated with a richly illuminating or seductively persuasive, if unconvincing, analysis, presented by Marx, arguably J.M.R. showed greater understanding than Marx of the more positive aspects and potentialities of capitalism.

The distinguished German historian Theodor Mommsen – a

future recipient of the Nobel Prize for Literature (1902) – was the subject of criticism by both Marx and Robertson. In a Note in *Capital*, Vol. 1 (Part 2, Chapter 6, 2013 Wordsworth Editions, p. 1029), Marx accused the author of *The History of Rome* of committing "one blunder after another" (mainly, it seems, in the field of economics); whereas J.M.R. in *Patriotism and Empire* (1899) – and, before that, more extensively in *The Saxon and the Celt* (1897) – berated Mommsen for being "degraded by race prejudice" (Mommsen's targets included Jews). On the preceding page (p. 112) in *Patriotism and Empire* to that comment about Mommsen's race prejudice Robertson included Marx and Ferdinand Lassalle in a list of German thinkers, writers and artists in diverse fields who, he believed, "had in their various ways a specifically *moral* influence in Europe, over and above their vogue on other grounds" (his emphasis). Lassalle's inclusion in this list was doubtless connected with Robertson's feeling that Lassalle had been insufficiently acknowledged as Marx's forerunner as a German workers' leader (see *The Meaning of Liberalism*, 1925 ed., pp. 146, 148-9). Outside that list Marx and Robertson both referred with apparent approval to aspects of the work by the nineteenth century German historian Georg Ludwig von Maurer on the ancient Germans or Germani (see Marx, *Capital*, Vol. 1, Part 1, Chapter 1, Notes, Wordsworth Editions, 2013, p. 1011; and J.M.R., *Courses of Study*, 1904 and 1932 eds.). In 1888 Engels praised von Maurer's contribution to an understanding of common land ownership and use in ancient society (see Engels' second note in the text of the 1888 English edition of *The Communist Manifesto*, reproduced in Penguin Classics, 2002, p. 219).

For at least two months towards the end of 1866 Marx enthused – predominantly, it seems, to Engels – about a recently published book by a French amateur scientist who travelled widely in North Africa called Pierre Trémaux, whose work as a whole has otherwise been largely forgotten. Declared Marx: "In its historical and political application, the book is much more important and copious than Darwin. For certain questions, such as nationality, etc., a natural basis is found only in this work." Trémaux apparently believed, in Leslie Page's words, that "the beauty, energy, level of civilization, and intellectual faculties of peoples and races were, in general, related directly to the geological age of the soil on which they lived" (see Leslie Page, *Karl Marx and the Critical Examination of His Works*, Part 1, 1987, p. 127 etc.).

The British historian H.T. Buckle – a contemporary of Trémaux's – had also highlighted the role of the soil, but from a different angle. As Robertson explained: "the statement of Professor Jevons that 'Buckle referred the character of a nation to the climate and the soil of its abode' … completely misrepresents him [Buckle]. What he taught was that climate and soil in early civilizations determined (a) the food supply, and so (b) the degree of population, and (c) their economic condition" (from J.M.R.'s Introduction to Buckle's *Introduction to the History of Civilization in England*, 1904 ed., p. vii). Trémaux's conclusion that, in Marx's approving words, "the common Negro type is only a degeneration of a much higher one" has no equivalent or counterpart in Buckle's *Introduction* (where Robertson's index has no entry for Negro, Africa, black, or race). Arguably Trémaux's views could have seemed acceptable to the later Nazi propagandists with their Blut und Boden (Blood and Soil) policy and racist contempt for Negroes and Africans. As *Das Kapital* had appeared years after Buckle's death, and as Marx had worked independently of Buckle, it was one of the more striking features of Robertson's 1895 book that, albeit briefly, tentatively and unsystematically, he compared aspects of the work of Buckle and Marx and pointed towards possible ways in which their respective interpretations of history could be regarded as mutually complementary.

In the twenty-first century beset by issues associated with climate change, climate could well seem a more important and crucial factor than class in humanity's struggle for survival and security as a species. In any event, Robertson would deserve much credit for his work with two substantial books – *Buckle and His Critics* (1895) and his edition (1904) of Buckle's *Introduction* – in emphasizing the importance of climate in human history and Buckle's contribution in that field. Subsequent historians based in Britain who drew attention to the role of climatic catastrophe featured Vere Gordon Childe and, later, Arnold J. Toynbee, although their books *The Most Ancient Near East* (1928) and *A Study of History* (after Robertson's death), respectively, were published at least twenty-four years after J.M.R.'s second book devoted to Buckle. The Marxist materialist conception of history clearly appears to have been accepted by the pro-Soviet Communists Gordon Childe and Toynbee's son Philip, of whom the latter became an old friend and drinking companion of the notorious Soviet spy Donald Maclean (as Christopher Andrew has confirmed).

Following his enthusiastic discovery of Trémaux's work Marx caustically dismissed "superficial nonsense" which he associated with Ludwig Büchner's lectures on Darwinism (see Leslie Page, op. cit. 1987, p. 131); whereas Robertson, who stayed with Büchner at his home in Germany for some weeks in the late 1880s, seemed distinctly more respectful of the German freethinker's work as a whole (see *Courses of Study*, for instance). As a historian of popular freethought in Britain explained: "Darwinian 'materialism' entered freethought by way of Germany, in the writings of Ludwig Büchner … it was really Huxley's *Evidence as to Man's Place in Nature* (1863) that marked out the battleground" (Edward Royle, op. cit. 1980, pp. 171-2). In Britain Huxley was known as "Darwin's bulldog"; and Robertson hailed Huxley's *Man's Place in Nature* as "the most courageous and the most important act of his life" (*A History of Freethought in the Nineteenth Century*, 1929, p. 321).

Huxley died only weeks before Engels during the summer of 1895, in Huxley's case in Eastbourne, a seaside resort that had become Engels' favourite holiday home from which he was transferred to London just before his own death in August. Up to at least June 1895 the *Freethinker* regularly devoted attention to Huxley's work; but while in that journal "there was a tendency to concentrate upon the controversies and the anti-theological implications of evolution rather than the biological details", in the *National Reformer* under Robertson's editorship a pseudonymous contributor – possibly J.M.R. himself – paid tribute in its front page opening article on 25 September 1892 to "Professor Huxley's best achievements, his work in biology for example" (see Jim Herrick, *Vision and Realism*, 1982, p. 23; and *NR*, 25.9.1892, p. 193). Both Robertson and Engels read Huxley, whose controversies they followed. As atheists both men were critical of Huxley's Agnosticism, which Engels dubbed "shamefaced materialism" (for which see Archibald Robertson, *Man His Own Master*, 1948, p. 107); and both referred in an unsupportive way to Huxley's designation of Comtism as Catholicism minus Christianity (see *Marx and Engels: Basic Writings*, ed. Lewis Feuer, 1969 ed., pp. 486-7; J.M.R., *The Dynamics of Religion*, 1926 ed., pp. 288-9, inter alia).

Later J.M.R.'s *History of Freethought in the Nineteenth Century* presented the Young Hegelian Arnold Ruge –

who had been friendly with Marx and Engels – in quite a sympathetic light. Whereas Marx, with at least half an eye on Hegel, had highlighted "the negation of negation" (*Capital*, Vol. 1, Part 8, Chapter 32, near end), J.M.R. had an eye on Darwinism when he declared in 1889 that "the problem of the future is 'the struggle *against* the struggle for existence'" (see *BRUG*, p. 42). Among left-wing works linking Darwinism and Marxism following Marx's death was Enrico Ferri's *Socialism and Positive Science* (1894; 1905), which was briefly noticed in *Courses of Study* (1932 ed., p. 409), where Robertson alluded to his critical discussion of one aspect of Ferri's book in *The Reformer* (December 1901) as he disapproved of Ferri's hostile attitude to the emancipation of women. But Ferri's work was also noteworthy for offering an early indication of Marx's serial misrepresentation, in this case through the false suggestion that the English philosopher Thomas Hobbes had located the "war of all against all" – *bellum omnium contra omnes* – in "civil society" instead of at an earlier stage of human development. (Marx was found guilty between 1885 and 1984 of grossly manipulating and distorting, for his own polemical anti-capitalist purposes, the meaning of contributions to public discourse provided by the British Parliamentary Blue Books, Gladstone, Malthus, and Adam Smith: see Leslie Page, op. cit. 1987, pp. 46-9, 59-60, 94, 124-6, 133, etc.)

Committed to the search for truth, Robertson was concerned to give an honest and reliable account and appraisal of Hobbes, to whom he devoted quite a lot of attention, for example in *Pioneer Humanists* (1907) and *A Short History of Morals* (1920), seeing him as a pioneering exponent of determinism, whereas Engels tended to emphasize Hobbes's contribution as "the first modern materialist (in the eighteenth-century sense)" (letter from Engels to Conrad Schmidt, 27.10.1890:

see Lewis Feuer, ed., op. cit. 1969, p. 444. On p. 88 Feuer claimed that Marx and Engels mistakenly attributed what Engels regarded as the first form of materialism to Duns Scotus instead of to William of Ockham).

Engels had already been castigated in 1958 by two rigorous and meticulous scholars, W.O. Henderson and W.H. Chaloner, for having presented information in his *The Condition of the Working Class in England* (1845) as if it were up-to-date or contemporary when it was sometimes needlessly years, even decades, out of date or misleadingly and avoidably incomplete in other respects: the two authors identified at least twenty-three distorting errors of fact or of transcription from his sources in one section alone (see Paul Johnson, *Intellectuals*, 1989 paperback ed., pp. 64-6 and 347-8 for details). Robertson was accordingly on the right track by 1925 when, after criticising Engels' flawed gift of prophecy in his 1845 book, he censured its author: "Unabashed by the knowledge that he had confidently given to the world utter delusion as scientific truth, he still posed as prophet and sought to 'bluff' mankind in the name of science" (*The Meaning of Liberalism*, p. 145). Engels' book was unreservedly acclaimed by Marx in his published Notes to Vol. 1, Part 3, Chapter 10 ("The Working-Day") of *Capital*.

During the later stages of the Soviet era the politically active Russian mathematician Igor Shafarevich maintained: "The concept of 'the scientific method' was of extraordinary importance for the development of nineteenth-century socialism … the theses of socialist doctrine thereby acquired the appearance of objectivity and a certain inevitability" (*The Socialist Phenomenon*, Eng. ed. 1980, pp. 211-12, quoted by Leslie Page, op. cit. 1987, pp. 121, 138). On that basis, it may be argued, Robertson, who as a public intellectual was a notable late Victorian and Edwardian exponent of the scientific method, tried to respect and adhere to its rigorous canons with greater consistency than did Marx and Engels with their not infrequent spasms of sweeping intellectual exuberance and extravagance.

Marx had been more enthusiastic than Engels regarding Pierre Trémaux's work. The distribution of enthusiasm was more balanced in the 1880s in the reaction of Marx and Engels to *Ancient Society* (1877), an anthropological study located in America by Lewis H. Morgan, whose book was used extensively by Engels in composing *The Origin of the Family, Private Property and the State* (1884). Between 1904 and 1932 Robertson commended Morgan's work, whose attraction for J.M.R. may have partly related to what Engels' biographer Tristram Hunt would call its "hybrid mixture of Darwinism and materialism" (*The Frock-Coated Communist*, 2010 ed., p. 308). In 1973 Marx's biographer David McLellan, without elaboration, would describe Morgan as "a once much-respected writer whose scholarly reputation has not survived subsequent research" (*Karl Marx*, 1976 paperback ed., p. 424). Forty years earlier, J.M.R. praised *Ancient Society* as "valuable" (*Courses of Study*, 1932, p. 7), but he did not claim its author was "scholarly". In April 1964 a contributor to *Current Anthropology* maintained that Marx and Engels had misrepresented Morgan.

In his essay "On the History of Early Christianity" – first published in *Die Neue Zeit* not long before his death in 1895 – Engels described Lucian of Samosata as "one of our best sources on the first Christians". Robertson – whose major books on Christianity and ancient religions very largely appeared after Engels' death – may have read this essay, but is not known to have cited it. Had J.M.R. read it he might have recoiled at Engels' statement that "the history of early Christianity has notable points of resemblance with the modern working-class movement" (see Feuer, op. cit. 1969, p. 209; and p. 211 regarding Lucian). However, in 1902 Robertson wrote of Lucian in what seems to have been an appreciative way in *A Short History of Christianity*.

In *The Germans* (1916) Robertson did not focus on Engels' *The Peasant War in Germany* (1850), possibly because he may have felt it was not particularly suitable for his purposes. Tristram Hunt would suggest that Engels' book was marred by "crassness" and a "bludgeoning" approach (op. cit. 2010, p. 218). Rather surprisingly, the Communist Germanist academic Roy Pascal did not mention Engels' work in *The Social Basis of the German Reformation* (1933), although both Pascal in his book and J.M.R. in *The Germans* did consult and cite a work by the Marxian socialist Karl Kautsky: *Communism in Central Europe* (which also featured in J.M.R.'s *HF*, 1936 ed., p. 480, and *Courses of Study*). However, a possible reading of *The Germans* may have partly influenced Roy Pascal or, more plausibly, the Marxian H.M. Hyndman, who had met J.M.R. and knew of his work: for in his book Robertson referred (pp. 150-1) to Luther's "brutal" denunciation of the peasants and, only six lines later, to Luther's "fury", which may be compared with Hyndman's comments, four years later, on Luther's "brutality" and "Luther abusing the latter with a fury" (both on p. 211) in *The Evolution of Revolution* (the title itself a possible echo of J.M.R.'s *The Evolution of States*). From 1914 onwards both Hyndman and Robertson supported the war effort against German aggression.

The two men had a mutual friend or acquaintance in George Bernard Shaw, who in the course of three articles in 1887 in Bradlaugh's *National Reformer* refuted Marx's theory of value

(G.B.S. was apparently inspired to do so by reading the British economist Stanley Jevons). In an unsigned article (attributed by Edward Royle to J.M.R.) in the 4 December 1892 *National Reformer*, Robertson apparently contested Engels' claim that Marx's alleged discovery of surplus value made socialism "scientific". The article writer also disapproved of Engels' "heavy-footed satire" aimed at the rival German socialist Eugen Dühring, although in *Courses of Study* (1932 ed., p. 219) J.M.R. would slate Dühring's (anti-Semitic) *The Jewish Question* (1881) as a gross disservice to sociology. Robertson ruefully commented in 1913 that at the dawn of the twentieth century "there was not a single chair of sociology in a British university" (*A Short History of Christianity*, second ed., p. 317). J.M.R.'s rueful comment was partly echoed and elaborated after fifty-five years by the Communist Eric Hobsbawm (*Industry and Empire*, 1981 reprint, p. 169, para. 2).

One British University where there was much discussion touching on sociological issues during the 1930s was Cambridge, where a Communist circle and cell developed, in effect encouraged to a large extent by the Communist fervour and commitment of the Cambridge don Maurice Dobb, who specialised in economics. Some of Dobb's works – though not *Russian Economic Development since the Revolution* (1928) – were referred to in Robertson's *Courses of Study* (1932 ed.), which also mentioned, without disapproval and, no doubt, in all good faith, works by Emile Burns, a committed Communist, and Professor Arthur C. Pigou, a Communist sympathiser, both passing through the doors of Cambridge University (see John Costello, *Mask of Treachery*, 1988, pp. 169, 181). Although J.M.R. may have met the Cambridge-educated, future Soviet spy Donald Maclean through the latter's prominent Liberal father, Robertson died years before the treachery of members of the Cambridge cell became a practical reality. However, in view of the allegedly impeccable social class background of leading Communist agents at Cambridge during the 1920s and 1930s such as James Klugmann, Anthony Blunt, Kim Philby, Guy Burgess, Maclean, and also J.B.S. Haldane (who, according to John Costello, passed British wartime military secrets to the Soviets), Robertson showed rather remarkable insight or prescience when just a year after the Bolshevik Revolution in Russia he referred to British "Upper-Class Bolshevism" in *Mr. Hughes: A Study* (which, although published anonymously in late 1918, has been attributed on good authority to J.M.R. by at least three informants). If Robertson had any suspicion about the willingness of such privileged undercover or overt Bolsheviks at Cambridge, or Oxford, University to consider secretly aiding an extremely hostile foreign power, this could have strengthened his belief from about 1929 onwards that contemporary Britain was beset by growing signs of decadence and decay. Between April 1943 and June 1945 Anthony Blunt could gain rare and sensitive information from across the security service while drafting top secret monthly wartime reports to Prime Minister Winston Churchill (see Nigel West, 2018, pp. 17-8). (For Communist outlets at Cambridge during the 1920s see John Costello's *Mask of Treachery*, 1988, pp. 117, 155, 167, 189-91, Peter Wright, *Spy Catcher*, 1987, p. 259 (on the pioneering Soviet atomic scientist Peter Kapitza at the Cavendish Laboratory), Russell Campbell's *Codename Intelligentsia*, 2018, pp. 34, 63, 153 (including Eisenstein's 1929 Cambridge visit), and Guy Clutton-Brock, *Cold Comfort Confronted*, 1972, p. 15-16; and for similar 1920s outlets at Oxford see Costello, pp. 220-22; David Burke, *The Lawn Road Flats*, 2019 ed., p. 189; and Chapman Pincher, *Too Secret Too Long*, 1985 ed., p. 16 - on the GRU at Oxford - and *Treachery*, 2012 ed., pp. 35-40.) Ironically, J.B.S. Haldane, Jack Lindsay, Archibald Robertson, Tom Bell,

Terry Eagleton and Harold Laski were among the Marxists, Communists and fellow-travellers in Britain who were aware of J.M.R.'s work, took account of it and, in some cases, were influenced by aspects of it.

INDEX